THE STATE OF
BLACK AMERICA 1993

Published by **National Urban League, Inc.**

January 1993

THE STATE OF BLACK AMERICA 1993

Editor

Billy J. Tidwell, Ph.D.

Copyright © National Urban League, Inc., 1993

Library of Congress Card Catalog Number 77-647469

ISBN 0-9632071-1-3

Price $24.95

The cover art, "New Generation," is the creation of Elizabeth Catlet "New Generation" is the seventh limited-edition lithograph in the "Gre Artists" series on African Americans commissioned for the National Urba League by the House of Seagram.

⊜ National Urban League, Inc.

The Equal Opportunity Building • 500 East 62nd Street • New York, New York 10021

Founded in 1910, the National Urban League is the premier social service and civil rights organization in America. The League is a nonprofit, community-based organization headquartered in New York City, with 112 affiliates in 34 states and the District of Columbia.

The mission of the National Urban League is to assist African Americans in achieving social and economic equality. The League implements its mission through advocacy, bridge building among the races, program services, and research.

Dedication

The eighteenth edition of *The State of Black America* is dedicated to "twenty-first century African-American children." The Urban League Movement is resolved to ensuring that every African-American child is prepared to meet the challenges and demands of a rapidly changing world. The next generation's development is crucial to the future well-being of both the African-American community and the nation as a whole.

TABLE OF CONTENTS

About the Authors

DR. WILLIAM D. BRADFORD
Associate Dean for Academic Affairs
Professor of Finance
Business School
University of Maryland - College Park

Dr. William D. Bradford served as Assistant and then Associate Professor of Finance at Stanford University before coming to the University of Maryland as Professor of Finance in 1980. During his 12-year tenure at College Park, he has also chaired the Finance Department.

Dean Bradford has been Visiting Professor at New York University, Ohio State University, Yale University, and the University of California at Los Angeles. He has served as Visiting Scholar at the Federal Home Loan Bank Board and the Board of Governors of the Federal Reserve System.

Dr. Bradford is a member of the Affordable Housing Advisory Council of the Federal Home Loan Mortgage Association.

Professor Bradford has published numerous books and articles on minority business development, entrepreneurship, corporate finance, and financial institutions. His teaching interests include financial institutions, corporate finance, and financial theory.

Dr. Bradford earned his bachelor's degree in economics from Howard University and his M.B.A. and Ph.D. degrees in finance and economics from Ohio State University.

DR. LYNN C. BURBRIDGE
Deputy Director
Center for Research on Women
Wellesley College

Dr. Lynn C. Burbridge, a trained economist, is an administrator and a researcher at Wellesley College. Her current research focuses on employment, welfare, and education issues with an emphasis on women of color.

Before assuming her position at Wellesley in 1989, Dr. Burbridge spent eight years as a researcher and policy analyst at The Urban Institute and—for a year—the Joint Center for Political and Economic Studies, both in Washington, DC.

Dr. Burbridge has written and published extensively, primarily about the impact of public policies on minorities, low-income women, and youth. She is strongly committed to public service and has served on a variety of boards and advisory committees of professional organizations, nonprofit service agencies, and special commissions.

Dr. Burbridge earned her bachelor's degree—with honors—in social and political theory from the University of California at Berkeley; she earned her master's and doctoral degrees in economics from Stanford University.

T. WILLARD FAIR
President and Chief Executive Officer
Urban League of Greater Miami, Inc.

T. Willard Fair has headed the Urban League of Greater Miami, Inc., for nearly 30 years. He is also President of the Council of Urban League Executives.

Under his tutelage, the Miami Urban League affiliate has crafted innovative programs and demonstration projects to ensure that the total needs of black family units are recognized and attended to, such as the establishment of the Clara B. Knight Early Childhood Learning and Developmental Center; the M&M Maison Townhouse Demonstration project, designed for single female heads of households; the Rainbow Club, an early prevention and intervention prototype for women who are either pregnant or have a child under the age of one; and Covenant Palms, a 137-unit housing complex for the elderly and handicapped.

A former adjunct professor at Bethune-Cookman College and Florida International University, Mr. Fair serves on numerous boards and committees. He has hosted television and radio talk shows. He has received several awards and citations for his achievements, including the 1989 Exemplar from the National Association of Social Work Managers.

Mr. Fair earned his bachelor's degree—cum laude—in sociology from Johnson C. Smith University and his M.S.W. degree from the Atlanta University School of Social Work.

DR. CHARLES V. HAMILTON
Wallace S. Sayre Professor of Government
Department of Political Science
Columbia University

Dr. Charles V. Hamilton is one of America's most widely respected political scientists. Before assuming his distinguished professorship at Columbia University, he taught at several other universities, including Tuskegee, Rutgers, Lincoln (PA), and Roosevelt—his undergraduate alma mater.

Professor Hamilton has been published extensively in national periodicals and journals. He is the author of six books on American government, race, and politics; the most recent is *Adam Clayton Powell, Jr.: The Political Biography of an American Dilemma* (Atheneum, 1991). The book with which he first gained national acclaim was *Black Power* (Random House, 1967), which he co-authored with Stokely Carmichael. His current research—in collaboration with his wife, Dr. Dona C. Hamilton—is a study of socioeconomic policies of civil rights organizations from the New Deal to the present.

Dr. Hamilton has received numerous awards and honorary degrees for scholarship and distinguished teaching, including the American Political Science Association's Urban Politics Award in 1989.

Dr. Hamilton earned his B.A. degree from Roosevelt University, his J.D. degree from Loyola University School of Law, and his M.A. and Ph.D. degrees from The University of Chicago.

DR. LENNEAL J. HENDERSON
Distinguished Professor
Government and Public Administration
University of Baltimore

Dr. Lenneal J. Henderson is a fiscal policy expert. In addition to his professorship, he is a Senior Fellow in the William Donald Schaefer Center for Public Policy and a Henry C. Welcome Fellow at the University of Baltimore.

Before assuming his current positions, Dr. Henderson was Head and Professor of Political Science at the University of Tennessee - Knoxville, a senior faculty member at the Federal Executive Institute in Charlottesville, VA, and a professor in the School of Business and Public Administration at Howard University.

Other academic accomplishments include his being a Ford Foundation/ National Research Council Postdoctoral Fellow at the Johns Hopkins School of Advanced International Studies, a Kellogg National Fellow, and a Rockefeller Research Fellow. He recently received the Distinguished Chair in Teaching at the University of Baltimore for 1992-93.

Professor Henderson has lectured or consulted in Canada, Europe, Japan, Mexico, sub-Saharan Africa, Egypt, Israel, India, Peru, the Caribbean, the former Soviet Union, and the People's Republic of China.

He has published or edited five books and numerous articles in many publications, including *The Urban League Review, The Review of Black Political Economy, The Annals, Policy Studies Journal, Howard Law Journal*, and *The Black Scholar*.

Dr. Henderson earned his B.A., M.A., and Ph.D. degrees from the University of California at Berkeley.

DR. JEFF P. HOWARD
President
The Efficacy Institute, Inc.

Dr. Jeff P. Howard is a psychologist who—as part of his graduate studies—developed a theory of the psychological foundations of intellectual development. He combined that theory with a training method developed by Professor David McClelland, a Harvard psychologist specializing in motivation and achievement training. This synthesis resulted in the "Efficacy Seminar," a training process to enhance academic performance and intellectual development.

The Efficacy Institute, incorporated in 1985, is a not-for-profit educational service organization involved in promoting the overall development of children of color. It works with both public school systems and social service agencies across the country. The Institute has developed curricula for elementary and high school teachers to instruct their students in the process of development. It also develops and supports programs that use adult volunteers from African-American and Hispanic professional communities to serve as role models and to provide direction to minority youth.

Dr. Howard is also chief executive officer of J. Howard and Associates, a management consulting company working with Fortune 500 clients to accelerate professional employee development, to increase retention and performance of minority and female professionals, and to improve managerial leadership skills.

Dr. Howard earned his undergraduate and Ph.D. degrees from Harvard University, where he initially enrolled as part of the first wave of black students sent to Harvard in the mid-1960s as a result of the Civil Rights Movement.

DR. DAVID H. SWINTON
Dean of the School of Business
Professor of Economics
Jackson State University

Dr. David H. Swinton is a nationally known economist and education administrator. He is recognized as a leading expert on the economics of social policy and minority groups and is often invited to testify before the U.S. Congress and national commissions.

As the chief academic officer for the Business School, Dean Swinton is directing the program through a major effort to develop a distinguished School of Business. Under his leadership, the school has introduced a quality assurance program to ensure that all graduates have the skills, competencies, and attitudes required for success in corporate America.

The former Director of Research for the Black Economic Research Center in New York, Dr. Swinton has also lectured at City University of New York; State University of New York - Stony Brook; and The Urban Institute in the District of Columbia.

Dr. Swinton is the former Director of the Southern Center for Studies in Public Policy and Professor of Economics at Clark College in Atlanta. While at the policy center, he was the principal fundraiser and architect of the research program.

Professor Swinton has published several books, monographs, and major research reports, as well as scores of articles. He is active in the profession and has served on the board or has been an officer of numerous professional organizations and journals, including a term as President of the National Economics Association.

Dr. Swinton earned his Ph.D. and M.A. degrees in economics from Harvard University, and his B.A. degree in economics—with honors, including Phi Beta Kappa—from New York University.

DR. BILLY J. TIDWELL
Director of Research
National Urban League, Inc.

Dr. Billy J. Tidwell is the Director of Research for the National Urban League, a position he has held since 1985. A widely respected commentator on social issues, Dr. Tidwell has authored numerous reports on the socioeconomic conditions of African Americans, including *Stalling Out: The Relative Progress of African Americans* and *The Price: A Study of the Costs of Racism in America*. Dr. Tidwell also authored the National Urban League's influential report, *Playing to Win: A Marshall Plan for America*, which outlines a strategy for improving the nation's economic productivity and competitiveness.

Dr. Tidwell is editor of *The State of Black America*, the National Urban League's highly regarded annual assessment of the well-being of African Americans; he is a frequent writer of articles for edited volumes, journals, newspapers, and other publications. Among other affiliations, he is a member of the 2000 Census Advisory Committee and the Council on Diversity of the Cooperative Extension System.

A practitioner of public policy research for more than 20 years, Dr. Tidwell was formerly a Senior Researcher with Mathematica Policy Research, a private consulting firm in Princeton, NJ. He served in a similar capacity with the Gary Income Maintenance Experiment in Gary, IN, in association with Indiana University. Dr. Tidwell is also noted for having founded the Watts Summer Festival and Sons of Watts Community Enterprises in Los Angeles following the civil disturbances that occurred there in 1965.

Dr. Tidwell earned his B.A. and M.S.W. degrees from the University of California at Berkeley and his Ph.D. degree in social welfare from the University of Wisconsin at Madison.

DR. MICHAEL B. WEBB
Director
Education and Career Development
National Urban League, Inc.

As Director of Education and Career Development, Dr. Michael B. Webb oversees the National Urban League's educational programs and projects, needs assessments, research, and program development. He is also director of the International Youth Leadership Institute at the Teachers College, Columbia University, where he develops and coordinates seminars on global studies and overseas programs for African-American and Hispanic high school students. Further, he is a Senior Research Associate at the Institute for Urban and Minority Education at Teachers College.

Dr. Webb is an avid Africanist who worked for two years at the American University in Cairo; he also spent a semester as a guest lecturer in the Gumel Advanced Teachers College in Nigeria.

Dr. Webb has held research and policy positions with the Far West Laboratory for Educational Research and Development, the Governor's Advisory Committee for Black Affairs, and the State University of New York African American Institute.

Dr. Webb's writings have appeared in professional and educational journals, monographs, and the Educational Resources Information Center (ERIC) Clearinghouse, where he served six years as Associate Director of Urban Education.

Dr. Webb earned his B.A. degree in English/African studies from St. John Fisher College, his M.A. degree in educational technology from San Francisco State University, and his Ed.D. degree from Columbia University.

Black America, 1992:
An Overview

John E. Jacob
President and Chief Executive Officer
National Urban League, Inc.

At the risk of oversimplifying, I would categorize the state of Black America in 1992 as one of bleak despair countered by fresh hope.

The despair was rooted in the effects of a long, debilitating recession that drove many black families deeper into poverty and diminished already stagnant employment opportunities.

The hope was based on the election of a new administration pledged to chart a different course for the nation and on a new thrust toward empowerment through self-development within the African-American community.

The recession exacerbated the most intractable problem faced by African Americans—disproportionate employment.

Since the start of the recession, black unemployment climbed by better than 16 percent. Officially, black unemployment was just over 14 percent in the third quarter of 1992, more than double the white rate. But adding discouraged workers and part-time workers who want full-time jobs to the officially unemployed brings total joblessness in the African-American community to almost four million, or more than one of every four black workers.

As Dr. David H. Swinton documents in his article, "The Economic Status of African Americans During the Reagan-Bush Era: Withered Opportunities, Limited Outcomes, and Uncertain Outlook," the erosion of the black economy continued throughout the economic boom of the 1980s and accelerated in this recession. The long slowdown's effects cut across virtually all demographic and occupational categories, imperiling the survival of the many millions of low-income African-American families while undermining the vulnerable, insecure middle class.

At year's end, many economists were saying that the recession was ended and that the recovery was underway. But there was also a consensus that the resultant economic growth would be at half the rate of previous recovery periods; too feeble to make much of a dent in unemployment. That view is reinforced by almost daily reports of new plant closings and large-scale corporate layoffs.

As an example of the changed economic environment, in a normal recovery period, we would expect a company like General Motors to rehire 100,000 laid-off auto workers. Instead, GM announced that it will be downsizing over the next several years, eliminating 74,000 more jobs. Add to that the

1

shrinking of the defense industry and the reduction in our military forces, which were prime sources of employment opportunities for African Americans, and prospects for the black economy looked very bleak indeed.

So Black America in 1992 was in the throes of a devastating economic depression whose effects will be felt throughout the remainder of the decade.

It is small comfort to realize that white Americans are similarly situated—our economy is experiencing structural dislocations that affect all, regardless of race. Those powerful economic changes have been largely responsible for the decline in real incomes experienced by American workers over the past two decades.

But while economic distress cuts across race and class lines, African-American workers have been hit hardest, by virtue of their concentration in the most marginal and vulnerable sectors of the economy, thanks to discriminatory patterns that retain their powerful role in shaping our lives.

Survival in a new global economy characterized by the relatively unhindered flow of goods, capital, and jobs across international borders will require major structural changes in our society that make us more productive and competitive. Those changes have often been narrowly defined in terms of greater public investments in the infrastructure and in the advanced technology that supports economic growth. But perhaps more relevant are changes that develop the human resource infrastructure—those that advance the education and skills of the work force and create a societal environment in which America's diversity is honed into a competitive strength. Dr. Billy J. Tidwell's article, "African Americans and the 21st Century Labor Market: Improving the Fit," is illuminating and hard-hitting on this issue.

Our failure to see beyond the narrow confines of the present to build for the future and our terrible failure to develop all the resources represented by all our people have led not only to economic decline but also to a serious erosion of the bonds that tie our society together.

Those failures underlie the troubling racial tensions that plague our society and led to the despair that erupted in the Los Angeles riots in April.

The immediate cause of the riots was a familiar one: a miscarriage of justice that sent a message to African Americans that their lives and their rights are expendable. The acquittal of the policemen who brutally beat an unarmed black man despite overwhelming evidence of their guilt led not only to the Los Angeles riots but also to disturbances in many other cities.

What is remarkable about those disorders is not that they took place but that there were so few of them, for the conditions of despairing anger that drove so many Los Angelenos into the streets were duplicated in virtually every city in this nation. The Los Angeles experience was predictable and inevitable; it could have happened in almost any of our communities.

Many Americans would resist that conclusion, and yet it is proved by the way so many cities went on red alert as soon as word spread of violence in outhern California; even Wall Street was literally shut down, as businesses closed early and sent employees home.

And while Los Angeles is thought of as an explosion of African-American protest, it actually was America's first interracial, multicultural riot. More Latinos than blacks were arrested, and one of every seven people taken into custody by the police was white—a reminder that while racism condemns disproportionate numbers of African Americans to lives of poverty and despair, anger based on economic inequality cuts across racial and ethnic lines.

Many preferred to interpret the riots as simple lawlessness, but others understood that when people loot and burn under the noses of the same police force that beat Rodney King half to death, they are telling us through their behavior that they have so little hope that they feel they have nothing to lose. Any society is in deep trouble when so many of its citizens feel they have no stake in it and are so angry that they will strike out regardless of the consequences.

Unfortunately, there seems to be little evidence that the nation is willing to respond adequately to the challenge of reconnecting masses of alienated citizens to the societal mainstream. The riot was followed by a presidential visit, and, just as in the 1960s, there was a commission report, some small-scale efforts to improve conditions, a feeble urban aid bill in Congress, and a bit of some pious rhetoric followed by a monumental national silence. Surely a more positive response was demanded by this test of whether our nation of diverse peoples can learn to live together with respect and dignity for all.

The riots—and America's inadequate response to the cries of pain they represented—demonstrate once again that the state of Black America is deeply influenced by the state of White America's continuing prejudice and stereotypes. It is increasingly clear that all Americans need to understand that issues such as race, ethnicity, poverty, and the survival of our cities will determine our national future for good or for ill.

Los Angeles was also a test of America's diversity, and America failed that crucial test. The riots exposed to view a complex network of interethnic rivalries and frictions that set group against group—African Americans against Koreans and Latinos from Central America against Latinos from Mexico, among others. Such rivalries poison the environment in many of our major cities, increasing tensions and questioning whether our diversity is a national strength or a weakness.

The answer to that question will be critical for African Americans and for the nation's future. For we are evolving into a society in which there will be no single "majority" racial group. Before the decade is out, the majority of Californians are expected to be members of a racial minority—black, Asian, and Latino. The United States as a whole is expected to have a "minority majority" sometime around the middle of the next century.

3

So Rodney King's questioning plea during the riots: "Can't we all just get along?" transcends the boundaries of its time and place to suggest the key challenge faced by a nation undergoing vast demographic transformations.

Many people found a hopeful answer to the challenge of diversity in the election of a presidential candidate who appeared to have mastered the ability to unite Americans of vastly different ideologies, races, and ethnic and economic backgrounds into a winning electoral coalition. Some of the important dynamics of this election and the strategic importance of the black vote to the outcome are examined astutely by Dr. Charles V. Hamilton in his essay, "Promoting Priorities: African-American Political Influence in the 1990s."

While an election campaign is very different from governing, and winning votes from diverse groups is very different from constructing firm biracial, multi-ethnic alliances, it is still remarkable how much hope has been sparked by the Clinton victory. Even among hardened cynics, there is a feeling that— for the first time in years—the nation has a leader who not only believes in diversity but also is willing to champion it with youthful vigor and powerful communication skills. Whether these expectations will be realized remains to be seen, but a note of guarded hope for the future characterizes the state of Black America at year-end.

That hope got a lift from the sudden popularity of reformist ideas that had been ignored for too long, ideas such as universal health insurance, a national youth service, a revived civilian conservation corps, preschool learning programs, neighborhood-based skills training centers, and encouragement for job-creating small businesses.

But that hope is also tempered by a new realism within the African-American community. It recognizes the limits of what government can do to improve the state of Black America—but it also recognizes the considerable amount that government *can* do. This volume contains a broad range of thoughtful suggestions, including those in Dr. Lynn C. Burbridge's chapter, "Toward Economic Self-Sufficiency: Independence Without Poverty"; the article by Dr. Lenneal J. Henderson, "Empowerment through Enterprise: African-American Business Development"; and the essay by Dr. William D. Bradford, "Money Matters: Lending Discrimination in African-American Communities." The National Urban League's policy proposals across different areas are presented in the Recommendations section of this book.

The legacy of a dozen years of conservative rule has left a huge federal budget deficit that serves as a barrier to ambitious social programs. But that legacy also includes two other important positive features that, if acted upon, can enhance government's role in empowering minority people to control their own future.

First, the realization that government's role is critical to creating a climate for better race relations. African Americans are convinced that the manipulation of racial fears for political purposes characterized recent administrations

4

and fostered racial tensions. They now expect the new president—who speaks eloquently about racial justice, who won the black vote by overwhelming margins, and who counts among his top advisers former Urban League officials Vernon E. Jordan, Jr., and Ronald H. Brown—will work to create an environment that is favorable to civil rights and improved race relations.

A second feature that engenders hope is the growing national consensus behind the need to invest in our human resources—a need born of an extended period of public disinvestment in the nation's productive assets, especially in its people.

President Clinton campaigned on an economic renewal strategy that included heavy new investments in both the physical infrastructure that undergirds a nation's productive capacity and the human resources that determine a nation's competitiveness.

The National Urban League has urged a Marshall Plan for America that would make similar investments; there is considerable convergence between our plan and the Clinton economic strategy. The Urban League's Marshall Plan is a coordinated, targeted, accountable investment strategy to develop our nation's physical and human resources to make this nation competitive again. Both the Urban League's Marshall Plan and the Clinton economic strategy share the same rationale: that such investments are necessary to improve the nation's economic productivity and competitiveness in a global economy. Both emphasize the importance of increasing productivity of our work force through training and education, including preschool, elementary, and secondary education, with a strong emphasis on meeting the needs of disadvantaged children.

But the League's plan is bolder: it would commit more resources for a longer time frame and would be structured in a more accountable fashion, with a Cabinet-level Marshall Plan coordinator who would have expanded authority and responsibility for the plan's components.

The basic difference, however, is that the Marshall Plan for America would be sharply targeted to improving education, skills training, and job opportunities for the disadvantaged. That would empower minorities to shape their economic futures, and it would pull all Americans into the mainstream. That targeting feature separates the Marshall Plan from a piecemeal approach that could easily bypass the areas of greatest need. And it is the key to America's renewal, for improving America's productivity and making its diversity into an economic competitive strength require the full utilization of its shamefully neglected disadvantaged people, especially its black and minority populations.

The Clinton administration should build on the existing similarities between its campaign proposals and the Urban League's Marshall Plan for America. Even if it does not adopt our entire plan, the administration must develop a sound economic strategy that sharply targets the poor and minorities. Its policies in this regard will be seen by the African-American community as an indicator of the validity of its hopeful expectations for a significant reversal of the national policies that erode black economic security.

In a straitened economic environment, the annual $50 billion price tag for the Marshall Plan for America may seem beyond reach, but given the tremendous long-term economic payoff, it is an investment that is necessary for our future. And allocating that relatively modest sum from a trillion-dollar federal budget should not be a difficult task, especially when our global economic rivals are spending far more to secure their own economic futures. Germany is investing a trillion dollars to develop the former East Germany and integrate it into its economy. Japan has embarked on an ambitious infrastructure development program, and even tiny Taiwan is committed to a six-year, $300 billion development program.

So there is a well-founded hope in the African-American community that America, too, will embark on a development program that yields a healthier economy and that will be based not on discredited trickle-down theories but on the "percolate-up" theory—that if you help the people on the bottom to move up, everyone will benefit.

But Black America is not hopeful solely because of its expectations of what government may do. It is also hopeful because the multiple problems afflicting our communities have sparked grass-roots concern and a new determination to solve those problems that are within our ability to influence. We know that all of our problems cannot be solved by a Marshall Plan or by enlightened social policies. Those are necessary but insufficient.

There is a growing realization within the African-American community that its biggest challenge will be to survive in the new, high-performance world of the future, a world that will require technological skills, self-confident mastery of knowledge, and lifelong development and learning. In such a world, what people know and how they perform will be more important than class and race. Therefore, it is imperative to overcome centuries of destructive racist stereotypes that many of us have unfortunately internalized.

Those persistent negative racial stereotypes have sapped too much of our energies, undermined our self-confidence, retarded risk-taking, and led too many of our young people to see academic achievement as a "white thing" and failure as a "black thing."

It is a phenomenon accurately noted many years ago by the renowned African-American historian, Carter G. Woodson, who wrote: "When you control a man's thinking, you do not have to worry about his actions. You do not have to tell him to stand here or go yonder. He will find his 'proper place' and will stay in it. You do not need to send him to the back door. In fact, if there is no back door, he will cut one for his special benefit. His education makes it necessary."

6

Many African Americans, of course, have rejected that insidious form of societal brainwashing and have demonstrated that black excellence is widespread even in a society governed by negative racist stereotypes. But many others of us are joined in a demoralized community of despair instead of a renewed community of resolve. The pervasive sense of hopelessness and helplessness in so many of our communities requires a radical regeneration of the way we think and the way we act.

In recent years, there has been a growing understanding of the way such internalized stereotypes have sapped our community's strength and of the need to rebuild the self-confidence necessary to individual and group achievement in our society. The rejection of the "big lie" of black inferiority has led many African Americans to challenge institutions and individuals who hold us to the lower standards and lower expectations that reinforce negative stereotypes, and it has encouraged a resolve to take control of our own lives—developing our individual potential to the fullest while marshalling our resources as a community. Dr. Jeff Howard, in the compelling article, "The Third Movement: Developing Black Children for the 21st Century," expounds upon this new awakening.

Thus, in 1992, there was an identifiable beginning of a movement for African-American excellence that promises to reach into every black community and every black home. It is founded on the belief in the continuous development of African Americans as a self-confident people whose effective efforts can change our lives and our nation.

The National Urban League believes such a movement must begin with our children, and it has resolved to be the catalyst for a nationwide effort dedicated to the development of African-American children, preparing them to become model citizens of the twenty-first century.

We believe that the same children who are bombarded with messages of racial inferiority, who are shunted into special education classes, who are prepared for lifetimes of failure can be helped to excel and to lead the rest of the nation into a bold new future. That belief is based on the conviction that our children are as capable of learning and of developing their talents as any in the world. And it is based on historical lessons—of an America that took immigrant peasants from the backwaters of Europe and molded them into a people that led the world and of a Japan, Korea, and Taiwan who took people racked by poverty and devastated by war and developed them into global economic powerhouses in one generation. Surely then, a committed, dedicated, African-American community can help its children develop into the most intelligent and most skilled people on the face of the earth.

The Urban League considered what it would take for our children to develop into outstanding twenty-first century citizens. The answer, adopted from the model formulated by Dr. Jeff Howard of the Efficacy Institute, focuses on four basic criteria that will be necessary to meet the challenging demands of the future:

- **Every African-American child should graduate from high school with the ability to do calculus.**
- **Every African-American child should be fluent in a foreign language.**
- **Every African-American child should be able to research, organize, and write a 25-page essay on a challenging topic.**
- **Every African-American child should live by strict, high ethical standards.**

These criteria, of course, apply to all Americans, for the 21st century's demands transcend race. No longer can this nation get away with categorizing and stereotyping children . . . with developing a small white elite and writing off African-American children. That's a prescription for suicide in the world of the 21st century.

Developing our children to excel in the next century is a tremendous challenge for us. We will have to confront the institutions that are miseducating our children today. Perhaps more importantly, we will have to engender a spirit of community involvement and concern. Ensuring that our young people excel in school and develop to the fullest requires the involvement of all African Americans. The Urban League's multifaceted education programming, described in Dr. Michael B. Webb's article, "Programs for Progress and Empowerment: The Urban League's National Education Initiative," exemplifies the kind of effort that is needed.

While government can be an enabling agent for black empowerment, ultimately we—the African-American community—must develop our own vision of the future and implement that vision. There are some exciting examples of communities doing just that, and I would draw particular attention to the activities of one of our own Urban League affiliates, as chronicled by T. Willard Fair in the case study, "Coordinated Community Empowerment: Some Experiences of the Urban League of Greater Miami."

Although we have been the victims of racism and discrimination, we also have enjoyed the fruits of a democratic system that enlarges our scope for positive action and have developed the tools to effect widespread positive change.

The African-American community has economic strength in some $300 billion in purchasing power; it has institutional strength in a powerful network of churches, colleges and universities, fraternal and civic organizations, a vocal press, national and community-based civil rights organizations, and social welfare organizations. It has political influence through its voting power and cultural influence through the worldwide popularity of its arts. And it has a growing, critical mass of educated, concerned people with outstanding professional, business, and academic skills.

Given those strengths, it is within our power to help shape the destiny of our children; to project a vision of the future and their role in that future; and to help our young people to secure the educational tools and the mindset they will need to empower them to excel in the twenty-first century.

Thus, the state of Black America in 1992 turned a hopeful, expectant face to the future, even as the terrible conditions of the present led to despair and rebellion. The African-American community is turning inward to develop itself and its children for the future, even as it turns outward to insist that government and the private sector fulfill the long-delayed social contract that binds all of America's diverse people together in a society free from discrimination and negative stereotyping.

I want to express my heartfelt gratitude to the authors in this eighteenth edition of *The State of Black America.* Their contributions reaffirm the high quality standards the National Urban League ascribes to this publication.

The Third Movement: Developing Black Children for the 21st Century

Jeff P. Howard, Ph.D.

This generation of black Americans and all who will follow us are beneficiaries of two of the most successful social movements in history, movements that gave many of us unprecedented access to education, jobs, and the best that America has to offer. The first movement, conceived and led by Charles Hamilton Houston (and brought to its conclusion by Thurgood Marshall after Houston's death), was the legal struggle to end segregation which, after nearly a quarter century battle, did just that. The *Brown v. Board of Education* decision of 1954 removed the protective cover of laws that had lent respectability to racist exclusion since 1896. The Civil Rights Movement finished the job with boycotts, marches, and voter registration campaigns that rendered the remaining traditional practices of segregation too expensive to maintain. The "two movements" were brilliant in their planning and execution. Both had clear compelling objectives—clearly articulated missions with which people strongly identified. Each mobilized a broad base of support among black folk too, by defining clear operational approaches that generated belief in our capacity to achieve our objectives.

THE EQUAL OPPORTUNITY GENERATION AND THOSE LEFT BEHIND

Given this history, the present conditions endured by black children living in the core cities of America are tragic and more, they are a disgrace. It is disgraceful that the United States and all of its citizens have allowed racism, discrimination, and apathy to breed conditions where whole communities feel abandoned, and where children cannot so much as walk to and from school without fear. More importantly, lack of effective action in the face of the deteriorating circumstances endured by black children brings disgrace upon black adults, especially those of us who are educated and often well-positioned, but who have not, as a group, leveraged the privilege won for us toward creating better conditions for our younger brothers and sisters. No child deserves the kind of treatment many of our children receive: from schools that presume to judge their intelligence and classify many as too dumb to learn; from the streets where they are terrorized from an early age by renegade teenagers and young adults; or from the home itself, where many of our children are being raised by verbally and physically abusive adults, who were themselves abused and mistreated in the same manner when they were children.

This transgenerational abuse mirrors the historical mistreatment of African Americans at the hands of whites. It is painfully clear that their disregard for us has poisoned the child-rearing practices of many black families. Far too many black people may now be counted on to abuse one another, including children, in the same fashion that we have been historically abused. The situation has become powerfully self-perpetuating, and its results are devastating to the affected children. Without effective intervention, those who are growing up in these conditions will live, at best, as marginal inhabitants of the domestic society and international economy of the 21st century—poor, angry, contemptuous of their own kind, and generally despised. But they are unlikely to endure their desperation and poverty quietly. Many of these injured children will grow up to become lawless and violent young adults, or they will bear children that they are neither financially nor emotionally equipped to rear to successful adulthood. The fate of these children and of *their* children is bound to ours; the status and the regard in which all black people are held and our self-esteem as a people are tied to their conditions and behavior. Continuation of these conditions and continued expansion of the numbers of children who endure them will be utterly destructive to the remaining fabric of civility and decency in inner-city black communities around the country.

We are confronted daily with news stories of crisis: from police violence to gang violence to domestic violence, children are often the innocent victims guilty only of living in the wrong places at the wrong time. Many of us who have left these violent places cannot avoid being drawn into the news about them. We often feel as if we are drowning in the numbers that describe the depressing story of what has happened to black people in the last half of the century. But just as the children cannot escape the very real conditions described by these numbers, there can be no escape for those of us who care, and those who ought to care, from the terrible statistics that chart what is happening, right now, to black children:

- In 1988, 63.7 percent of black children were born out of wedlock.
- 68 percent of black girls have had sexual intercourse by the age of 15, and 40.7 percent of black girls become pregnant by the age of 18.
- 44 percent of black children live below the poverty line.
- In my experience, many urban school systems report official dropout rates approaching 50 percent; actual rates may be much higher, approaching two-thirds in some cities.
- Blacks account for 45.3 percent of the inmates in state and federal prisons, while only 23.4 percent of our 18-to-24-year olds were enrolled in institutions of higher education in 1989.
- The mortality rate for black males between the ages of 15 to 25 is 3.25 times that for black women, with the main cause of death being gunned down by a member of their own race.

12

- 56 percent of all black households are headed by women, and 56 percent of these households had incomes below the poverty level.
- 39.8 percent of black families are receiving aid for dependent children.[1]

The Problem of Those Left Behind

The circumstances of life for poor black children have become so overwhelmingly negative that the news can no longer be repressed. That was not always the case. Through the 1970s and for much of the 1980s, America, including much of Black America, repressed the news very successfully, choosing not to know fully what was happening. Many human service workers and educators, and some of our national leaders, did understand (John Jacob, for example, drew public attention to the rates at which black children were being born out of wedlock at the beginning of his tenure as Executive Director of the National Urban League a decade ago and pushed for a coordinated effort to address the issue). These people dared to look and were deeply unsettled by what they saw. They tried to tell us, but they ran afoul of a strong human tendency to avoid the implications of a life-threatening illness until we are forced to confront the full-blown disease. In light of the optimism spawned by successes of the movements and the real gains in income and status enjoyed by those of us who benefitted most directly from these successes, this tendency toward repression of news that might spoil our good feelings about our accomplishments became very widespread.

The fact is that two very distinct groups of African Americans were left in the wake of the two movements. One might be called the "Equal Opportunity Generation," the offspring of families who emerged from the Great Depression and World War II sufficiently developed and economically strong to take advantage of the unprecedented opportunities available after 1964. It is the other, much larger group whose situation we are discussing here. These folks, who might be called "Those Who Were Left Behind," were essentially unaffected by the movements. Slavery and the era of Jim Crow undermined their family structures. Many were then brutally exploited as sharecroppers or fled to conditions that were little better in urban centers. In this weakened state, these families were essentially unprotected from the economic ravages of the Great Depression.[2] Their children were in no position to take advantage of the new opportunities, and the conditions of their lives have been steadily deteriorating since the 1960s.

Open discussion of the magnitude of their problems or of any responsibility the rest of us might have to do something about them came to be regarded in many circles of the Equal Opportunity Generation as bad manners, an indicator of bad taste. This sort of avoidance of bad news is very human, and should be understood as the defense mechanism it is: the truth of the growing desperation of the black poor offends on a number of levels. We are shamed by the fact that it is *our* children who behave this way—our children who live this way. We wonder how such neglect reflects on those of us who live better, often much better. And the way they live reminds us of something else that is deeply disturbing: the way that we, the privileged ones, are treated suggests that the places where *we* live are not that far from the places where they live. Their feelings of alienation mirror our own when our comments are ignored or patronized at meetings, when we are hassled by police, experience humiliating difficulties during real estate transactions, when we are followed around in department stores, seated by the kitchen door in restaurants, or otherwise disregarded or treated as undesirable. All of this has been too depressing to contemplate, and it made many of us in the Equal Opportunity Generation angry to be confronted by anyone who tried to force us to face it. We were successful enough at shutting out the news that, on a day-to-day basis, we could live as if what was happening wasn't actually happening.

But repressing the news did not alter the underlying dynamic; it probably only strengthened and accelerated it. As we moved into the 1980s, the reality insisted on getting worse and worse and intruded upon our peace with a voice that was louder and louder, until we were obliged to put forward some sort of explanation. For more than a decade, the dominant interpretation of events and the attendant prescription for change were, "*they* created these conditions, so let them do something about it." The litany is familiar to anyone who has lived through these times. "Our young people are unemployed because of discrimination in employment. Our children are unemployable because the school systems fail to educate them. Our children are unmotivated in school because even if they do learn, no one will employ them. Our children are violent because they have no hope for getting a job, and because *they* are bringing drugs into our communities, and controlling drug turf is the only way many of these kids can 'make it.' Our children use drugs because they have been effectively closed out and they live without hope for 'making it' in American society. Many of our children, including preteens, loiter on the streets at all hours because there are no recreational facilities for them. Our children become unwed mothers because they have no hope of 'making it' in American society. Many parents do not effectively raise their children because no one has ever taught them how, and even if they knew how, they have no hope that anyone will give their kids jobs. So many people were left behind by the Civil Rights Movement because *they* had a quota on how many of us they wanted integrated into American society."

Statements such as these have validity, in the sense that they represent theory, or general explanation, that can be used to understand the data about behavior, attitudes, and conditions of black children; but it is only one explanation, or perhaps only a partial explanation, and it has become increasingly unsatisfying. It is an explanation that tends to focus blame for causing the problems and responsibility for resolving them on forces outside of our ommunities over which we have little or no direct control. As is usually the case, the theory about the cause of a problem dictates the search for a fix. Given the perceived external locus of the causes of our difficulties, it has appeared self-evident to many black people that only an attack on these external causes could redress the situation. These forces have also been perceived as powerful. For many, "powerful" is an understatement; they believe the entire weight of the most powerful forces of American society are arrayed against us. To confront such forces, we would need an equally powerful ally. The federal government, perhaps with the support of some players in big business, enlightened by their own self-interest, came to be regarded as our primary hope of influencing the forces that controlled us. "The problem," went this line of thought, "is a problem of power. White people have a monopoly on power, and much of that power is hostile to our interests and opposed to our advancement. Black people, confronting such formidable adversaries, are essentially powerless." Given such a profound imbalance of power, it stands to reason that influencing powerful, progressive white people to intercede on our behalf and attack the powerful, negative forces that stand against us was the only feasible line of attack.

This perspective on how to solve the problems has itself been problematic. The idea that only white people have the power to change the conditions that afflict our children is very potent because belief in it profoundly limits our options for action. The theory of the problem that leads us to invest our belief in the power of others to change our circumstances has led to paralysis; it has been a formula for immobilization. It is a mind-set that has been widely shared at all levels of black society, captured nicely by the opening lament to a very popular recent song:

"I had some problems, and no one could seem to solve them . . ."

The young man who sang that song has not yet learned that you can get very old waiting for someone to solve your problems for you. Our situation is analogous to his. We cannot find solutions to our problems by suppressing open discussion of the statistics that shame us, or by conferring on someone else the power to make the transformation.

The dip in the national fortunes has provided that final, clarifying slap in the face, bringing new lucidity to our view of our situation. By the early 1990s, as community after community across the country became unlivable, the truth dawned clear enough for virtually everyone to see: successive local and national political regimes, regardless of whether they seemed for us or against us, were similarly ineffectual at slowing the course of decline in black communities. And when these national leaders (powerful icons of white male superiority and dominance) could be induced to discuss the issues at all, it became obvious that they had not a clue about "what is *wrong* with these people," or what to do about it, even if we presume that they care enough to want to do anything at all. And then a broader truth began to emerge: it was not just black folk in trouble. The American economy was in decline. The government was spending far more than it was taking in; bank were failing at a rate not seen since the Great Depression; white kids were no longer learning much in school; the country seemed to be falling apart literally; and the dominant white males who run things were gridlocked and immobilized. As the impotence of national leadership became undeniable the strategy of "holding white folks' feet to the fire" until they came up with solutions for our problems, a strategy revealed to me approvingly by member of the Congressional Black Caucus a decade ago, was itself revealed as a most unpromising approach to changing the conditions of black people in America. *They* could not solve what they understood to be their own problems, even as those problems reached crisis proportions. Clearly the could not be counted on to champion useful solutions for ours. The way thus opened for a search for a different theory of what was wrong and for a very different kind of strategy to bring about change.

There can be no real peace for this generation of black adults, nor pride in our status as beneficiaries of the two movements, unless we take control.

THE ISSUES: DEVELOPMENT AND MOBILIZATION

Our situation will change only when we assume the power to change it. No power flows from attributing problems to forces over which one has no control. Power comes from identifying causative factors which we have the power to impact—searching for sources of leverage and control that are in our hands or within our reach. I will propose a way of understanding the present situation of black children, a theory of our problem, that puts power in the hands of black adults to control the conditions within which black children grow up. I will not suggest that we can control most of the decision about hiring and firing that will determine whether and how they will be employed. But there are many crucial aspects of black children's existence that black adults can control, if we have a theory of the nature of their condition that disposes us to act in a focused, aggressive manner and that capitalizes on all of our potential power.

The current condition of black children is a function of two kinds of failures:

- **Failures of development**—Too many black children grow up without the skills, capabilities, and values they will need to function in this society. Underdevelopment is the most basic reality; it is the very heart of the problem. As long as black children remain underdeveloped, no other solution to the problems black people face will change the basic condition of our communities. Failures of development are a function of failures of education and training, and these are remediable.

* **Failures of mobilization**—The available resources within black communities, the assets available to us with which we could take charge of our situation, have not been mobilized to address the problems of development of the mass of black children. Failures of mobilization are functions of psychological and organizational problems, and these too, are remediable.

These are failures within our power to remedy. We will address them in turn.

The Problem: Underdevelopment. The Solution: Development

There is a simple, unpleasant reality at the heart of the problems that most of our children face, and the problems that many of them cause: far too many black children are underdeveloped, many of them grossly so. They lack the skills, capabilities, and values they will need to thrive as citizens of the 21st century. Many are not proficient in the particular brand of English usage that prevails in the marketplace where they must seek employment; they cannot write a coherent paragraph; they have, at best, rudimentary mathematical skills and so are closed out of the science and technology that drive the modern economy. Too many have not been taught how to behave with ethics and humanity. A minority (but a dangerously organized one) is engaged in criminal behavior—physical and psychological violence most often directed at other black people, particularly other black children.

The failures of training in skills, values, and proper behavior define their underdevelopment and must be squarely faced; but this is not to be confused with "blaming the victim." I am most assuredly not blaming the children for their behavior or their lack of skills. Children are not underdeveloped because they want to be. They are underdeveloped because they have been allowed to be, and the responsibility for the breach lies exclusively with adults. It is not black children who have failed. They have been failed—by their society which, in its own sickness, behaves as if black children do not deserve humane conditions; by their community and its leadership, which have failed to mobilize the resources at our disposal to take the situation into our own hands; by their teachers, who allow schools to become places where black children are made to feel stupid, instead of places where they become smart;[3] and by their parents, who have been poorly served by their culture— who have never been taught an effective model of child-rearing with which to raise 21st century citizens. Arguments about proper shares of the blame for this situation, when so many have already been lost, when the carnage proceeds unabated, and when there is so much blame to go around, are a waste of time. In a circumstance where so many young souls are being destroyed before our eyes, the only question for any serious person is, "who will take responsibility?"

The Objective: 21st Century Standards of Development

Responsibility is facilitated by a clear, simple statement of what we ar trying to do: *the objective must be to develop black children to 21st centur standards of skills, capabilities, and values.* We have translated this objec tive into three specific outcome targets, which we have dubbed the "Efficac 21st Century Educational Objectives," to which I will add a fourth suggeste by John Jacob. To attain the status of true citizenship in the world they wi inherit and full participation in the 21st century economy, by the end of hig school, children must:

- Master calculus (or any substitute form of mathematics certified by math ematicians as equivalent) at the advanced placement level.
- Achieve fluency in at least one language in addition to English.
- Demonstrate a capacity to write a literate, well-structured, well-researche twenty-five page essay on any topic deemed important by teachers an interesting to the student.
- Demonstrate a capacity to "live by strict, high ethical standards."[4]

All educational approaches and programs must demonstrate that they ca produce measurable changes in the direction of these ultimate educationa outcomes. These objectives are based on respect for the actual intelligenc and decency of our children—on accurate understanding of the capacity c virtually all of them to develop to very high levels of intellectual proficienc and ethical standards. These four categories of learning will, of course, no be the exclusive focus of 18 years of education and development. They ar outcome objectives, representing demonstrations of mastery of a wide arra of learning.

Development to the level of these standards is not based on some innat trait. It is a long-term process of building capabilities, values, and conf dence. The following is a formal definition of development that we hav found very useful:

Development is a process of building: a constructive personal identit (including a sense that "I am a decent person," and "I am a perso committed to learning"); the ethics and character required to be a construc tive factor in the lives of others; the analytic and operational capabilit required to function in the world of work; and the self-confidence tha serves as the psychological underpinning for a lifelong commitment t growth and learning.

What is most important and empowering about this definition is the notio that development is a process, rather than a fixed trait. Processes can b managed. If we can learn to manage effectively the process of development, we can build the skills and capabilities of all our children. But there are important obstacles to overcome.

The Innate Ability Paradigm

The idea of development as process is in direct contradiction to the prevailing ideas about intelligence and educability in American education and American society in general. The fact that many black people buy into the prevailing ideas (how could it be otherwise, since we, too, were raised under their shadow) represents a formidable psychological obstacle to taking charge of our children's development. As such, we will address the prevailing assumptions in some detail.

The way we treat children in American society is based on powerful assumptions we share about the distribution of intelligence and its relationship to learning capacity. These assumptions generate educational practices that enter the child's experience as critical events, introducing the conditions for failures of confidence and disrupting the motivation to work at learning. They may be summarized:

- There is a distribution of intelligence within what is considered the "normal" human population; some individuals are highly intelligent (kids would say "very smart"), some are moderately intelligent ("sorta smart"), and some are not very bright ("kinda dumb").
- We can specify how much intelligence is needed to learn particular skills and concepts in school and to fulfill particular vocational or professional functions in adult life.
- We can employ standardized tests to measure the intelligence of children and then predict who will be able to master which skills and assume which functions. Ability placements matching curricula to the judged intelligence of individual children are made on the basis of these measurements.
- We can *infer* levels of intelligence in the absence of formal test data by assessing which material the child seems to be able to master and which s/he cannot and by assessing the rate of mastery of new ideas, concepts, and operations. Thus, assessments of ability need not be left exclusively to experts and standardized test scores; they may reasonably be made by classroom teachers, parents, and other adults as well, relying upon their own observations. Inferences drawn in this way operate with the same force as test data in subsequent judgments about a child's intelligence and ability placements in the schools.

These beliefs constitute a paradigm—a more or less universally accepted, taken-for-granted theory which organizes perception and behavior. The core idea of this paradigm is the belief that intelligence controls the capacity of a individual to develop intellectually and ethically. Intelligence is thought t be an innate endowment, fixed at birth, apportioned to different people i different quantities. The relationship between intelligence and learnin capacity may be modeled:

Innate Intelligence ⟹ Development

Thus, the standard operating assumption in the great majority of America schools is that development is tied to a fixed trait, understood to be beyon our influence. *All the intelligence a child is ever to have is fixed at th moment of birth.* This is a radical notion and should be understood as suck It leads directly to the practice of assessing intelligence in very youn children, then making life-shaping decisions about their educability based o those assessments. This strange notion and the destructive practices spawns have become the central operating principle of American educatior We have lived with it for so long that we accept it without reflection; much c its power, in fact, derives from its status as an unquestioned, taken-for granted aspect of "the way things are."

As long as this fundamental idea remains unquestioned, it will continue t shape a set of destructive attitudes, policies, and behavior toward childrer American children in general—and black children in particular—are ratec sorted, and boxed like so many potatoes moving down a conveyor belt. I schools, we presume to "test" their intelligence using paper and pencil test developed by academics and assessment merchants. Children are then place or "tracked" according to these assessments of their intelligence. There is th "gifted and talented" or advanced placement track for those few (exceedingl few when it comes to black children) considered highly intelligent. There ar the regular programs for those of more modest endowment, and the voca tional and special education classes for those considered "slow." Onl children in the gifted programs can expect the kind of education that will giv them access to the challenges and rewards of the 21st century. Placement i vocational or special education programs is tantamount to a sentence o economic marginality at best, and for many, a lifetime of unemploymen welfare, or involvement in the underground economy of crime and drugs.

School systems organized around the innate ability paradigm become, a best, places where only *some* children are expected to learn; at worst, the become mean, dispirited places. Educators who are convinced that the poo children they work with are incapable of higher learning have no incentive t learn effective instructional approaches to teaching them. When schoo administrators, teachers' union officials, and school board members in sucl systems debate school policy, "they talk," says Jerome Harris, former super intendent of the Atlanta public schools, "about everything *but* kids." Th innate ability paradigm induces people to give up on our children. Once the

20

o, they tend to fight over issues of concern only to grown-ups. Schools ecome places, in fact, where children get little consideration. In the atmophere of futility that pervades urban public education, school policies are ften decided on the basis of what is most convenient for adults.

The idea of fixed traits shapes children's destinies outside of school, too. the home, the community agency, and on the street, adults make assessents of children's behavior and decide which ones are smart, which are ood, which are disruptive or "at risk," and label them, often publicly, ccordingly. Children routinely referred to as "bad" or "dumb" tend to ccept the designations we give them as if they were true. They internalize om an early age the idea that innate, fixed limitations of intelligence and haracter control their destinies. Kids who have learned that they are bad or umb, or both, expect to be that way for life. The sense that these character-tics are immutable has profound negative consequences for their subse-uent behavior and confidence about future prospects.

umors of Inferiority

There is another complicating factor—a factor that is deeply disturbing to lack people. It is a small jump from the idea that intelligence and character re distributed unequally among individuals to the conclusion that they may e distributed unequally among different population groups, too. In the tmosphere generated by the innate ability paradigm on the one hand, and cism on the other, African-American children are routinely subjected to ery negative expectations about their intellectual capabilities. There is a mor of inferiority about black people—a major legacy of American racism—at follows black children to school, especially racially integrated schools.[5] lack children enter the school environment under a general expectation that ey have less intelligence and are severely overrepresented in slow, or special education" classes. Black students make up 16 percent of public chool students, yet make up almost 40 percent of those placed in special ducation or classified as mentally retarded or disabled.[6] They are even more everely underrepresented in the upper end of the placement hierarchy, the advanced placement" or "gifted and talented" classes. These children are lso subject to a range of forces outside the school, including negative peer ressure, that oppose any commitment to intellectual development.

The academic difficulties displayed by many black people, children, and dults are rooted in the fears and self-doubts engendered by the constant rojection of strong negative stereotypes about black intellectual capabili-es. The most recent expression of this theme is the ongoing race/IQ ontroversy, which amounts to a highly public discussion of genetic intellec-al inferiority for black Americans. The embarrassment and self-doubt that re the inevitable by-products of exposure to this kind of public spectacle enerate, in many people, a sequence of avoidance, evasion, and general

unwillingness to commit to intellectual engagement. Such behavior shoul
be understood to be a less-than-conscious reaction to the psychologic
burden of the terrible rumor:

*"If you keep your mouth shut, people might think you're stupid.
If you speak up, they'll know for sure."*

To avoid being proven stupid, many young black people have devise
preventive measures. They drop out or otherwise evade and disparage th
academic situations where their worst fears might find confirmation. In to
many cases, they are encouraged to do so by schools that are predisposed t
view them as intellectually limited. Allowing children to avoid intellectu
engagement is a setup. They forfeit the possibility of the kind of develop
ment that could quiet their fears, create a meaningful possibility of employ
ment, and set the stage for group progress. Avoidance is an understandab
reaction to the rumor of inferiority, but it carries unacceptable consequence
It is time to mount a national movement to set new expectations for blac
children. We must expect nothing less than committed effort and superi
performance in all arenas of endeavor.

The "Get Smart" Paradigm

The definition of development we are proposing here gives us back contr
of the development of our children. It is empowering; the capabilities c
children, including high order intellectual capabilities, can be deliberatel
built up. *The most important single factor controlling learning capacity
children is the ability to view development as a process that adults have th
power to manage.* Taking responsibility for the development of childre
depends on willfully breaking the link in our minds between a child'
learning capacity and crude measures of intelligence. *All children can lear
if the process of learning is effectively organized and managed by adults.*
black community organized around this central idea will be moved by th
examples of educators—inside and outside of schools—who have alway
known that it was true and will incorporate their techniques into an effecti
movement to reform our educational process.

A new framework for thinking about education will include three critic
elements: we must replace the old, destructive ideas about intelligence wi
a new, constructive conception of development; we must build children
self-confidence through positive expectations and emotional support; and w
must instruct them in a general technique for development, applicable acro
the range of academic and character-building domains.

Teach Children a Constructive Theory of Development. The destructive idea that we have put in the heads of our children—that development is the province of an innately gifted few—must be replaced with a new idea that will provide a psychological foundation for confidence and omitted study. An empowering idea, explicitly taught as a part of the formal school curriculum, will define intellectual development as an ongoing process of building analytic and operational capability through effort:

$$\text{Think You Can} \longrightarrow \text{Work Hard} \longrightarrow \text{Get Smart}$$

This model[7] underlines the notion of intelligence as something constructed, something one can build. It is an idea easily taught to young children: "if you believe in yourself, if you 'think you can,' then you will be able to 'work hard' at what you are trying to learn. And if you really work, if you don't give up, you will learn. You will "get smart." This is an alternative, *constructive* notion about the basis of development that can be summed up in a single sentence:

> "Smart is not something that you just are,
> smart is something that you can *get*."

If development is understood by the child to be built up through the expenditure of effort, then the child is in control—the decision about becoming smart is in his or her own hands. Children are empowered and energized by the notion that they can choose to get smart. Instilling confidence that "smart is something that you can get" and training students in techniques associated with getting smart should be primary objectives of early education, at home and in school.

Build Up Children's Confidence Through Belief and Emotional Support. Lack of confidence is the intangible at the core of the educational problems experienced by so many of our children. Building confidence in their learning capabilities will be an essential part of the cure. Strong confidence generates positive attitudes toward development and positive feelings between teacher and student, energizes effort, and allows attention to focus on strategic approaches to the work of learning and teaching. With proper emotional support, all children can learn to believe in their own capabilities. A confident child can confront difficulties without giving up. A child who can stay with it, who can continue to work, will eventually blossom in his/her own time.

Positive expectations and emotional support are powerful tools that adults can use to shape the confidence of children. Jon Saphier[8] suggests a three-part communication combining the two:

23

- This schoolwork I am asking you to do is important.
- I know you can do it, and
- I won't give up on you.

The belief in the child expressed in this kind of communication is experi enced emotionally. It is a gift, an embrace: "I believe in you, and I won give up on you." Children need love and affirmation to grow confident an strong, and they respond to expressions of support and belief from authori figures. Building confidence must become a major objective of all instruc tion, especially in early education. Each child should finish every academi year not only with an increased knowledge base, but also with a stronger fait that "I am the kind of person who can learn whatever is taught to me i school."

Teach Children the Efficacy of Effective Effort, Step-by-Step. Childre who believe that they can learn are able to give their full commitment t learning the *process* of learning; they are, in fact, eager to do so. What w have characterized as the "step-by-step process of development" represen one simple, easily learned technique for "getting smart." It begins wit teaching a child to choose an appropriate starting point, one that matches th difficulty of the material to be learned with the present capabilities of th individual. Initial objectives should be somewhat challenging (involving stretch and some real possibility of failure), but very realistic (failure may b a possibility, but the goal is within the range of what is realistically attain able). Goals that are both challenging and realistic stimulate effective effo and greater satisfaction with the work. A starting point that is realisticall geared to the present capabilities of the child stimulates a belief that "I can d this" and engenders stronger commitment of effort to the task. The per ceived challenge or difficulty involved results in feelings of satisfaction wit eventual success and increased confidence.

Confidence and satisfaction with the results of previous efforts drive th next stage of the process: incrementally increasing the level of challenge o difficulty of the objective and engaging again. Each success generate increased confidence and satisfaction and energizes a more challengin objective for the next attempt. As goals become more challenging, the evoke greater focus; the child becomes increasingly absorbed, immersed i the detail and the work. This heightened involvement alters the experience o the task. The work becomes enjoyable, learning is accelerated, understand ing is deepened. Increasing challenge stimulates changes in the approach t the work, too. As objectives become more difficult, but success still seem possible, the child is strongly motivated toward strategic thinking. Prioritiz ing action steps, working collaboratively with others, more innovative, mor economical, and more pragmatic approaches to the work will often result.

A failure in this system is not viewed as an indication of the limits of one's abilities (how many of us, raised in the innate ability theory of development, reacted to our first real difficulty in mathematics—often in algebra or geometry—by declaring ourselves unequal to the demands of math and carefully avoiding it thereafter?). Failure is simply feedback about one's readiness to accomplish this particular objective. It stimulates corrective action, an increase in intensity of effort, a review of basic concepts, a search for help, or a reexamination of strategies, with no destructive loss of confidence or self-esteem.

These principles of managing development—teaching a constructive theory of intelligence, building confidence through emotional support, and encouraging use of a step-by-step process of development—can be applied wherever we make institutional contact with children. Parents may use them in the home, youth workers can employ them in their day-to-day contact with children using their agencies, and they may become the new operating principles for our public schools. If we are to substitute the "Get Smart" paradigm for the destructive ideas about intelligence that presently control our institutions, a major mobilization will be necessary: an organized effort to bring together all the skill, knowledge, money, and commitment that are available to us.

Mobilization

> *A precipice in front, wolves behind.*
> Erasmus

This is an apt, and evocative, metaphor for our position; we deliberately approach the precipice—the unknowns involved in taking responsibility and assuming accountability when there is no guarantee of success—only when the wolves draw very near. The consequences of doing nothing are now so frightening that they have effectively neutralized our anxieties about taking the full weight of responsibility upon our shoulders. When we take responsibility, we expose ourselves to the psychological hazards of possible failure ("What does it mean if we try, but we can't do it?"). Most people will approach the precipice only when they have to, and, as a people, we have now reached a situation where the wolves are so close that there is a growing consensus that we have no choice but to take the leap.

The pieces of a tremendously successful third movement, quite possibly the final movement, lie all about us. We have much more to work with now than previous generations did—more money, more know-how, more position power. We know more about how this society works, and there are many more of us who are well-positioned to use that knowledge. This is, of course, no accident. Putting us in this position must be precisely what Charlie Houston had in mind, what he and so many others expended their lives

working for. It helps to approach our challenges with some sense of th
resources at our disposal for dealing with them. Black America has:

- Educated people. Nearly 13 percent of our population is college educate
  These people are engaged in every sector of American institutional ar
  economic life. As of 1989, 23.4 percent of 18-to-24-year olds are enroll
  in institutions of higher education. Twenty-six percent are majoring
  social sciences and psychology. In 1989, blacks earned 5.7 percent of a
  bachelor's degrees awarded, 5.1 percent of all medical degrees, and 4
  percent of all law degrees.
- An institutional base, including 67,000 churches, human service agenci
  in every city focused on health care, youth services, and community actio
  The people who operate these institutions understand the community ar
  its people.
- School systems run with significant black participation, and in many case
  outright control. Many urban systems have black superintendents, majo
  ity black school boards, and predominantly black faculty. As of 1985, the
  were 15,036 black faculty in higher education in America.[9]
- Black colleges, with a long history of service that includes training ke
  leadership in the previous movements for change.   There are 99 "histor
  cally black" colleges in the United States.
- National organizations, including the National Urban League, the NAAC
  fraternities, sororities, and various professional organizations.
- Political leadership at the local, state, and federal levels in a position
  fight for strategic policies and legislation favorable to the interests of bla
  children. As of January 1988, there were over 6,829 black elected officia
  in the United States. Recent elections bring the total in the U.S. Congre
  to 40, including the first black woman elected to the Senate.
- Corporate professionals in banks and other financial institutions, loc
  companies, and multinational corporations. These people operate in th
  functional heart of the economic structure of society. They are in produ
  development and design, manufacturing, marketing, finance. They are
  a position to learn how things work and how to get things done.
- Black women near or at parity with whites in earnings given comparab
  educational backgrounds. For every $1,000 a white person with four yea
  of college earns, a black woman with four years of college earns $1,00
- Professional women. Among employed black women, 63 percent are
  professional positions, and 55 percent of those are in managerial position
- Professional people positioned in government, foundations, and other l
  cal and national not-for-profit institutions. Over a third of all black lawye
  work for governmental departments, as do 30 percent of black scientist
- Individuals who are well-positioned in the huge, worldwide sports a
  entertainment industries. There has been important recent progress
  black ownership and control in this arena.

- Small businesses whose annual receipts average $50,000. Approximately 425,000 of this nation's small businesses are owned by African Americans.
- Disposable income, money that must be regarded as a critical source of potential contributions to a cause the people embrace. Nearly 30 percent of black families earn over $35,000, with 14.5 percent earning over $50,000. Blacks make up 7.8 percent of the total personal income earned in this country. There are three blacks on the Forbes list of the 400 richest men and women in the United States.[10]

How a group fares in this society is less a function of how many assets it has and more a function of "how well used." Our community has the resources it needs to take the initiative. Others may have more, but the fact is that we have more now than we did during the times when we mounted the two previous, highly successful social movements. It is the capacity to organize effectively and to mobilize available resources that separates successful generations from less successful ones. In these terms, the two previous generations were successful because they effectively mobilized the limited resources available to them and achieved major change—in the face of powerful opposition. Despite our considerable endowments, the Equal Opportunity Generation, which benefitted most directly from the two movements and who should be expected to lead us to the other side, has not yet mobilized to do so. The ideas and displays of commitment that could galvanize us are not yet in evidence. But the problem is remediable; the failure to galvanize and to organize is not a problem of inability or powerlessness. It is not that our generation lacks the resources, it is simply that we have not yet assembled, organized, and focused those resources.

The great challenge for this privileged generation is to set the foundation for a new mobilization. We must take the methods of the first two movements as our model. As their successes have demonstrated, mobilization requires: articulation of a clear, compelling mission; unshakable belief in our own capacity to take control of the situation; and a plan, an operational approach, that people believe can work.

The Mission: Take Control of the Development of Black Children

The Equal Opportunity Generation will be galvanized by the declaration of a mission it regards as correct—it will be moved when we put forward a feasible approach to solving fundamental problems. The mission must be clear, simply stated, and very compelling; once stated, it will seem obvious to people that it is something we must do. *I propose that the mission for this generation must be to take control of the development of black children—all black children, not just the biological children of the privileged. We must systematically mobilize all the resources we have been given and then efficiently deploy them toward the task of preparing our children to meet the*

27

challenges of the 21st century—as constructive citizens in their own communities and full participants in the international economy.

The twenty-first century educational objectives cited earlier in this paper—calculus, fluency in at least one additional language, capacity to write an excellent 25-page essay, and demonstration of high ethical standards—represent targeted outcomes our children must reach. Given our positions and resources on the one hand, the requirements for safe, healthy communities and the imperatives of the competitive international job market on the other, nothing less is acceptable. This is a mission that will move black people. A focus on empowering their children is the most compelling mission any people can have. Almost all healthy adults are subject to powerful protective impulses toward children, and nothing could be more motivating than a mission to correct the inexcusable conditions faced by black children in America.

Belief

Belief in the goodness, wisdom, and intelligence of black people, and faith in the power of our own leadership to mobilize and organize us will drive this mission. We must believe so devoutly in a vision of what black people could become that we can dare to be openly dissatisfied with what we presently are. There can be no ambivalence on this point. Underdevelopment and immobilization are unacceptable conditions. They lead nowhere and reduce our stature in our own eyes and in the eyes of the world. Excuses and rationalizations only aggravate the problem by communicating to our people that we expect nothing better. We must believe in ourselves enough to demand the highest standards of development for black children and to expect full mobilization of black adults to ensure it. We can accept nothing less. It bears repeating: *underdevelopment and immobilization are unacceptable for a people with the resources and the potential we possess.*

The capacity of any group to take control of its destiny is a function of the quality and commitment of its leadership. The belief of our leadership in their own capabilities and their belief in the qualities of black people will be reflected by their willingness to accept responsibility and accountability for a mission to change our conditions. In light of our failure to do so thus far, those of us in leadership positions must face two basic questions: Do we believe it can be done? Do we believe that *we* can do it? If we believe it can be done, then it is our responsibility to build a movement to do it. There can be no excuses. The only shield from accountability is to take the position that it cannot be done, that we are powerless to do it. We should ask ourselves this question: "Should people who do not believe that a mission can be accomplished be given authority to lead it?" Questions about our capacity to take power can no longer be allowed to stand in the way of mobilization. The most formidable enemy is no longer *them*; it is doubts and fears that we harbor within ourselves, often expressed within our own councils by those who argue that *their* overwhelming power is the source and solution to all our problems. There can be no mobilization based on the sense of inadequacy that such a position implies. The new movement must be declared and organized by leaders who are inspired by belief—in ourselves, our people, and our mission.

When people believe that something is possible, they can learn how to do it, even if they don't know how to do it right now. This was clearly demonstrated by those who strategized the first two movements. It is not a matter of magic, or of waiting for some savior of superhuman endowment to come and tell us what to do. People can "get smart." When ordinary people have the courage to confront a great challenge—a difficult set of problems within their capacities to master—they can always work out solutions if they believe in their own power to do so.

An Operational Approach

No movement can come alive without an operational approach that gives it substance. An effective approach gives momentum; the forward motion it generates spawns learning, greater confidence, and belief. The operational approach of the first movement deployed trained constitutional lawyers in a well-planned assault on the legal underpinnings of segregation.[11] The Civil Rights Movement used a two-pronged operational approach. Marches and demonstrations were employed to shine a harsh light on the traditional practices of segregation and to influence national and international public opinion for basic change.[12] Voter registration campaigns were simultaneously mounted to break the political stranglehold of our adversaries.[13] In both cases, the approaches used were simple in concept and terribly effective in practice. They were created by people who took it upon themselves to make change, who would not take "no" for an answer, and who figured out what to do.

I propose a three-phased operational approach for the third movement. In phase one, we will mount demonstration projects in selected cities to prove that it is possible, under initiatives planned and organized by local black leadership, to change specific outcomes of black children in targeted communities. Demonstration projects can begin only when a group of local leaders have embraced the mission to develop black children and are prepared to publicly declare their own accountability for achieving it. The Efficacy Institute and the Urban League of Eastern Massachusetts have begun such a project to demonstrate the mobilization process in a real community—Boston. We are using Efficacy training programs for community leadership as a primary organizing tool. To date, we have succeeded in getting over 70 leaders in Boston human service agencies to buy into the mission and are planning a public announcement of objectives and accountability in the spring of 1993. In addition to the Boston demonstration, Urban League affiliates in Springfield, Massachusetts, and Miami, Florida, have introduced the Efficacy approach into their local public school systems and are planning to introduce the approach into the human service network as well. By early 1994, we expect to have reportable results on these and other interventions.

Every demonstration project should operate in two venues: public school systems and human service agencies. Schools are an obvious choice. Children spend their best waking hours, five days a week, 180 days a year, in institutions that are mandated to educate them. A training process designed to get their teachers to reject the innate ability paradigm and to adopt a constructive, "get smart" approach to instruction has been demonstrated to have dramatic effects on the academic performance of children.[14] There have been, in fact, a number of programs that have demonstrated positive effects on academic performance of children in urban schools, including (1) the work of Superintendent Jerome Harris in both New York City District 13 and the Atlanta public schools; (2) Jaime Escalanate's successes in teaching calculus to poor Hispanic students in Los Angeles; (3) the work of Dr. John C. Chen, who uses summer crash courses to teach higher mathematics to Philadelphia high school students; and (4) anonymous classroom teachers in cities across the country who consistently teach their poor urban children to the highest standards. These successes prove that our children can learn if public education is organized to make sure that they do.

Human service agencies will be an equally important venue. They have the dual advantage of being places where children go to receive services and recreation, thus facilitating our access to them, and they are institutions that attract as workers many of the most socially committed people in the society. Human service workers have skills in working with people, knowledge of the day-to-day realities our children face, and commitment to making things better. The heads of these agencies, along with top school officials, are generally among the most respected and influential people in the community; as such, their declaration of the mission is likely to draw attention to what we are doing. Successful outcomes for these demonstration projects will, under these circumstances, be duly noted by a cross-section of the community—increasing hope, generating belief in the mission, and credibility for its leadership.

Success must be clearly defined; it will be measured in terms of changes in outcomes on key variables that affect the life chances of children, including academic development in school, and what might be called quality of life indicators, such as statistics on crime, teen pregnancy, and drug use. The focus on measurable changes in outcomes dictates that we start by defining which statistics we will use to describe the conditions of black children. I propose that, over the next year, we establish a "Black Community Children's Index" of key variables we will use to chart our progress. Once the index has been agreed upon, each community will establish baseline data (where are we now on these critical variables?), set concrete objectives for change ("we will get _% improvement on x, y, and z variables by December 31, 19_"), and report on a regular basis (perhaps annually) on the results of the intervention.

Phase two begins once we can show clear successes in the demonstration projects. In this phase we will leverage our successes to expand greatly the number of black people who believe in the mission and who are prepared to support it. Success in phase two will be the basis of a transition from demonstration projects to the real work of building the basis for a national movement. It will be vital that we integrate a broad base of the Equal Opportunity Generation into the planning and execution of the movement at this stage. The combination of demonstrated successes and their own participation will allay the cynicism and disbelief that are the legacy of the deterioration of the last quarter century. Once these folk learn to believe that we can do it, and get excited about the mission, they will commit their time, their money, and their know-how to the building of a movement. It is also vital that we work to integrate the parents of the children we serve. Black parents are frightened by the violent conditions their children face and frustrated by their poor educations and limited prospects. Most are deeply committed to their kids' well-being, even when they don't know how to ensure it. A movement to develop children will find many ready to contribute in any way that they can, and with some prepared to assume leadership roles. To build a broad base of consensus, belief, and commitment, all elements of the community must be part of the planning and execution of the mission.

Once we have demonstrated what is possible and have a critical mass of believers and solid experience at making these interventions work, we will move into phase three: the public launch of a national movement with bold objectives and timetables. A movement launched by black leaders and educators at the local and national levels, willing to accept responsibility for the outcomes of black children, will be taken very seriously by everyone. The world, literally, will be watching, and we will have crossed a point of no return. But that is appropriate, because if we do nothing, there will be no meaningful future for black children.

This phased approach will work. The specifics of each phase await discovery; the point is that experienced, committed, and confident people have the wherewithal to work out the details. Building a movement is fundamentally a creative process. We will fill in the details as we go along, as we confront the problems. Effective people are those who believe intensely in what they are doing and their own capacity to figure out how to do it. They do not demand prefabricated, highly detailed blueprints as a prerequisite to beginning. They immerse themselves in the work, and as issues and problems arise, they are able to find creative solutions and discover new resources, motivation, and sources of power with which to manage a continuous stream of unforeseen challenges and opportunities.

A movement focused on the development of children in no way diminishes the importance or the need for the whole range of human service support activities that dedicated people are presently engaged in. Rather, we are proposing that these initiatives be placed in the context of an organized thrust to take control of the development of our children. This is in keeping with a general *outcomes orientation* that we advocate: the ultimate indicator of a healthy community is its capacity to see the development of its children as its most important outcome. Successful achievement of this outcome requires a mobilized community that is crime-free, has a strong economic infrastructure, is politically active (especially in the arena of education), is characterized by strong families and effective parenting, has a strong tradition of civic-minded volunteerism, etc. These elements of a mobilized community demand activist approaches to changing the present, negative realities. The overall thrust is to build the kind of community that can take care of its children; and that community-building encompasses the whole range of activities that socially committed people presently engage in. In effect, articulating *as our ultimate mission* the imperative to develop children to 21st century standards of education and ethics contextualizes these other critical activities and gives them sharper focus.

There are inherent risks in such an approach. Taking responsibility for changing specific outcomes and accepting accountability for doing so are bold moves. They represent putting our reputations on the line. But taking such risks is essential for generating credibility for those who have accepted the challenge and for stimulating belief in the feasibility of the mission. It will be clear to people that those of us who have accepted accountability would never have done so unless we believed in what we were doing. Once we achieve results, the fact that we are people who have decided to take control of our own situation will be self-evident to all. Building a movement is exciting, challenging work. It is a privilege, not a burden; and it is given only to those who believe.

STAND AND DELIVER

We can, whenever and wherever we choose, successfully teach all children whose schooling is of interest to us. We already know more than we need to do that.

Whether we do or not must finally depend on how we feel about the fact that we haven't so far.

Ron Edmonds

The tremendous psychic injuries of slavery are still with us. We are a people violently dislocated from home, brutalized in bondage, and despised and isolated in emancipation. The effects of centuries of physical and psychological violence on the institutional structure of the group and the self-concepts of individual people should not be underestimated. Such injuries do not heal by themselves, nor will they ever be healed by the descendants of those who caused them. The first two movements broke the isolation and opened opportunities for inclusion into this society. The third movement must use the powers we have gained as a result to heal the damage done to the people, to enable all to take advantage of the opportunities won for us. A new movement focused on development—and the mobilization it requires—represents a concerted, organized effort at self-healing. The process will be therapeutic for all involved. To make sure the children of this generation are not left behind, we must teach them to meet appropriate standards of character and skills, creating a basis for a healthy community and inclusion into the 21st century economy. For the Equal Opportunity Generation, whose injuries are often less visible, success in mobilizing our people and our resources to give our children what they deserve is the minimum requirement for self-respect. We will never be able to hold our heads high until we create the conditions they need to move into the light.

We have all been affected by what our people have endured. Becoming the most developed people in this society should be understood as the proper response to what has been done to us, and the defining task of this generation. The commitment to develop our children will give meaning to the dark past, give purpose to our present accomplishments, and give this generation great stature in the eyes of those who will follow us. History will remember us well when we finish what is before us.

ENDNOTES

[1] All statistics from Andrew Hacker, *Two Nations: Black and White, Separate, Hostile, Unequal* (New York: Charles Scribner's Sons, 1992), and the *1991 Digest of Educational Statistics* (Washington, DC: U.S. Department of Education, Office of Educational Research and Improvement, 1992).

[2] Harold Cruse, *Plural But Equal* (New York: William Morrow and Company, 1987).

[3] Jeff Howard, *Getting Smart* (Lexington, MA: The Efficacy Institute, Inc., 1990).

[4] John E. Jacob, *Keynote Address*, National Urban League Conference, San Diego, CA, July 26, 1992.

[5] Jeff Howard and Ray Hammond, "Rumors of Inferiority," *The New Republic*, September 9, 1985.

[6] Andrew Hacker, *Two Nations: Black and White, op. cit.,* p. 164.

[7] This model was devised for elementary-aged children by a colleague, Verna Ford, as a variant of a more general model previously developed for older children and adults:

Confidence $\Longrightarrow$ Effective Effort $\Longrightarrow$ Development

[8]John Saphier and Robert Gower, *The Skillful Teacher,* 4th Ed. (Carlisle, MA: Research for Better Teaching, Inc., 1987).

[9]*Statistical Record of Black America*, Carrell, Peterson, Horton, Jeffie, Carney, Smith, eds. (New York: Jale Research, Inc., 1990), p. 115.

[10]Statistics taken from Andrew Hacker, *Two Nations.*

[11]Richard Kluger, *Simple Justice* (New York: Alfred A. Knopf, 1976).

[12]Taylor Branch, *Parting the Waters* (New York: Simon and Schuster, 1988).

[13]From conversations with Bob Moses, who led the voter registration campaigns in Mississippi.

[14]In Peoria, Illinois, 21 Efficacy classrooms were established in 14 primary buildings of the public school system during the '90-'91 school year. The intent of the program was to increase reading achievement to a degree greater than would be expected in a typical classroom. Comparisons of the percentile scores obtained in the spring indicated that 16 classrooms had exceeded the projected outcome.

In Detroit public schools, during the '89-'90 school year, 900 third-grade students were in Efficacy classrooms. A study by the Detroit public schools to evaluate the performance of Efficacy students in comparison to a control group of non-Efficacy students indicated that Efficacy students showed a 2.4 percent increase in mean grade equivalent units (GEU) in comparison with non-Efficacy students who showed only a 0.4 percent increase in mean GEUs on the reading portion of the California Achievement Tests. On the mathematics portion of the California Achievement Tests, Efficacy students showed a 1.8 percent increase compared with a 0.7 percent increase for non-Efficacy students.

Detroit also conducted this study at the middle school level during the '90-'91 school year, where 1,400 sixth graders have been in Efficacy classrooms. The study found significant differences in the Efficacy students compared with the non-Efficacy students in reading and mathematics on the California Achievement Tests, grade point averages, and citizenship.

African Americans and the 21st Century Labor Market: Improving the Fit

Billy J. Tidwell, Ph.D.

INTRODUCTION

The importance of human capital to the nation's economic well-being has thrust to the forefront of public policy discussion. Preoccupation with the issue reflects a growing recognition of some serious weaknesses in the U.S. economy and the need to rectify them with vision, decisiveness, and dispatch. The overarching problem is lack of competitiveness. Compelling evidence documents a pronounced decline in America's competitive position in the rapidly developing global economy. Even the latest recession, which continues to spread hardship and insecurity across a broad cross-section of the population, may be regarded as a manifestation of the more fundamental problems that have impaired the general welfare and greatly jeopardized our economic future. Hence, the pervasive adverse effects of this recession have intensified the policy deliberations over rising international competition and what it means for our long-term needs and prospects.

The competitiveness problem is complex, the result of interplay among multiple forces and exigencies, here and around the world. An effective response, therefore, requires a multifaceted strategy. However, the central requirement is to improve the quality and utilization of the nation's human resources. In the changing economic environment, the premium is on enhanced people skills and the productivity derived from personal proficiency in the workplace. Economic growth in the decades ahead will be driven by the engine of human ingenuity.

By the same token, individual economic well-being in the modern era is determined by the match between one's acquired aptitudes and the more discriminating demands of the economy. Moreover, the dynamics of global competition are increasingly unsympathetic to persons who lack the versatility to adapt to ongoing vicissitudes in the labor market.

The implications of these trends for African Americans are at once promising and perilous. On the one hand, the changing demography of the labor force may combine with the mounting centrality of human resources to expand employment opportunity for the group. As African Americans and other minorities comprise a growing share of the available labor pool, the prospect is that employers may have to draw more heavily from this segment of the population for their human capital.

> If companies are to meet their labor needs, they will have to broaden the ethnic and gender makeup of their work forces. In other words, "affirmative action" will no longer be a matter of social responsibility, but of economic necessity.[1]

Thus, there is a manifest convergence between the needs of African Americans and the nation's economic interests. "The needs of the American workplace and the needs of the disadvantaged," echoes *BusinessWeek*, "may be merging for the first time in recent history. The drive to raise productivity and increase international competitiveness is transforming the debate over social equity into a discussion about economic growth."[2] Theoretically, African Americans are strategically positioned to benefit. On the other hand, as intimated, the contemporary labor market is much different from that which existed during the heyday of industrialization when one's pursuit of economic well-being was well served by physical muscle. In the new era, *intellectual* muscle—i.e., the ability to think analytically, compute, comprehend instructions, make decisions, communicate clearly, interact effectively in group endeavor, etc.—is the ticket to prosperity. In this connection, there continues to be an unsettling *lack* of convergence, a bad fit, between the overall conditions of African Americans and the human capital that the changing economy needs. One writer has made this point in stark, poignant terms.

> Black Americans have outlived their usefulness. Their raison d'etre to this society has ceased to be a compelling issue. Once an economic asset, they are now considered an economic drag. The wood is all hewn, the water all drawn, the cotton all picked, and the rails reach from coast to coast. The ditches are all dug, the dishes are put away, and only a few shoes remain to be shined.[3]

The fact that the disadvantages that cloud the economic future of African Americans are largely consequences of the blatant racial oppression of the past and the persisting institutional deprivation and neglect of the present offers little consolation. For the divergence between their conditions and today's imperatives for economic success is a reality that has neither memory nor conscience. However, it will also be unforgiving if we are not more aggressive about improving the fit.

Set in the context of the competitiveness challenge, this multi-sided human resource issue is examined in detail in the pages to follow, using the latest available data. In the end, we conclude that the economic future of *all* Americans hinges on how the human resource question, in terms of the fit problem, is resolved. The primacy of mutual dependence and enlightened self-interest simply cannot be denied.

At the same time, the analysis leaves no doubt that African Americans must be much more astute and proactive on behalf of their own development and participation in the economic mainstream. In particular, we stress the importance of ensuring that development institutions prepare African-American youth to be creative labor market participants and not just afford them the skills needed to land a decent job in a given segment of the economy at a given point in time. "African-American children," in the words of John Jacob, "must be trained to see and seize opportunity in the chaos of the changing domestic marketplace. We must cultivate a new mind-set."[4]

U.S. COMPETITIVENESS: LAPSES, LAGS, AND LOSSES

The United States no longer enjoys the distinction of being the world's indisputed economic superpower. Led by Japan and Germany, other industrialized nations have made remarkable advances that have altered radically the global economic order. The erosion of American preeminence appears in several key indicators of economic performance.[5]

- The U.S. productivity growth rate has slowed dramatically, falling behind that of major international competitors. From 3.1 percent in the 1960s, U.S. productivity growth dropped to 1.1 percent in the 1980s. Japan's productivity growth in the last decade was more than triple the U.S. rate.

- The real gross domestic product (GDP) in the United States rose by just 2.6 percent per year in the 1980s, compared to 2.8 percent in the 1970s and a robust 3.8 percent in the 1960s.

- U.S. trade deficits over the last decade totaled $1 trillion. In 1980, the United States was the world's largest creditor nation, to the tune of about $400 billion. By 1990, we were the largest debtor nation by an even larger amount, much of it borrowed from Japan.

- The United States now trails other industrialized countries—including Japan, Germany, Canada, and the United Kingdom—in national saving rate. The saving rate in Japan more than doubles the U.S. rate. Likewise, the U.S. investment rate is less than half that of Japan and lags well behind that of other competitor nations.

- The federal budget deficit has skyrocketed to $300 billion, while the national debt has soared to $4 trillion. The debt averages to about $50,000 for every American family.

There are still other, equally revealing correlates of economic weakness that fuel concerns about U.S. economic competitiveness.

Real wage growth has dipped sharply, down by 12 percent since 1969. Manufacturing workers have been especially hard-hit. Meanwhile, wages in competitor nations have been on the rise.

Family incomes in the United States have stagnated, but income inequality has widened. Families in the upper fifth of the income distribution have progressed; those in the lower fifth have lost ground. There now is more income inequality in the United States than in any other industrial nation. Unemployment in the 1980s rose over average levels in the 1960s and

1970s, and it remains above 7 percent at this writing. Similarly, the poverty population expanded during the past two decades. In 1991, 35.7 million persons, 14.2 percent of the U.S. population, were poor. The 1991 poverty rate was well above the recent low of 11.4 percent in 1978.

In combination, these conditions and trends bespeak a reduction in the American standard of living and have even more ominous implications for the future. Although African Americans have suffered disproportionately and face the bleakest prospects, the loss of competitiveness will continue to have painful bread-and-butter repercussions across all race and ethnic groups. We all have a stake in reversing the slide.

Among the many factors associated with the long-term competitiveness decline, none is more salient than the decrease in productivity growth. Thus, in the years ahead, the extent to which we achieve productivity gains relative to our major competitors will be the chief determinant of America's status in the international marketplace and the living standard we are able to maintain. The quality of the nation's human resources is absolutely critical in this regard.

In recent decades, expansion of the U.S. economy was largely propelled by the addition of new workers to the labor force. The sheer increase in the number of workers drove up the production of goods and services. However, our *rate* of productivity growth spiraled downward, settling at an anemic one percent during the 1980s. During the same period, productivity growth contributed much less to U.S. economic expansion than it did in other industrialized countries, while an enlarging work force had a relatively stronger role.

In the 1980s, for example, only 62 percent of America's economic growth derived from increased worker productivity, while 38 percent occurred because more people were working. By contrast, in Japan, productivity gains accounted for almost 90 percent of growth in the economy.[6]

As discussed in the next section, we no longer can rely on an expanding work force to move the economy forward. The new imperative for competitiveness is to obtain more output per person-hour of work by upgrading the nation's human capital.

While some American firms have sought to be more competitive by downsizing and otherwise reducing production costs, the gains have come at the expense of lost jobs, lower wages, and declining living standards. Moreover, as a long-term strategy, the cost reduction option is doomed to fail. "If all we're looking at is productivity increases by downsizing," one analyst warns, "it's 'game over' for America."[7]

Thus, the human resource strategy holds the greatest promise, provided we make the right responses to the changing demographics. That means more investment in people, targeted to maximize the payoffs. African Americans are an integral part of the winning scenario. Or are they?

38

THE NEW DEMOGRAPHICS: COUNTS, COLORS, AND CONTINGENCIES

As mentioned, an expanding civilian labor force has been key to U.S. economic growth. Figure 1 shows a marked increase in the labor force growth rate during five-year intervals between 1960 and 1980. The proliferation of baby boomers and a sharp rise in the labor supply of women spurred the escalation. However, a precipitous drop in growth rate occurred in the 1980s and, according to the latest projections by the Bureau of Labor Statistics (BLS), the downward trend will continue through the year 2005. The projected 1995-2005 rate would represent slower growth than in any comparable period since 1960.[8] Over the longer 1990-2005 time frame, overall labor force growth is expected to be just 21 percent, compared to 33 percent over the previous 15 years. These trends mirror changes in the growth of the U.S. population as a whole.

FIGURE 1
Labor Force Change 1960-90 and Projected Change to 2005

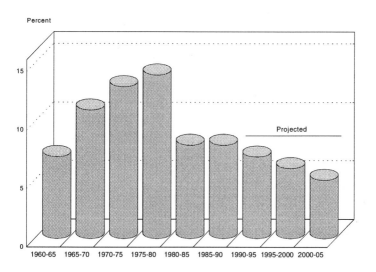

Source: Bureau of Labor Statistics, Bulletin 2402, May 1992, p.3.

In their highly influential report, *Workforce 2000: Work and Workers in the 21st Century*, Johnston and Packer identify three likely economic impacts of the expected slow growth:

1. *The national rate of economic growth will fall well below what it would be if the nation's population and workforce were increasing at the rates of the 1960s and 1970s.* Slower population growth will lead to less demand for population-sensitive products. . . .

2. *Economic growth will depend more directly on increased demand for income-sensitive products.* . . . Companies will focus more on capturing a larger share of disposable income, rather than on serving a greater share of households.

3. *Labor markets will be tighter, due to the slower growth of the workforce and the smaller reservoir of well-qualified workers.* [F]ewer well-educated workers will be available than during the 1960s and 1970s . . .[9]

Although the extent to which the population and labor force growth trends threaten a skills shortage has been debated, there is broad consensus that the projected changes have crucial implications for human resource policy.[10] These implications come into clearer focus in light of some corresponding changes in the racial and ethnic composition of the work force.

While the growth of the overall work force is slowing, the African-American share, along with that of other minorities, is on the rise. African-American workers accounted for 9.9 percent of the total in 1975 and 10.8 percent in 1990. By the year 2005, their proportion is expected to reach 11.8 percent. By contrast, the proportion of whites slipped from 88.3 percent in 1975 to 85.9 percent in 1990, and it is expected to decline further, to 83.4 percent by 2005 (Table 1).

The underlying dynamics of the projected reconfiguration are captured in Table 2. The data speak to the relative proportions of labor force *entrants, leavers,* and *stayers* between 1990 and 2005. Variation in the demographic composition of new entrants from the makeup of the current labor force, combined with the characteristics of those who leave and those who stay during the next 15 years, will determine the racial and ethnic profile of the labor force in 2005.

If the projections hold, about 65 percent of all new entrants between 1990 and 2005 will be non-Hispanic whites, a proportion that is substantially smaller than their 78 percent share of the labor force in 1990. During the same period, non-Hispanic whites are projected to comprise 82 percent of all leavers. The net effect is a 5 percentage point decrease in total representation—from 78 percent in 1990 to 73 percent in 2005.

The outlook is much different for African Americans. Excluding Hispanic blacks, African Americans are expected to account for 13 percent of all new entrants, which well exceeds their 10.7 percent share of the 1990 labor force.

Only 10.5 percent of African Americans are projected to leave during the period, raising their share of the 2005 labor force to almost 12 percent. The data indicate a similar pattern for other minorities.

Table 1
Percent Distribution and Annual Growth Rate of Civilian Labor Force, by Race and Hispanic Origin: 1975-2005

Group	Percent distribution			Annual growth rate (%)	
	1975	1990	2005^	1975-1990	1990-2005^
Total, 16 years and over	100.0	100.0	100.0	1.9	1.3
White	88.3	85.9	83.4	1.7	1.1
African American	9.9	10.8	11.8	2.5	1.9
Hispanic*	N/A	7.7	11.1	5.9	3.8
Asian and other	1.8	3.3	4.8	6.2	3.8

^Projected

*Persons of Hispanic origin may be of any race.

Source: Bureau of Labor Statistics, Bulletin 2402, May 1992, Table 4, p. 5.

Table 2
Percent Distribution of Civilian Labor Force, 1990 and 2005, and Projected Entrants and Leavers, 1990-2005, by Race and Hispanic Origin

Group	Labor force, 1990	Entrants, 1990-2005^	Leavers, 1990-2005^	Labor force, 2005^
Total	100.0	100.0	100.0	100.0
White, non-Hispanic	78.5	65.3	81.8	73.0
African American	10.7	13.0	10.5	11.6
Hispanic	7.7	15.7	5.2	11.1
Asian and other	3.1	6.0	2.4	4.3

^Projected

Source: Bureau of Labor Statistics, Bulletin 2402, May 1992, Table 5, p. 39.

For our purposes, the demographic trends pose two related issues:

(1) To what extent does the current African-American work force "fit" the economy of the 1990s and beyond?

(2) What attributes will new African-American entrants bring to the labor market over the next 15 years, and how well will these attributes mesh with what the changing economy demands? Both issues necessitate a closer look at the economic transformations alluded to in the opening

INDUSTRIAL SHIFTS: GOODS TO SERVICES

The inexorable shift from the production of goods to the production of services is arguably the most profound economic change to occur in the United States since the Industrial Revolution. Measured in terms of shares of total nonfarm wage and salary employment, goods-producing industries dropped from 30 percent in 1975 to 23 percent in 1990. By contrast, the employment share for service-producing industries rose from 70 percent to 77 percent (Table 3). The restructuring was underway well before this recent period. In 1919, for example, the earliest year for which payroll records are available, the services-producing sector encompassed slightly more than half of all nonfarm employment, leaving goods production accounting for less than half.[11]

The point to stress here is that the trend is expected to continue. As Table 3 shows, the goods-producing share of employment is projected to be just 19 percent in 2005, while the proportion for service industries climbs to 81 percent. Although goods-producing industries are expected to create 284,000 new jobs by that time, this net growth stems from a projected gain of 923,000 jobs in construction. Manufacturing, the predominant goods-producing industry, is expected to experience almost 600,000 job losses, continuing the long-term contraction. Meanwhile, service industries are expected to add *23 million* jobs, which represents 99 percent of the projected overall expansion of the nonfarm employment base.

There has been much commentary about the adverse consequences the historical decline of manufacturing has had for the well-being of African Americans and their communities. William Julius Wilson's analysis in *The Truly Disadvantaged* is particularly insightful. He concludes that the loss of manufacturing jobs is the chief factor behind the emergence of the so-called "black underclass" and the rapid economic deterioration of the nation's inner cities where African Americans remain heavily concentrated. African-American males, says Wilson, have been especially hard-hit, resulting in a shrinking pool of "marriageable" men to form and maintain economically viable families.[12] As recently as 1982-1987, New York City lost 93,000 manufacturing jobs; Chicago, 56,000; and Philadelphia, 29,000.[13]

The cities have lost manufacturing jobs in two ways. First, some plants have simply closed down, unable to survive changing markets and competi-

Table 3

U.S. Employment by Industry: 1975, 1990, and Projected to 2005
(numbers in thousands)

Industry	Number 1975	Number 1990	Number 2005	Percent 1975	Percent 1990	Percent 2005	Change 1990-2005
Total							
Nonfarm	76,680	109,319	132,647	100.0	100.0	100.0	23,328
Goods	22,600	24,958	25,242	29.5	22.8	19.0	284
Services	54,080	84,363	113,168	70.5	77.2	81.0	23,042

Source: U.S. Department of Labor, Bureau of Labor Statistics, Bulletin 2402, May 1992, Table 1, p. 44.

tion. Second, many manufacturing plants have relocated—from urban areas to the suburbs or from the densely populated Northeast and Midwest to other parts of the country where wage rates and taxes are relatively low. Whether they move to the suburbs or the Sunbelt, the jobs in many companies are often physically inaccessible to residents of the areas from which they departed.[14]

And what does the industrial restructuring portend for African Americans in the future? The prospects are less than sanguine. African Americans continue to be greatly dependent on the manufacturing sector, accounting for more than 10 percent of all manufacturing workers in 1991 (Figure 2). By comparison, they represented only 6.6 percent of all workers in the growing construction industry. Hence, there is a "bad fit" between the current distribution of the African-American work force and the reconfiguring industrial base. This point is underscored by observed racial differences in the incidence of job displacement in manufacturing industries and in the post-displacement experiences of affected workers, especially males.

Empirical study shows that African-American male manufacturing workers, particularly those in durable goods production, are significantly more likely to be displaced than are their white counterparts.[15] Between 1979 and 1986, for example, the displacement rate among African-American male durable goods workers was a full eight percentage points higher than the rate for whites.[16] Analysis of the outcomes of displacement during this period revealed the following:

• African Americans were less likely than whites to be reemployed after displacement.

• Displaced African Americans experienced much longer jobless spells than did whites.

43

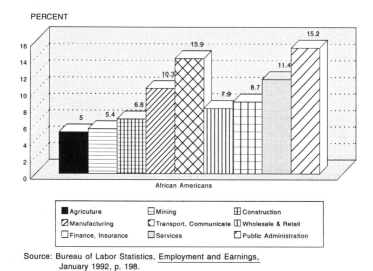

FIGURE 2
African American Proportion of Workforce
by Major Industry: 1991

Source: Bureau of Labor Statistics, Employment and Earnings,
January 1992, p. 198.

- Following displacement, African Americans were less likely than whites to be reemployed in manufacturing.
- African Americans were less likely to regain employment in the same area of manufacturing from which they were displaced.

As the researcher points out, the "postdisplacement differences [between African Americans and whites] occurred despite many similarities in labor market characteristics prior to displacement."[17] Thus, the industry-related fit problem is compounded by the apparent effects of racial discrimination.

In any event, restructuring of the economy's industrial base has brought disproportionate hardship to the African-American work force. Under present conditions, there is little reason to expect this circumstance to improve. The parallel pattern of occupational changes could have even more ominous implications.

OCCUPATIONAL SHIFTS: BRAWN TO BRAINS

Johnston and Packer are widely credited with having raised public awareness of the changing occupational structure and related work-force issues.[18] The central proposition generated by their trend analysis is that "the skill mix of the economy will be moving rapidly upscale, with most new jobs demanding more education and higher levels of language, math, and reasoning skills."[19]   More recent projections by the Bureau of Labor Statistics support this forecast.

According to the BLS, the U.S. employment base is expected to expand by 20 percent between 1990 and 2005, which translates to about 25 million new jobs.   During this period, occupations that require higher levels of education or training are projected to grow significantly faster than those having less demanding requirements.   Although employers will continue to need workers at all education and skills levels, "the fact remains that workers with higher levels of education or training usually will have more options in the   job market and better prospects for obtaining the higher paying jobs."[20]

Table 4
Percent Distribution of Employment by Major Occupational Group, 1990 and Projected 2005, and Percent Change, 1975-90 and 1990-2005

Occupation	1990	2005	Percent Change 1975-1990	Percent Change 1990-2005
Total	100.0%	100.0%	37.4%	20.1%
Exec., admin., & mgr.	10.2	10.8	83.1	27.4
Prof. spec.	12.9	14.2	59.9	32.3
Tech. & related support	3.4	3.9	75.7	36.9
Mkt./sales	11.5	11.9	55.1	24.1
Adm. support, including clerical	17.9	16.9	33.9	13.1
Service	15.7	16.9	36.1	29.2
Agri., forestry, & fishing	2.9	2.5	-9.8	4.5
Precision prod., craft, & repair	11.5	10.8	28.9	12.6
Opers., fabricators, & laborers	14.1	12.2	6.7	4.2

Source: Extrapolated from Bureau of Labor Statistics, Bulletin 2402, May 1992, Table 1, p. 63.

As Table 4 shows, of the major occupational groups, technical and related support jobs are projected to grow fastest (37 percent), followed by professional specialists (32 percent); service workers (29 percent); and executives, administrators, and managers (27 percent). The projections for the technical, professional, and executive positions are particularly noteworthy, inasmuch as these occupations are recognized to entail relatively extensive amounts of education and training. Combined, they account for 41 percent of the projected expansion of the U.S. employment base between 1990 and 2005. However, it is noteworthy, also, that the growth rate of managerial occupations has slipped from first in the 1975-90 period to a projected fourth in the ensuing 15 years. We return to this observation later.

At the other extreme, the operators, fabricators, and laborers category, which comprised 14 percent of total employment in 1990 and grew at the rate of less than 7 percent between 1975 and 1990, is expected to continue bringing up the rear. These relatively low-skill occupations are projected to expand by just 4 percent during the 1990-2005 period, reducing their share of total employment to about 12 percent. The projections reflect the continuing vulnerability of workers in the declining manufacturing sector of the economy.

The higher-than-average rate of increase in the number of professional workers—in both the 1975-90 and 1990-2005 periods—is pronounced in the services industry, where 80 percent of all new professional jobs between 1990 and 2005 are expected to materialize. To a comparable degree, the pace-setting growth of the technical and related support occupational group is also expected to center in the services industry. The progressive ascendancy of the services sector is readily apparent as one reviews the industry-occupation matrix on which the projected occupational shifts are based.[21]

Equally illuminating data are provided in Tables 5 and 6, which show, respectively, the 20 fastest growing occupations and the 20 that are expected to generate the most jobs between 1990 and 2005, based on the new BLS projections. Most striking is the overwhelming predominance of service industry occupations—led by home health aides, which, at a 92 percent growth rate, are expected to nearly double in number by 2005. Likewise, the paralegal profession shows remarkably rapid growth (85 percent). The lowest growth rate—for medical records technicians—is an impressive 54 percent (Table 5).

Ranked by projected absolute growth, the number of retail sales workers is expected to climb by almost 900,000, while registered nurses should add close to 800,000 jobs to the employment base during the next 15 years. Seven other members of the top 20, constituting a reasonable cross-section of American industry, have projected job growth of well over half a million. (See Table 6.) Although several of the most prolific occupations are relatively low-skill and/or low-pay types, others are highly positioned in

46

Table 5
Twenty Fastest Growing Occupations
(Numbers in thousands)

Occupation	Projected employment growth, 1990-2005	
	Number	Percent
Home health aides	263	91.7
Paralegals	77	85.7
Systems analysts and computer scientists	366	78.9
Personal and home care aides	79	76.7
Physical therapists	67	76.0
Medical assistants	122	73.9
Operations research analysts	42	73.2
Human services workers	103	71.2
Radiologic technologists and technicians	103	69.5
Medical secretaries	158	68.3
Physical & corrective therapy assts. & aides	29	64.0
Psychologists	79	63.6
Travel agents	82	62.3
Correction officers	142	61.4
Data processing equipment repairers	50	60.0
Flight attendants	59	58.5
Computer programmers	317	56.1
Occupational therapists	20	55.2
Surgical technologists	21	55.2
Medical records technicians	28	54.3

Source: Extrapolated from Bureau of Labor Statistics, Bulletin 2402, May 1992, Table 3, p. 79.

Table 6
Twenty Occupations with the Most New Jobs,
1990-2005
(Numbers in thousands)

Occupation	Projected employment growth, 1990-2005	
	Number	Percent
Salespersons, retail	887	24.5
Registered nurses	767	44.4
Cashiers	685	26.0
General office clerks	670	24.5
Truck drivers	617	26.1
General managers and top executives	598	19.4
Janitors & cleaners, including maids & housekeepers	555	18.5
Nursing aides, orderlies and attendants	552	43.4
Food counter, fountain, & related workers	550	34.2
Waiters and waitresses	449	25.7
Teachers, sec. school	437	34.2
Receptionists and information clerks	422	46.9
Systems analysts and computer scientists	366	78.9
Food preparation workers	365	31.6
Child care workers	353	48.8
Gardeners/groundskeepers	348	39.8
Accountants and auditors	340	34.5
Computer programmers	317	56.1
Teachers, elementary	313	23.0
Guards	298	33.7

Source: Extrapolated from Bureau of Labor Statistics, Bulletin 2402, May 1992, Table 4, p. 80.

both respects. For example, almost 600,000 more general managers and top executives are expected to be added to the work force, along with 366,000 systems analysts and computer scientists.

Of signal importance to the present analysis are the educational requirements of the fastest growing and most populous occupations. Those that require education or training beyond high school are prominent in both distributions. Moreover, jobs that generally require a college education or more—e.g., systems analysts/computer scientists, physical therapists, operations research analysts, psychologists, teachers—are well represented.

Contrasted against the growth occupations are those whose work forces are expected to shrink (data not shown). The manufacturing sector encompasses a disproportionate number of these occupations. Recall that manufacturing industries are projected to lose some 600,000 jobs between 1990 and 2005.

Table 7
African-American Share of Major Occupations in
1991 and Projected Occupation Growth Rates,
1990-2005

Occupation	African American Percent in 1991	Occ. Growth Rate 1990-2005
Total	10.1	20.1
Exec., admin., & managerial	5.7	27.4
Prof. specialty	6.7	32.3
Technicians and related support	9.3	36.9
Sales	6.6	24.1
Admin. support, including clerical	11.4	13.1
Service	17.2	29.2
Precision prod., craft, & repair	7.8	12.6
Opers., fabricators, & laborers	15.0	4.2
Agri., forestry, fishing, etc.	6.4	4.5

Sources: Bureau of Labor Statistics, *Employment and Earnings, January 1992*, Table 22, pp. 185-190; Bulletin 2402, May 1992, Table 1, p. 63.

And what about the "fit"? What about the convergence between where African Americans are and the shifting occupational structure? What about the match between the human capital of African Americans and the upscaling requirements of the labor market? Table 7 provides a partial answer. It compares the representation of African Americans in the major occupational categories in 1991 to the projected 1990-2005 growth rate for each occupation.

Again, the fit is not very good: African Americans are greatly underrepresented in the fastest growing occupations and overrepresented in those having the slowest projected growth. For example, in 1991, African Americans accounted for just 9 percent of the employed work force in the front-running technical and related support occupations, which are expanding at a 37 percent rate. By contrast, the African-American share of the shrinking operators, fabricators, and laborers group was nearly four times the minimal 4 percent growth rate for these occupations.

With respect to human capital characteristics, the contemporary African American profile is similarly unfavorable. In particular, their educational status puts them at a serious disadvantage in the competition for the high growth, high-paying jobs. In 1991, the proportion of African Americans who had completed high school was more than 20 percentage points below that of whites. Only 29 percent of African Americans had attained one or more years of college education, compared to 46 percent of whites. And

FIGURE 3
Years of School Completed by Persons 15 Years and Older by Race: 1991

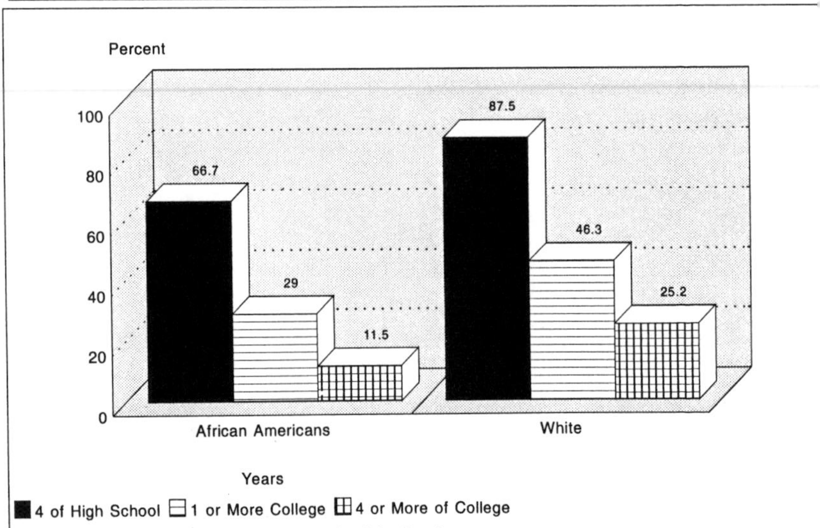

Percent

| | 4 of High School | 1 or More College | 4 or More of College |

African Americans: 66.7, 29, 11.5
White: 87.5, 46.3, 25.2

Years

■ 4 of High School ⊟ 1 or More College ⊞ 4 or More of College

Source: Bureau of the Census, Current Population Reports, "Educational Attainment in the United States: March 1991 and 1990," (Series P-20, No. 462), pp. 15-28.

African Americans were less than half as likely to have attained four or more years of college (Figure 3). More discouraging, perhaps, is the fact that the high school dropout rate among African-American youth (ages 16-24) is 53 percent higher than the rate for their white counterparts.[22]

In short, the shifting occupational structure does not bode well for the economic future of African Americans. Both their current placement in the labor market and their relative position on the hierarchy of educational attainment are major constraints. Relieving these constraints, i.e., "improving the fit," is essential to the overall economic well-being of the African-American community in the years ahead. But the challenge may be even more complicated than that.

PAINS OF PROGRESS: WORK, WORKERS, AND WORKPLACES

It was mentioned earlier that the growth rate for executive, administrative, and managerial occupations, while still robust, dropped from the highest ranking between 1975 and 1990 to a projected fourth in the ensuing 15-year period. (See Table 4.) This development is another by-product of the broad-scale economic restructuring phenomenon, and it has yet to run its course. Just as many frontline workers, in manufacturing and elsewhere, have been impacted adversely by the fundamental industrial and occupational changes in the economy, so, too, have persons higher up the occupational ladder—i.e., persons who are relatively well educated. Only during the latest recession has this aspect of the situation commanded widespread attention. It could have—indeed, has had—a tremendous bearing on the labor market prospects for African Americans and is, therefore, an important subject for discussion here.

In the drive to become more competitive, American companies are tending toward a flatter, leaner organizational form. This downsizing (or "rightsizing," as corporate heads prefer to call it) has resulted in the elimination of hundreds of thousands of jobs—management jobs. In just the last few months, such blue-chip companies as General Motors, Federal Express, and IBM have led the general trend. The IBM case is particularly notable, in that its announced 25,000 job cuts worldwide in 1993 include provisions for laying off workers for the first time in "Big Blue's" 78-year history.[23] The response to global competition is serious business, indeed.

In practical terms, the organizational flattening involves abolishing many middle-management and supervisory positions. The process is aided by advancements in computer technology that render superfluous whole tiers of managers and their staffs. Once eliminated, these positions are gone for good, their decision-making and other functions being moved to lower level employees who, supported by the new technology, are equally capable of executing them. This is the workplace of the future, and the future is now.

> Entire layers of management and supervision will be erased from the organizational chart. Traditional ideas about a "span of control" where a manager or supervisor was needed for every four, five, or six employees are being discarded. Instead of a narrow span of control, companies are now beginning to look at a much broader span of communication or span of information as the basis for establishing the number and levels of management. ˌ No longer are [sic] the number of employees per manager constrained by how many he or she can "control." Rather, the constraining factor is "how many he or she can communicate with effectively."[24]

Some of the labor market effects of this streamlining can be surmised from unemployment statistics. For example, while the nation's overall unemployment rate rose by 21 percent between 1989 and 1991, unemployment among executives, administrators, and managers jumped by 28 percent. African Americans in these occupations in 1991 were 1.6 times as likely as their white counterparts to be jobless.[25] In other words, management personnel are being hit hard by the corporate restructuring, and African-American managers are experiencing a disproportionate impact. The "last hired, first fired" principle is alive and well in this context.[26]

The upshot of this discussion is threefold. First, credentials that formerly served management-oriented African Americans well may no longer assure their economic success. Second, African Americans must guard against being trained for positions that either no longer exist or whose disappearance seems imminent. Third, the shift of responsibility to lower level workers demands that they possess strong human capital attributes. As Boyett and Conn explain, the realignment of responsibilities:

> . . . will exert enormous pressures on employees and companies alike to invest in education and retraining. Continuous learning will become commonplace to create a more flexible work force, provide employees with the skills necessary to take advantage of rapidly changing technology, and prepare employees for new jobs inside or outside the company when their old jobs are replaced by technology or eliminated due to changes in customer demands.[27]

They drive home the point by emphasizing that:

> Since continuous learning will be required to just maintain a position and will be even more critical for advancement, a solid basic education will be mandatory for any American to have a hope of succeeding. Obviously, basic literacy—reading, writing, arithmetic—will be essential. Much more than basic literacy will be required for success in the new organization. Americans will need to know how to solve problems, think creatively, and work effectively in a group.[28]

With these considerations, the "fit" problem takes on additional complexity. Recall John Jacob's sagacious pronouncement: "*African Americans must be trained to see and seize opportunity in the chaos of the changing domestic marketplace . . .*" It is helpful to examine more closely the kinds of "chaotic" conditions he has in mind and what they imply for African

American participation in the economic mainstream. Boyett and Conn are exceedingly instructive in this regard. Below are some of their most telling points.[29]

- Americans who process information, analyze information, and/or make routine decisions are likely to find their positions in danger within the next decade. Responsibilities will be shifted to workers and their peers for planning, scheduling, organizing, directing, and controlling their own work process.

- No job will be entirely secure, whether inside or outside of a large company. Because of their high failure rate, small entrepreneurial companies will continue to be volatile places to work. The average American will most likely work in ten or more different types of jobs and at least five different companies.

- Adaptability and creativity will be more important for success than seniority and loyalty. There will be fewer opportunities for promotion to management or supervisory ranks. Hence, traditional paths of career advancement will be closed to most people. The most valued employees will be those who are flexible and can perform a wide range of functions.

- Success will flow to those who can effectively use data presented to them to modify their own behavior or to identify new opportunities for the organization. Americans who want to succeed will need the ability to analyze data, draw conclusions, and present recommendations.

- Whole groups of American workers will lose their jobs or find their association with a particular company terminated as major companies "disintegrate" and refocus on a "core business" where they can be really good.

Although these observations focus on the private economy, most describe the modern public sector workplace as well. In addition, of course, the private economy will continue to account for the overwhelming majority of jobs. Also, it bears emphasizing that the trends toward "chaos" are already well underway, propelled by the irresistible dynamics of global competition.

So where is the opportunity in the chaos? Where are the passages to progress for African-American workers in the changed environment? To begin with, there will continue to be attractive, well-paying positions in large corporations for versatile individuals who covet authority and responsibility. While such positions are becoming less plentiful and the requirements for occupancy more stringent, they remain integral to American business.

Second, there is the opportunity to pursue entrepreneurial "micro-businesses," i.e., enterprises that are undertaken with fewer than four employees. Such businesses are often launched by corporate executives and mid-level managers who lose their position to downsizing or expect the axe to fall.[30]

Third, there is the prospect of establishing a small firm with venture backing from a large company. As Boyett and Conn point out, "Such arrangements increased dramatically in the 1980s (from only 32 in 1980 to 477 in 1987) and are likely to become even more popular in the 1990s."[31]

Finally, one might look to start an "intrepreneurial" venture inside a big corporation. Some companies have formed special units or earmarked funds to encourage innovative employees to develop their own businesses, within the corporate framework. The Colgate-Palmolive Company and S.C. Johnson & Sons, Inc., are two notable examples.[32]

Thus, the most fruitful opportunities for professional and financial advancement are linked to one's ability to recognize and exploit openings to create new small business enterprises within large companies or as independent entities. The contemporary corporate restructuring phenomenon, therefore, brings bad news *and* good news.

> On one side, the elimination of layers of management drastically reduces opportunities for promotion. On the other hand, the expansion of small businesses and the creation of entrepreneurial business units within large organizations greatly expand opportunities for enterprising Americans. . .[33]

Whether they are inclined to entrepreneurship, to management within the corporate setting, or simply to the role of productive employees, it is clear that African Americans must be much better prepared to participate in the changing economy than they have been to date. It is clear that "improving the fit" presents a tremendous challenge to the nation as well as to African Americans themselves.

CONCLUSIONS: IMPROVING THE FIT

This paper has examined several issues related to what we call a lack of "fit" between the contemporary conditions of African Americans and the changing U.S. economy. Three main conclusions emerge. First, there is indeed a fit problem of substantial magnitude. It is impairing the economic well-being of African Americans in the short-term as well as threatening their long-term prospects.

Second, the problem is more complex than is generally recognized. It is not simply a matter of one's ability to get a job.

Third, the fit problem as it concerns African Americans has its locus in a

54

pervasive set of conditions that jeopardizes the economic future of the work force and nation as a whole. Although African Americans are at disproportionate risk, the quality of our human resources in general is inadequate to meet the mounting challenge of global economic competitiveness.

The National Urban League has been in the forefront in enhancing public understanding of the competitiveness issue as it pertains to human resource development and other domestic needs. Likewise, the League has been forthcoming and aggressive in proposing policy initiatives to deal with the situation.[34] Key to these efforts is the assessment of mutual dependence between the interests of African Americans and broader national interests. Given the new demographic realities, America will be hard-pressed to improve its competitive position if it does not put priority emphasis on the needs of African Americans and other disadvantaged minorities, within the framework of a national human capital development strategy.

The National Urban League is joined in its concerns— about the competitiveness challenge, in general, and the human resource question, in particular—by a growing cross-section of public officials, corporate leaders, academicians, public interest groups, political commentators, and the popular media.[35] Most important, President Bill Clinton campaigned on a platform which had as its centerpiece the necessity to restore economic competitiveness, and he brings to his leadership ideas that are more than compatible with those of the League.[36] The new president's overriding concept of "putting people first" effectively represents the League's own perspective on the problem and the policy imperatives. It remains now to actualize the concept through initiatives such as those the League has proposed.

At the same time, whatever happens on the policy level, African Americans must be resolute about furthering their own development vis-a-vis the labor market changes we have reviewed. Ensuring that all African-American children have the intellectual, emotional, and moral wherewithal to produce and progress in the new environment is paramount. In the final analysis, "improving the fit" comes down to that.

* * * * *

The author would like to thank Djenaba Kai Tidwell and Marcus Gordon for their assistance in preparing this paper.

ENDNOTES

[1] U.S. Department of Labor, *Opportunity 2000: Creative Affirmative Action Strategies for a Changing Workforce* (Washington, DC: U.S. Government Printing Office, 1988), p. 16.

[2] *BusinessWeek*, September 19, 1988, p. 103.

[3] Samuel F. Yette, *The Choice: The Issue of Black Survival in America* (New York: G.P. Putnam's Sons, 1971), p. 18.

[4] Personal communication with the author, December 3, 1992.

[5] Sources include David Alan Aschauer, *Public Investment and Private Sector Growth: The Economic Benefits of Reducing America's "Third Deficit"* (Washington, DC: Economic Policy Institute, 1991); Samuel Bowles et al., *After the Wasteland: A Democratic Economics for the Year 2000* (Armonk, NY: M.E. Sharpe, Inc., 1991); *BusinessWeek*, 1992 Special Bonus Issue, "Reinventing America: Meeting the New Challenges of a Global Economy"; Anthony Patrick Carnevale, *America and the New Economy* (Alexandria, VA: American Society for Training and Development, 1991); Competitiveness Policy Council, *Building a Competitive America* (Washington, DC: Competitiveness Policy Council, 1992); Cuomo Commission on Competitiveness, *America's Agenda: Rebuilding Economic Strength* (Armonk, NY: M.E. Sharpe, Inc., 1992); Lawrence Mishel and David Frankel, *The State of Working America, 1991-92 Edition* (Armonk, NY: M.E. Sharpe, Inc., 1992); Billy J. Tidwell, *Playing to Win: A Marshall Plan for America* (New York: National Urban League, Inc., 1991).

[6] Tidwell, *op. cit.*, p. 11.

[7] Stephen S. Roach, senior economist at Morgan Stanley & Company, as quoted in *BusinessWeek*, "Reinventing America," *op. cit.*, p. 22.

[8] U.S. Department of Labor, Bureau of Labor Statistics, *Outlook: 1990-2005*, Bulletin 2402 (Washington, DC: U.S. Government Printing Office, 1992), p. 3..

[9] William B. Johnston and Arnold H. Packer, *Workforce 2000: Work and Workers for the 21st Century* (Indianapolis: The Hudson Institute, 1987), pp. 78-79.

[10] For example, see Lawrence Mishel and Ruy A. Teixeira, *The Myth of the Coming Labor Shortage: Jobs, Skills, and Incomes of America's Workforce 2000* (Washington, DC: Economic Policy Institute, 1991) and John Bishop, "Is a Skills Shortage Coming?," *Workforce* (Spring 1992), pp. 15-30. Bishop finds that the available data seriously underestimate the future need for well-educated, high-skilled workers, while Mishel and Teixeira draw more moderate conclusions.

[11] Janet L. Norwood, "Projections 2005," *Workforce* (Spring 1992), pp. 12-14.

[12] William Julius Wilson, *The Truly Disadvantaged: The Inner City, the Underclass, and the Public Policy* (Chicago: The University of Chicago Press, 1987).

[13] U.S. Department of Commerce, Bureau of Census, *Census of Manufacturing, 1982 and 1987* (Washington, DC: U.S. Government Printing Office, 1987).

[14] For relevant discussion, see John F. Kain, "Housing Segregation, Negro Employment, and Metropolitan Decentralization," *The Quarterly Journal of Economics (May 1968)*, pp. 175-97. Also, Wilson, *op. cit.*, and Charles L. Betsey and Bruce H. Dunson, "The High Tech Revolution and Its Implications for Black America," in James D. Williams (ed.), *The State of Black America 1984* (New York: National Urban League, Inc., 1984), pp. 25-42.

[15] Lori G. Kletzer, "Job Displacement: Black and White Workers Compared," *Monthly Labor Review*, July 1991, pp. 17-25.

[16] *Ibid.*, Table 1, p. 18.

[17] *Ibid.*, p. 24.

[18] Johnston and Packer, *op. cit.*

[19] *Ibid.*, p. 96.

[20] George Silvestri and John Lukasiewicz, "Occupational Employment Projections," in Bureau of Labor Statistics, *Outlook 1990-2005, op. cit.*, p. 62.

[21] *Ibid.*, p. 64.

[22] *Digest of Education Statistics, 1992* (Washington, DC: National Center for Education Statistics, 1992), Table 98, p. 109.

[23] "IBM Plans More Job Cuts, Calls Its First Layoffs Likely," *The Washington Post*, December 16, 1992, pp. A1, A8.

[24] Joseph H. Boyett and Henry P. Conn, *Workplace 2000: The Revolution Shaping American Business* (New York: Plume, 1992), pp. 28-29.

[25] U.S. Department of Labor, Bureau of Labor Statistics, *Employment and Earnings, January 1990* (Washington, DC: U.S. Government Printing Office, 1990); *Employment and Earnings, January 1992* (Washington, DC: U.S. Government Printing Office, 1992). Racial unemployment gap in 1991 computed from unpublished race and occupation data.

[26] Similar changes are occurring in the public sector, as governments struggle with budget deficits and seek to improve operational efficiency. Of course, African Americans continue to be greatly dependent upon government employment and, therefore, have been hit hard by the public belt-tightening.

[27] Boyett and Conn, *op. cit.*, p. 7.

[28] *Ibid.*, p. 8.

[29] *Ibid.*, Chapters 1 and 2.

[30] "More Execs Strike Out On Their Own," *USA Today*, May 10, 1988, p. B1.

[31] *Op. cit.*, p. 36. See also Joel Kotlin, "Natural Partners: A New Source of Start-Up Financing," *Inc.*, June 1989.

[32] "Consumer-Product Giants Relying on 'Intrepreneurs' in New Ventures," *The Wall Street Journal*, April 22, 1988.

[33] Boyett and Conn, *op. cit.*, p. 44.

[34] Tidwell, *Playing to Win: A Marshall Plan for America, op. cit.*; "Serving the National Interest: A Marshall Plan for America" in Billy J, Tidwell (ed.), *The State of Black America 1992* (New York: National Urban League, Inc., 1992), pp. 11-30.

[35] In addition to citations previously mentioned, see Commission on the Skills of the American Workforce, *America's Choice: High Skills or Low Wages* (Rochester, NY: National Center on Education and the Economy, 1990); Ray Marshall and Marc Tucker, *Thinking for a Living* (Rochester, NY: National Center on Education and the Economy, 1992); The Secretary's Commission on Achieving Necessary Skills, *What Work Requires of Schools* (Washington, DC: U.S. Department of Labor, 1991); Robert B. Reich, *The Work of Nations: Preparing Ourselves for 21st Century Capitalism* (New York: Alfred A. Knopf, 1991). Among popular news magazines, *BusinessWeek* has been particularly informative on the issues. The 1992 Special Bonus Issue, "Reinventing America: Meeting the New Challenges of a Global Economy," was preceded by a 1987 issue entitled "Can America Compete?" and a 1988 edition on "Human Capital."

[36] Bill Clinton and Al Gore, *Putting People First: How We Can All Change America* (New York: Times Books, 1992).

Promoting Priorities: African-American Political Influence in the 1990s

Charles V. Hamilton, Ph.D.

AN ELECTORAL STRATEGY

It was not difficult to notice an obvious feature of the 1992 presidential election regarding the issues of racism and civil rights. More than a few commentators and political activists called attention to the relative absence of specific reference from either major candidate to matters of racial discrimination and segregation. In fact, this was the first presidential election since 1944 where the civil rights of African Americans was not dealt with in some overt form. Even more significant, neither was this omission expected to redound to the detriment of either political party. That is, both parties concluded in 1992 that it was best to subordinate the issue of racism to other concerns. Both parties concluded, for different reasons, of course, that no mileage could be gained by addressing the issue explicitly. The Republicans could hardly resurrect the despicable Willie Horton-race-baiting tactic of 1988 for fear of alienating decent *white* voters who saw such advertising as deplorable. Plus, such an approach just might activate some anti-Republican black voters in strategic electoral college states. At the same time, the Democrats, intent on winning back the "Reagan Democrats" and aware that talk of civil rights and affirmative action was not the best way to do that, made a conscious effort to mute the issue.[1]

No one believed that the black vote was unimportant, and certainly no one believed that if blacks turned, out they would vote overwhelmingly for any other than the Democratic ticket. Therefore, 1992 presented the rather anomalous political situation wherein the votes of African Americans were wanted and needed by one party, but could not be too openly courted. And on the other hand, the votes of African Americans were feared by the other party, but could not be openly challenged or insulted. The Democrats had been told that they were losing white votes because the party was being perceived as too much under the dominance of "special (read, minority) interests" and especially of leaders such as the Reverend Jesse Jackson. This was a sure way to continue the exodus of centrist, moderately conservative Democrats into the Republican Party ranks. Unless those voters were reclaimed, the analysis went, the Democrats would continue to lose the presidency, a fate they had experienced five out of the last six elections. What developed throughout the primary season into the general election campaign was an election where civil rights per se would not be on the table for discussion. It was certainly acceptable to champion equal rights for all in broad, general language and to call for all people to come to respect each other, etc. But if the discussion came to specific civil rights remedies to correct past and present discriminatory wrongs, this would open up a can of politically sensitive worms that had best be left covered up.

This was a recognition, some explained, of the "political realities" of the 1990s. There were still latent, if not manifest, feelings of racism, and it was best not to arouse those negative political sentiments. First, the party most African Americans had been supporting substantially since 1936 had to win office before it could do anything worthwhile for black people. And apparently, *talking* about doing things for blacks was precisely what was sending whites out of the party. Therefore, the 1992 presidential race became a visible contest for the votes of whites and an invisible quest for the votes of blacks, at least as far as the Democrats were concerned.

In all fairness, this was not a strategy fostered on many black leaders without their knowledge or consent. More than a few political observers eagerly pointed out that this strategy occurred under the adept chairmanship of the Democratic Party's first black chairman, Ronald Brown, and with the active understanding and counsel of many other African-American leaders. This was seen as a manifestation of the virtues of enlightened, sophisticated political pragmatism and leadership in a complex pluralist system.

The emphasis would be on those socioeconomic policies that helped *everyone*, not just blacks. Therefore, there would be health care programs for *all* those 37 million-plus without care—blacks and whites. There would be job training and job-creating policies for *all* unemployed, not just for blacks. Student loans for all, etc. This was the "universal" approach to social policy as opposed to "race-specific" policies. Surely, this approach would not be interpreted as favoring blacks, even though blacks would benefit substantially, and surely, many whites would see their self-interest being served by such enlightened, all-inclusive programs. There would be no emphasis on "divisive" policies of affirmative action, especially "quotas."

This "universal" emphasis has been referred to in some instances as a "hidden agenda." And to its proponents, it made eminent political sense. What better way to build coalitions of support? This was the way to overcome the zero-sum effects of targeted social benefits. Broaden the scope of benefits to include *all* those in need, and you broaden the base of potential political support. It might not solve all the economic, jobless problems, but, so the thinking went, it was better to appeal to the whites in Middle America in such terms in order to gain their votes.[3] This argument was not new—a point to return to later. But first let's look at what happened. What do the voting numbers tell us in terms of the efficacy of the strategy?

WHAT HAPPENED?

Apparently, for the Democrats, the strategy worked. The Clinton-Gore ticket won. Blacks gave the Democrats 82 percent of their votes (Bush, 11 percent; Perot, 7 percent).[4] But once again, the Democratic candidate, as had been the case since 1968, received fewer overall white votes than the Republican candidate (in 1992, whites voted 39 percent for Clinton; 41 percent for Bush; 20 percent for Perot).[5] Governor Clinton was winning important electoral college votes on the strength of two important factors: very heavy support from blacks and an apparently decent performance by Ross Perot.

Looking at the margin of victory in several states, we see an interesting phenomenon. There were 18 states (with a total of 199 electoral votes) that were decided between Clinton and Bush by 5 points or less. Clinton won 11 (with a total of 107 electoral votes; Bush won 7 (with a total of 92 electoral votes). And in each case, the Perot vote was reasonably substantial, gaining percentages such as 21 percent in Ohio (where Clinton won over Bush by 1 percentage point); and in New Jersey, Perot got 16 percent (while Clinton beat Bush by only 2 points). Likewise, while Perot was doing well in such states, Clinton was gaining overwhelming black support, sufficient to provide the slight margin of victory in critical electoral states. It is obvious that if blacks divided their votes along lines similar to that of whites in critical electoral college states, Governor Clinton would not have won. While the black vote in 1992 was only 8 percent of the total vote, that 8 percent is so strategically located in important electoral college states that its influence can be—indeed, was—magnified when mobilized and concentrated. (The last time this was similarly demonstrated was in 1976 with Jimmy Carter's victory over Gerald Ford. Then, blacks voted 83 percent for Carter, 16 percent for Ford. Whites went 47 percent for Carter, 52 percent for Ford.) These data and results provide interesting material for assessing the views of pundits who were, during the 1980s, admonishing blacks for "isolating" themselves in one party and for not being more evenly balanced in their party support. Another factor to consider, while looking at size and location of vote, is how the electoral college system enhances the influence of some groups where those groups are strategically located in close, competitive, *and large* states, and *if* the group's votes are mobilized and turned out.

It is also important to look at what happened regarding the strategy's effort to win back the so-called "Reagan Democrats." Recall, the object was to be more "centrist," to play down the volatile, potentially divisive issue of race, and to talk in terms that would appeal to the more moderate and conservative Democrats who had been deserting the Democratic Party in droves over the past two decades.

How successful was this approach for the Democrats? Initially, one might suggest that it was quite successful: the party *did* win. But combining the above data with a look at four other categories reveals a most interesting picture. For purposes of analysis, assume the "Reagan Democrats" would be those identified in exit polls as: Moderate Democrats; Conservative Democrats; Moderate Independents; Conservative Independents. Table 1 shows the electoral behavior of these four groups from 1976 through 1992—five presidential elections.

In each category, just looking at 1992 and 1988, Clinton received *fewer* votes than the Democratic *loser,* Dukakis, in 1988! Also important, however, is that Bush received *considerably* fewer in 1992 in each category than

Table 1
"Reagan Democrats," 1976-1992

| | 1976 | | 1980 | | | 1984 | |
	Carter	Ford	Reagan	Carter	Anderson	Reagan	Mondale
Moderate Democrats	77%	22%	27%	67%	5%	22%	78%
Conservative Democrats	64%	35%	39%	56%	4%	46%	54%
Moderate Independents	45%	53%	53%	30%	14%	57%	42%
Conservative Independents	26%	72%	75%	18%	6%	85%	13%

| | 1988 | | 1992 | | |
	Bush	Dukakis	Clinton	Bush	Perot
Moderate Democrats	18%	81%	76%	10%	14%
Conservative Democrats	34%	65%	60%	24%	16%
Moderate Independents	51%	47%	42%	28%	30%
Conservative Independents	77%	20%	18%	54%	28%

Source: *The New York Times*/CBS News poll, November 5, 1992.

he received four years earlier. Where did these voters go in 1992? Not so much to Clinton, but apparently to Perot! (Exit poll data indicated that 38 percent of all those who voted for Perot said their second choice was Clinton, and 38 percent said Bush was their second choice, with 24 percent saying they would not vote or did not know how they would vote if they did not have a Perot option.) In 1992, these four voter categories accounted for 47 percent of the total vote—no insignificant amount by any calculation.

Another important voter group for the Clinton campaign strategy was the union household. Long a strong component of the Democrats' coalition stretching back to the New Deal of the 1930s, organized labor's support was needed, but it had been falling off over the past several elections, taking the same outward flight as the Reagan Democrats. In fact, some saw considerable overlap in composition between the Moderate and Conservative Democrats and union rank-and-file members. Once again, Clinton got fewer of such votes than Dukakis (55 percent to 57 percent), and again, it was Bush who suffered the biggest loss: 42 percent union support in 1988; 24 percent in 1992. Where did those votes go in 1992? To Perot, 21 percent.

This electoral pattern was repeating itself in other categories that were clearly targets of the Democrats' 1992 strategy. Obviously, the South would be watched with intense interest. For the first time in modern memory, a major presidential ticket abandoned the usual balance-the-ticket practice and nominated two people who were ideological, chronological, physical, and regional twins. The latter, region—namely, the South—was the area the Democrats hoped to regain. But this really meant regaining the *white* votes in the South, because southern blacks had been supporting the Democratic presidential ticket since they began voting in large numbers after the mid-1960s. Once again, the strategy was risky. In 1988, whites in the South gave Dukakis 32 percent of their vote (Bush got 67 percent). In 1992, whites in the South gave Clinton 34 percent of their vote (Bush got 48 percent, and Perot got 18 percent). Whites in the South left Bush, but they really did not stop off at Clinton-Gore; they went to Perot. Blacks in the South dropped from 86 percent for Dukakis in 1988 to 82 percent for Clinton in 1992.

The strategy was working, but barely. Absent the clearly unpredictable intervening Perot variable, and absent the continued solid voter support from African Americans, the success of the Democrats' strategy would likely have been highly problematic. It obviously was a risk the Democratic Party decided to take in the face of what many were saying for several years, namely, that "political realities" dictated such centrist moves. This would certainly involve not getting caught up in a discussion of such issues as affirmative action, and certainly not quotas or school desegregation or other volatile debates having to do with civil rights legislation against discrimination. The strategy would be to deal with problems of poverty, bad housing, education, lack of health care, and unemployment in a manner that was race neutral.[6] In this way, it was argued, policies would be proposed that others, especially the middle class, could relate to and, indeed, benefit from. There would be no need or aim to favor blacks over whites, inasmuch as both groups would be helped, forming the basis, it was hoped, for a broadened, enlightened coalition. This strategy was reminiscent of and predicated on the kinds of programs and incentives that constituted the New Deal coalition under Franklin Roosevelt, continued with Harry Truman, was revived a bit with John Kennedy, and reached its pinnacle in the election of Lyndon Johnson in 1964. This was the hope based on that historical understanding of how the Democrats had been winning presidential office the relatively few times (only four out of 11 elections) since President Roosevelt died in 1945.

Issues of race and civil rights were always vexing and potentially disruptive to the intraparty harmony the Democrats hoped to achieve. At the same time, the 1992 strategy of muting the issues of racism and civil rights was by no means a new one. The strategy *appeared* to be new to those unfamiliar with Democratic Party history since the New Deal. In 1992, some blacks and whites felt that the most liberal of the two major parties was now overtly abandoning its progressive position and moving to the center/right, chasing after former supporters who had gone over to the Republicans. Others winked and said no, that this was only an *electoral* strategy, an effort to come to terms with "political realities," namely, the party needs those old supporters in order to win. Otherwise, there will be no chance for a viable, potentially progressive *governance* strategy. Therefore, the script called for campaigning excessively where the white "Reagan Democrats" were— ideologically, regionally, programmatically, and campaigning on "universal" issues that cut across race lines. Propose policies that would help not only the poor and truly disadvantaged, but also those in the middle class who also needed help and would therefore be inclined to support such a coalition. Help the poor by helping those not poor. The latter are in the majority, and ultimately that is what electoral politics comes down to— numbers. This, then, is the strategy of the "hidden agenda" as it was pursued in the 1992 presidential election.

THE DUAL AGENDA

As the options and choices have been framed over the years, one notices a strong tendency to talk in terms of either/or: *either* race *or* class is the important factor in understanding the plight of African Americans: *either* civil rights *or* economic policies are the main means for alleviating that plight. Articles and columns in newspapers focus on this dichotomous way of understanding problems facing African Americans. "Civil Rights Act of 1991 Targets the Wrong Problems" was the headline of a column by one syndicated columnist.[7] The most important problems facing Black America, William Raspberry wrote, are joblessness, despair among the young, dissolution of families, crime, drugs, and "the economic marginality of our people." He concluded: "And the Civil Rights Act of '91 won't do a blessed thing about these problems." He agreed that the 1991 Act should be enacted, focusing as it did on lawsuits aimed at proving racial and gender discrimination. But he (and many others, incidentally) simply wondered whether such intense interest on such matters was really "of such overriding importance that they should constitute the No.1 priority of our leaders." And he emphatically concluded: "I don't think so."

Several other political observers, policy analysts, and journalists have reached similar conclusions. The priorities are all wrong or at least ought to be reexamined, they admonish. For policy and political reasons, it is better to focus on economic issues, especially jobs, and to frame future policy in less divisive, less zero-sum terms; that is, not to push for certain kinds of laws or remedies that will aggravate tensions and, as Raspberry writes, "threaten(s) to divide America along racial lines. . . ."

This is a formulation of priorities that has gained increasing currency in recent years. Calling for the need to build coalitions, William Julius Wilson writes:

> . . . Since an effective coalition will in part depend upon how the issues are defined, it is imperative that the political message underline the need for economic and social reforms that benefit *all* groups in the United States, not just poor minorities. Politicians and civil rights organizations, as two important examples, ought to *shift* or *expand* their definition of America's racial problems and broaden the scope of suggested policy programs to address them. They should, of course, continue to fight for an end to racial discrimination. But they must also recognize that poor minorities are profoundly affected by problems in America that go beyond racial considerations.[8]

Interestingly enough, this is an old admonition in the history of civil rights and African-American leadership. There has always been a debate about what the priorities should be, what tactics and strategies to pursue, and generally how much energy and resources should be placed on dealing with explicit race-oriented civil rights, antidiscrimination issues. These issues were raised in the throes of the Great Depression in the 1930s, in the post-World War II days in the fight for a Full Employment Act *and* a Fair Employment Practices Bill, in the 1950s over the Powell Amendment to withhold federal funds from segregated facilities (a tactic not all liberals supported because they felt it would jeopardize passage of other worthwhile liberal legislation such as aid to education, hospitals, and housing). There has not been a time in African-American history when black leaders have not been faced with these issues. At the same time, the historical record will show that the civil rights organizations *have* attempted to deal simultaneously with both sets of problems. They have always understood that there are problems specifically related to racial discrimination and segregation, and there are problems that stem from the structural nature of the socioeconomic system. The fact is that a careful reading of African-American history will indicate that this "dual agenda" (civil rights *and* economics) has always been a part of the black struggle. It only *seems* new and unique in 1992, because most commentators are unaware of that history.

Thus, the frustration that creeps into the perennial responses of African-American leaders is understandable. Two letters, 57 years apart, tell the sad story of this effort to make clear what the *dual* struggle is about. In 1937, Walter White of the NAACP had to reprimand gently a Congressman with whom he had corresponded. White had written seeking support for a pending wages and hours bill. The Congressman, seeing the NAACP stationery, assumed the letter was seeking support for antilynching legislation, and responded to Walter White in that vein. White corrected his misunderstanding of the NAACP's letter and added: "I am not surprised that you assumed that my communication had reference to the antilynching bill since that has been the subject of our correspondence for so long a time. *But you can see from my letter of the 21st that after all I can write about other matters.*"[9]

The need to remind others that African-American groups *do* have multiple agendas and are not focused only on race per se was evidenced in John E. Jacob's letter to *The New York Times* in 1991. Responding to an article that suggested lack of adequate attention by civil rights groups to economic issues, Jacob patiently pointed out: "Those who accuse civil rights groups of ignoring the crucial economic problems of African Americans or who condemn them for not transcending black concerns conveniently choose to ignore the National Urban League's Urban Marshall Plan proposal. . . .We object to articles that misinform the public into believing that civil rights and social problems represent an either/or choice for the civil rights movement. Both need to be pursued and both are being vigorously pursued."[10]

The "vigorous pursuit" of both agendas is a matter of historical record, including the efforts to get national health care in the 1940s; a full employment bill in the 1940s, as well as the National Urban League's continuing concern with that issue (see the proceedings of the 1974 League Conference, which was devoted entirely to that issue), etc. The lack of awareness of these efforts is not a function of a failed public relations process, but rather ignorance of the intricate, complex civil rights struggle over time. In addition, such ignorance might also stem from the fact that the civil rights groups had so very few liberal/progressive allies in supporting the meaningful socioeconomic measures they were proposing. This was certainly the case in the 1960s with the National Urban League's first Domestic Marshall Plan. It was certainly the case in the 1970s when the League proposed sensible welfare reform measures, as well as means to developing a viable work force in the inner-city communities. These efforts were made even as attention was also paid to problems of racial discrimination.

This history will also show how the same concern for adapting to "political realities" that preoccupied the 1992 strategists has been a long-standing concern. Civil rights organizations were asked to support the Full Employment Bill in 1945 and specifically asked *not* to raise the issue of racial discrimination in employment because that would make the passage of the bill politically unlikely. The organizations agreed. Civil rights groups were asked to support national health care in the late 1940s and, again, *not* to insist on the end to segregated health facilities, because that would put the bill in further political difficulty. The organizations agreed. Throughout the years, the civil rights struggle has had to accommodate arguments that "political realities" would not permit certain actions or at least would counsel caution on the racial agenda. Therefore, when this was raised in 1992, it was hardly new or, to the informed, not even surprising or unexpected. African-American leaders have known for a long time that, to most white Americans, a black face is a red flag! And they did not need a 1992 "hidden agenda" strategy to tell them how to navigate that treacherous racial mine field. They have known, precisely because they have been dealing with the "dual agenda" and "political realities" all the time.

The point now, after the election, is to move forward.

PUTTING THE MARSHALL PLAN FOR AMERICA INTO PLAY

One concrete means of moving the struggle to another level and, at the same time, of making it clear what the dual agenda means is to translate the proposals of the National Urban League's Marshall Plan for America into specific draft legislation. (I am pleased that the League has already taken important steps through its Policy and Government Relations Department.)[11] This plan has virtually all the elements of a relevant focus the critics of civil rights groups have called for. It pays careful attention to two basic needs: investment in human resources and rebuilding the nation's infrastructure. These are hardly race-specific concerns, but no one denies that, if developed properly, the proposals will certainly benefit African Americans. Is this a "hidden agenda" approach? Perhaps so, but the National Urban League and other groups have been talking this way long before now! The problem is that there were few listeners. Now, there is a new administration, poised to pursue a "universal" strategy, and dedicated to the proposition that the way to deal with socioeconomic problems of blacks is to help whites and blacks. Now, there is a new administration that won the election on the tacit agreement that if the *civil rights* agenda was not raised, then surely the *social welfare policy* agenda would be addressed, once elected. Now is the time to test those political propositions. But the best way to do that is by being as specific as possible. It is not sufficient to ask the new administration for a rhetorical commitment to a "fair urban policy," etc. The best way to exact political accountability is to focus the attention.

There should be a specific piece of draft legislation introduced in the 103rd Congress containing the specific features of the Marshall Plan for America. This should be endorsed and cosponsored as widely as possible. It should become the focal point for renewed mobilization in local communities around the country—mobilization that goes beyond election day, mobilization that points toward constituents pressuring their representatives and senators *and* state and local officials to support the specific legislative proposal. There would be hearings, modifications, and all the other manipulations that constitute politics and policy-making in the American political process. No one is naive to believe that it would be the only such proposal or even the one initially preferred by the administration and potential allies. *But the plan would be in play*, and there would be a specific way to link pre-election promises with post-election performance.

Whatever else is known about the struggle for racial justice and economic equity in this country, black history will reveal that African Americans have been more successful when they have been more focused. At times this concentration has been on achieving favorable court decisions; on particular boycott targets; on mass action directed at specific conditions or practices such as segregated facilities and unconstitutional voting requirements; on passing specific civil rights legislation in the 1960s. Now is the time to bring that focus to bear on specific proposed legislation aimed at implementing the proposals and recommendations in the Marshall Plan for America. Now is the time to test the efficacy of the 1992 presidential strategy. Now is the time to move the struggle to the next stage, to cash in on the meaning of those political numbers discussed earlier in this paper.

Now is decidedly *not* the time for more "agenda setting" meetings issuing yet again "detailed position papers" accompanied by inspirational speeches about what "ought" to happen. Neither is this the time to engage in time-consuming dialogue about race vs. class or about civil rights vs. economics or about who should be doing what. The fact is that some groups will work in one arena, others in another, and still others in several. That is both expected and wise, and the historically uninformed debates about the efficacy of one strategy or another should end. The problems in the 1990s are vast enough to accommodate the particular priorities, styles, and temperaments of various groups.

ENDNOTES

[1] See "Clinton Waves at Blacks as He Rushes By," by Gwen Ifill, *New York Times*, September 20, 1992, section 4, p. 1. The article quoted Congressman Charles B. Rangel of New York regarding the Clinton campaign's treatment of blacks: "It appears that at this point we are on the back burner. We are on an 'as needed' basis." Columnist Carl Rowan wrote: "Bill Clinton cannot win the presidency unless he wins a lot of electoral votes in the South. I sense that Clinton knows this, which is why he is following a strategy of not embracing black Americans to the point that he provokes the 'bubbas' of the old slave states' vote against him," *Daily News of Virgin Island,* September 24, 1992, p. 12. A.M. Rosenthal of *The New York Times* wrote: "Democrats are pushing race relations into the background because they do not want Jesse Jackson in the foreground. Republicans don't see political capital in talking about it at all," *The New York Times,* October 30, 1992, p. A31.

[2] Thomas Byrne Edsall and Mary D. Edsall, *Chain Reaction, The Impact of Race, Rights, and Taxes on American Politics* (New York: W.W. Norton & Company, 1991).

[3] See William Julius Wilson, *The Truly Disadvantaged: The Inner City, The Underclass, and Public Policy* (Chicago: The University of Chicago Press, 1987); Margaret Weir, A.S. Orloff, and Theda SkocPol, *The Politics of Social Policy in the United States* (Princeton: Princeton University Press, 1988). Wilson describes the universal/targeted emphasis in the following way: "As the universal programs draw support from a wider population, the targeted programs included in the comprehensive reform package would be indirectly supported and protected. Accordingly, *the hidden agenda for liberal policy makers is to improve the life chances of truly disadvantaged groups such as the ghetto underclass by emphasizing problems to which the more advantaged groups of all races and class backgrounds can positively relate,"* p. 155. (Emphasis in original.)

[4] All voting data are from the Voter Research and Surveys and surveys conducted by *The New York Times* and CBS News reported in *The New York Times*, November 5, 1992, p. B9.

[5] Data on Hispanics: 61 percent for Clinton; 25 percent for Bush; 14 percent for Perot.

[6] Other terms have been used to describe the same approach: deracialization; universal rather than targeted policies; crossover candidates and issues.

[7] "Civil Rights Act of 1991 Targets the Wrong Problems," William Raspberry, *The Herald-Sun,* Durham, NC, March 19, 1991, p. A11.

[8] Wilson, *Truly Disadvantaged, op. cit.,* p. 155 (emphasis added).

[9] Dona Cooper Hamilton and Charles V. Hamilton, "The Dual Agenda of African-American Organizations Since the New Deal: Social Welfare Policies and Civil Rights," *Political Science Quarterly,* Fall, 1992, Volume 107, Number 3, pp. 435-452.

[10] Letter to the Editor, John E. Jacob, President and Chief Executive Officer, National Urban League, *The New York Times*, April 12, 1991, p. A28.

[11] See "Special Supplement to *The Urban League News*—Playing To Win: A Marshall Plan for America," prepared for the National Urban League Annual Conference, San Diego, California, July, 1992. See also: Supplement to the *Urban League News* on the Marshall Plan, September 1992.

Toward Economic Self-Sufficiency: Independence Without Poverty

Lynn C. Burbridge, Ph.D.

INTRODUCTION

Much has been written in the past two decades about the need for poor women to attain economic self-sufficiency, free from dependency on the U.S. social welfare system. African-American women, either explicitly or implicitly, have been the target of much of this literature.[1] Although the welfare system was originally designed to help women remain at home with their families whenever they were without a male breadwinner, this is no longer the case.[2] Staying at home and raising one's children are not considered "real" work, and those who do so are often considered irresponsible and feckless, at least if they are poor. While many have appropriately criticized the hypocrisy of conservatives who have insisted that welfare recipients work while extolling the virtues of remaining at home in the name of "family values" for white, middle-class women, one cannot deny overall changing expectations regarding women and work. The irony, of course, is that African-American women have historically had a much stronger attachment to the labor force than any other group of women and continue to work in great numbers, including those who are public assistance recipients.

In examining the issue of self-sufficiency for African-American women, this chapter begins with three fundamental premises. First, economic independence is meaningless if one is in poverty, particularly if one is responsible for the well-being of children as well as one's own self. Poverty makes women and families vulnerable to a variety of social ills, regardless of their dependence on or independence from social welfare programs. The relationship between poverty and "rotten outcomes" has been well-documented.[3] Thus, the concept of self-sufficiency has to be broad enough to include economic well-being as well as economic independence.

Second, it is argued that African-American women desire and seek economic self-sufficiency. African-American women have ambitiously pursued economic opportunities when they have been presented to them and will continue to do so as long as these opportunities are available to them. There is little to suggest that black women do not want to work in the labor market when, in doing so, it does no harm to them or their children. If a recent poll is any indication, all women, including those of African descent, value having a job and money of their own.[4] The problem involves providing options that will lead to true self-sufficiency, to independence without poverty.

Finally, it is argued that African-American women face increasing barriers to their hopes for economic self-sufficiency. Not only have the wages of African-American women stagnated, but also black women have been confined to sectors of the economy characterized by unstable employment or slow growth. Further, there are indications that discrimination against black women increased in the 1980s. These barriers, combined with the deteriorating economic situation of black men, are making it difficult for African-American women to achieve self-sufficiency either singly or in combination with their male counterparts.

GAINS AND LOSSES

While some of the economic literature have focused on the problems faced by many poor black women, other books and articles have noted the extraordinary occupational gains they have made, particularly since World War II.[5] Black women would appear to be between the proverbial rock and a hard place: described as both doing extremely well (especially when compared to black males) and as doing extremely poorly (especially with respect to welfare receipt). Both scenarios are correct to some extent; there have been many important breakthroughs for some African Americans—both male and female—and severe disappointments for others. Yet most African-American women have been marginalized in the U.S. economy, including the more successful professionals. In this section, some of the gains and losses experienced by African-American women are discussed. This will be followed by an examination of the relationship of black women to the social welfare system and implications for public policy.

Occupational and Wage Gains

The National Research Council's examination of black economic progress indicates that African-American women of the 1980s shared a common characteristic with African-American women of the 1930s: their relatively lower earnings when compared to African-American men and to white men and women.[6] But while black women remained at the bottom of the pile, they made tremendous earnings gains relative to other groups. Their weekly wages went from 41 percent of white women's weekly wages to 97 percent in the mid-1980s; from 57 to 78 percent of black men's weekly wages; and from 27 to 53 percent of white men's weekly wages.

Much of this wage growth was driven by dramatic changes in the occupational distribution of black women. As indicated in Table 1, the occupational distribution of white women changed very little between 1950 and 1980, in spite of the fact that labor force participation rates have increased by over 50 percent for this group. For black women, the changes have been dramatic. But this change primarily involved a shift from the low-wage services, particularly private household services, to the low-

Table 1
Change in Occupational Distribution of
Black and White Women, 1950-1980

Occupation	Distribution in 1980		Change 1950-1980	
	White	Black	White	Black
Professional/ Technical	18.2	14.9	4.9	9.9
Managerial	7.3	3.7	2.6	2.4
Clerical	36.0	28.8	5.7	24.8
Sales	7.2	2.8	-2.2	1.5
Craft	2.0	1.8	.4	1.2
Operatives	11.9	17.8	-7.9	3.3
Laborers	1.2	1.8	.5	.3
Service	17.2	30.8	1.8	-29.6
Farm Related	.8	.4	-2.1	-5.0

Source: U.S. Bureau of Census, 1950 and 1980 Census of the Population.

Note: Estimates were made for 1980 occupations to make them comparable to 1950. Figures may not total 100 percent because of rounding.

wage, female-intensive administrative support occupations that are and have been dominated by white women.

Among those black women who have not completed high school, service work still dominates. Sixty percent of black women without a high school diploma are in service occupations, compared to 33 percent of similar white women, 18 percent of their black male counterparts, and 10 percent of white men without high school diplomas. According to Julianne Malveaux, an analysis of detailed occupations indicates even greater segregation among black women.[7] Forty-one percent of black women in service occupations can be found in only four types of jobs: chambermaids, welfare service aides, cleaners, and nurse's aides. Thus, dropping out of high school severely limits the opportunities of African-American women.

Nevertheless, labor force participation rates of black women have climbed 19 percent since 1970 (to 59 percent), compared to a 7 percent decline of labor force participation among black males (to 71 percent). Further, because of earnings gains of black women, coupled with the slowdown in black male wages, the earnings of African-American women have come to represent an increasing proportion of family income: in two-parent, two-earner families, a wife's earnings now represent 50 percent of black family income, compared to 40 percent of Hispanic family income and 35 percent of white family income.[8]

In documenting these gains, however, some important caveats are in order. First, there is evidence that earnings gains of African-American women dissipated over the 1980s, and black women's wages have begun to diverge from white women's wages after years of convergence. A study by Elaine Sorenson indicates that the probable explanation for this change is discrimination, since neither changes in human capital nor in the industrial structure were sufficient to explain this new trend.[9] Second, by other measures, they do considerably less well than white women: they have considerably less total income and wealth, even when their labor earnings are similar; their unemployment rates are two-and-a-half times that of their white counterparts; and they must work longer hours in order to achieve earnings parity with white women.[10] Finally, the gains of African-American women have been limited to certain sectors of the economy. Research indicates that 80 percent of professional black women work for either the government (federal, state, or local) or the nonprofit sector.[11] Even the most skilled of African-American women have been locked out of the private, for-profit sector.

Constraints and Losses

Unfortunately, the gains made by black women have been counterbalanced by the tremendous growth in female-headed households, resulting in many African-American women being left alone to fend for themselves and their families. The growth in black female-headed households is often cited as one of the most significant demographic phenomena of recent decades and as a reason for the failure of black family poverty rates to decline significantly. In 1989, almost 44 percent of black families were headed by a woman with no husband present. Black female-headed households have increased over 134 percent since 1940 and by 70 percent since 1965. In comparison, only 13 percent of white families are headed by females with no husband present (although this, too, represents a significant increase).[12]

This trend is largely explained by a rise in divorces and separations and an increase in out-of-wedlock births, particularly among very young women. One of the most striking numbers often cited is that as many as 68 percent of births to black women between the ages of 15 and 24 are outside of marriage. There is also a larger proportion of women forming independent households than in the past. (In other words, women with children and no husbands are more likely to form their own households rather than live with parents or within the context of the extended family.) The growth in black female-headed households has occurred in spite of declining overall fertility rates.[13]

While some have attributed the increase in female-headed households to AFDC receipt, most studies do not find a statistically significant relationship.[14] In those studies in which a relationship between female headship and AFDC receipt is found, the effect is usually small and weak.[15] Some that have focused on illegitimacy also find no relationship between out-of-wedlock births and AFDC receipt.[16] Although still a hotly debated topic, it appears that if there is an impact, it is more than likely extremely small.

While there has been a resurgence of interest in the impact of male joblessness on family structure,[17] the idea is not altogether new.[18] Statistical studies have consistently found a relationship between male joblessness or low wages on marital dissolutions or nonmarriage. This result has been found using individual or geographic data.[19] The study by Ross and Sawhill is instructive in that they found no "pure income effect"; rather, fluctuations in income were important.[20] In other words, income instability has a major impact on marital instability.

William Wilson's recent book places great emphasis on structural economic transformations affecting the availability of jobs in the inner city.[21] He focuses on the loss of manufacturing employment and the spatial mismatch of jobs—blacks do not reside where the jobs are being created—as an important explanation of changes in the inner city, including increases in female headship.

While the poor labor market performance of many men has been cited as a cause of marital instability, the increasing opportunities for women have been cited as well; in other words, women are now better able to "opt out" of a bad marriage. Many studies have found that with greater opportunities for women, there does appear to be more female-headed households.[22] It is not clear, however, what the direction of causality is; it may be that greater marital instability is causing greater female labor market participation.[23] Generally, however, these impacts are found only for white women. Black women, it seems, more often work to supplement their husbands' incomes rather than to have a cushion when a marriage falls apart.

A related issue is the low male-to-female sex ratio among blacks which William Wilson—one of the principal proponents of this view—discusses extensively in his book.[24] The discussion not only focuses on the absolute number of black males, but also on the availability of "marriageable black males." In other words, not only are there fewer black men because of high mortality rates, but also high rates of unemployment, incarceration, and substance abuse reduce the number that are really eligible for marriage. A study by Darity and Myers, using time-series data, finds that the formation of female-headed households shows a statistically significant relationship to the male-female ratio, the female age distribution, and the nonwhite male mortality rate.[25]

Whatever the reason, fewer African-American women are marrying. Table 2 gives the expectations of marrying for different cohorts of women. African American women born in the early 1950s have significantly less likelihood of marrying than those born in the late 1930s. African-American women born in the 1950s with less than a high school education have the least likelihood of marrying: 69 percent compared to 84 percent of those with more than a high school education. While there have been declines in the percentage of white women ever marrying, the decline has been considerably less; 90 to 93 percent of those in the 1950s cohort are expected to marry. Further, a recent study by Hatchett found significant differences between black men's and women's attitudes toward marriage. Black women were

Table 2
Expectations to Ever Marry, 1985

| | Date of Birth | | | |
	Late 1930s	Early 1940s	Late 1940s	Early 1950s
Black Women				
Less than high school	84.3	82.4	75.2	68.9
High school	88.8	88.6	79.2	77.8
More than high school	98.5	95.4	92.3	83.7
White Women				
Less than high school	95.1	94.8	92.7	91.3
High school	96.9	97.1	95.8	92.9
More than high school	94.0	96.8	95.2	90.1

Source: Estimates derived from Neil G. Bennett, David E. Bloom, and Patricia H. Craig, "The Divergence of Black and White Marriage Patterns," *American Journal of Sociology* 95(3), 1989.

nore likely to value financial security as a reason to marry, while black men were more likely to emphasize the socio-emotional aspects of marriage.[26] These differences between African-American men and women further complicate the picture.

The decline in marriage not only has consequences for African-American women, but also for their children. Child poverty rates are very high in female-headed households: 47 percent for whites and 72 percent for blacks (Table 3). Among single-parent families headed by a woman without a high school diploma, childhood poverty is virtually guaranteed: 87 percent for blacks and 77 percent for whites. Thus, limited education not only lowers opportunities for women but also jeopardizes the well-being of their children.

Differences in long-term poverty are even more dramatic. One national study has found that, on average, a black child can expect to spend five of

Table 3
Child Poverty Rates by Family Type,
Race, and Education: 1982-1983

	Black	White	B/W Ratio
Married-couple families	20.9	11.3	1.85
Father's education only:			
Failed to complete high school	39.6	29.0	1.37
Completed high school	13.1	7.3	1.79
High school diploma only	17.5	10.1	1.73
Completed some college	6.9	4.8	1.44
Father and mother's education:			
Neither completed high school	44.9	36.8	1.22
Only mother completed high school	32.8	18.6	1.76
Only father completed high school	29.7	18.6	1.60
Both completed high school	11.1	6.2	1.79
Single female-headed families	71.5	47.4	1.51
Mother's education:			
Failed to complete high school	86.8	76.8	1.13
Completed high school	61.6	34.4	1.79
High school diploma only	67.6	41.0	1.65
Completed some college	47.3	22.7	2.08

Source: Committee on Ways and Means, U.S. House of Representatives, *Overview of Entitlement Programs: 1992 Green Book* (Washington, DC: U.S. Government Printing Office, 1992).

his or her first 15 years in poverty compared to 0.8 years on average for a white child.[27] These figures are particularly compelling when one considers Marian Wright Edelman's statement that "poverty is the greatest child killer in the affluent United States. . . .[M]ore American children die each year from poverty than from traffic fatalities and suicide combined."[28]

In addition, a life of single parenthood or low earnings has consequences for black women when they pass their childbearing years. Older black women are more likely than any other group to be poor or near poor (Table 4): 50 percent of older African-American women are poor or near poor, followed by black men (39 percent), Hispanic women (38 percent), Hispanic men (27 percent), white females (21 percent), and white men (10 percent). The most impoverished group, black women, has poor or near-poor rates five times that of the most advantaged group, white males.

Poverty rates are high for older black women in spite of evidence of a great commitment to the labor market because of lower earnings in their prime-age years and insufficient pension coverage in the jobs they have

Table 4
Percent of Elderly Who Are
Poor or Near-Poor, 1990

	Black	White	Hispanic
Females			
65 and over	49.6	20.9	38.2
65 to 74	45.3	15.8	35.0
75 and over	55.8	27.8	44.5
Males			
65 and over	38.5	10.2	27.0
65 to 74	34.7	8.5	26.0
75 and over	46.4	13.2	29.2

Source: U.S. General Accounting Office, *Elderly Americans: Health, Housing, and Nutritio Gaps Between the Poor and Nonpoor*, GAO/PEMD-92-29, June 1992.

held. Since minority men also experience low incomes and often di younger than white males, minority women had fewer opportunities tha white women to enhance their earnings with those of a male partner wit greater earnings potential. Thus, savings, social security benefits, and th accumulation of assets were much lower.

In addition, the black aged also provide support to their families: they are more likely to take in grandchildren, nieces, nephews, and other family members.[29] While this may provide them a greater sense of purpose, it also may add more stress and stretch the already limited incomes of many of these seniors. Households headed by a woman 65 years old or over, with no spouse present and with children under the age of 18, have poverty rates of 48.4 percent for blacks, 35.4 percent for Hispanics, and 23.5 percent for whites.[30]

Although African-American women from the "baby boom" generation will have higher earnings than the current generation of older black women, they will still have less access to wealth and pension income than their white counterparts because of the kinds of jobs they have and the fewer marriage opportunities available to them. Since marriage rates have declined so precipitously, black women will increasingly have to rely on their own incomes for savings, contributions to social security and pension income, and the accumulation of assets.[31] This will counterbalance many of the gains they have made in earnings.

BLACK WOMEN AND THE SOCIAL WELFARE SYSTEM

Because of the problems African-American women have encountered in terms of occupational segregation, low earnings, and declines in marriage, they are more likely to have to fall back on the social welfare system in times of economic distress. The income support system helps poor, black women with families through Aid to Families with Dependent Children (AFDC)—particularly single-parent families—and provides supplemental social security (SSI) to older black women who were never able to accumulate the needed assets to retire graciously. In addition, many African-American women depend on the social welfare system for jobs in both the government and nonprofit sectors; this is particularly true if the "social welfare system" is interpreted broadly to include both health and human service fields, where there is a preponderance of black women. The great irony of the past 45 years is that African-American women have struggled so hard to make such dramatic gains in earnings and occupations, only to find themselves overwhelmingly marginalized in U.S. society.

Welfare Receipt

Although women of all races receive welfare, in the minds of many, dependence on welfare has been overwhelmingly and erroneously associated with African-American women. The derogatory attitudes many hold regarding welfare are often synonymous with derogatory attitudes towards black women. Nevertheless, African-American women are disproportionately reliant on welfare benefits. Forty percent of families receiving welfare are black, although blacks are only 12 percent of the total population.[*] The proportion of welfare families that are black has declined 13 percen[t] since 1969. Nevertheless, at this rate of decline, it would be the year 210[3] before the percentage of black welfare recipients was equal to the percent[-] age of blacks in the total population (assuming that the black populatio[n] stabilizes at 15 percent of the total U.S. population).

While many in the African-American and wider communities would lik[e] to see black welfare receipt drop more quickly than this, efforts to reduc[e] rates of welfare receipt have not been entirely successful. While fe[w] studies have focused specifically on African Americans, an examination o[f] evaluations of welfare-employment programs will give a sense of the diffi[-] culties involved in reducing welfare dependency.

Welfare-Employment Programs

Since 1967, states have been required to operate welfare-employmen[t] programs for recipients of AFDC. From the original Work Incentive (WIN[)] program to the current JOBS program, these work-welfare programs hav[e] gone through a variety of changes: strengthening mandatory participatio[n] requirements, emphasizing and then de-emphasizing the importance [of] intensive training and services, and, perhaps more importantly, experiencin[g] fluctuating funding levels. Throughout the history of welfare-employme[nt] programs, evaluations have been conducted of their effectiveness. Table [.] presents results from studies of the 13 welfare-employment program[s] conducted by the Manpower and Development Research Corporation (MDR[C) in the mid-1980s and the results from a study of the ET Choices progra[m] performed by the Urban Institute.[33]

The table presents characteristics of and outcomes from these programs. It indicates that the net gains for participants in these programs tend to b[e] very small. Further, increases in employment are often offset by reductio[n] in AFDC benefits, leaving many poor families still poor. The table als[o] indicates little or no relationship between program outcomes and the ma[n-] datory nature of the program or its employment of sanctions. The mo[st] stringent programs produced a mix of outcomes, as did the least stringe[nt] programs. There is no evidence from the evaluations that workfare pr[o-] grams (requiring recipients to work off their grants) or those imposing stri[ct] sanctions for nonparticipation produced better results in the form of i[n-] creased employment or reduced cost to taxpayers than did other types [of] programs.

Even high-intensity training programs, which overwhelmingly result i[n] greater earnings for those in the program, do not necessarily translate in[to] high welfare savings, at least in the short run. This reflects the difficulti[es] low-income women face in making enough income from paid work in ord[er] to achieve permanent self-sufficiency from welfare, even when they make

Characteristics of Work-Welfare Programs

	PROGRAMS			ANNUAL IMPACT AT FOLLOW-UP PERCENT DIFFERENCE IN:	
	Job Search	Workfare	Intensive Training	Earnings	AFDC Payments
Mandatory Programs					
With High Sanction Rate					
Cook County WIN Demonstration	X			1%	-1%
San Diego I	X	X		23%	-8%
San Diego II (SWIM)	X	X	X	21%-29%	-8% to -14%
With Low Sanction Rate					
Arkansas WORK Program	X	X		23%-33%	-13% to -19%
Baltimore Options	X	X	X	10%-17%	-2%-0%
Louisville WIN Lab I	X			18%-20%	-3%-10%
Louisville WIN Lab II[a]				43%	-2%
West Virginia CWEP		X		4%	0%
Virginia ESP	X	X	X	5%-14%	-2% to -9%
Voluntary Programs					
Maine OJT		X	X	8%-38%	-1%-4%
New Jersey OJT[b]			X	14%	-6% to -11%
National Supported			X	23%-327%	-10% to -39%
Work Demonstration ET Choices[ac]	X		X	32%	-8%

Note: Ranges indicate the lowest and highest impact for various years studied. The ET evaluation figures represent the percent difference between participants and a nonparticipant comparison group over the period of study (6 months to 2 years).

[a] Impacts presented based on six months follow-up period.

[b] Results available only from second year of follow-up.

[c] Measurement used to calculate welfare reductions is not comparable to other evaluations.

Sources: Daniel Friedlander and Judith M. Gueron, "Are High-Cost Services More Effective Than Low-Cost Services? Evidence from Experimental Evaluations of Welfare-to-Work Programs," paper prepared for Evaluation Design for Welfare and Training Program Conference in Airlie, VA, April 1990; and Demetra Nightingale et al., *Evaluation of the Massachusetts Employment and Training Program* (Washington, DC: The Urban Institute, 1991).

strong commitment to the labor market. These results may also reflect the short time frame used for all of these studies; a longer follow-up period could possibly produce more unequivocally positive outcomes. The one high-intensity program targeted on those with little labor market experience—Supported Work—produced the most dramatic results in terms of increased employment and in terms of welfare savings, however. While costly, intensive training programs like the Supported Work Demonstration can produce dramatic increases in employment and the most welfare savings. The supported work component in ET Choices also showed large reductions in AFDC payments and large increases in employment.

Not obvious from this table is the fall-off in employment and earnings that is often found in follow-ups of many welfare-employment programs. In addition, while welfare savings have come from reductions in the number of months spent on welfare, many families eventually return to the welfare rolls. This reflects the extraordinary problems involved in producing long-term self-sufficiency for women confined to the low-wage labor market. They are in jobs that are unstable and that do not pay enough to support themselves and their families and where there are few benefits, particularly health insurance.

Work by Mary Jo Bane and David T. Ellwood documents the fragility of periods of self-sufficiency for women who have received welfare.[35] Thus findings of little impact on caseload size, in spite of gains in employment and reductions in welfare spell lengths, could reflect returns to welfare by those whose earnings made them ineligible in the short run. It should be noted again, however, that an intensive program like the Supported Work Demonstration resulted in sizeable decreases in welfare expenditures. Most important, those in the treatment group had a 14 percent decrease in receipt of *any* welfare during the third year of the program.[36]

None of the studies estimated reductions in poverty as a result of welfare employment programs. The authors of an MDRC summary of the studies state, however, that there is little evidence welfare-employment programs reduced poverty.[37] Even in programs like Supported Work, which had substantial earnings impact, studies found that earnings gains were virtually offset by benefit reductions. While high-intensity services tend to result in more job stability and better job quality for recipients, these jobs alone do not reduce poverty.

Unfortunately, only one study is currently available which examines the impact of post-secondary education on welfare recipients, and it focuses on a small sample of AFDC recipients in New York.[38] All of the four-year college graduates interviewed (100 percent) were able to get off welfare compared to 81 percent of the two-year graduates. Since the New York study was based on a small, nonrepresentative sample, much more research is needed on the effect of education programs—from basic skills to college—in order to assess their effectiveness.

While welfare-employment programs—taken as a whole—have been less than successful, there is considerable evidence that most welfare recipients are either receiving welfare for a short period of time (1-2 years) or would be willing to take jobs if they could provide a decent standard of living for their families.[39] The Urban Institute study of ET found that in 1987, nearly 70 percent of all adults on AFDC volunteered for the ET program; this was higher than the national average. In addition, a study by Hartmann, Spalter-Roth et al. found that a significant proportion of welfare recipients already works in the labor market, either directly combining work with welfare or cycling between welfare and work.[40] Where studies examined racial differences, there was no evidence that African-American women were any different than other women in this regard. The study by Bane and Ellwood found that the primary reason minority women have longer spells on welfare than white women is because minority women are less likely to marry, not because they are less likely to take jobs in the labor market.[41]

Employment

Beyond the issue of welfare, employed African-American women may be overly reliant on jobs within the social welfare system and on other government and nonprofit jobs. This has been driven largely by discrimination against African-American women in the for-profit sector, combined with the tremendous growth in expenditures for health and human services—as directly provided by the government or via nonprofit intermediaries.[42] (This is not to discount the strong commitment of African-American women to public service as well.) But recent trends suggest an increasing emphasis on cost containment within the government as well as efforts to encourage private-sector initiatives—particularly in the past 12 years. Even with a new administration, budget deficits and concerns about cost will limit the extent to which black women can rely on government jobs for upward mobility.

Occupational trends indicate that only the health fields will provide significant opportunities for women in traditionally female jobs.[43] But spiraling health costs, government cost containment strategies, and a continuing backlash to government spending will encourage the utilization of cheap labor. The number of less-skilled health workers—home health aides, licensed practical nurses, and nursing and psychiatric aides—is expected to grow more than the number of registered nurses, for example. The lowest-paying health occupation—home health aides—is one of the fastest growing occupations in the country. (On average, home health aides make less than poverty-level wages.) Those in low-skilled occupations will have greater difficulty increasing their earnings, particularly if—as the incoming Labor Secretary Robert Reich has argued—declines in the manufacturing sector will increase the number of workers competing for these jobs.[44]

Thus, unless African-American women can find greater opportunities for advancement in the private, for-profit sector, they may see their past gains eroded. Even those who are highly skilled may discover that they have been cut off from the mainstream, with serious consequences for their earnings and potential for advancement.

In discussing welfare recipients and African-American women employed in health and welfare fields, it was not the intention of this paper to ignore black women productively working in other sectors. The purpose is to demonstrate the restrictions many African-American women face in their efforts to achieve economic self-sufficiency. If black women are to be subject to exhortations to become more independent, the limited opportunities available to them cannot be ignored. The only way of achieving independence without poverty is to expand the range of options available.

IMPLICATIONS FOR PUBLIC POLICY

Taking independence without poverty as the theme of this chapter, what can public policy do? Clearly a range of policy efforts is needed. Policies are required to increase the human capital of those who do not have the education and training needed to obtain decent jobs. Policies are needed to expand the number and range of jobs that are available. And policies are needed to reinforce the social welfare system to ensure that families that encounter economic distress are able to stabilize their situation and move on.

Increasing Human Capital

There can be little doubt that African-American women can benefit from renewed efforts to increase the human capital of the American population. The new administration's emphasis on education and training is encouraging. But it is important to note that studies indicate that the greatest benefits went to those who received long-term training. Among those with limited experience in the labor market, Supported Work—intensive counseling combined with supervised work experience—produced the greatest benefit. Even with Supported Work, however, many recipients were able only to *reduce* their dependency on welfare, not to end it. Among those with a high school education, complete dissociation from the welfare system often required a four-year college degree.

Thus, the new administration's emphasis on a two-year limit on welfare is of concern since it often takes longer than two years to obtain the human capital necessary to obtain self-sufficiency: independence without poverty. While it is possible to force women into low-wage jobs that will keep them and their families in poverty, such efforts—in the long term—will not be beneficial to them, their families, or society as a whole.

In all fairness, there are many in the new administration who acknowledge the importance to the country of having a highly educated work force with access to well-paying jobs and who promote efforts to provide more education opportunities to those who have had little access to them in the past.[45] Nevertheless, welfare recipients often get lost in the shuffle when real policy decisions are made about how to earmark scarce dollars.

Expanding the Availability of Jobs

Another area of concern surrounding the new administration's welfare proposals is the emphasis on replacing welfare with access to public service jobs. There can be little doubt that public service jobs are of great value and that public job creation is an important public policy tool. But it has also been pointed out that black women—even highly skilled black women—have encountered serious difficulties obtaining employment outside of the public and nonprofit sectors. Unless job creation is combined with efforts to assist welfare recipients in making the transition to unsubsidized jobs in the private sector, the result may be to replace dependency on welfare benefits with dependency on public jobs.

Thus, the self-sufficiency of African-American women depends on strenuous enforcement of antidiscrimination laws that will open doors for them to move beyond the sectors within which they have been confined because of their race and their sex. Otherwise, black women will continue to "bunch up" in relatively few occupations and industries.

Beyond this, expanding the availability of unsubsidized jobs to many black women will entail the revitalization of many of the communities within which they live. Too often welfare policy has been considered separately from economic development policy when there are clearly benefits from one that can accrue to the other.

Reinforcing the Social Welfare System

Even if many poor women are able to obtain an education and training, and even if African-American women can obtain greater access to more and better jobs, there will still be a need for a social welfare system that provides social services and income support. It is not realistic to expect any modern, industrial society to exist without a strong social welfare system.

First, women with children need child care if they are to work in the labor market. They need health care to provide for the well-being of their families. For example, Sweden—which has one of the highest labor force participation rates for women—provides universal child care and a national health care system.[46] Discussions of self-sufficiency are vain unless a social infrastructure is in place to make this possible. There clearly seems to be recognition of this in the new administration and some movement in the direction of more health and child care is expected.

Second, some families will continue to need income support, regardless of all these other efforts. Little attention has been paid to the fact that a significant proportion of those receiving AFDC are physically or mentally disabled. Those who are disabled will benefit considerably less from the efforts discussed above.[47] Others may be unable to obtain jobs that will keep them out of poverty. Any blanket rule specifying how long people can receive AFDC ignores the great heterogeneity of the welfare population. Those who may be incapable of work in the labor market will require continued support.

Those who are unable to find jobs that will keep them out of poverty may require a wage supplement to enhance their income. Again, this is not inconsistent with what is done in other Western, industrialized countries.[48] Low earners—whether receiving welfare or not—would also benefit from an increase in the minimum wage and an expansion of the Earned Income Tax Credit. Raising the income floor may do more to benefit those receiving income support than any welfare-employment program.

And What of Black Men?

This paper has had African-American women as its primary focus. But it has also indicated the difficulties in separating issues affecting African-American women from those affecting their male counterparts. The decline in marriage among African Americans affects everyone: men, women, and children alike. But this author has argued elsewhere that marriage, per se, cannot and should not be manipulated by public policy, if for no other reason than the decision to marry is a private one.[49]

Public policies can affect the economic situation of both black men and women, however, which will affect marriage rates, at least if the research on this subject is correct. Most of the same policies discussed above will apply to African-American men: the need for investments in human capital, antidiscrimination and job creation strategies, and social support.

In addition, increased efforts to provide jobs and training for men need to be coupled with efforts to encourage or require greater child support. Poor families will not benefit from the improved economic situation of poor men if noncustodial parents do not contribute to the well-being of their children. Currently, only 34 percent of poor African-American women who qualify for child support have a child support award. Of those with a child support award, only 50 percent receive partial payments or no payment at all.[50] However, calls for greater child support may be in vain without efforts to improve the economic situation of African-American men.

Community-Based Efforts

Finally, it is important to note that there are many community-based organizations attempting to grapple with these issues. Expectations for change cannot rest solely with federal, state, and local governments. Many people on the community level are concerned with the issue of self-sufficiency and carry with them the credibility and moral authority to carry out many innovative programs to generate this.

For example, there are several locally based efforts to encourage business development for low-income women. Women for Economic Justice in the Boston area is helping poor women develop cooperative businesses in a variety of areas: child care, health care, building maintenance, catering, and so on. One of the principal barriers to be overcome is various welfare rules, such as those limiting the earnings and assets these women can have, while they attempt to get their businesses off the ground.

In Milwaukee, the New Hope Project is a demonstration project developed by a coalition of business and community leaders to deal with the issue of chronic low wages facing those in poor communities. By providing income supplements to those who cannot earn enough to get out of poverty and short-term public service jobs for those who cannot find work, the New Hope Project aspires to encourage better strategies for dealing with poverty and underemployment. It is not only unique because of the nature of the project, however, but also because of the coalition of persons from all walks of life that made it possible.

CONCLUSION

This paper has covered a wide spectrum of issues. Its unifying theme is how to achieve self-sufficiency, defined as independence without poverty. The focus has been on African-American women, but much of what has been written can apply to many other groups that have found themselves outside of the mainstream.

The challenge for the next century is how to turn a country with a very diverse population into a true community where the needs and contributions of others are respected and valued. Across America, there are many efforts—some large, some small—to bring a community response to the issue of how to achieve self-sufficiency for families in a changing society. Government support of these efforts should include both financial support and a willingness to bend the rules to make them possible. Respect for and encouragement of community-based efforts is also an important role for public policymakers. Self-sufficiency is only possible where everyone has an equal chance to achieve it.

ENDNOTES

[1]For example, see Charles Murray, *Losing Ground: American Social Policy, 1950-1980* (New York: Basic Books, Inc., 1984).

[2]Mimi Abramovitz presents a history of the welfare state in *Regulating the Lives of Women: Social Welfare Policy from Colonial Times to the Present* (Boston, MA: South End Press, 1988).

[3]For example, see Lisabeth Schorr, *Within Our Reach: Breaking the Cycle of Disadvantage* (New York: Doubleday, 1989).

[4]Ms. Foundation for Women and Center for Policy Alternatives, *A Polling Report, Women's Voices: A Joint Project* (New York: Ms. Foundation for Women, 1992).

[5]For example, see Claudia Goldin, *Understanding the Gender Gap: The Economic History of American Women* (New York: Oxford University Press, 1990); Gerald D. Jaynes and Robin M. Williams, Jr., *A Common Destiny: Blacks and American Society* (Washington, DC: National Academy Press, 1989); and Frank Levy, *Dollars and Dreams: The Changing American Income Distribution* (New York: W.W. Norton and Company, 1987).

[6]Jayne and Williams, *A Common Destiny, op. cit.*.

[7]Julianne Malveaux, "The Economic Status of Black Families," in Harriet Pipes McAdoo (ed.), *Black Families* (Newbury Park: Sage Publications, 1988).

[8]U.S. Commerce Department, Bureau of the Census, *Statistical Abstract of the United States, 1991* (Washington, DC: U.S. Government Printing Office, 1991).

[9]Elaine Sorenson, *Why the Gender Gap Declined in the 1980s* (Washington, DC: The Urban Institute, 1991).

[10]Jaynes and Williams, *A Common Destiny, op. cit.*, Bureau of the Census, *Statistical Abstract of the United States, 1991.*

[11]Lynn C. Burbridge, *Careers of Women in the Nonprofit Sector*, paper presented at the national conference on "Women, Power, and Status in the Nonprofit Sector," Menlo Park, CA. November 15-18, 1992.

[12]Bureau of the Census, *Statistical Abstract of the United States, 1991, op. cit.*

[13]Time and space do not permit a more detailed discussion of the demographic makeup of black female-headed households. The interested reader is referred to William Julius Wilson's exhaustive review of the literature in *The Truly Disadvantaged: The Inner City, The Underclass, and Public Policy* (Chicago: The University of Chicago Press, 1987).

[14]For example, see Joseph J. Minarik and Robert S. Goldfarb, "AFDC Income, Recipient Rates, and Family Dissolution," *Journal of Human Resources*, Spring 1976; William Darity and Samuel Myers, Jr., "Does Welfare Dependency Cause Female Headship: The Case of the Black Family," *Journal of Marriage and the Family*, November 1984.

[15]For example, see Sheldon Danziger et al., "Work and Welfare as Determinants of Female Poverty and Household Headship," *Quarterly Journal of Economics*, August 1982.

[16]For example, see the summary in Kristin A. Moore and Martha R. Burt, *Private Crisis Public Cost: Policy Perspectives on Teenage Childbearing* (Washington, DC: Urban Institute Press, 1982).

[17]The notable example being William Wilson's *The Truly Disadvantaged* (see footnote 13).

[18]For example, Daniel Moynihan suggested as much in his controversial work, *The Negro Family: The Case for National Action* (Washington, DC: U.S. Government Printing Office, 1965).

[19]For example, see Kristin A. Moore et al., "The Consequences of Early Childbearing," (Washington, DC: Urban Institute, 1977); Jaynes and Williams, *A Common Destiny, op. cit.*, Mark Testa, Nan Marie Astone, Marilyn Krogh, and Kathryn Neckerman, "Employment and Marriage among Inner-City Fathers," *Annals of the American Academy of Political and Social Science*, January 1989; Neil G. Bennett, David E. Bloom, and Patricia H. Craig, "The Divergence of Black and White Marriage Patterns," *American Journal of Sociology*, Volume 95, Number 3 (November 1989).

[20]Heather L. Ross and Isabel V. Sawhill, *Time of Transition: The Growth of Families Headed by Women* (Washington, DC: The Urban Institute, 1975).

[21]Wilson, *op. cit.*

[22]For example, see Danziger et al., "Work and Welfare," *op. cit.*

[23]Robert Michael, "Consequences of the Rise in Female Labor," presented at the Conference on Trends in Women's Work, Education, and Family Building, Sussex, England, May 31-June 3, 1983.

[24]Wilson, *op. cit.*

[25]Darity and Myers, "Does Welfare Dependency," *op. cit.*

[26]Shirley J. Hatchett, "Women and Men," in James S. Jackson (ed.), *Life in Black America* (Newbury Park: Sage Publications, 1991).

[27]Committee on Ways and Means, U.S. House of Representatives, *Overview of Entitlement Programs, 1992 Green Book* (Washington, DC: U.S. Government Printing Office, 1992).

[28]Marian Wright Edelman, *Families in Peril, An Agenda for Social Change* (Cambridge: Harvard University Press, 1986), p. 29.

[29]Zev Harel, Edward A. McKinney, and Michael Williams, eds., *Black Aged: Understanding Diversity and Service Needs* (Newbury Park: Sage Publications, 1990).

[30]Bureau of the Census, *Poverty in the United States: 1990*, Current Population Report, Series P-60 No. 175 (Washington, DC: U.S. Government Printing Office, 1991).

[31]James S. Jackson, Linda M. Chatters, and Robert Joseph Taylor, *Aging in Black America* (Newbury Park: Sage Publications, 1993).

[32]Committee on Ways and Means, *Overview of Entitlement Programs, op. cit.*

[33]Results from the MDRC's studies come from their summary paper: Daniel Friedlander and Judith M. Gueron, "Are High-Cost Services More Effective Than Low-Cost Services? Evidence from Experimental Evaluations of Welfare-to-Work Programs," paper prepared for Evaluation Design for Welfare and Training Program Conference in Airlie, Virginia, April 1990. The ET Choices evaluation data come from Demetra Nightingale et al., *Evaluation of the Massachusetts Employment and Training Program* (Washington, DC: The Urban Institute, 1991).

[34]The MDRC studies compared the outcomes of a group with access to welfare-employment programs ("experimental group") to a group with similar demographic characteristics but without access to the specified program ("control group"). The ET program, evaluated by the Urban Institute, also tracked two groups of women with similar characteristics: a group of women who did not participate in ET beyond registration and orientation and a group that fully participated in the ET program. The major difference between the MDRC and Urban Institute procedures was that the MDRC randomly assigned individuals into control or experimental groups while the Urban Institute studied those who self-selected to participate beyond registration versus those who did not.

[35]Mary Jo Bane and David T. Ellwood, *The Dynamics of Dependence: The Routes of Self-Sufficiency*, report prepared for Assistant Secretary for Planning and Evaluation, Office of

Evaluation and Technical Analysis, Office of Income and Security Policy, U.S. Department of Health and Human Services, Contract No. HHS-100-82-0038, 1983.

[36]Stanley H. Masters and Rebecca Maynard, *The Impact of Supported Work on Long-Term Recipients of AFDC Benefits* (New York: Manpower Demonstration Research Corporation 1981).

[37]Friedlander and Gueron, "Are High-Cost Services," *op. cit.*

[38]Marilyn Gittell, Margaret Schehl, and Camille Fareri, *From Welfare to Independence: The College Option*, report to the Ford Foundation, March 1990.

[39]David Ellwood and Lawrence Summers, "Poverty in America: Is Welfare the Answer or the Problem?," in Sheldon Danziger and Daniel Weinberg (eds.), *Fighting Poverty: What Works and What Doesn't* (Cambridge: Harvard University Press, 1986).

[40]Roberta Spalter-Roth, Heidi I. Hartmann, Linda Andrews, and Usha Sunkara, *Combining Work and Welfare, An Alternative Anti-Poverty Strategy*, report to the Ford Foundation, 1991.

[41]Bane and Ellwood, *op. cit.*

[42]Lester M. Salamon, *America's Nonprofit Sector: A Primer* (New York: The Foundation Center, 1992).

[43]U.S. Department of Labor, Bureau of Labor Statistics, *Outlook 2000*, Bulletin 2352, April 1990.

[44]Robert B. Reich, *The Work of Nations: Preparing Ourselves for 21st Century Capitalism* (New York: Alfred A. Knopf, 1991).

[45]For example, Robert Reich—an economic policy adviser of the new president and his Labor Secretary-designate—makes a strong case for this in his book, *The Work of Nations*.

[46]Sheila B. Kamerman and Alfred J. Kahn, *Mothers Alone: Strategies for a Time of Change* (Dover, MA: Auburn House Publishing Company, 1988).

[47]For example, see Barbara Wolfe and Steven Hill, "Health, Welfare, and Work," paper presented at the Third Women's Policy Research Conference, Washington, DC, May 15-16 1992.

[48]Kamerman and Kahn, *op. cit.*

[49]Lynn C. Burbridge, "Policy Implications of a Decline in Marriage among African Americans," in Claudia Mitchell-Kernan and M. Belinda Tucker (eds.), *The Decline in Marriage Among African Americans: Causes, Consequences, and Policy Implications* (Newbury Park Sage Publications, Inc., forthcoming).

[50]Data from Committee on Ways and Means, *Overview of Entitlement Programs*, *op. cit.*

Empowerment through Enterprise: African-American Business Development

Lenneal J. Henderson, Ph.D.

INTRODUCTION

Enterprise has always been referred to as a fundamental source of African-American empowerment. Regardless of ideological, regional, or economic status, ownership of business has been regarded by African-American leaders as a source of individual financial wealth, community capital formation, self-esteem for business owners and employees, skills and capacity-building, and even political power. Empowerment represents the simultaneous development of these consequences of business ownership and development. Consequently, the objectives of this discussion are: (1) to develop and to apply the concept of empowerment to entrepreneurship in Black America, (2) to review the current status of African-American business enterprise as it relates to both present and future prospects for African-American community empowerment, and (3) to identify near- and long-term challenges to African-American empowerment through entrepreneurship and enterprise.

THE CONCEPT OF EMPOWERMENT

Empowerment is a complex and comprehensive concept consisting of at least five interrelated components:

(1) The formulation of strategic goals and objectives by individuals and institutions that focus on the creation, expansion, distribution, and utilization of human, financial, technological, and information resources,[1] particularly for a given group or organization;

(2) The mobilization of those resources through strategic interaction with individuals/institutions within and beyond the current range or field of interaction to achieve even higher levels of resource attainment;

(3) As resource mobilization generates higher levels of resource attainment, entrepreneurs build skills, capacities, and networks that position them for even greater resource development and diversification.

This is the economic concept of "multiplier effect" applied to psychological, socioeconomic, and institutional outcomes as well as financial consequences;

(4) As resource development and diversification occurs, entrepreneurs are able to transact, contract, and interact across more and more community, financial, institutional, and other boundaries both within and beyond their own locations, further extending their networks, skills, and resource base; and

(5) The enabling and building of the individual, organizational, and institutional network, of which the empowered organization is part. In other words, when one force is empowered, most forces connected with it are actually or potentially empowered as well.

Specifically, these five interrelated characteristics of the concept of empowerment suggest that African-American entrepreneurs begin to empower themselves by first *deciding* to become entrepreneurs and then *generating* the necessary financial, human, information, technological, and physical capital to actualize that decision. The act of generating capital and resources reflects the strategic capability of the entrepreneur, the ability of the entrepreneur to interact with various individuals and institutions with some "clout," or power, and the consequent development of the entrepreneur's interactive, managerial, financial, and technical knowledge; experience; and skills. Assuming that the entrepreneur is effective, the resource generation that results from business activity impacts not only the firm but also the network of relationships established by the firm.

Among the essential network of relationships presumed to be affected, if not enhanced, by African-American entrepreneurs is the economic well-being of African-American communities. Employment generation, capital development, and the increased production of goods and services to African-American individual households and neighborhoods by African-American businesses are among the benefits hypothesized to accrue from entrepreneurial activity. However, many have argued that majority businesses and institutions benefit far more substantially from African-American entrepreneurs than African Americans themselves do. The suggestion is that African-American entrepreneurs generate interest payments on business loans, purchase equipment and supplies, utilize information and data networks, consult expertise, and pay taxes to the majority community in greater quantities than to their own communities. The balance of trade and, hence, the balance of power are overwhelmingly negative. Consequently, the concept of empowerment for African-American entrepreneurs includes a two-dimensional imperative: (a) conception, development, and enrichment of economically and socially productive enterprising *organizations* and (b) mutually enriching and collectively productive relationships between African-American *enterprise organizations* and African-American *individuals, households*, and *communities*.[2]

92

ENTREPRENEURIAL MEASURES OF EMPOWERMENT

A major challenge to the analysis of these mutually enriching and socially productive relationships between African-American entrepreneurs and the African-American community is the development of workable measures of empowerment.[3] How do the stakeholders in African-American communities perceive and define "empowerment"? How do we know when empowering relationships are initiated, pursued, developed, and enhanced? What are depowering relationships; that is, relationships that fail to progress into mutually productive exchanges and may subtract power from the parties? What indicators of empowerment are useful and appropriate?[4]

Taking the last question first, it is initially useful to examine data on African-American business enterprises to examine current descriptions, measures, and indicators of business activity potentially able to illumine the concept of entrepreneurial empowerment.[5] According to the Census Bureau's *Survey of Minority-Owned Business Enterprises*, the number of firms owned by African Americans increased by 37.3 percent, higher than the 26.2 percent increase for all U.S. firms.[6] Based largely on the quantitative indicators matrixed in Figure 1, the suggestion is that African-American business enterprises are a growing but essentially small influence in American business enterprise.[7] Tables 1, 2, and 3 explicate some of these quantitative indicators in greater detail.

Table 1 describes the distribution of the number and receipts of African-American owned businesses by legal status. Given that more than 90 percent of these firms are sole proprietorships, it appears that these firms operate on a very small scale, that relationships between these enterprises and community institutions are circumscribed, that their financial and organizational power is limited, and that the investment of majority and minority institutions in these institutions is insubstantial.[8] However, an alternative view is that these sole proprietorships are the struggling seedlings of potentially larger and more diverse firms or the offspring of larger African-American owned enterprises. Hence, no matter how small the enterprise, the potential for larger scale business activity and empowerment always exists.[9]

The second pie chart in Table 1 describes the distribution of receipts among African-American-owned sole proprietorships, partnerships, and S corporations. The $19.8 billion generated by these enterprises in 1987 represent nearly one-third of the $74.8 billion generated by all minority-owned businesses in 1987.[10] However, although sole proprietorships are more than 90 percent of all African-American businesses, they generate only 51 percent of the gross receipts generated by all African-American businesses. Clearly, to the extent that businesses reach the level of maturation of fully corporate institutions, they are more likely to both generate more receipts and to leverage resources more effectively. Indeed, the magnitude and growth of African-American corporate institutions are among the indices of entrepreneurial empowerment.[11]

Figure 1
Summarized Matrix of Quantitative Indicators of African-American Business Power/Influence

Indicator	*Quantitative Measures*
Percent of total U.S. business enterprises that are African American	*3.1 % or 424,165 in 1987.*
Growth rate of African-American firms compared to overall growth rate of U.S. firms	*37.3% for African-American firms; 26.2% for all firms in 1987.*
Concentration/Distribution of African-American and U.S. firms by type of industry	*63% of African-American firms are concentrated in the services and retail trade industries.*
Level of capitalization of African-American and U.S. firms firms.	*African-American firms enjoy 1/2 of the level of capitalization of all U.S.*
Geographical concentration/ distribution of African-Americanand U.S. businesses	*States with largest African- American population have largest proportions of African-American businesses.*
Employment intensity of African-American and U.S. firms paid	*17% of African-American firms have paid employees; 25% of all U.S. firmshave employees.*
Percent of sales and receipts African-American firms account for in the United States	*African-American firms account for only 1% of sales/receipts of all U.S. firms.*
Percent of African-American and U.S. businesses that are sole proprietorships, partnerships, or corporations	*94% of African-American firms are organized as sole proprietorships, 3% partnerships, 3% sole corporations.[a]*

Source: Adapted from the U.S. Department of Commerce, Bureau of the Census, *Minority-Owned Business Enterprises - Black* MB 87-1 (Washington, DC: U.S. Government Printing Office, 1990).

[a] A sole corporation is a special designation of the Internal Revenue Service of a legally incorporated business with 30 or fewer shareholders, who, because of tax advantages, elect to be taxed as individuals rather than as corporations.

94

Table 1

Distribution of the Number and Receipts of Black-Owned Firms by Legal Form of Organization in 1987

Number	Receipts
Total = 424,165	Total = $19.8 Billion

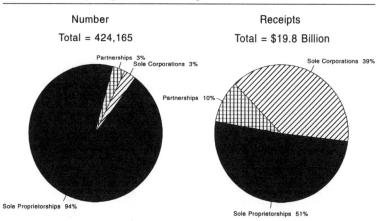

Source: Adapted by the U.S. Small Business Administration, Office of Advocacy, from data published in U.S. Department of Commerce, Bureau of the Census, Minority-Owned Business Enterprises Black MB87 -1(Washington, D.C.: U.S. Government Printing Office, 1990), Table 7.

Source: Adapted by the U.S. Small Business Administration, Office of Advocacy, from data published in U.S. Department of Commerce, Bureau of the Census, *Minority-Owned Business Enterprises Black* MB87-1(Washington, DC: U.S. Government Printing Office, 1990), Table 7.

Table 2

Industry Distribution of Black-Owned Firms (1987)
and All Small Firms (1988)

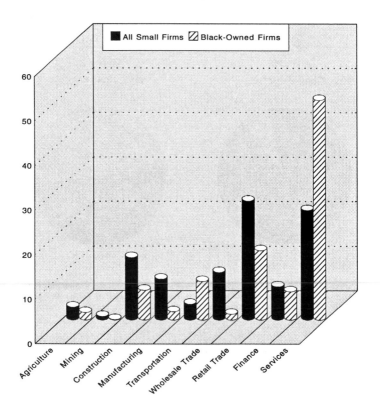

Source: Adapted by the U.S. Small business Administration, Office of Advocacy, from data published in U.S. Department of Commerce, Bureau of Census, Minority-Owned Business Enterprises-Black MB87-1 (Washington, D.C.: U.S. Government Printing Office, 1990), Table 1.

Source: Adapted by the U.S. Small Business Administration, Office of Advocacy, from data published in U.S. Department of Commerce, Bureau of the Census, *Minority-Owned Business Enterprises Black* MB87-1(Washington, DC: U.S. Government Printing Office, 1990), Table 1.

Table 3
States with the Highest Percentage of Total Sales
and Receipts Generated by Black-Owned Firms in 1987

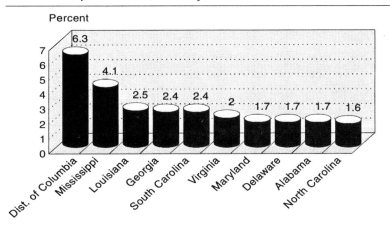

Percent

Sorce: Adapted by the U.S. Small Business Administration, Office of Advocacy, from data published in: U.S. Department of Commerce, Bureau
of the Census,Minority-Owned Business Enterprises Black MB87 1 (Washington, D.C.: U.S. Government
Printing Office, 1990) Table 2.

Source: Adapted by the U.S. Small Business Administration, Office of Advocacy, from data published in
           U.S. Department of Commerce, Bureau of the Census, *Minority-Owned Business Enterprises Black*
           MB87-1(Washington, DC: U.S. Government Printing Office, 1990), Table 2.

Table 2 describes the distribution of African-American firms among various industries in relation to all small business firms. Nearly 50 percent of all African-American firms are involved in services. Fewer are involved in agriculture, mining, construction, wholesale trade, or manufacturing. Empowerment in business is not just the leveraging of influence in a single or several industries, but a constructive presence in most industries. Since industries tend to be operationally independent, the concentration of business resources and influence in a few industries results in dependency on other industries.[12]

Table 3 describes the states with the highest percentage of African-American business sales and receipts generation. The concentration of sales and receipts generally reflects the demographic concentration of the African-American population in the states. However, far more significant in the context of the concept of empowerment are:

(1) The power and influence of non-African-American firms in establishing and maintaining the context in which African-American firms thrive;

(2) The glaring disparity between the proportion of African Americans in the states' population and the revenues generated by African-American owned firms;

(3) The meager patronage of both majority and African-American consumers purchasing goods and services from African-American firms. For example, in the District of Columbia, 69 percent of the population is African American. Although it is safe to hypothesize that the vast majority of the sales and receipts generated by African-American firms derives from the African-American community, it is clear that African-American consumer patronage is not sufficiently strong to elevate those businesses even to the level of 50 percent of all sales and receipts generated in the District of Columbia. Thus, the potential of the mutual empowerment of African-American business and consumers is circumscribed by the greater influence, persuasion, and resources of majority entrepreneurs.[13]

Indeed, a closer view of the largest African-American businesses suggests both the kind and the size of businesses that are most influential in African-American communities (Table 4). The business type, staff size, location, and sales volume suggest that the largest firms are located in metropolitan areas and are small; even in relation to the definition of "small business" used by the federal government, they represent a diversity of types of business activity. Only two of these enterprises employ over 1,000 individuals, and only one exceeds $500 million in sales volume.[14] The entrepreneurs who own and operate these businesses exert some influence on the national, regional, and local African-American communities, but they are just as connected to a network of majority lending institutions, suppliers, patrons, and consumers as they are to African Americans. Empowerment certainly requires this versatility in influence and dependency, particularly at the level of sales. But equally essential are the continued efforts of these firms to empower African Americans through additional business development; investment of time, talent, and money in educational, youth, and other institutions in the community; and the use of social and political influence to persuade majority institutions to further empower them and the African-American community.

Table 4

Black Enterprise 100 Largest African-American Firms by Type and 1989 Sales Volume:

Top Five Firms in Each Category Industrial/Service Companies

BUSINESS	LOCATION	STAFF SIZE	1989 SALES VOLUME IN MILLIONS OF DOLLARS	BUSINESS TYPES
TLC Beatrice International Holdings	New York, NY	6,000	$ 1,514,000	Processing and distribution of food products
Johnson Publishing Co.	Chicago, IL	2,370	$ 241,327,000	Publishing, broadcasting
Philadelphia Coca-Cola Bottling Co., Inc.	Philadelphia, PA	985	$ 240,000,000	Soft-drink bottling
H.J. Russell & Company	Atlanta, GA	985	$ 132,876,000	Construction; communication; food; and beverages
The Gordy Company	Atlanta, GA	70	$ 100,000,000	Entertainment
AUTO DEALERS				
Shack-Woods & Associates	Long Beach, CA	400	$ 138,000,000	Ford Dealership
Jerry Watkins Cadillac-GMC Truck, Inc.	Winston-Salem, NC	70	$ 107,916,000	GM Dealership
S & J Enterprises	Charlotte, NC	216	$ 97,882,000	Ford Dealership
Dick Gidron Cadillac & Ford, Inc.	Bronx, NY	283	$ 57,500,000	GM-Ford Dealership
Mel Farr Automotive Group	Oak Park, MI	160	$ 52,100,000	Ford-Toyota Dealership

Source: *Black Enterprise*, Special Issue, 1990.

Consequently, the characteristics of the concept of empowerment discussed in the context of these data tend to go beyond the orientation of studies of African-American business. As Frank Fratoe,[15] Pat Roberson-Saunders,[16] William O'Hare,[17] Timothy Bates,[18] and others have argued, these studies tend to fall into four general categories, each corresponding to a major analytic field: economics, business management, psychology, and sociology. Fratoe argues that the economy approach focuses on financial characteristics of these firms and the economic environment in which they operate. Financial/capital resources, profit and loss dynamics, and debt-equity ratios tend to characterize the economic approach.

The business management approach examines nonfinancial characteristics of these firms, such as their management methods, planning processes, operations management approach, marketing strategies, and human resource management. The concern is both with the efficiency and effectiveness of management systems and processes and with the need for additional technical assistance from both business and government to better management of the firm.

The psychological approach examines the personal characteristics of African-American entrepreneurs. The concern is with the individual human resources that each entrepreneur brings to the enterprise, particularly personality, experiential, occupational, or leadership qualities. The frequent assumption of this approach is that there are recurring traits that make for good or poor entrepreneurs, particularly achievement motivation, risk-taking, tenacity, and energy level.

Finally, the sociological approach to the study of nonwhite entrepreneurial behavior is more comprehensive and process-oriented. It suggests that business ownership is a group-level phenomenon dependent upon social group resources for its development. The individual entrepreneur is seen as the most visible member of a self-help network of supportive kinship, peer, and community subgroups. Indeed, the implication is that some groups seem to be more effective at mobilizing the resources of their groups to support entrepreneurship than others.[19]

Entrepreneurial measures of empowerment incorporate characteristics of each of these four approaches into a normative but macroanalytical approach that examines both the internal development and performance of African-American enterprises and their external relations with a variety of African-American and external communities and institutions. Consistent with Swinton's approach (see his chapter in the *State of Black America 1992*), it is concerned with monitoring the overall wealth generation of the African-American community (Table 5) and the contributions of enterprises to that wealth generation. Although community self-actualization and reliance is a priority, strategic, effective, and mutually productive exchanges with non African-American communities and institutions are also fundamental to the long-term efficacy and success of African-American entrepreneurs.[20]

100

THE PERSISTENT ROLE OF GOVERNMENT

Clearly, one glaring dilemma for empowerment through African-American entrepreneurship is the role of government. Given the historical exclusion of African-Americans from significant ownership and control of American corporations and the contemporary minor role that African-American businesses maintain in corporate power and influence, the disproportionate role of government in the birth, life, and death of African-American businesses is a major challenge to African-American empowerment. On the one hand, without government, particularly federal support through procurement processes, many African-American businesses would not be solvent or viable. On the other hand, government accounts for more than 60 percent of sales and receipts generated by these businesses. The Small Business Administration's (SBA) 8(a) program, a specialized procurement program for minority-owned, including African-American, businesses which sets aside government work exclusively for eligible firms, represents clearly the dependency of many firms on public support (Table 5).[21]

However, as Malveaux and others indicate, the *Richmond v. Croson* decision severely challenged the validity of local minority-business set-aside programs making municipal sponsorship of these programs difficult.[22] More fundamentally, the court's determination comes at a time when the influence of African-American elected officials is growing, particularly at the local level. Following the 1992 elections, the number of African-American elected officials exceeds 8,000; more than 90 percent of these officials will serve at the local level of government and, for the first time in U.S. history, African-American members of Congress will reach 40, including the first African-American female and Democrat in the U.S. Senate.[23] Nevertheless, the immediate challenge for these officials and for African-American entrepreneurs is to enhance the public policy environment for entrepreneurs so that the linkage between entrepreneurship and empowerment is firmly established.

Moreover, the election of Bill Clinton as President and Al Gore as Vice President of the United States in 1992, combined with the election of 40 African-American members of Congress, potentially provides African-American entrepreneurship with a new and vibrant political and administrative environment. President Clinton's emphasis on equitable strategies for economic restoration and Vice President Gore's experience with African-American businesses, particularly with the Tennessee Valley Center for Minority Business Development, provide the White House with unusual experience in and exposure to potentially empowering enterprise-oriented public policy strategies.

Budget and tax policies, strategies to stimulate business activities, policies to revitalize the economies of cities, and trade policies will be of most critical

Table 5
Wealth Ownership 1988
(in millions of 1990$)

	Mean		% Wealthholders Owning		Per Capita		Aggregate		B/W	Aggregate Gap
	Black	White	Black	White	Black	White	Black	White		
Total Net Worth	26,130	111,950	100.00	100.00	8,981	43,164	268,568	8,862,993	.21	1,022,208
Interest-Earning at Financial Institutions	4,806	20,870	44.48	76.58	735	6,162	21,979	1,265,262	.12	162,289
Regular Checking	789	1,193	30.11	50.92	82	234	2,452	48,048	.35	45,454
Stock & Mutual Funds	4,050	31,266	6.97	23.92	97	2,884	2,901	592,180	.03	83,342
Equity in Business	27,880	73,511	3.66	13.57	351	3,846	10,496	789,711	.09	104,515
Equity in Motor Vehicle	4,384	7,080	64.67	89.15	974	2,434	29,127	499,781	.40	43,660
Equity in Home	40,624	70,888	43.46	66.72	6,068	18,236	181,458	3,744,453	.33	363,872
Equity in Rental Property	45,031	92,090	4.55	9.61	704	3,412	21,052	700,596	.21	80,980
Other Real Estate	18,132	42,505	4.37	11.35	272	1,860	8,134	381,919	.15	47,488
U.S. Savings Bonds	1,118	3,444	11.01	18.47	245	203	1,256	50,307	.17	60,705
IRA or Keoghs	6,136	18,242	6.87	26.43	1,714	1,714	4,336	381,714	.08	51,255

Aggregate gaps = white per capita - black per capita * 1988 black population.
Inequity Index (B/W) = black per capita/white per capita.
Source: U.S. Department of Commerce, Bureau of the Census, *Household Wealth and Asset Ownership: 1988*, December 1990.

Category	Number of Participants		Percentage*	
	1991	1992	1991	1992
African American	1,779	2,040	48.5	47.5
Hispanic American	884	1,018	24.1	23.7
Asian American	615	793	16.8	18.5
American Indian	238	267	6.5	6.2
Puerto Rican	100	105	10.5	2.4
Eskimo/Aleut	6	7	.2	.7
Undetermined	2	29	.1	.7
Other	41	33	1.1	.7
Total	3,665	4,292	100.0	100.0

Source: U.S. Department of Commerce, Bureau of the Census, *Minority-Owned Business Enterprise -Black* MB87-1.

importance to both the Clinton administration and African-American entrepreneurs. Among the most essential budget and tax options the Clinton administration is now considering that are also fundamental to the increased success of African-American entrepreneurs include:

(1) Short-term federal budget deficit reduction policies. Policies which simply reduce budget outlays without a stimulus program will retard small and African-American business growth. A program to convert carefully reductions in military outlays to infrastructure, human capital, housing, and economic development strategies, particularly in large central cities, offers substantial, diverse, and comprehensive opportunities for African-American enterprise;[24]

(2) Monetary policies which carefully balance short-term increase in money supply, incremental reductions in reserve requirements for Federal Reserve member banks, and lower interest rates with attention to inflationary consequences could significantly ease the availability of capital to African-American businesses; and

(3) Tax reforms which (a) carefully restore the investment tax credit, particularly for small and nonwhite firms; (b) provide a partial restoration of the tax deduction for consumer installment debt; (c) reward business for investment in central city infrastructure. Thus, employment, housing, neighborhood, and economic development resulting from these reforms could significantly boost African-American businesses while encouraging a more systemic development of urban African-American communities.[25]

Foreign policies, particularly trade policies, do and will have a significant impact upon the empowerment of African-American businesses. The continuing struggles of European nations to reach accord on the tariff reduction; labor policy and business development aspects of trade; the recent economic difficulties faced by Japan; the continuing transformation of Eastern Europe and the former Soviet Union; continued tumult in the economies and politics of Africa, Asia, and Latin America; and the prospect of a new foreign assistance program in the Clinton administration will all directly affect the empowerment equation in the African-American community. Levels of immigration, competition between international and domestic college students—particularly those who are African-American, continuing overseas investments by U.S. companies, and overseas investments in the United States all contain major stakes for the empowerment of African-American firms.

Three immediate examples of international challenges to African-American enterprise are apparent. First, the recent signing of the North American Free Trade Agreement by former President Bush reduces tariff and other barriers to trade among the United States, Mexico, and Canada. Competition among firms in these nations will accelerate, particularly in consumer goods, small manufacturing, and service industries. Empowerment of African-American firms will mean an enhanced ability to transact successfully across cultural and language, as well as national, boundaries. Co- and joint ventures, subcontracting and prime contracting, and other modes of partnerships will be essential.

Second, as foreign-owned firms expand investment in the United States, empowerment of African-American firms will mean both competition and partnership with these firms. For example, the Nissan automobile plant in Smyrna, Tennessee, will continue to require raw materials, parts, and services. African-American firms can and should become part of that commercial complex. Indeed, according to Jimmy Hydel, State Director of the Department of Economic Development in Mississippi, European and Asian firms are now seriously investing in states like Mississippi because labor land, and other costs are now competitive with those overseas and because state and local fiscal incentives are more encouraging. Both existing and emerging African-American entrepreneurs can globalize the concept of empowerment by working with these firms.

Third, many cities are pursuing new opportunities for major economic development, including the development of electronics, information-based, telecommunications, biotechnological, and infrastructural industries. Baltimore, Houston, New Orleans, and Boston are developing large-scale biomedical complexes. Public policy support not only from the local and state levels but also from the Clinton administration can accelerate the progress and the productivity of these initiatives. The channeling of existing and emerging African-American scientific, medical, health, and business expertise into experienced and new firms owned by African Americans not only empower the African-American community but also shape and transform the direction, content, and impact of these initiatives.

In addition to these fiscal, foreign, and trade policies, the Clinton administration's policies toward specific federal programs designed to empower African-American business will be essential. Examples of these programs include:

(1) The Small Business Administration's minority set-aside 8(a) program;[26]

(2) Support for the roles of small and disadvantaged business utilization programs in federal agencies;

(3) Constructive reshaping of the role of the Minority Business Development Agency (MBDA) in the Commerce Department;

(4) Increased support for the Office of Minority Economic Impact in the U.S. Department of Energy; and

(5) Increased support for the "Gray amendment," a statutory provision requiring minority business participation in foreign assistance and foreign affairs programs.

Public policy will continue to be essential to African-American empowerment through enterprise. Not only are supportive public policies essential, but also even for the largest U.S. firms, government is a large and growing consumer of business goods, services, and expertise.

SUMMARY AND CONCLUSIONS

Given the role of entrepreneurship in the empowerment of the African-American community, it is essential to understand the concept of empowerment. Empowerment involves decisions, strategies, mobilization of resources, transactions across diverse boundaries and institutions, and the cultivation of both internal and external resources. Resources generated by the enterprise must be constructively multiplied within the African-American community and not dissipated outside the community. Employment development, capital growth, increased production of goods and services, and investment in the basic institutions of the community are all presumed benefits of increasing African-American entrepreneurial activity.

Given the modes of measuring enterprise effectiveness, African-American businesses continue to grow and diversify but remain significantly below both their demographic representation in the U.S. population and their small business peers. There is disproportionate representation of African-American businesses in the service industries and minimal employment, assets, and capital development. Most African-American businesses are sole proprietorships and, although the representation of these firms is significant, particularly in states with sizeable African-American populations, African-

American consumer support for these firms remains significantly low.

Consequently, the challenge of empowerment through entrepreneurship in the African-American community is fraught with stubborn realities and difficulties. Under-capitalization, meager human and technical resources, a growing and reliable consumer base, and extensive dependency upon the public sector are among those challenges. Not only must individual entrepreneurs exhibit unusual personal characteristics, including business acumen and management skills, but also individual enterprises must continue to invest in capacity building in increasingly distressed inner-city and rural African-American communities.

RECOMMENDATIONS

(1) That either the SBA or the MBDA develop a complete, updated list of existing African-American businesses by Standard Industrial Classification (SIC) code, business specialty, and business type (sole proprietorship, partnership, corporation);

(2) That African-American businesses accelerate an "invest in African America" campaign to more comprehensively empower African-American community, human, physical, technical, and financial development;

(3) That African-American organizations and institutions, such as the National Urban League, *Black Enterprise*, or the Black Business League accelerate a national "buy African-American" campaign to further empower African-American community, human, physical, technical, and financial development.

(4) That existing and recently elected federal, state, and local officials rigorously support minority set-aside programs for the continued development of African-American businesses and to facilitate their entry into all industrial and service categories;

(5) That the fiscal policies of the Clinton administration support investment in new firms, expansion of existing firms, and investment tax credits and fiscal incentives for investing in urban and rural African-American communities;

(6) That the U.S. Trade Representative inculcate policies encouraging the involvement of African-American businesses; and

(7) That President Clinton's economic stimulus package include more substantial investment in human and physical infrastructure, particularly in the nation's largest cities.

* * * * *

The author wishes to thank Diane Aull of the Schaefer Center and Janice Harris of the Small Business Administration for their tireless and generous help in the preparation of this paper.

ENDNOTES

[1] On the concept of resources, see Warren Ilchman and Norman Uphoff, *The Political Economy of Change* (Berkeley and Los Angeles: University of California Press, 1969).

[2] Robert Suggs, *Recent Changes in Black-Owned Business* (Washington, DC: The Joint Center for Political Studies, 1986).

[3] William Bradford and Timothy Bates, "An Evaluation of Alternative Strategies for Expanding the Number of Black-Owned Businesses," *The Review of Black Political Economy*, Vol. 5, No. 4, Summer 1975, pp. 376-385.

[4] Arthur G. Woolf, "Market Structure and Minority Presence: Black-Owned Firms in Manufacturing," *The Review of Black Political Economy*, Vol. 14, No. 4, Spring 1986, pp. 79-90.

[5] Timothy Bates, *Black Capitalism: A Quantitative Analysis* (New York: Praeger Books, 1973), chapter 2.

[6] U.S. Department of Commerce, Bureau of the Census, *Minority-Owned Business Enterprise - Black* MB87-1 (Washington, DC: U.S. Government Printing Office, 1990).

[7] *The State of Small Business* (Washington, DC: U.S. Government Printing Office, 1991).

[8] *Ibid.,* p. 279.

[9] See, for example, Minority Business Development Agency, *Minority Business Enterprise Today: Problems and Their Causes* (Washington, DC: U.S. Department of Commerce, 1982).

[10] *State of Small Business, op. cit.,* p. 279.

[11] Pat Roberson-Saunders, *Segmented Research: Minorities and Women*, unpublished paper, 1992.

[12] *State of Small Business, op. cit.,* p. 279.

[13] *Ibid.,* p. 285.

[14] *Black Business Enterprise: One-Hundred Largest Black Firms, 1990* (New York: *Black Enterprise Magazine,* June 1990).

[15] Frank A. Fratoe, "A Sociological Analysis of Minority Business, " *The Review of Black Political Economy*, Vol. 15, No. 2, Fall 1986, pp. 5-30.

[16] Roberson-Saunders, *op. cit.,* pp. 2-24.

[17] William P. O'Hare, "Black Business Ownership in the Rural South," *The Review of Black Political Economy*, Vol. 18, No. 3, Winter 1990, pp. 93-104.

[18] Timothy Bates, "Characteristics of Minorities Who Are Entering Self-Employment," *The Review of Black Political Economy*, Vol. 15, No. 2, Fall 1986, pp. 31-50.

[19] See John H. Johnson, "What Black Business Leaders Can Do for the Black Community," *The Urban League Review*, Vol. 9, No. 1, Summer 1985, pp. 68-71.

[20] Fratoe, *op. cit.,* p. 8.

[21] The *Croson* decision was aimed primarily at minority set-aside programs sponsored by local governments. The federal Small Business Administration's minority set-aside program was not directly affected.

107

[22] Julianne M. Malveaux, "The Parity Imperative: Civil Rights, Economic Justice, and the New American Dilemma," in Billy J. Tidwell (ed.), *The State of Black America 1992* (New York: National Urban League, Inc., 1992), pp. 299-300.

[23] The Joint Center for Political Studies, *National Roster of Black Elected Officials*, 1990.

[24] See Lenneal J. Henderson, "Budget and Tax Strategies: Implications for Blacks," in Janet Dewart (ed.), *The State of Black America 1990* (New York: National Urban League, Inc., 1990), pp. 53-71

[25] *Ibid.*, pp. 62-66.

[26] On the advantages and disadvantages of set-aside programs, see Samuel L. Myers, "Who Benefits from Minority-Business Set-Aside and Why: The Case of New Jersey," paper presented at the Association for Public Policy and Management Annual Research Conference, October 30, 1992, Denver, Colorado.

Money Matters:
Lending Discrimination In
African-American Communities

William D. Bradford, Ph.D.

INTRODUCTION AND SUMMARY

Do African Americans experience discrimination when they attempt to obtain credit? If so, what are the public policy and private policy remedies? Economists have long identified the existence and access to financial markets as contributing to the quality of life and economic development of the participants in an economy. To the extent that African Americans are discriminated against in their participation in these markets as borrowers, then the quality of life of African Americans is unduly inhibited, and the economic development of their communities will be limited.

To summarize the conclusions of this paper, based upon analysis of the available information, there is indeed evidence that the financial markets discriminate against black households with regard to credit. But the available evidence is insufficient to specify which agents in the homebuying process discriminate and the extent to which they discriminate. For example, the Home Mortgage Disclosure Act (HMDA) data of the Federal Reserve clearly detail the disparity in loan rejection rates for black applicants compared to white applicants at all income levels, but the HMDA data do not provide sufficient information about black and white applicants to detail the exact nature of the differential treatment.[1]

The clearest evidence of credit discrimination against black applicants (Hawley and Fujii, 1991) is not specific in terms of what types of loans blacks are less able to borrow from lenders. In this regard, consider the case of mortgage loans, which are the dominant source of debt for black households. As noted, HMDA data show that commercial banks and other lenders reject loan requests from black households at a higher rate than from white households at all income levels observed. In fact, the rejection rate of high-income black households (i.e., income greater than 120 percent of the Metropolitan Statistical Area (MSA) median) is higher than the rejection rate of low-income white households (income less than 80 percent of the MSA median). But the HMDA data do not provide information on the loan amount requested, the down payment offered by the applicant, or other information (such as credit history and credit rating of the applicant) which would be necessary in order for the lender to make a reasonable decision on the application for a loan.

The determination of the fundamental causes of the unequal treatment of blacks in borrowing requires consideration of the agents with whom the prospective homebuyer interacts in the process, including sales agents, real estate appraisers, loan originators, and loan purchasers, among others. With regard to real estate sales agents, results of HUD audit surveys show that sales agents treat blacks differently with regard to providing as much information as whites on financing, and sales agents (in providing information on mortgage loans to the homebuyers) steer black borrowers more toward FHA-VA loans. Such loans suffer problems in longer processing times, limits on the loan amount, higher transaction costs, and fewer institutions which lend these types of loans. There is also evidence, but less definitive, that appraisers discriminate against black households in valuing their homes. The lower the appraised value of the home, the lower the amount that the lender is willing to extend.

The most attention concerning credit discrimination has been on the lenders themselves. In this regard, it has been felt that financial institutions may be contributing to the decline of certain black neighborhoods by failing to provide adequate home financing to qualified applicants on reasonable terms and conditions. This belief has generated concern among community leaders, regulators, and elected officials. The significant role of financial institutions in providing credit for home purchases was recognized by Congress in the 1970s with the passage of both the Home Mortgage Disclosure Act (HMDA) in 1975 and the Community Reinvestment Act in 1977. The HMDA data mentioned earlier are a first step at attempting to quantify the extent of the disparity in lending.

Given the conclusions previously specified, the following recommendations can be deduced:

1. Expand HUD's equal housing enforcement staff. There has been an increase in the work of the staff, but no additional resources have been supplied to support the additional work.

2. Create metropolitan area-wide antidiscrimination agencies across the United States. These could be nonprofit organizations which funded and/or conducted studies concerning lending discrimination in their communities.

3. Expand direct testing activities. The studies cited herein show the effectiveness of direct testing, in which a black customer (auditor) and a white customer (auditor) with the same financial background seek housing and housing financing. Direct testing of discrimination could be sponsored at the local level by the antidiscrimination agencies, local government agencies, federal agencies (e.g., the U.S. Department of Housing and Urban Development (HUD) or the Federal Reserve), or a combination of these organizations.

4. Eliminate the caps on damages for illegal credit discrimination. States place caps on damages. From an economic standpoint, if the cost of an act is sufficiently high, a business, in its own self-interest, will not undertake that act.

5. Determine, using the HMDA data and any other sources of data available, those institutions which support community residents through lending to community households. Community residents should then place deposits in those institutions which do not practice discrimination and withdraw their deposits from those which do. By doing so, there is a penalty which discriminating institutional lenders must absorb. This will reduce their willingness to withhold lending to community residents.

6. Ascertain the degree of bias in other types of consumer loans. Federal agencies can do this by increasing the information which lenders must report on their loan decisions. Consumer loans are also undertaken for purchase of consumer durables and for unsecured personal loans. To what extent is there discrimination in this segment of lending?

THE CREDIT DECISION

Before turning to the evidence on the experience of blacks borrowing in the financial markets, it is helpful to review how institutional lending decisions are made. First, an applicant applies to a lending institution for credit. The lending institution then assesses whether the applicant is a good or a bad risk. Credit decisions are typically made on the basis of credit scoring systems, which attempt to distinguish between good and bad risks on the basis of applicant characteristics. These characteristics may include length of residence in an area, length of employment, income, net worth, whether or not the applicant is a homeowner, past credit experience, and other objective characteristics of the applicant. A credit applicant's supplied information and perhaps credit reports are then scored, and credit is awarded or denied depending upon whether the applicant's score exceeds a target score.[2] The criteria by which points are awarded and the number of points themselves may vary from lending institution to lending institution, depending upon management's criteria.

The framework above describes a consumer lending decision made by an institutional lender, whether a personal loan (unsecured or secured; i.e., with an asset such as an automobile for collateral) or a real estate mortgage loan. The latter is characterized by real estate as collateral, a larger loan amount, and a longer repayment period (e.g., 15 years) than other consumer loans.

With regard to personal loans, very little work has been done to examine credit discrimination in this segment. However, a recent study by Hawley and Fujii (1991) provides information on applications for loans among which were personal loans. The Survey of Consumer Finances (SCF) is a

111

large random sample of U.S. households, for which the Federal Reserve Board gathers data on family finances, including household data on income, employment history, and other indicators of credit worthiness. The SCF also contains answers to questions concerning credit denial. Based upon responses of 3,665 households (81 percent white, 19 percent nonwhite) in the 1983 SCF data, Hawley and Fujii found that minorities are more likely to report being denied credit, controlling for income, net worth, previous debt repayment problems, job tenure, auto and home ownership, checking account status, tenure of local residency, age and marital status, credit and balances owed, and monthly loan expenses owed. In the context of the credit scoring framework discussed above, this means that to the extent that these variables are used to score loan applicants, a black applicant with the same financial background as a white applicant will be more likely to be rejected for credit than the corresponding white applicant. This study refers to all applications for loans, including both personal and mortgage loans, since the type of credit for which the SCF respondent applied was not in the questionnaire.

For black households, the ability to borrow in the mortgage market is more important than borrowing in the personal loan market, because real estate composes a higher proportion of assets and wealth for black households than any other single category of asset. To illustrate this relationship, Table 1 and Table 2 show the asset categories by income levels for black and white households in 1984 (the latest data available in this detail). The own home equity is the largest fraction of wealth at all income levels for both black and white households. But there is no consistent increase in the fraction in own home as income increases. But at the highest income level, black households hold almost half of their wealth in their own homes. With regard to other real estate equity, the fraction of wealth in this category increases as income increases for both black and white households. In addition, black households hold less than white households for all income levels except the highest income level, in which black households hold 13.6 percent of their wealth in other real estate, compared to 10.1 percent for white households.

To assess the impact of discrimination in mortgage markets requires that we consider the overall process of buying a home. Prospective homebuyers encounter—directly or indirectly—numerous agents in the homebuying process: advertisers, sellers, sales agents, loan originators, appraisers, insurers, investors, and secondary market intermediaries. Our concern is how these agents interact with the black homepurchaser with regard to obtaining credit to purchase a home.

In order to induce the lender to lend, the ratio of debt to the market value of the home must be sufficiently low. If the loan defaults, the lender will use the property to get the money owed. If the property has low value, then the lender will less likely be repaid fully. In turn, the market value of the real estate which will be collateral is estimated by the professional real estate appraisers. Although the appraiser is an important agent in the homebuying process, perhaps the most important person which a homebuyer encounters in this process is the real estate agent. Sales agents come into contact with the prospective homebuyer before the sale is made, and thus are guides to the entire process of purchasing the home, including obtaining financing. The next section will discuss findings on discrimination in the appraisal of homes and also the results of research on steering by sales agents with regard to financing the home being purchased.

Of course, the dominant discussion with regard to differential treatment in the lending decision has been focused on the lending outcomes of institutional lenders. Thus, we will examine the research on lending discrimination by discussing general findings and the findings of the HMDA data.

UNEQUAL TREATMENT REGARDING CREDIT THROUGH THE APPRAISAL PROCESS AND THROUGH SALES AGENT STEERING

With regard to appraisers, in order for a homebuyer to borrow the amount required to purchase a home, the lending institution must value the home at a sufficiently high amount such that the loan-to-value ratio is at some desirable level. The lower the home appraises, the lower the lender is willing to lend.

As recently as 1970, Prentice-Hall published a text in which appraisers were instructed to report to lenders the racial characteristics of areas in which properties were appraised because "mixing of residents with diverse historical backgrounds within a neighborhood has an immediate and a depressing influence on value" (Ring, Valuation of Real Estate, cited in Dennis and Pottinger, 1980).[3] Anecdotal evidence abounds in discrimination with regard to appraisals. Joseph Boyce, a senior editor at the *Wall Street Journal*, was trying to sell his home and was surprised to find a white appraiser valuing his home at $15,000 less than the other homes in the racially mixed neighborhood. Mr. Boyce hired another white appraiser, but this time had his family leave the house before the appraiser arrived and took out all pictures indicating that a black family owned the house. Instead, he placed photos of his white secretary and her son throughout the house. The appraisal came in $12,500 higher.[4]

Another agent with whom the homebuyer has contact is the real estate agent. In fact, for most homebuyers, the real estate sales agent is the first and most important person in the homebuying process. Only for sales agents has there been direct measurement of discriminatory treatment of prospective homebuyers on a broad scale. These data on sales agents provide us with information on credit steering.

In 1977, HUD's Office of Policy Development and Research conducted the first national study of housing market discrimination. This Housing Market Practices Survey (HMPS) used the audit methodology to observe directly differential treatment of black and white homeseekers. Specifically, pairs of auditors—one white and the other black—posed as otherwise identical homeseekers. They responded separately to advertisements randomly selected from the major newspapers of 40 metropolitan areas and recorded their treatment on standardized forms. Because audit teammates were identically qualified as homebuyers, systematic differences in treatment could be attributed to their race.

In 1988, HUD initiated a second national audit study of housing market discrimination. This study—the Housing Discrimination Study (HDS)—contains data on 3,800 paired tests completed in 25 metropolitan areas during the late spring and early summer of 1989. The HDS audits did not extend far into the process of obtaining financing for home purchase. However, the information and assistance on financing the purchase provided by agents to minority and majority homebuyers were considered as part of the HDS. HDS auditors were matched with regard to both assets and liabilities, and both members of an audit team provided agents with equal information about their financial status, if and when asked. HDS results indicate that real estate agents provide substantially different information to minority and majority customers about potential sources of financing and are more likely to offer assistance to white Anglos in obtaining financing. The index of unfavorable treatment with respect to credit assistance is 39 percent for black homebuyers. Four specific indicators reflect key areas of differential treatment and are incorporated into the overall index of treatment with respect to financing assistance: (1) Did the agent offer to help in obtaining financing? (2) Did the agent tell the auditor he or she was not qualified for a mortgage? (3) Did the agent say that conventional fixed rate financing was available? and (4) Did the agent say that adjustable rate financing was available?

As shown in Table 3, real estate agents provide substantially different information to blacks than to white Anglos about sources of financing and are much more likely to offer assistance to Anglos in obtaining financing. In more than 20 percent of the audits, an offer to help in obtaining financing was made to the white Anglo auditor only. In addition, black auditors are less likely to be told about conventional and adjustable rate mortgages than are comparable Anglo homebuyers. As in other audit studies, the HDS found that blacks were more frequently told about FHA and VA financing than were their white counterparts. These government-based financing sources have more transaction costs, require more processing time, and fewer institutions participate in this market as loan originators compared to conventional mortgages. In addition, there is a maximum amount which can be borrowed under these programs.

114

Associated with these findings on steering toward FHA-VA mortgages, Canner, Gabriel, and Woolley (1991) used the 1983 SCF data to find that the average minority household obtaining a mortgage in a minority neighborhood is only about one-third as likely to obtain a conventional loan as a comparable white household in that neighborhood, even controlling for several objective measures of default risk. Canner and Gabriel (1992) find similar patterns in the 1990 HMDA data.

UNEQUAL TREATMENT REGARDING CREDIT BY LOAN ORIGINATORS

In May 1972, HUD released the results of a survey of savings and loan associations in 50 cities. Nearly 1,000 institutions admitted that they considered neighborhood racial composition in evaluating loan applications; almost 100 admitted that they considered the race of the prospective borrower; over 400 admitted they made no loans in areas of minority concentration (U.S. Senate Committee on Banking, Housing and Urban Affairs, 1976).[5] Although this survey was made before passage of the Equal Credit Opportunity Act, the Community Reinvestment Act, and the HMDA, it was well after passage of the Fair Housing Act of 1968 (and over 100 years after the Civil Rights Act of 1866 prohibited racial discrimination in any form of contracting, including loan contracts).

A tremendous amount of research has been conducted on discrimination in mortgage lending by loan originators. But numerous questions still remain about the degree of illegal discrimination by lenders. Research in discrimination in mortgage markets can use a direct or an indirect approach to determine if discrimination has occurred. The research has been almost exclusively indirect, attempting to infer discrimination from observable differences in loan amounts, types, and terms and differences in consumer attitudes. In the late 1970s and 1980s, several studies analyzed various unpublished data sources showing loan application dispositions by characteristics of the borrower. These econometric studies showed that in some, but not all, metropolitan areas investigated, race was of only moderate statistical influence in explaining rejection rates when other legitimate financial characteristics were controlled for.[6]

The weakness of these findings was indicated by Maddala and Trost (1982), who showed that the statistical models used by the authors overstated the significance of race. Another indirect method has attempted to determine if lenders may encourage or insist that more risky borrowers, such as minorities, apply for government insured (and thus default risk-free) mortgages. As noted, Canner, Gabriel, and Woolley (1991) and Canner and Gabriel (1992) found that minority households utilized more government-insured mortgages than comparable white households. These results are consistent with the hypothesis of lender bias (to be discussed in the next section). But both studies observe that they are also consistent with difference in preferences for FHA vs. conventional financing among different racial or ethnic groups, the effect of steering by real estate agents, or market specialization by mortgagors. The HDS finding that real estate agents were more likely to provide information about conventional loans to white testers and information about government-insured loans to minority testers adds support to this hypothesis.

Benston and Horsky (1990) have employed a different indirect approach to measure the existence of mortgage discrimination through opinion surveys of owners and the prospective buyers of homes. Their interviews in Atlanta revealed that homesellers in a putatively "redlined" inner-city neighborhood did not perceive that prospective buyers were limited by their inability to obtain financing or that they, themselves, had any difficulty in receiving home improvement loans. Prospective buyers, for their part, did not perceive financing as a limitation on where they wished to buy homes or perceive any spatial variation in the types of loans or their terms.

Very little direct evidence has been available on discrimination by loan originators. Four experiments employed paired testers to probe the behavior of lenders before formal applications were made. These experiments were conducted in Pontiac, Michigan (1984-85); Louisville, Kentucky (1988); Chicago (1990); and New York City (1991) and are reviewed in Galster (1992). They revealed some incidents when loan officers provided more information, assistance, and encouragement to the white auditor and tended to direct the minority teammate toward government-insured loans. However, these are only pilot studies and could not conform to the typical standards of scientific investigations.[7]

Testing offers a significant amount of potential for resolving some of the gaps emerging from the above statistical studies. Neither methodological nor operational issues seem to be insuperable barriers. There may even be possibilities for pursuing (perhaps nonpaired) testing beyond the pre-application stage. Unfortunately, the federal regulatory agencies have refused to employ direct testing as a tool for investigating lending practices. The Comptroller of the Currency turned down proposals to do so in 1979 and 1990, as did the Federal Reserve in 1991.[8] Direct testing offers the only methodological device for investigating possible discouragement or product-steering discrimination at the pre-application stage because by definition no paper trail is left for subsequent statistical analysis.

EVIDENCE ON UNEQUAL TREATMENT IN THE LOAN ORIGINATION PROCESS PROVIDED BY THE HOME MORTGAGE DISCLOSURE ACT DATA

An important set of information on the lending decisions of financial institutions is provided by the Home Mortgage Disclosure Act of 1975. The

Act requires all banks, savings and loan associations, mortgage companies that are subsidiaries of depositories, and credit unions with more than $10 million in assets to disclose the number and dollar amount of their housing loans within their Metropolitan Statistical Area (MSA) by census tract. With the 1989 amendments to the HMDA, 1990 data also include loan applications and denials by race, gender, and income of loan applicants. In addition, as of 1990, many independent mortgage companies, formerly exempt from HMDA reporting, were required to report for the first time. To assure broad range reporting, HUD was added as an enforcement agency for mortgage lenders unaffiliated with financial institutions.

These mortgage lenders are required to report lending activity, per application, on a loan/application register format. For each loan applicant, information is collected on the applicant's race, sex, and income, and whether or not the loan was granted. Lenders may, but are not required to, identify the reasons for denying loan applications.

The 1990 HMDA data include information pertaining to roughly 6.5 million loan and application records. Covered lenders reported on 5.41 million loan applications—3.16 million for home purchase, 1.05 million for refinancing, 1.15 million for home improvement, and the remainder for loans on 44,300 multifamily properties (dwellings for more than four families). The 1990 HMDA data also contain information on roughly 1.1 million loans that were purchased by reporting lenders.

Previous analysis of the 1990 HMDA data has documented differences in the experiences of home loan applicants grouped by their racial and income characteristics and by the racial composition and the median family incomes of the neighborhoods in which they sought to buy or improve homes. That analysis revealed that larger proportions of black applicants than of white applicants with similar incomes are denied home loans. The analysis also revealed that home loan applicants seeking to buy homes in low- or moderate-income neighborhoods and areas with significant minority populations are denied credit more frequently than are applicants seeking homes in areas whose residents have higher incomes or that are predominantly white.

These patterns are reflected in Tables 4 and 5, which provide information on lending by financial institutions for home purchase and refinancing arrayed by applicant race and income attributes, and for neighborhoods categorized by the racial composition, median family income, and central city (Table 4) or noncentral city (Table 5) location. The data indicate substantial variation in origination rates across applicant racial groups and income classes.[9] Origination rates for black applicants are significantly lower than the rates for other racial groups. Further, these findings appear to be robust to controls for applicant income class. For example, for central city location, mortgage origination rates for black and white households are 55 percent and 70 percent, respectively, in the lowest income group (households with less than 80 percent of the MSA median income). Although origination rates rise to 61 percent and 77 percent for black and white households, respectively, among applicants with incomes higher than 120 percent of the MSA median income, the differential between these racial groups remains sizable. The same general relationships follow for noncentral city locations.

The 1990 HMDA data indicate that the rate of loan denial increases as the proportion of minority residents increases. Table 6 reports the origination rates data on all types of loans, by percent minority and by income for central city locations. Table 7 is the corresponding information for noncentral city locations. For central city locations, the origination rate is 76 percent for areas with less than 10 percent minority residents and declines to about 56 percent for areas with 80 percent or more minority residents. The pattern of loan denial for government-backed loans is virtually the same as that for conventional loans, and the noncentral city location results are consistent with central city results.

The difference in denial rates across neighborhoods of different racial composition is roughly the same even when differences in neighborhood median family income levels are considered. For the most part, whether the neighborhood is low or moderate income, middle income, or upper income, the proportion of home purchase loan applicants denied credit increases as the percentage of minority residents increases. This pattern is present for applications for both conventional and government-backed forms of credit.

The secondary mortgage market entities can purchase home loans only from the pool of originated loans, and the underwriting guidelines of the government-sponsored agencies can have a profound effect on the borrower or neighborhood characteristics of home purchase loans that are originated. The basic underwriting guidelines—including maximum acceptable monthly payment-to-income ratios, maximum loan-to-value ratios, and charter limitations on the size of loans—differ significantly among the secondary market institutions. The Government National Mortgage Association (GNMA) accepts less stringent guidelines involved in the underwriting of FHA and VA home purchase loans; accordingly, the GNMA portfolio is composed of relatively high proportions of loans originated among lower-income and minority homebuyers and neighborhoods. In contrast, the Federal National Mortgage Association (FNMA) and the Federal Home Loan Mortgage Corporation (FHLMC) together account for 70 percent of the secondary market acquisitions of conventional home purchase loans. It follows then that only a small percentage of the purchase of each of those federally charged agencies derives from black borrowers.

In this regard, an ICF study (1991) provides insights into the purchase of mortgages of black and low-income borrowers. Focus groups of lenders representing 133 lending firms in 12 cities revealed the following perceptions about secondary market lending guidelines: (1) They posed distinct "challenges" for community efforts; more time was needed to determine whether such loans were salable. (2) Although they urged flexibility in principle, lenders were not convinced of the need for flexibility in practice. (3) Numerous guidelines, such as those dealing with source of down payment, acceptable documentation of credit histories, employment stability, multi-unit structures, and structures needing rehabilitation, were criticized as having adverse impacts.[10]

Of course, in addition to differences in underwriting standards, other factors may influence the distribution of home loan purchases among the secondary market agencies. As suggested above, for instance, steering of black homebuyers to FHA-insured loans by real estate agents and possibly by lending institutions may further influence the distribution of home loan purchases.

The 1990 HMDA data document differences in the experiences of loan applicants grouped by their personal characteristics or by the characteristics of the neighborhood in which they seek to purchase or improve homes. Most prominently, the data indicate that black applicants are denied home loans more frequently than are white or Asian applicants who have similar incomes.

CONCLUSIONS AND RECOMMENDATIONS

There is sufficient evidence, although still insufficient for scientific verification, to conclude that African Americans experience discrimination in borrowing in the financial markets. Further research is required in order to detail the agents and the extent to which the differential treatment is illegal. The following recommendations result from the findings cited in this chapter.[11]

1. *Expand HUD's Title VIII enforcement staff.* Under the 1988 amendments to Title VIII, many groups were added to the protected status concerning housing. Originally, the protected status consisted primarily of racial minorities. But there has not been an increase in HUD's staff for investigating and implementing Title VIII concerns. Complaints from these incremental groups are crowding out those concerning racial discrimination in housing markets. To avoid a decline in the emphasis on eliminating racial discrimination efforts in housing markets, HUD's enforcement staff should be increased.

2. *Create metropolitan area-wide antidiscrimination agencies across the United States.* Since racially discriminatory acts in the housing market are clearly illegal everywhere, those who criticize such acts do not need the permission of local governments to do so within the boundaries of such governments. Therefore, antidiscrimination agencies designed to operate throughout an entire metropolitan area can be created without gaining the

political consent of all or any local governments. Such agencies could be private nonprofit agencies, such as Woodstock, which now operates in the Chicago metropolitan area. This situation makes adoption of a regional strategy concerning racial discrimination activity possible in a way that is not possible concerning most other social problems within large metropolitan areas.

3. *Expand HUD-sponsored direct testing activities.* Direct testing of behavior patterns by key actors in housing markets has proved to be the most effective means of detecting and rooting out discrimination practices. Therefore, this approach should be greatly expanded, not only into more geographic areas, but also into mortgage financing transactions and other parts of the decision process that have not yet been subjected to testing. The ultimate objective should be for testing programs in each metropolitan area to be an ongoing part of the real estate industry's normal operations there— until repeated tests show almost no racially discriminatory behavior is occurring.

4. *Require state agencies to abolish caps on damages.* If a state agency dealing with racial discrimination in housing qualifies as "substantially equivalent" to HUD's antiracial discrimination department, then HUD turns over enforcement activities and responses to individual complaints to that state agency. But some states have had relatively low limits on the amount of damages that plaintiffs could receive. HUD should change its rules so that no state with such limits can qualify as substantially equivalent to HUD. Then the real estate industry in an area cannot evade being subject to strongly deterring penalties by having enforcement shifted from HUD to its own state agency.

5. *Add other types of loans to the data collected to determine differential treatment in those types of loans.* Although the largest size of loan for black households is for borrowing to purchase real estate, black and other minority consumers apply for automobile loans and other personal loans. Information on lending in these areas would enable a more complete analysis of discrimination in lending.

6. *Community residents should observe and publicize the lending patterns of local institutions and place their deposits in those which are more supportive of lending in the community.* One way to implement empowerment is through withdrawing funds from nonsupportive lenders and placing funds into the deposits of supportive lenders. In this way, those institutions which avoided discrimination would be able to expand their lending activities, and those which practiced discrimination would have less funds to allocate.

ENDNOTES

[1]See Canner (1991) for an analysis of the 1990 HMDA data and Thomas (1992) for an analysis of the 1991 HMDA data. There are relatively minor changes between the HMDA data for 1990 and 1991.

[2]This discussion follows that of Hawley and Fujii (1991), p. 22.

[3]Wienk (1992), p. 218.

[4]Sands (1992), p. A13.

[5]Wienk (1992), pp. 218-219.

[6]See Black, Schweitzer, and Mandell (1978); Schafer and Ladd (1980); Wiginton (1980); King (1981); and Warner and Ingram (1982).

[7]The studies are cited in Galster (1992), p. 651.

[8]*Ibid.*

[9]The origination rate is the amount of loans created divided by the amount of loan applications. The typical reason for which a loan application does not result in a loan creation is rejection of the application. Other applications will be withdrawn or not taken down if approved.

[10]Galster (1992), pp. 657-658.

[11]The first four recommendations have been previously suggested in Downs (1992), pp. 739-740.

REFERENCES

Barry Leeds and Associates, Inc. 1992. *Mortgage Pre-Application Bias Survey: Summary.* New York: Barry Leeds and Assoc. February 12.

Benston, G. 1981. " Mortgage Redlining Research: A Review and Critical Analysis." *Journal of Bank Research* 12:8-23.

Benston, G. and D. Horsky. 1990. "Is Anti-Mortgage Redlining Regulation Justified?" Atlanta, GA: Unpublished paper, Emory University.

Black, H. and R. Schweitzer. 1985. "A Canonical Analysis of Mortgage Lending Terms." *Urban Studies* 22:13-19.

Black H., R. Schweitzer, and L. Mandell. 1978. "Discrimination in Mortgage Lending." *American Economic Review* 68:18-91.

Canner, G. 1991. "Home Mortgage Disclosure Act: Expanded Data on Residential Lending." *Federal Reserve Bulletin,* November.

Canner, G. 1981. "Redlining and Mortgage Lending Patterns." In *Research in Urban Economics,* edited by J.V. Henderson. Greenwich, CT: JAI Press, Inc., pp. 67-101.

Canner, G. and S. Gabriel. 1992. "Market Segmentation and Lender Specialization in the Primary and Secondary Mortgage Markets." *Housing Policy Debate* 3:2, pp. 241-332.

Canner, G., S. Gabriel, and J. Woolley. 1991. "Race, Default Risk, and Mortgage Lending." *Southern Economic Journal* 58:249-62.

Clapp, J. 1980. "A Model of Localized Lending Behavior." *American Real Estate and Urban Economics Association Journal* 8:229-62.

Downs, A. 1992. "Policy Directions Concerning Racial Discrimination in U.S. Housing Markets." *Housing Policy Debate* 3:2, pp. 655-745.

Fishbein, A. 1992. "The Ongoing Experiment with 'Regulation from Below': Expanded Reporting Requirements for HMDA and CRA." *Housing Policy Debate* 3:2, pp. 601-638.

_____. 1990a. "Racial Steering by Real Estate Agents: A Review of the Audit Evidence." *Review of Black Political Economy* 18:105-29.

____. 1990b. "Racial Discrimination in Housing Markets in the 1980s: A Review of the Audit Evidence." *Journal of Planning Education and Research* 9:165-75.

____. 1990c. "Racial Steering by Real Estate Agents: Mechanisms and Motivations." *Review of Black Political Economy* 19:39-63.

Galster, G. 1992. "Research on Discrimination in Housing and Mortgage Markets: Assessment and Future Directions." *Housing Policy Debate* 3:2, pp. 639-683.

Green, R., and G. von Furstenberg. 1975. "The Effects of Race and Aging on Housing on Mortgage Delinquency Risk." *Urban Studies* 12:85-89.

Hawley, C. and E. Fujii. 1991. "Discrimination in Consumer Credit Markets." *Eastern Economic Journal* 17:21-30.

ICF, Inc. 1991. *The Secondary Market and Community Lending through Lenders' Eyes.* Fairfax, VA: ICF Report to Federal Home Loan Mortgage Corp.

Keest, K. 1991. *Second Mortgage Lending: Abuses and Regulation.* Boston, MA: National Consumer Law Center.

King, A.T. 1981. *Discrimination in Mortgage Lending.* New York: New York University Graduate School of Business Administration, Monograph Series in Finance, 1980-84.

Kohn, E., C. Foster, B. Kaye, and N. Terris. 1992. *Are Mortgage Lending Policies Discriminatory? A Study of 10 Savings Banks.* New York: New York State Banking Department, Consumer Studies Division.

Maddala, G. and R. Trost. 1982. "On Measuring Discrimination in Loan Markets." *Housing Finance Review* 1:245-68.

Ohls, J. 1990. *Secondary Mortgage Market: Information on Underwriting and Home Loans in the Atlanta Area.* Washington, DC: U.S. General Accounting Office/GA0-RCED-91-2.

Sands, David R. 1992. "Borrowing Bias." *The Washington Times.* January 21, p. A13.

Schafer, R. and H. Ladd. 1980. *Equal Credit Opportunity Accessibility to Mortgage Funds by Women and Minorities.* Washington, DC: U.S. Department of Housing and Urban Development/PDR-551-1.

Shlay, A. 1989. "Financing Community: Methods for Assessing Credit Disparities, Market Barriers, and Institutional Reinvestment Performance in the Metropolis." *Journal of Urban Affairs* 11:201-24.

Staff of the Board of Governors. 1991. *A Feasibility Study on the Application of the Testing Methodology to the Detection of Discrimination in Mortgage Lending.* Washington, DC: Federal Reserve System.

Thomas, Paulette. 1992. "Blacks Can Face a Host of Trying Conditions in Getting Mortgages." *Wall Street Journal,* November 30, p. 1+.

Turner, M., R. Struyck, and J. Yinger. 1991. *The Housing Discrimination Study: Synthesis.* Washington, DC: The Urban Istitute and Syracuse University.

Warner, A. and J. Ingram. 1982. "A Test of Discrimination in a Mortgage Market." *Journal of Bank Research* 13:116-24.

Wienk, R. 1992. "Discrimination in Urban Credit Markets: What We Don't Know and Why We Don't Know It." *Housing Policy Debate* 3:2, pp. 217-240.

Wiginton, J. 1980. "A Note on the Comparison of Logit and Discriminant Models of Consumer Credit." *Journal of Financial and Quantitative Analysis* 15: 757-770.

Table 1
Median Asset Holdings by Income Level (%)

Annual Income: $000		< 10.8			10.8 - 24.0		
		White HH	Black HH	Black/ White	White HH	Black HH	Black/ White
Int. Earn Assets at Fin. Inst.	Owning	0.508	0.221		0.718	0.457	
	Median	2800	400	0.14	3000	649	0.22
Other Int. Earn Assets	Owning	0.027	0.008		0.066	0.017	
	Median	7748	650	0.08	10000	1000	0.10
Stocks	Owning	0.069	0.007		0.131	0.040	
	Median	4000	4000	1.00	4000	4000	1.00
Business Equity	Owning	0.074	0.014		0.087	0.025	
	Median	10000	2500	0.25	11000	2500	0.23
Motor Vehicles	Owning	0.634	0.399		0.913	0.746	
	Median	1750	1500	0.86	3350	2013	0.60
Own Home	Owning	0.482	0.296		0.602	0.421	
	Median	31350	20000	0.64	37830	22000	0.58
Other Real Estate	Owning	0.090	0.041		0.137	0.083	
	Median	20600	15000	0.73	20000	11000	0.55
IRA or Keough	Owning	0.046	0.010		0.123	0.045	
	Median	4000	4000	1.00	4000	2600	0.65
Other Assets	Owning	0.455	0.147		0.613	0.373	
	Median	398	141	0.35	450	263	0.58
Net Worth	Median	19500	5104	0.26	30350	6599	0.22

Table 1 (Cont.)
Median Asset Holdings by Income Level (%)

Annual Income: $000		24.0 - 48.0			> 48.0		
		White HH	Black HH	Black/ White	White HH	Black HH	Black/ White
Int. Earn Assets at	Owning	0.842	0.701		0.927	0.779	
Fin. Inst.	Median	2886	999	0.35	7499	2598	0.35
Other Int. Earn	Owning	0.103	0.027		0.223	0.131	
Assets	Median	6000	833	0.14	11999	2450	0.20
Stocks	Owning	0.244	0.090		0.457	0.256	
	Median	3500	2760	0.79	8275	4000	0.48
Business	Owning	0.110	0.035		0.216	0.140	
Equity	Median	13930	5750	0.41	30000	29500	0.98
Motor	Owning	0.972	0.909		0.975	0.889	
Vehicles	Median	4950	3737	0.75	7500	6436	0.86
Own Home	Owning	0.739	0.587		0.866	0.809	
	Median	42500	28100	0.66	65000	35917	0.55
Other Real	Owning	0.201	0.105		0.355	0.303	
Estate	Median	25000	36500	1.46	40000	57000	1.43
IRA or	Owning	0.268	0.107		0.538	0.189	
Keough	Median	4400	2000	0.45	6500	4000	0.62
Other	Owning	0.730	0.629		0.791	0.792	
Assets	Median	550	400	0.73	1350	1000	0.74
Net Worth	Median	47925	16203	0.34	113377	59957	0.53

Source: Bureau of the Census, SIPP data.

Table 2
Wealth Composition by Income Level

Annual Income: $000	< 10.8		10.8 - 24.0	
	White HH	Black HH	White HH	Black HH
Int. Earn Assets at Fin. Inst.	18.33	10.37	16.75	13.64
Other Int. Earn Assets	0.61	0.16	1.40	0.53
Stocks	1.33	0.22	1.74	1.16
Business Equity	2.74	0.90	2.55	0.76
Motor Vehicles	29.09	35.60	28.38	39.21
Own Home	35.77	42.97	37.91	34.23
Other Real Estate	3.93	3.31	4.74	4.10
IRA or Keough	0.69	1.00	1.43	1.68
Other Assets	7.51	5.47	5.10	4.69
Total	100.00	100.00	100.00	100.00

Table 2 (Cont.)
Wealth Composition by Income Level

Annual Income: $000	24.0 - 48.0		> 48.0	
	White HH	Black HH	White HH	Black HH
Int. Earn Assets at Fin. Inst.	12.97	10.75	12.15	6.78
Other Int. Earn Assets	1.49	0.24	2.78	0.57
Stocks	2.96	1.76	6.25	1.44
Business Equity	2.70	0.56	5.63	4.88
Motor Vehicles	21.89	34.28	11.48	16.15
Own Home	44.98	41.57	43.22	43.35
Other Real Estate	6.21	4.67	10.10	13.61
IRA or Keough	2.32	1.63	3.71	0.90
Other Assets	4.48	4.54	4.68	6.32
Total	100.00	100.00	100.00	100.00

Source: Bureas of the Census, SIPP data.

Table 3
Incidence of Unfavorable Treatment of Blacks in
Financing Assistance for Homebuyers*

	Percent
Share of Audits with Unfavorable Treatment of Blacks:	
Told fixed-rate conventional financing was available	32.7
Told adjustable-rate financing was available	23.1
Told auditor not qualified for financing	2.1
Assistance with financing volunteered	24.4
Index of Financing Assistance	39.1

Source: Turner, Struyck, and Yinger (1991). p. 22.

*: All values reflect the gross incidence of unfavorable treatment, using weighted data. All reported estimates are statistically significant at a 95 percent confidence level.

Table 4
Home Loan Activity by Applicant Characteristics
(All Lenders, Central City)

Applicant Characteristics	Origination Rate(%)	Distribution (%)
Race/Ethnicity		
American Indian	64.1	.5
Asian	66.8	4.8
Black	57.0	6.6
Hispanic*	61.8	7.1
White	74.3	78.2
Other	61.7	.6
Joint (White/Minority)	71.3	2.2
Total	71.2	100.0

(Number of Loans: 832,669)

Income and Race		
< 80% MSA Median Income		
American Indian	58.5	.1
Asian	67.6	.6
Black	54.6	2.5
Hispanic*	58.4	1.8
White	69.8	14.8
Other	59.9	.1
Joint (White/Minority)	66.5	.3
Total	66.1	20.3
80% - 99% MSA Median Income		
American Indian	70.0	.1
Asian	69.9	.5
Black	60.1	1.1
Hispanic*	66.5	1.1
White	76.7	10.3
Other	66.5	.1
Joint (White/Minority)	73.4	.3
Total	73.7	13.4

Table 4 (Cont.)
Home Loan Activity by Applicant Characteristics
(All Lenders, Central City)

Applicant Characteristics	Origination Rate(%)	Distribution (%)
100% - 120% MSA Median Income		
American Indian	67.9	.1
Asian	71.0	.5
Black	60.6	.8
Hispanic*	66.2	1.0
White	77.6	9.6
Other	65.2	.1
Joint (White/Minority)	73.3	.3
Total	74.6	12.4
> 120% MSA Median Income		
American Indian	66.7	.2
Asian	67.6	3.1
Black	60.5	2.2
Hispanic*	64.8	3.2
White	76.5	43.5
Other	62.3	.4
Joint (White/Minority)	73.3	1.4
Total	74.1	54.0
Total (All)	72.3	100.0

Total Number of Loans: 805,396

*: Persons of Hispanic origin may be of any race.

Source: Canner and Gabriel (1992).

Table 5
Home Loan Activity by Applicant Characteristics
(All Lenders, Noncentral City)

Applicant Characteristics	Origination Rate(%)	Distribution (%)
Race/Ethnicity		
American Indian	68.3	.4
Asian	68.4	4.0
Black	60.4	3.2
Hispanic*	62.7	4.7
White	75.7	85.2
Other	64.4	.5
Joint (White/Minority)	72.1	1.9
Total	73.9	100.00
(Number of Loans: 1,319,384)		
Income and Race		
< 80% MSA Median Income		
American Indian	61.2	.1
Asian	66.5	.3
Black	54.9	.8
Hispanic*	58.6	.7
White	70.2	13.4
Other	61.4	.1
Joint (White/Minority)	66.3	.2
Total	68.4	15.5
80% - 99% MSA Median		
American Indian	70.3	.1
Asian	73.3	.3
Black	62.8	.5
Hispanic*	65.4	.6
White	77.7	11.0
Other	65.3	.1
Joint (White/Minority)	73.1	.2
Total	76.0	12.8

Table 5 (Cont.)
Home Loan Activity by Applicant Characteristics
(All Lenders, Noncentral City)

Applicant Characteristics	Origination Rate(%)	Distribution (%)
100% - 120% MSA Median		
American Indian	74.0	.1
Asian	72.7	.4
Black	65.1	.5
Hispanic*	66.7	.7
White	79.2	11.4
Other	68.8	.1
Joint (White/Minority)	74.4	.2
Total	77.5	13.3
> 120% MSA Median		
American Indian	70.7	.3
Asian	69.4	2.9
Black	63.8	6.4
Hispanic*	65.8	2.8
White	77.7	49.4
Other	64.5	.3
Joint (White/Minority)	73.8	1.3
Total	75.9	58.5
Total (All)	74.9	100.0

(Total Number of Loans: 1,278,414)

*: Persons of Hispanic origin may be of any race.

Source: Canner and Gabriel (1992).

Table 6
Home Loan Activity by Census Tract Characteristics
and by Geographical Location of Property
(All Lenders, Central City)

Census Tract Characteristics	Origination Rate(%)	Distribution (%)
Racial Composition		
< 10% Minority	75.5	50.6
10 - 19%	69.6	19.3
20 - 49%	65.7	17.7
50 - 79%	61.9	6.6
80 - 100%	56.2	5.7
Total	70.0	100.0
(Number of Loans: 873,755)		
Income and Racial Composition		
Low/Moderate Income		
< 10% Minority	70.3	3.3
10 - 19%	68.1	2.3
20 - 49%	74.2	4.7
50 - 79%	60.9	3.6
80 - 100%	55.2	4.2
Total	62.6	18.2
Middle Income		
< 10% Minority	75.9	27.6
10 - 19%	69.3	10.9
20 - 49%	65.9	10.9
50 - 79%	62.6	2.7
80 - 100%	59.2	1.4
Total	71.1	52.8
Upper Income		
< 10% Minority	75.9	19.7
10 - 19%	69.7	6.1
20 - 49%	67.6	2.8
50 - 79%	69.1	.3
80 - 100%	58.5	.1
Total	73.4	29.0
Total (All)	70.0	100.0

(Number of Loans: 873,755)

Source: Canner and Gabriel (1992).

Table 7
Home Loan Activity by Census Tract Characteristics
and by Geographical Location of Property
(All Lenders, Noncentral City)

Census Tract Characteristics	Origination Rate(%)	Distribution (%)
Racial Composition		
< 10% Minority	76.2	67.4
10 - 19%	68.7	17.3
20 - 49%	66.4	10.9
50 - 79%	62.6	3.2
80 - 100%	58.6	1.2
Total	72.9	100.0
(Number of Loans: 1,357,715)		
Income and Racial Composition		
Low/Moderate Income		
< 10% Minority	69.5	2.7
10 - 19%	65.2	1.1
20 - 49%	64.0	1.8
50 - 79%	59.7	1.1
80 - 100%	57.0	.8
Total	64.5	7.4
Middle Income		
< 10% Minority	76.2	41.8
10 - 19%	69.4	10.3
20 - 49%	66.9	6.9
50 - 79%	63.6	1.7
80 - 100%	59.3	.3
Total	73.3	61.1
Upper Income		
< 10% Minority	77.0	22.9
10 - 19%	68.2	5.8
20 - 49%	67.2	2.1
50 - 79%	66.8	.4
80 - 100%	68.0	.1
Total	74.3	31.5
Total (All)	72.9	100.0

(Number of Loans: 1,357, 715)

Source: Canner and Gabriel (1992).

The Economic Status of African Americans During the Reagan-Bush Era: Withered Opportunities, Limited Outcomes, and Uncertain Outlook

David H. Swinton, Ph.D.

INTRODUCTION

This latest in the annual series of reports on the economic status of African Americans comes at the end of the Reagan-Bush era and the beginning of the Clinton-Gore era. It is, therefore, appropriate, as we examine the latest available data, that we also take a retrospective look at the impact of the 12 years of Reagan-Bush on the economic status of African Americans. Although the final numbers are not yet in, the general conclusion is nonetheless apparent. The past 12 years have been a period of no progress towards achieving the long-sought-after goal of economic parity for African Americans. To be sure, some African Americans have advanced. However, the central tendency for the group as a whole has been stagnation or retrogression in absolute status and increased disparities in relative status.

The latest data from 1991 and 1992 on income, poverty, and labor market status reveal a continuation of the disadvantaged status of blacks. The Reagan-Bush era closed as it began: with an economy gripped by recession or, at best, in a very anemic recovery. However, for African Americans, the entire period has been characterized by conditions that would be considered depression level if they were experienced by all Americans. The data at the end of the period—as they have throughout the Reagan-Bush era—reveal the persistence of second-class economic status for African Americans. The standard indicators of economic status to support the above conclusions will again be reviewed in some detail. These data on income, poverty, and labor market status will show that the African-American population made no progress in reducing its low and unequal status during the Reagan-Bush era.

The lack of progress in reducing the racial gaps in economic status during the past 12 years is no accident of history. Rather it reflects a failure of Reagan-Bush policy to address effectively the underlying factors which perpetuate the unequal economic status of African Americans. Indeed the era started with an explicit policy of dismantling and reducing emphasis on effective equal opportunity and affirmative action efforts. The Reagan-Bush policy of neglect and deregulation was based on their strong belief in the virtues of the market and self-help. The failure of 12 years of the Reagan-Bush approach to advance the absolute and relative economic status of African Americans will be apparent after review of the data.

Persisting relative inequality in the current economic status of African Americans reflects the persistence of limited economic power. Economic power flows from ownership of human and nonhuman capital. The tremendous gaps in ownership have been repeatedly pointed out in previous reports in this series on the "Economic Status of African Americans." This situation was especially stressed in last year's report. Given the overall theme for this volume, empowerment, we will repeat much of last year's presentation on the limited ownership of wealth. Policies to reduce the glaring disparity in wealth ownership have been neglected not only during the Reagan-Bush era but also throughout American history. Yet, as we have argued previously, it is unlikely that economic parity could ever be obtained in our capitalistic economic system without significant attenuation of the racial gaps in ownership.

The presentation will focus on three major aspects of economic status. In the first section, we will review data on ownership. Although data are limited, it will be apparent that limited progress in closing the ownership gaps has been made. Second, we will review the evidence on income and poverty. These data will show that income levels and poverty rates stagnated in absolute terms while inequality remained relatively constant. Finally, we will review labor market data which will reinforce the conclusion from the other analyses; namely, that little progress was made in improving the absolute or relative status of African Americans in the labor market during the Reagan-Bush era. Indeed, in many respects, the absolute and relative labor market position of African Americans worsened.

The review of the facts will clearly establish the proposition that society made little or no progress towards the goal of attaining racial equality in economic life during the Reagan-Bush era. African Americans continue to bear the heavy burden of the historic legacy of slavery, Jim Crowism, and discrimination. Therefore, at the end of our review, we will have some concluding remarks concerning the implications of this experience for future efforts to improve the relative economic status of African Americans.

AFRICAN-AMERICAN OWNERSHIP OF WEALTH: FINANCIAL ASSETS, BUSINESS, AND EDUCATIONAL CAPITAL

The importance of ownership in a capitalistic economy is perhaps obvious to all. However, despite its obvious importance, little attention has been

136

given to the limited African-American ownership position and its relationship to the perpetuation of the disadvantaged economic status of African Americans. The relatively limited current economic status of African Americans is well known. However, the much larger disparities in ownership have been widely neglected by researchers and policymakers alike. Yet, empowerment of the African-American community to obtain and maintain economic parity through its own efforts will be impossible without the elimination of the large and glaring disparities in wealth ownership.

As suggested in last year's report, ownership is an important determinant of the absolute and relative economic status of an individual or group for two reasons. First, ownership provides income either in the form of the earnings from assets or in the form of the services provided by the asset. Thus, one earns profits from the ownership of businesses, dividends, and interest from the ownership of financial assets, rents from the ownership of real property, and greater wages or salaries from the ownership of human capital. In addition, household assets such as houses, cars, and furnishings provide valuable consumption benefits throughout their lifetime. Thus, the individual or group that owns more will also have higher income and consumption, all else equal. Second, ownership of wealth is important because owners organize and control production either directly or indirectly in a capitalistic system. They determine the quantity, location, and nature of investment; how much, what type, and whose resources to employ; and they determine how much, what type, and whose goods and services to purchase. Thus, ownership enables an individual or group to have greater influence on the development, employment, and remuneration of their human and nonhuman resources. Limited ownership of wealth by African Americans leads to lower current consumption, earnings, and employment, and lower ability to develop their human and nonhuman resources.

Financial Assets

Data on wealth ownership by race are extremely limited. The latest available data, for 1988, are displayed in Table 1. The Census Bureau has recently begun to publish data on wealth ownership every four years. The current series started in 1984; therefore, no consistent historical series exists yet. Moreover, there are well-known problems with the estimates of household wealth holdings. However, the bias in the estimates would appear to be in the direction of lowering estimates of racial inequality in wealth ownership. In any case, the relative disparities are so large that improved data would probably not affect our broad conclusions. Nevertheless, the Census Bureau data are the only readily available source for recent information on wealth holdings.

Two surveys were reported for the Reagan-Bush years. Presumably new survey data will be published for 1992. However, in view of recent trends in

Table 1
Wealth Ownership, 1988
(in millions of 1991$)

	Mean Wealth Holdings		Percent Owning Each Type of Wealth		Per Capita Wealth Holdings			Aggregate Wealth Holdings		
	Black	White	Black	White	Black	White	B/W	Black	White	Gap
Total Net Worth	$27,230	$116,661	100.00%	100.00%	$9,359	$44,980	20.81%	$279,870	$9,235,958	$1,065,224
Interest Earning at Financial Institutions	5,008	21,748	44.48	76.58	766	6,421	11.93%	22,904	1,318,506	169,118
Regular Checking	822	1,243	30.11	50.92	85	244	35.04%	2,555	50,070	47,367
Stocks & Mutual Funds	4,220	32,582	6.97	23.92	101	3,005	3.36%	3,023	617,100	86,849
Equity in Business	29,053	76,604	3.66	13.57	366	4,008	9.13%	10,938	822,943	108,913
Equity in Motor Vehicle	4,568	7,378	64.67	89.15	1,015	2,536	40.02%	30,353	520,812	45,497
Equity in Home	42,334	73,871	43.46	66.72	6,323	19,003	33.27%	189,094	3,902,024	379,184
Equity in Rental Property	46,926	95,965	4.55	9.61	734	3,556	20.63%	21,938	730,078	84,388
Other Real Estate	18,895	44,294	4.37	11.35	283	1,938	14.62%	8,476	397,991	49,486
U.S. Savings Bonds	1,165	3,589	11.01	18.47	51	212	23.95%	1,309	52,424	63,260
IRA or Keoghs	6,394	19,010	6.87	26.43	174	1,786	9.73%	4,518	397,777	53,412

Aggregate gaps = white per capita - black per capita * 1988 black population (29,904,000).

Inequality Index (B/W) = black per capita/white per capita.

Source: U.S. Department of Commerce, Bureau of the Census, *Household Wealth and Asset Ownership: 1988*, December 1990, Table 3.

capital markets, these data will most likely reveal a deterioration in the value of wealth holdings. In any case, the African-American disadvantage for 1988 stands out clearly. First, we note that African Americans have a mean net worth of only $27,230 compared to $116,661 for whites. On a per capita basis, blacks have a net worth of $9,359 versus $44,980 for whites. In 1988, blacks had a net worth of only 20.81 percent of the amount required for parity.

As is apparent from the data in Table 1, the disadvantage for African Americans arose because smaller proportions of African Americans had each type of wealth, and those African Americans who had the various types of wealth had smaller mean wealth holdings. For example, 76.58 percent of white households had assets which earned interest at financial institutions, but only 44.48 percent of black households had this type of wealth. Moreover, those blacks who had interest-earning assets at financial institutions had mean holdings worth $5,008 compared to $21,748 for white households. The net result of these two facts is that blacks had only $766 per capita in interest earning assets at financial institutions compared to $6,421 for whites. The inequality index for this type of asset was only 11.93 percent. This means that blacks had only 11.93 percent of the amount of assets earning interest at financial institutions as would be required to have parity in this type of asset.

Looking at each type of asset, the reader can easily observe that inequality in wealth is pervasive. Using the B/W index for the various categories, it is obvious that the greatest equality occurred in the ownership of motor vehicles, housing, and regular checking accounts. These are basically consumption-oriented assets. However, even in these categories, African Americans owned only between 33 and 40 percent of the amounts required to have parity. African Americans had only one-third as much equity in housing as did white Americans. Greatest inequality existed for ownership of stocks and mutual funds, equity in business, and IRAs and Keoghs. Blacks owned only between 3 and 10 percent of the amounts required for parity in these types of assets. Ownership of interest-bearing assets at financial institutions and other real estate were also very limited. In these cases, the parity index is between 10 and 15 percent. The last two categories, equity in rental property and U.S. savings bonds, have parity indexes between 20 and 25 percent.

The aggregate implications of this limited ownership are shown in the column labeled "Aggregate Wealth Holdings Gap." The aggregate shortfalls in wealth ownership are very large. Overall, the African-American community had a wealth gap of 1.065 trillion dollars. Moreover, in view of the well-known underreporting of certain categories of wealth ownership, this is a conservative estimate of the gap. The gaps for individual categories range from a low of $47 billion for regular checking accounts to a high of $379 billion for equity in housing. The gap in business ownership is $108 billion, and there is an $86 billion shortfall in the ownership of stocks and mutual funds.

As previously stated, very little data exist to examine the trends in wealth ownership. Comparing the results for 1988 to the results for 1984 reported in *The State of Black America 1989*, we note that, after adjusting for inflation, both blacks and whites made modest gains in their per capita net worth. In 1991 dollars, per capita net worth in 1984 was $8,967 for blacks and $42,842 for whites. However, most of the gain in net worth was attributable to an increase in equity in homes. In fact, the data indicate that net worth for both blacks and whites in several asset categories (regular checking, stocks and mutual funds, equity in business, and equity in rental property) either declined or barely changed.

Overall, there was almost no change in inequality as measured by the B/W index. The value in 1984 was 20.93 percent compared to the 20.81 percent already cited for 1988. In general, this implies that during the period of greatest growth during the Reagan-Bush era, no progress was made in reducing racial inequality in wealth ownership. While the pattern for individual items is mixed, there were notable reductions in equality between 1984 and 1988 in business equity and equity in rental property: the parity index dropped from 13.44 percent to 9.13 percent and 28.99 percent and 20.63 percent, respectively.

The aggregate parity gap increased between 1984 and 1988 from about 954 billion dollars to 1,065 billion dollars. Thus, there was a 112 billion dollar increase in wealth inequality over this four-year period. In general, the parity gap increased in every individual category except equity in business. In this case, the sharp decline in business equity for both blacks and whites resulted in a decline in the aggregate inequality gap despite the fact that relative inequality increased.

The wealth gaps remained extremely high during the Reagan-Bush era. Indications are that relative inequality during the middle Reagan-Bush period remained about constant. However, the absolute gap increased a great deal. It is clear that the Reagan-Bush era did nothing to move African-Americans towards parity in wealth ownership.

Business Ownership

Table 2 displays the latest data on black business ownership during the Reagan-Bush era. These data make it very clear that inequality in business ownership remained at a very high level. Blacks are disadvantaged by owning relatively fewer businesses, and the businesses they do own tend to be very small in comparison to all businesses. In 1987, blacks owned 424,000 businesses compared to 17,526,000 businesses in the nation as a whole. There were only about 14 firms per 1,000 black persons compared to 73 firms per 1,000 persons for the country as a whole. Blacks were 12.1

Table 2
Receipts (in billions of 1991$) and Number of Firms (1,000s) in 1987 by Industry

	Black Receipts	Total Receipts	B/T**	Black Firms	Total Firms	B/T***	Receipts per Firm Black	Receipts per Firm Total	Receipts per Firm B/T	Receipt Gap	Firm Gap
Total	$22.8	$11,893	1.6%	424	17,526	19.8%	53,774	678,592	7.92	$1,427	1,713
Construction	2.6	616	3.7%	37	560	53.9%	70,270	1,100,000	6.34	72.9	32
Manufacturing	1.2	3,185	0.3%	8	642	10.2%	150,000	4,961,059	3.02	387.7	70
Trans. and Public Util.	1.8	909	1.7%	37	735	41.2%	48,649	1,236,735	3.93	108.4	53
Wholesale Trade	1.5	1,466	0.9%	6	641	7.0%	250,000	2,287,051	10.93	177.2	73
Retail Trade	6.7	1,802	3.2%	66	2,658	20.4%	101,515	677,953	14.97	212.6	258
Finance, Ins., & Real Estate	0.9	1,814	0.4%	27	1,426	15.5%	33,333	1,272,090	2.62	220.9	147
Selected Services	7.1	996	6.0%	210	7,095	24.2%	33,810	140,381	24.08	114.6	656
Other Industries*	0.9	1,105	0.7%	34	3,769	7.5%	26,471	293,181	9.02	134.4	425

Note: 1987 dollars were converted to 1991 dollars using CPI-U-X1.

*: Includes Agriculture, Mining, and Industries not elsewhere classified.

**: (Black Receipts/Black Population) divided by (Total Receipts/Total Population).

***: (Black Firms/Black Population) divided by (Total Firms/Total Population).

Black population in 1987: 29,417,000; total population in 1987: 241,187,000.

Source: U.S. Department of Commerce, Bureau of the Census, *Survey of Minority-Owned Businesses: Black, 1987*, and *The Statistical Abstract of the United States, 1990*, Table 859, p. 521.

percent of the population in 1987 but owned only 2.4 percent of the businesses. As the inequality index (B/T) indicates, blacks owned only 19.8 percent of the number of firms required for numerical ownership parity.

Moreover, the small size of black-owned businesses is indicated by the fact that all of them together generated receipts of only $22.8 billion compared to receipts of $11,893 billion for all businesses. Black businesses accounted for only 0.19 percent of total receipts. Black businesses had total receipts of $775 for each black person compared to $49,310 per person for the economy as a whole. The B/T inequality index suggests that black businesses generated only about 1.6 percent as much revenue as would be required to have ownership parity as measured by receipts. The picture of limited parity holds for each of the major industry types. Relative equality in number of firms was highest in the construction and the transportation and public utility sectors. In construction, blacks owned about 37,000 firms, which is 53.9 percent of the number of firms required for parity. In transportation and public utilities, they owned about 37,000 businesses, or 41.2 percent as many firms as would be required for parity. However, these firms, though relatively numerous, were very small in comparison to the typical firm in these industries. The average black construction firm, for example, had revenues of only $70,270 compared to $1,100,000 for the average construction firm in general; the average black firm in the transportation and public utility sector grossed $48,649 compared to $1,236,735 for the average total firm.

Examining the B/T numbers for each of the other industries indicates the large degree of inequality in number of firms owned that existed in all industries during the Reagan-Bush era. Moreover, a comparison of the receipts per firm for African-American businesses and total businesses reveals that the typical black-owned firm in each industry was orders of magnitude smaller than the typical nonblack-owned firm. Small numbers and small size lead to limited generation of receipts. Indeed, the closest blacks came to parity in 1988 was in the selected services sector; here, black-owned businesses generated only $7.1 billion out of a total of $996 billion. This amounted to only seven-tenths of 1 percent of total receipts and only 6 percent of the amount required for parity. The situation in the other industries can be read from the table.

In the aggregate, business ownership inequality was very large. The gap in number of firms owned in 1987 was over 1.7 trillion enterprises. The receipts gap was a startling $1.4 billion. Obviously, the African-American business sector was a long way from business ownership parity. The gaps in each major industry were also large.

A new survey will be taken for 1992. In view of the general business slowdown, and taking 1982 as a guide, we can expect a deterioration in the already very marginal position of black-owned businesses. The limited trend data that are available suggest that the black-owned business sector may have lost ground during the Reagan-Bush years. For example, inflation-adjusted receipts reported in the Commerce Department's *Survey of Minority Businesses* show that after the data are adjusted for inflation, aggregate receipts of black-owned businesses fell between 1977 and 1982 from $19.6 billion to $17.7 billion. The 1982 inflation-adjusted level of black receipts was actually below the 1972 level of $18.2 billion. Aggregate receipts recovered somewhat in 1987 to $22.8 billion.

However, on a per capita basis, the receipts during 1987 of $775 were still slightly below the 1972 and 1977 levels of $784 and $790, respectively. The per capita receipt level in 1982 was only $650. Since the per capita receipts of all American businesses have risen since 1977, these results imply that the African-American business sector is generating a smaller share of total receipts. When the complete record is in, we suspect it will be very clear that 12 years of Reagan-Bush retarded progress towards parity in business ownership.

Educational Capital

The basic data on the educational attainment of the African-American population 25 years and over are shown in Table 3. In 1991, African Americans still had considerably less education than white Americans. This is reflected in the fact that considerably higher proportions of black males and females had not completed high school (32.97 percent and 31.82 percent, respectively) than white males and females (18.92 percent and 19.34 percent, respectively) had, and considerably smaller proportions had graduated from college (11.88 percent and 11.97 percent for black males and females versus 25.20 percent and 11.88 percent for white males and females). Overall, using an educational equality index calculated by using white male mean earnings, in 1991, black males had educational capital that was roughly 86.48 percent as much as white male educational capital. On the other hand, black females had an educational capital equality index of 90.94 percent using white female earnings and 91.33 percent using white male earnings. Thus, the level of equality in educational capital was much higher than it was for either wealth or business ownership. Of course, this is a very rough measure of educational equality which takes no account of differences in the quality of education.

African Americans also continued to make progress in improving their educational capital during the Reagan-Bush years. This can be seen by observing the declines in the proportions of African-American males and females with less than a high school education between 1980 and 1991. For males, the proportion dropped from 46.77 percent in 1980 to 32.97 percent in 1991; for females, the proportion declined from 47.40 to 31.82 percent. Moreover, the proportion of African Americans with four or more years of college increased during the Reagan-Bush era. Only 8.21 percent of males

143

Table 3
Distribution of Persons 25 Years and Older by Years of School Completed

Male

	1991 White	1991 Black	1990 White	1990 Black	1985 White	1985 Black	1980 White	1980 Black	1970 White	1970 Black
0-8 yrs.	9.16	14.44	10.30	17.01	12.75	20.76	15.67	26.66	25.47	43.98
1-3 yrs. HS	9.76	18.53	9.86	16.33	10.77	17.73	12.27	20.11	15.40	21.93
4 yrs. HS	33.70	36.42	36.07	38.33	35.17	34.28	34.10	31.10	31.64	23.25
1-3 yrs. COL	22.18	18.74	18.42	16.94	17.26	16.02	15.73	13.92	11.76	6.02
4+ yrs. of COL	25.20	11.88	25.35	11.41	24.05	11.19	22.24	8.21	15.73	4.81
4 yrs. COL	15.87	8.11	13.99	7.66	13.26	7.15	11.94	5.23	*	*
5+ yrs. COL	9.34	3.77	11.36	3.75	10.79	4.04	10.30	2.98	*	*
Median	12.9	12.5	12.8	12.4	12.8	12.3	12.6	12.1	12.3	9.8
B/W	86.48%		86.48%		86.13%		83.45%		80.61%	

Female

	1991 White	1991 Black	1990 White	1990 Black	1985 White	1985 Black	1980 White	1980 Black	1970 White	1970 Black
0-8 yrs.	8.91	12.34	9.54	13.83	12.36	18.01	15.58	25.00	23.60	38.71
1-3 yrs. HS	10.43	19.48	10.49	19.44	11.78	19.02	13.26	22.40	17.12	25.55
4 yrs. HS	38.81	35.05	41.83	37.22	42.54	36.64	42.39	32.06	39.47	25.16
1-3 yrs. COL	22.71	21.16	18.78	17.93	16.87	15.61	14.93	12.39	10.85	6.22
4+ yrs. of COL	19.14	11.97	19.32	11.57	16.44	10.73	13.83	8.15	8.96	4.36
4 yrs. COL	13.36	8.54	12.10	7.61	10.24	6.97	8.87	5.38	*	*
5+ yrs. COL	5.78	3.43	7.22	3.96	6.20	3.76	4.96	2.77	*	*
Median	12.8	12.5	12.7	12.4	12.6	12.4	12.5	12.1	12.2	10.3
B/W	90.94%		90.32%		91.31%		88.62%		85.55%	

* Included with 4+ yrs. in 1970.

B/W = Educational Equality Index.

Source: U.S. Department of Commerce, Bureau of the Census, Money Income of Households, Families, and Persons in the United States: 1991, August 1992, Series P-60, No. 180.

144

and 8.15 percent of females had four or more years of college in 1980; these numbers had increased to 11.88 percent and 11.97 percent, respectively, by 1991.

White Americans also made educational progress during the Reagan-Bush era. However, blacks progressed enough to close the educational gap a little more. For example, in 1980, the absolute gap between the proportion of blacks and whites who had not completed high school was 18.83 percentage points; this declined to 14.83 percentage points in 1991. However, the relative gap had grown slightly as black males were only 67 percent more likely to be a high school dropout in 1980 and about 74 percent more likely in 1991. The results at the lower levels of education were similar for African-American females. The absolute gap in high school dropout rates declined from 18.56 percentage points to 12.48 percentage points. The relative gaps remained about constant with the African-American female dropout rate, increasing from 64 percent more likely in 1980 to 65 percent more likely in 1991.

At the college graduate level, the gaps were reduced in absolute and relative terms between 1980 and 1991 for African-American males. There was a 14.03 percentage point gap between the proportion of black and white males with four years of college in 1980; this had declined slightly to 13.32 percentage points by 1991. However, in relative terms, the gain was greater since African-American males were only 36.9 percent as likely to have four or more years of college in 1980 and 47.1 percent as likely in 1991. The absolute gap between black and white females actually increased between 1980 and 1991 from 5.68 percentage points to 7.17 percentage points because of relatively large gains for white females. However, black females did make slight progress in closing the relative gap by increasing their likelihood of having four or more years of college from 58.9 percent as likely as white females in 1980 to 62.5 percent as likely in 1991.

However, while progress was made between 1980 and 1991, we should note that the rate of progress was somewhat slower than it had been between 1970 and 1980. For example, between 1970 and 1980, the proportion of African-American males with four or more years of college increased by 71 percent. However, the increase in the proportion of college graduates was only 45 percent between 1980 and 1991. However, more important was the slowdown in educational progress between 1985 and 1991. Increases in the proportion of both African-American males and females gaining college degrees slowed dramatically between 1985 and 1991—the latter half of the Reagan-Bush era. The proportion of black males increased by only 0.59 of a percentage point between 1985 and 1991, while the proportion of black females increased by only 1.24 percentage points. The rate of increase averaged only 1 percent over the six-year period for males and 1.9 percent for females. In contrast, the rate of increase averaged 7 percent for males and 8.7

percent for females between 1970 and 1980. The rate of increase in the proportion of African-American college graduates averaged 7.3 percent for males and 6.3 percent for females between 1980 and 1985. Progress in the rate of reduction of the proportion of high school dropouts also slowed, if not as dramatically.

The overall pattern of educational progress during the Reagan-Bush era is revealed by the educational equality index shown in the last line of the male and female panels of Table 3. As can be seen, the index improved between 1970 and 1980, and between 1980 and 1985 for African-American males and females. For males, the index increased from 80.61 percent in 1970 to 83.45 percent in 1980 and to 86.13 percent in 1985. However, between 1985 and 1991, the index barely moved, increasing from 86.13 percent to 86.48 percent. A similar pattern was observed for African-American females, except that the index actually declined slightly between 1985 and 1991, from 91.31 percent to 90.94 percent. Thus, for the last six years of the Reagan-Bush era, progress towards educational capital parity slowed to a halt.

Table 4 provides another perspective on progress at reducing educational capital gaps. This table provides years of school completed data for two younger age groups. The 25-to-64 age group excludes all those 65 and older. The educational distributions for these two groups were better than they were for the population as a whole for both blacks and whites. The younger groups had lower proportions who were high school dropouts. The black differentials are more favorable for the younger groups and the racial disparities are lower. This implies that as the older cohorts leave the work force, the proportions with very low education will continue to decline somewhat.

On the other hand, the differences between the proportions with college degrees were much less striking between the 25-to-64 and the 25-to-34 age groups. Moreover, the differences between these groups were even less marked for blacks. This implies that progress in increasing the proportions with college degrees will not be helped by a cohort effect. Additional gains in reducing the disparity in the proportions with college degrees will not occur automatically since more recent cohorts among African Americans apparently have not been attaining college degrees at a much faster pace than older cohorts.

The value of the educational shortfall in 1991 can be estimated from the earnings shortfall that can be attributed to the educational differences between blacks and whites. We estimated this shortfall by calculating what black males and females would earn if they had white educational distributions and African-American mean earnings at each educational level. For African-American males, this earnings shortfall for 1991 was about $32.0 billion; for African-American females, the earnings gap attributable to the educational gap was $14.4 billion. Education accounted for about 41 percent

Table 4
Years of School Completed in 1991
by Race, Sex, and Age

	Male 25 to 64		Male 25 to 34	
	White	Black	White	Black
0-8 yrs.	6.32	7.71	4.49	2.67
1-3 yrs. HS	8.71	18.84	9.20	15.13
4 yrs. HS	34.31	40.13	37.92	46.35
1-3 yrs. COL	23.73	20.35	24.33	23.59
4 yrs. COL	17.05	8.95	18.17	9.02
5+ yrs. COL	9.88	3.99	5.88	3.19
4+ yrs. COL	26.92	12.96	24.05	12.22
Median	13.0	12.6	13.0	12.7

	Female 25 to 64		Female 25 to 34	
	White	Black	White	Black
0-8 yrs.	5.37	5.66	3.78	2.47
1-3 yrs. HS	8.88	19.15	8.41	16.07
4 yrs. HS	38.73	37.96	36.64	41.33
1-3 yrs. COL	24.98	24.08	26.85	28.31
4 yrs. COL	15.32	9.50	19.33	10.14
5+ yrs. COL	6.72	3.15	4.99	1.64
4+ yrs. COL	22.04	13.13	24.32	11.79
Median	12.9	12.7	13.0	12.8

Source: U.S. Department of Commerce, Bureau of the Census, *Money Income of Households, Families, and Persons in the United States: 1991*, August 1992, Series P-60, No. 180, Table 29. Medians calculated by the author using linear interpolation.

of the total male earnings gap in 1991 and 96 percent of the total female earnings gap. The combined male and female educational earnings gap was $46.4 billion in 1991. Assuming a rate of return to educational capital of 11 percent, the value of the missing educational capital shortfall was $421.8 billion in 1991.

The large ownership gaps previously discussed have tremendous implications for the economic well-being of the African-American population and the continuation of racial inequality. The limited ownership and progress in improving the ownership position of African Americans are reflected in low absolute levels of income, high rates of poverty, low labor market status, and the size and persistence of the racial gaps in these indicators of current economic status. We, therefore, turn to review the facts concerning income and poverty of African Americans during the Reagan-Bush years.

AFRICAN-AMERICAN INCOME AND POVERTY DURING THE REAGAN-BUSH ERA

Income is generally the most widely utilized indicator of current economic status. It measures the flow of purchasing power during a particular period of time. We use annual income flows in this report. Income—at least earned income—may be viewed as an annual return to current stocks of capital. Differences in income are generated in large measure from differences in ownership of human and nonhuman capital.

The next several tables display data on annual income flows. Table 5 reports the latest data on aggregate and per capita income for African Americans. Before discussing these data, however, we should note that a change in the methodology of calculating inflation introduced at the Census Bureau in the 1980s was applied retroactively to the historical income series in 1990.

This rather unusual tampering with historical data had the effect of reducing previous estimates of inflation-adjusted income for the 1970s relative to income for the 1980s. As a result of this adjustment, income levels during the Reagan-Bush years have been made to appear higher relative to income levels during the 1970s. Data reported in this series through the 1992 edition continued to reflect the old inflation index adjustment which was used in published Census Bureau reports through 1990. In Table 5, the unrevised series for black per capita income is shown in parentheses; we have also included the unrevised black median family income series in Table 8. However, all the other tables include only the revised data. The text discussion will focus on the revised Census Bureau series.

In 1991, the latest year for which income figures are available, the Census Bureau reported that the per capita income of the African-American population of 31,438,000 was $9,170 (see Table 5). This implies that the African American population had aggregate income of $288.3 billion. African Americans were 12.5 percent of the total population of 251,434,000 but received only 7.84 percent of total income of $3,675.2 billion. In 1991, white Americans received $15,510 in per capita income. Thus, the income equality index (B/W) stood at 59.1. This implies that blacks received 59 cents for every dollar received by whites. In 1991, blacks had $6,340 less income per person than did whites. In the aggregate, black income was $199.3 billion less than would have been required to have per capita income parity.

Table 5 shows that income for blacks and whites declined for the second straight year in 1991. After peaking in 1989, black per capita income

Table 5
Per Capita Income, Aggregate Income,
and Income Gaps
(1991$)

	Aggregate Black Income (Billions)	Black	Per Capita Income *	White	B/W	Parity Per Capita	Aggregate Gaps (Billions)
1991	288.3	$9,170		$15,510	59.1	6,340	199.3
1990	290.3	9,396		15,907	59.1	6,511	201.2
1989	292.0	9,608		16,362	58.7	6,754	205.3
1988	284.7	9,522		15,999	59.5	6,477	193.7
1987	269.6	9,166		15,758	58.2	6,592	193.9
1986	259.1	8,956		15,350	58.3	6,394	185.0
1985	247.1	8,658		14,773	58.6	6,115	174.5
1984	231.6	8,228		14,340	57.4	6,112	172.1
1983	218.4	7,870	(7,865)	13,846	56.8	5,976	165.8
1982	208.2	7,636	(7,561)	13,573	56.3	5,937	161.9
1981	208.5	7,753	(7,679)	13,573	57.1	5,820	156.5
1980	210.3	7,950	(7,939)	13,625	58.3	5,675	150.1
1979	212.9	8,179	(8,336)	13,940	58.7	5,761	150.0
1978	203.8	8,140	(8,420)	13,715	59.4	5,575	139.6
1977	191.3	7,702	(8,030)	13,146	58.6	5,444	135.2
1976	184.4	7,535	(7,860)	12,740	59.1	5,205	127.4
1975	174.0	7,203	(7,519)	12,292	58.6	5,089	123.0
1974	169.7	7,133	(7,505)	12,274	58.1	5,141	122.3
1973	171.3	7,275	(7,724)	12,584	57.8	5,309	125.0
1972	163.6	7,055	(7,486)	12,172	58.0	5,117	118.6
1971	149.3	6,516	(6,932)	11,364	57.3	4,848	111.1
1970	143.1	6,164	(6,554)	11,061	55.7	4,897	113.7
1969	137.0	6,091	(6,554)	10,972	55.5	4,881	109.8
1968	127.8	5,708	(6,183)	10,419	54.8	4,711	105.5
1967	115.9	5,260	(5,718)	9,770	53.8	4,510	99.4

Aggregate income = per capita income * population.

*: Numbers in parentheses ( ) represent historical income figures adjusted based on unrevised consumer price index.

Source: U.S. Department of Commerce, Bureau of the Census, *Money Income of Households, Families, and Persons in the United States: 1991*, August 1992, Series P-60, No. 180, Table B-19. Aggregates and gaps calculated by the author.

declined 4.6 percent and white per capita income declined 5.2 percent. We suspect that when the data for 1992 are in, they will most likely show an additional decline in per capita income. Earlier in the Reagan-Bush years, from 1979 through 1982, there were three consecutive years of declining black aggregate and per capita. In the 11 years preceding the Reagan-Bush era, there were never back-to-back years in which per capita and aggregate income declined.

African-American aggregate and per capita income increased by 37 percent and 15 percent, respectively, during the 11 Reagan-Bush years. This was significantly slower than the corresponding increases of 54 percent for aggregate income and 31 percent for per capita income in the 11 years preceding the Reagan-Bush years. African-American income growth was definitely retarded by recent historical standards during the Reagan-Bush era.

Moreover, as can be seen from the inequality index and the two gaps, inequality did not improve during the Reagan-Bush years. The inequality index, which worsened during the first part of the period, improved during the second half. However, the level of inequality as measured by B/W at the end of the Reagan-Bush era was still around the level obtained during the latter half of the preceding 11 years. The per capita and aggregate gaps continued to rise for most of the periods with increasing income but declined at the end because of falling incomes. During the 1970s, African Americans made a little progress in improving relative equality as measured by the B/W index in comparison to the end of the 1960s. The Reagan-Bush years brought an end to this period of modest improvement in racial per capita income inequality.

Income Recipiency of Persons

The per capita income disadvantage for blacks comes from a number of factors. For one, blacks have smaller proportions of adults or potential earners in their population. In 1991, according to Census Bureau data, 32.92 percent of the black population was 18 years old or under, compared to only 24.98 percent of the white population. Thus, the proportion of blacks over 18 was about 12 percent lower than the corresponding proportion of whites. However, the proportion of persons 18 or under has declined for both black and white populations since 1974. The proportion under 18 was 39.68 percent for African Americans and 30.46 percent for white Americans in 1974. In 1980, at the beginning of the Reagan-Bush era, the proportions were 35.48 percent and 26.75 percent for blacks and whites, respectively.

The data in Table 6 provide additional insight into the reasons for the low income of blacks. Table 6 displays data on the percentage of persons with income and the ratio of males to females in the black and white populations 15 years or older. In 1991, smaller proportions of African-American males

Table 6
Percent of Persons with Income and
Ratio of Number of Males to Females
by Race and Sex

	Male			Female			Ratio of Males to Females		
	Black	White	B/W	Black	White	B/W	Black	White	B/W
1991	87.2	95.7	91.12%	87.3	92.1	94.79%	83.4	93.6	89.12%
1990	87.6	96.1	91.16%	88.1	92.4	95.35%	83.1	93.5	88.87%
1989	88.5	96.1	92.09%	88.4	92.2	95.88%	83.1	93.4	88.97%
1988	87.8	96.1	91.36%	88.1	92.2	95.55%	83.2	93.1	89.37%
1987	87.8	96.2	91.27%	87.1	92.1	94.57%	82.9	93.0	89.14%
1986	87.5	96.0	91.15%	85.8	91.1	94.18%	82.7	93.0	88.92%
1985	87.3	95.6	91.32%	85.3	90.6	94.15%	82.7	93.0	88.92%
1984	85.9	95.6	89.85%	85.3	90.7	94.05%	82.4	92.5	89.08%
1983	84.4	95.6	88.28%	83.5	89.8	92.98%	82.4	92.5	89.08%
1982	83.2	95.2	87.39%	83.5	89.5	93.30%	81.9	92.5	88.54%
1981	86.6	95.2	90.97%	81.0	89.9	90.10%	82.0	91.0	90.11%
1980	87.4	95.8	91.23%	83.3	89.6	92.97%	81.9	92.0	89.02%
1979	87.9	96.3	91.28%	81.4	89.7	90.75%	82.0	92.3	88.84%
1978	85.6	94.3	90.77%	80.4	81.3	98.89%	82.3	92.5	88.97%
1977	84.1	93.7	89.75%	78.1	74.6	104.69%	83.2	92.4	90.04%
1976	84.0	93.4	89.94%	75.8	73.1	103.69%	83.4	92.4	90.26%
1975	84.0	92.8	90.52%	75.2	71.2	105.62%	83.3	92.2	90.35%
1974	85.4	93.4	91.43%	74.9	71.0	105.49%	83.0	92.3	89.92%
1973	86.2	93.3	92.39%	73.7	68.8	107.12%	83.9	92.1	91.10%
1972	83.9	92.6	90.60%	72.8	66.7	109.15%	83.6	91.8	91.07%
1971	85.6	92.4	92.64%	73.0	65.4	111.62%	83.5	91.9	90.86%
1970	86.0	92.8	92.67%	72.7	65.8	110.49%	84.5	91.6	92.25%
1969	88.4	93.0	95.05%	73.1	65.0	112.46%	84.6	91.1	92.86%
1968	88.5	92.9	95.26%	73.7	63.8	115.52%	84.5	90.9	92.96%
1967	88.2	92.9	94.94%	72.3	62.0	116.61%	84.7	89.9	94.22%

Source: U.S. Department of Commerce, Bureau of the Census, *Money Income Households, Families, and Persons in the United States: 1991*, August 1992, Table B-14.

and females received incomes than did white males and females. In 1991, 87.2 percent of black males and 87.3 percent of black females received income compared to 95.7 percent and 92.1 percent of white males and females, respectively. The B/W index shows that black males were 91.12 percent as likely as white males to have income, and black females were 94.79 percent as likely as white females to have income.

Quick perusal of the other years in the table for males shows that, during the Reagan-Bush years, the absolute level of the proportion with income for both white and black males has fluctuated in a narrow band with the business cycle. There had been no significant trend in the proportion with income or in the degree of inequality for males during the Reagan-Bush years.

However, the absolute proportion of males with income may have been slightly higher during the Reagan-Bush years than during the 1970s, though the proportions for black males were higher during the latter part of the 1960s. The B/W measure of racial inequality for this indicator has been relatively constant during the past 11 years, though again inequality is higher than it was during the late 1960s and early 1970s. In short, black males did not gain any ground during the Reagan-Bush years in closing the rate of income recipiency gap, but they did not lose any ground relative to the 1970s either.

Perusing the data for females in Table 6, we can see that both black and white females continued the long-term trend of increasing their proportions with income during the Reagan-Bush era. The rate of increase in income recipiency was higher for black females. During the Reagan-Bush era, black females made some progress in closing the advantage developed by white women during the latter part of the 1970s.

It is noteworthy that inequality as measured by the B/W was significantly higher during the 1980s than during the 1970s. Indeed, for most of the 1970s, black women had higher income recipiency rates than white women. However, throughout the 1970s, white women were overtaking black women, and by the end of the 1970s, they had passed black women.

Nonetheless, black women did make steady progress in increasing their income recipiency rates throughout the 1970s. In fact, the increase of 14.0 percent for the 11 years after 1969 was greater than the 4.8 percent increase over the 11 years of the Reagan-Bush era. The relative gap between black and white women closed during the Reagan-Bush years primarily because of a slowdown in the rate of increase for white women. This slowdown was due to the fact that white women had almost obtained maximum income recipiency rates by the beginning of the Reagan-Bush years. In any case, the smaller income recipiency rates for black males and females is another significant cause of the aggregate income gap.

The final column in Table 6 shows the ratio of males to females for the black and white populations. There are fewer black and white males among the adult population than females. However, there are significantly fewer black than white males. In 1991, at the end of the Reagan-Bush era, there were 83.4 percent as many black males as females, but 93.6 percent as many white males as females.

During the past 11 years, there has been a slight increase in the proportion of black and white males in the adult population. For black males, the proportion increased from 81.9 percent in 1980 to 83.4 percent in 1991, while the increase for white males was from 92.0 percent to 93.6 percent.

Table 7
Median Income of Persons with Income
by Race and Sex
(1991$)

	Male Black	Male White	B/W	Female Black	Female White	B/W
1991	$12,962	$21,395	60.6	$8,816	$10,721	82.2
1990	13,409	22,061	60.8	8,678	10,751	80.7
1989	13,850	22,916	60.4	8,650	10,777	80.3
1988	13,866	22,979	60.3	8,461	10,480	80.7
1987	13,446	22,666	59.3	8,331	10,199	81.7
1986	13,449	22,443	59.9	8,160	9,643	84.6
1985	13,630	21,659	62.9	7,945	9,312	85.3
1984	12,385	21,586	57.4	8,080	9,109	88.7
1983	12,335	21,092	58.5	7,615	8,912	85.4
1982	12,591	21,011	59.9	7,498	8,501	88.2
1981	12,851	21,611	59.5	7,412	8,343	88.8
1980	13,254	22,057	60.1	7,580	8,187	92.6
1979	14,019	22,648	61.9	7,358	8,085	91.0
1978	13,844	23,110	59.9	7,480	8,307	90.0
1977	13,560	22,850	59.3	7,446	8,622	86.4
1976	13,719	22,785	60.2	7,791	8,268	94.2
1975	13,475	22,538	59.8	7,530	8,288	90.9
1974	14,397	23,235	62.0	7,385	8,180	90.3
1973	14,754	24,392	60.5	7,352	8,146	90.3
1972	14,519	23,970	60.6	7,497	8,025	93.4
1971	13,639	22,870	59.6	6,778	7,736	87.6
1970	13,709	23,121	59.3	6,803	7,473	91.0
1969	13,603	23,386	58.2	6,361	7,543	84.3
1968	13,432	22,641	59.3	5,957	7,511	79.3
1967	12,554	21,935	57.2	5,478	6,960	78.7

Source: U.S. Department of Commerce, Bureau of the Census, *Money Income of Households, Families, and Persons in the United States: 1991*, Series P-60, No. 180, August 1992, Table B-14.

The proportion of black males to females was generally higher than during the preceding 11-year period than it was during the Reagan-Bush era. However, this proportion was declining at the end of the preceding period; this downturn was reversed during the Reagan-Bush era. Relative inequality was generally lower during the Reagan-Bush era, yet the disparity was large at the end of the Reagan-Bush era. The lower ratio of black men to women implies that the adult black population was missing 1.093 million men in 1991. These "missing" black males are another reason for the continued income inequality.

Median Income of Persons

Table 7 provides data on the relative median incomes of black and white male and female income recipients. In 1991, both black male and female income recipients had lower median incomes than their white counterparts. First, we note that both African-American and white male workers had incomes during the Reagan-Bush era that were lower than they were during the preceding 11 years. For both groups, median income also declined during 1991 for the third consecutive year. The decline in income would have been even larger except for the change in the methodology of accounting for inflation. The median incomes of both male groups were lower at the end of the Reagan-Bush era than they had been at the beginning and considerably lower than they were during the peak periods of the preceding 11-year period.

As can be seen from the B/W index, inequality is very marked among males. In 1991, black male median income was $12,962 compared to $21,395 for white males. The B/W index indicates that the typical black male income recipient got only about 61 cents for every dollar received by the typical white male. This high degree of inequality persisted throughout the Reagan-Bush era. In general, income inequality among black and white males may have been slightly higher during the Reagan-Bush years than during the preceding 11 years. However, the important point is that inequality remained high and no progress was made in improving the degree of income inequality for African-American males.

The picture for females is somewhat different. First, female incomes for both groups generally increased throughout the period. In 1991, the median income of African-American female recipients was $8,816 compared to $10,721 for white females. Black female income was up from $7,580 in 1980—an increase of 16.3 percent. White female income was up from $8,187 in 1980—an increase of 31 percent. African-American female income increased by 19.2 percent during the 11 years preceding the Reagan-Bush era, while white female income increased by 8.5 percent during the same period. While females of both races gained ground on males, the data of Table 7 make it clear that the gaps were still large at the end of the period.

We can also see that black females received incomes that were substantially smaller than white female incomes. The B/W index for 1991 indicates that black females received only about 82 cents for every dollar received by white females. Recalling that the B/W index for males was 60.6 percent in 1991, it is apparent that racial inequality by this measure between females is less than it is between males. However, racial inequality by this measure increased substantially for females during the Reagan-Bush years. The B/W index for females was 92.6 percent in 1980, which had declined to 82.2 percent in 1991. This represents a substantial increase in racial inequality in income for females and reverses all of the gains made during the 1970s in lowering the racial gap in female incomes. In any case, the lower average incomes of African-American males and females is another important reason why the income gap persists.

A Decomposition of the Racial Income Gap

The preceding discussion suggests that racial income inequality can be decomposed into two basic components. The first component is that part due to the lower amount of income received by current recipients; the second component is the lower proportion of adult income recipients. During the Reagan administration, no progress was made in reducing the impact of these components. In fact, inequality for females generally worsened, while the larger gaps for males held steady.

As noted, the total income gap in 1991 was about $199.3 billion. We estimate that 73.95 percent of this gap—or $147.4 billion—was due to lower income recipiency rates. The remaining 26.05 percent—or $51.9 billion—was due to the smaller proportion of adults in the African-American population.

Lower income recipiency rates among African-American males resulted in a loss of $117.1 billion for the African-American population; this accounted for 79.46 percent of the gap due to lower income recipiency rates. Most of this income loss was attributable to the fact that black males had lower average incomes than white males. This factor accounted for $93.3 billion, or 79.7 percent, of this loss due to lower recipiency. The lower proportion of black males with incomes resulted in a loss of $14.7 billion, or 12.59 percent, due to lower recipiency among males. The remaining 7.7 percent of the lower recipiency loss for males was due to the interaction of the above-mentioned factors.

Lower recipiency rates among African-American females accounted for $30.3 billion, which was 20.54 percent of the loss due to lower income recipiency rates. Nearly $22 billion, or 71.6 percent of this loss, was due to the increasing differences between the average earnings of black and white females. The lower proportions of black females who had earnings resulted in a gap of $7.4 billion, explaining another 24.46 percent of this loss. The remaining 3.91 percent of the female lower recipiency gap—or $1.2 billion—was caused by the interaction of the above two factors.

Altogether, $115.037 billion dollars, or 57.72 percent, of the total income gap was due to lower average incomes among African-American income recipients. About $22.154 billion, or 11.12 percent, of the total income gap was due to lower percentages of the adult population receiving income. The remaining 5.12 percent of the gap, or $10.207 billion, was due to the interaction effect.

As noted, 26.05 percent of the income gap in 1991 ($51.916 billion) was accounted for by the smaller proportions of African-American adults in the population. This smaller proportion led to 1,643,000 fewer male income recipients and 459,000 fewer female income recipients. We estimate that 1,093,000 of the males are the so-called "missing" African-American males. These missing males generated an income gap of $30.023 billion, which accounted for two-thirds of the gap due to the shortage of adult males and 57.83 percent of the overall smaller adult population gap. The missing African-American males accounted for 15.06 percent of the overall income gap. The remaining part of the smaller African-American male population, due to the higher proportion of children in the African-American population, generated an income loss of $15.162 billion. This accounted for 20.58 percent of the total smaller adult population gap and 7.61 percent of the overall income gap. Finally, the smaller proportion of adult females generated a loss of $6.713 billion. The smaller number of adult females accounted for 12.97 percent of the smaller adult population gap and 3.38 percent of the overall gap.

The decomposition of the gap may be summarized as follows:

CAUSE OF LOSS	AMOUNT IN BILLIONS	PERCENT OF GAP
Lower Recipiency Rates		
Lower Average Income		
Males	$93.347	46.83
Females	21.690	10.88
Lower Percent With Income		
Males	14.749	7.40
Females	7.405	3.72
Interaction of Lower Average and Lower Percent W/Income		
Males	9.023	4.53
Females	1.184	0.59
Total Lower Recipiency Rates	147.398	73.95
Smaller Adult Population		
Smaller Male Population		
Missing Males	30.023	15.06
Other Male Shortfall	15.162	7.61
Smaller Female Adult Population	6.731	3.38
Total Smaller Adult Population	51.916	26.05
TOTAL ALL FACTORS	$199.314	100.00

Family Income Trends

The next several tables will be used to examine trends in family income during the Reagan-Bush years. Table 8 displays data on median family income. As previously noted, the numbers in parentheses represent the series based on the old methodology for adjusting inflation. As can be seen, these numbers increase the size of income in the 1970s relative to the 1980s. However, we will base our discussion on the revised series.

In 1991, the median income of African-American families was $21,548, and the median income of white families was $37,783, according to the Census Bureau. Median family income fell in 1991 for both groups from the previous year. African-American income declined by $777, or 3.5 percent, while white income fell by $685, or 1.8 percent. Thus, racial inequality increased in 1991 from the year before, as this index declined from 58.0 percent to 57.0 percent. The median black family had $16,235 less to spend than the median white family. The income differences in families translate into an aggregate gap of 136.6 billion dollars. The aggregate gap also increased during 1991 despite the fact that median income fell. We expect that the decline in median family income has continued during 1992.

Perusal of the table shows that although income rose during the second half of the Reagan-Bush years, the 1978 peak was not reached until 1987. (Indeed, the original unrevised data suggest that, during the 1980s, income never fully recovered to the peaks of the 1970s.) Moreover, even with the revised series, the level of income at the end of the decade was still below the 1978 level. Thus, African-American family income at best stagnated over the 11 years of data reported for the Reagan-Bush era and was lower for most of the 1980s than it was for most of the 1970s. The average median income for African Americans during the Reagan-Bush era was $21,189—just slightly above the 11 pre-Reagan-Bush years' average of $21,037, despite the impact of the data revision. White median family income averaged $37,368 for the Reagan-Bush years, which was up $1,764 from the $35,604 average of the pre-Reagan-Bush years.

Inequality in family income by the B/W measure also clearly increased in absolute and relative terms. The median gaps were generally larger during the Reagan-Bush years. The gap was $15,275 in 1980 and $16,235 in 1991. For the 11-year period as a whole, the gap averaged $16,179. In contrast, the median income gap averaged only $14,568 in the 11 years preceding the current period. The aggregate gap grew from $95.5 billion in 1980 to $136.6 billion at the end of the Reagan-Bush era. The aggregate gap averaged $120.1 billion during the Reagan-Bush years, in contrast to an average aggregate gap of $82.6 billion in the earlier period.

The B/W index indicates that relative inequality was also generally higher during the Reagan-Bush period. In 1991, the B/W index stood at 57.0, up

Table 8
Median Family Income and Inequality Indicators
for Selected Years
(1991$)

	Black	Median Family Income *	White	B/W	Median Income Gap	Aggregate Gap (Billion$)
1991	$21,548		$37,783	57.0	$16,235	136.6
1990	22,325		38,468	58.0	16,143	132.2
1989	22,197		39,514	56.2	17,317	139.4
1988	22,254		39,047	57.0	16,793	127.9
1987	22,068		38,828	56.8	16,760	127.4
1986	21,877		38,286	57.1	16,409	120.3
1985	21,248		36,901	57.6	15,653	114.0
1984	20,228	(20,230)	36,293	55.7	16,065	112.3
1983	19,912	(19,901)	35,331	56.4	15,419	106.6
1982	19,373	(19,183)	35,052	55.3	15,679	105.5
1981	20,054	(19,862)	35,550	56.4	15,496	99.2
1980	20,974	(20,944)	36,249	57.9	15,275	95.5
1979	21,302	(21,712)	37,619	56.6	16,317	98.2
1978	21,951	(22,707)	37,063	59.2	15,112	88.8
1977	20,609	(21,488)	36,076	57.1	15,467	88.0
1976	21,191	(22,107)	35,625	59.5	14,434	83.2
1975	21,276	(22,211)	34,578	61.5	13,302	77.3
1974	21,010	(22,107)	35,186	59.7	14,176	80.8
1973	20,975	(22,273)	36,344	57.7	15,369	84.1
1972	21,056	(22,341)	35,427	59.4	14,371	76.9
1971	20,351	(21,653)	33,725	60.3	13,374	70.1
1970	20,707	(22,019)	33,756	61.3	13,049	65.9
1969	20,738	(22,283)	33,856	61.3	13,118	65.7
1968	19,364	(20,979)	32,287	60.0	12,923	60.6
1967	18,291	(19,882)	30,895	59.2	12,604	58.9

Note: Aggregate gap is defined as the difference in mean income (not shown) times the number of black families (not shown). Median family income is in 1991 CPI-U adjusted dollars.

*: Numbers in parentheses ( ) represent historical income figures adjusted based on unrevised consumer price index.

Source: U.S. Department of Commerce, Bureau of the Census, *Money Income of Households, Families, and Persons in the United States: 1991*, Series P-60, No. 180, Tables B6 and B19.

from the 57.9 in 1980. However, the average value of this index was 56.7 for the Reagan-Bush period taken as a whole. This was down from the average of 59.1 in the pre-Reagan-Bush period. Family income inequality between African-American and white families clearly increased during the Reagan-Bush years. The black family income loss over the period as a whole totaled over $1.321 trillion.

Trends in the Family Income Distribution

Table 9 displays data on the distribution of family income. Several facts stand out. First, the black family income distribution has worsened over the past four years. The proportion receiving incomes under $10,000 rose from 24.1 percent in 1988 and 23.4 percent in 1989 to 26.4 percent in 1991. The majority of this increase has been at the very lowest income levels. Those African-American families receiving under $5,000 per year rose from 9.7 percent to 11.4 percent during this period. At the same time, the proportion receiving very high incomes, that is, over $50,000 per year, declined from 17.4 percent in 1988 to 14.8 percent in 1991.

It is also apparent that inequality is also marked in the income distribution. African Americans were 4.56 times as likely to have very low incomes under $5,000. At the other end of the income distribution, African-American families were less than 23 percent as likely to have incomes over $100,000. In numerical terms, in 1991, there were 7,716,000 African-American families. In comparison to parity, about 1.47 million more African-American families had incomes below $10,000, and about 1.49 million fewer African-American families had incomes over $50,000.

For the Reagan-Bush period as a whole, the proportion of blacks receiving low incomes increased. Over the 11 years of this period, the proportion of African-American families receiving incomes less than $10,000 averaged 25.0 percent, while the average for the 11 pre-Reagan-Bush years was only 21.9 percent. The average proportion of whites receiving such low incomes increased only slightly, from 6.9 percent to 7.4 percent. Thus, racial inequality increased at the lower end of the distribution. African Americans were on average 3.2 times as likely as whites to have these low incomes during the 11 years before Reagan-Bush and an average of 3.4 times more likely during the Reagan-Bush years.

On the other hand, the average proportion of blacks receiving incomes over $50,000 increased during the Reagan-Bush era, to 14.2 percent from 10.8 percent in the pre-Reagan-Bush period. Moreover, although the average proportion of whites receiving these high incomes also increased absolutely, from 40.1 percent to 43.7 percent, the relative gap was on average lower during the Reagan-Bush era. Blacks were about 40.1 percent as likely to have high incomes in the pre-Reagan-Bush era, and 43.7 percent as likely during the Reagan-Bush era.

Table 9
Percentage of Families Receiving Income:
Selected Ranges by Race

	Under $5,000		$5,000-$9,999		Less than $10,000		$10,000-$14,999		$10,000-$34,999		$35,000-$100,000 +		$50,000-$100,000 +		$100,000 and over	
	Black	White	Black	White	Black	White	Black	White	Black	White	Black	White	Black	White	Black	White
1991	11.4	2.5	15.0	4.8	26.4	7.3	11.1	6.7	44.0	38.3	29.6	54.4	14.8	34.1	1.4	6.1
1990	10.9	2.3	13.8	4.4	24.7	6.7	11.2	6.7	44.2	38.0	31.2	55.3	16.1	34.7	1.5	6.6
1989	9.7	2.3	13.7	4.5	23.4	6.8	12.6	6.5	45.2	36.7	31.4	56.7	16.8	36.0	1.6	7.0
1988	9.7	2.5	14.4	4.5	24.1	7.0	12.9	6.5	44.6	37.4	31.4	55.6	17.4	34.9	2.1	6.3
1987	9.9	2.3	14.8	4.8	24.7	7.1	11.7	6.2	45.1	36.9	30.1	55.9	15.8	34.8	1.8	6.1
1986	10.0	2.6	14.1	4.9	24.1	7.5	12.2	6.6	45.4	37.8	30.5	54.6	15.3	33.6	1.4	5.9
1985	9.2	2.6	15.2	5.2	24.4	7.8	12.1	6.8	47.1	39.4	28.6	52.7	13.7	31.9	1.1	5.2
1984	9.9	2.6	15.5	5.1	25.4	7.7	13.7	7.2	48.4	40.1	26.2	52.1	13.2	30.9	0.9	4.8
1983	10.3	2.9	16.4	5.3	26.7	8.2	12.8	7.3	47.5	41.5	25.8	50.2	11.7	28.9	0.5	4.3
1982	9.4	2.8	17.4	5.3	26.8	8.1	13.6	7.4	47.9	42.0	25.3	49.8	10.2	28.3	0.5	4.1
1981	8.4	2.4	16.2	5.0	24.6	7.4	13.5	7.2	49.2	41.9	26.2	50.7	11.6	28.5	0.3	3.5
1980	7.9	2.1	15.1	5.0	23.0	7.1	13.9	6.9	49.9	41.0	27.0	51.8	12.5	29.0	0.6	3.6
1979	7.1	1.9	15.1	4.4	22.2	6.3	13.8	6.7	49.3	39.6	28.6	54.1	13.2	30.5	0.6	4.2
1978	6.7	2.0	15.5	4.4	22.2	6.4	12.3	7.2	49.3	40.3	28.3	53.3	13.4	29.9	0.6	4.1
1977	6.8	2.0	14.8	4.7	21.6	6.7	15.1	7.4	52.5	41.9	25.9	51.5	11.3	28.2	0.6	3.5
1976	5.3	1.8	16.3	4.9	21.6	6.7	14.4	7.6	52.1	42.5	26.2	50.8	10.7	27.0	0.5	3.2
1975	5.8	1.9	16.0	5.2	21.8	7.1	14.6	7.9	52.9	44.0	25.4	48.9	9.6	25.1	0.4	2.9
1974	5.8	1.9	15.4	4.5	21.2	6.4	14.3	7.3	53.8	43.6	25.0	49.9	10.3	26.4	0.4	3.1
1973	6.1	1.8	14.9	4.8	21.0	6.6	15.2	7.0	54.5	42.0	24.5	51.5	10.0	27.6	0.6	3.4
1972	6.2	2.0	15.5	5.0	21.7	7.0	14.0	6.9	52.9	42.8	25.3	50.3	10.2	26.2	0.6	3.2
1971	6.0	2.3	16.2	5.4	22.2	7.7	13.7	7.2	55.5	45.8	22.3	46.4	8.7	22.6	0.4	2.4
1970	7.3	2.4	14.6	5.5	21.9	7.9	13.5	7.0	55.4	45.7	22.7	46.5	8.9	22.6	0.3	2.5
1969	7.3	2.3	13.1	5.5	20.4	7.8	15.1	6.9	58.3	45.6	21.1	46.7	7.7	22.5	0.2	2.4
1968	7.1	2.5	14.6	5.4	21.7	7.9	16.3	7.6	58.2	48.3	20.1	43.9	7.1	19.6	0.3	1.9
1967	8.4	2.8	17.1	6.4	25.5	9.2	15.1	7.3	57.8	50.5	16.7	40.3	5.9	17.5	0.5	2.0

Note: Total will not equal 100.0 due to overlap of categories. Data are 1991 CPI-U-X1 adjusted dollars.

Source: U.S. Department of Commerce, Bureau of the Census, *Money Income of Households, Families, and Persons in the United*

160

It is apparent, therefore, that the bottom of the African-American distribution got lower during the Reagan-Bush era. At the same time, the top got higher. Inequality within the population increased. Additional insight on the impact of the Reagan-Bush years on income at different levels of the African-American income distribution can be obtained by reviewing the data in Table 10.

Table 10
Mean Income of Families at Selected Positions
of the Income Distribution 1991, 1990, 1980, 1970
(1991$)

1991	Black	White	Black/White
Lowest Fifth	$4,369	$11,407	38.3%
Second	11,594	24,997	46.4
Third	21,585	37,773	57.1
Fourth	35,022	53,913	65.0
Highest Fifth	65,286	98,313	66.4
Top 5%	95,201	152,297	62.5
1990			
Lowest Fifth	$4,721	$11,834	39.9%
Second	12,325	25,778	47.8
Third	22,394	38,568	58.1
Fourth	36,295	54,723	66.3
Highest Fifth	67,860	101,161	67.1
Top 5%	99,563	159,082	62.6
1980			
Lowest Fifth	$5,519	$11,455	48.2%
Second	12,546	24,615	51.0
Third	20,966	36,234	57.9
Fourth	33,193	49,593	66.9
Highest Fifth	58,564	84,459	69.3
Top 5%	81,510	124,763	65.3
1970			
Lowest Fifth	$5,619	$10,909	51.5%
Second	12,990	23,721	54.8
Third	20,641	33,476	61.7
Fourth	30,604	44,712	68.4
Highest Fifth	52,867	76,724	68.9
Top 5%	74,580	117,172	63.7

Source: U.S. Department of Commerce, Bureau of the Census, *Money Income of Households, Families, and Persons in the United States: 1991*, August 1992, Series P-60, No. 180, Table B-7.

The data in this table are the mean income at each position of the income distribution. It is apparent that the income of African-American families at each position is substantially lower than the income for whites at corresponding positions. The mean income in 1991 for blacks at the lowest quintile was only $4,369, compared to $11,407 for whites. The top 5 percent of blacks had mean incomes of $95,201 compared to mean incomes of $152,297 for the top 5 percent of whites. For both blacks and whites, mean incomes at each position of the income distribution were lower in 1991 than in 1990. This is the second year in a row that mean incomes declined all along the distribution.

For the entire Reagan-Bush period, the data in Table 10 reveal that the higher the income class, the more the mean income had risen since the 1980s. Indeed, since 1980, the incomes of the two lowest groups of blacks have actually declined—by about 21 percent for the bottom fifth and 8 percent for the second fifth. On the other hand, the mean incomes of the top three positions increased by 3 percent, 6 percent, and 11 percent, respectively. The mean income of the top 5 percent increased most, by about 17 percent over this period. Thus, under Reagan-Bush, the poor literally got poorer while the rich got richer.

The last column of Table 10 shows that income inequality continued to be marked at all levels throughout the Reagan-Bush era. However, inequality was greatest for the poor. The B/W index indicates that blacks at the bottom had only 38.3 percent as high mean incomes as white families at the bottom, and black families in the second fifth had only 46.4 percent of the income of corresponding white families. The degree of inequality for poorer black families got much worse, as can be seen by comparing the 1980 and 1991 B/W indexes. The famed "safety net" clearly did not provide much protection for poor blacks during the Reagan-Bush era.

Although better off relative to whites and blacks at the bottom, the data in Table 10 make it very clear that inequality is still very high for better-off African Americans. In 1991, the mean income of the top three fifths ranged between 57.1 percent and 66.4 percent of the mean incomes of corresponding whites. Moreover, comparing the data for 1991 and 1980 shows that inequality rose for the top of the distribution as well as during the Reagan-Bush era. Thus, under Reagan-Bush, inequality increased for all blacks throughout the income distribution.

Family Income by Regions

Table 11 summarizes data on family income by region. Family income for blacks and whites declined in all regions during 1991. African Americans living in the West had the highest income— $28,298. They were followed in descending order by African Americans living in the Northeast, Midwest, and South, with median family incomes of $25,533, $20,860, and

Median Family Income by Region
(1991$)

	Northeast Black	Northeast White	B/W	Midwest Black	Midwest White	B/W	South Black	South White	B/W	West Black	West White	B/W
1991	$25,533	$41,815	61.1	$20,860	$38,224	54.6	$20,124	$35,226	57.1	$28,298	$37,610	75.2
1990	25,720	42,821	60.1	21,375	38,943	54.9	21,680	35,683	60.8	29,123	38,387	75.9
1989	27,889	45,023	61.9	20,102	39,310	51.1	20,901	36,180	57.8	28,196	39,700	71.0
1988	28,249	43,350	65.2	20,147	39,496	51.0	20,853	36,907	56.5	29,801	38,610	77.2
1987	24,836	42,410	58.6	20,124	38,612	52.1	20,204	36,252	55.7	24,774	39,047	63.4
1986	25,987	41,498	62.6	21,604	37,968	56.9	18,269	32,336	56.5	27,562	39,047	70.6
1985	22,892	39,861	57.4	20,197	36,663	55.1	20,020	34,308	58.4	30,953	38,277	80.9
1984	21,401	38,940	55.0	18,833	36,289	51.9	19,484	34,154	57.0	25,181	37,372	67.4
1983	21,317	37,953	56.2	17,843	34,916	51.1	18,909	33,455	56.5	24,911	35,569	70.0
1982	20,634	36,152	57.1	17,328	34,678	50.0	19,256	34,160	56.4	28,373	37,446	75.8
1981	20,026	37,321	53.7	22,428	36,107	62.1	18,568	33,333	55.7	25,081	36,769	68.2
1980	21,827	37,405	58.4	23,242	36,928	62.9	19,245	34,143	56.4	28,357	37,426	75.8
1979	22,129	39,268	56.4	23,977	38,823	61.8	19,764	34,683	57.0	24,148	38,729	62.4
1978	24,156	38,832	62.2	28,339	39,409	71.9	20,389	35,488	57.5	22,380	39,026	57.3
1977	22,165	37,287	59.4	23,038	37,134	62.0	19,314	33,880	57.0	21,372	36,604	58.4
1976	22,303	36,286	61.5	24,954	37,455	66.6	19,550	33,050	59.2	22,592	36,093	62.6
1975	19,800	35,996	55.0	28,372	35,986	78.8	21,222	31,694	67.0	24,943	35,138	71.0
1974	22,110	37,590	58.8	31,646	36,777	86.0	23,629	31,924	74.0	26,802	35,100	76.4
1973	22,398	38,176	58.7	26,285	37,882	69.4	18,566	33,207	55.9	23,757	36,534	65.0
1972	23,976	37,753	63.5	25,516	36,648	69.6	17,678	32,102	55.1	25,501	35,964	70.9
1971	24,020	35,681	67.3	24,026	34,821	69.0	17,109	30,672	55.8	24,089	34,138	70.6
1970	27,316	38,355	71.2	27,119	36,923	73.4	18,363	32,468	56.6	28,114	36,482	77.1
1969	23,890	35,485	67.3	26,708	35,239	75.8	17,239	30,296	56.9	26,556	35,250	75.3
1968	23,342	33,671	69.3	24,964	33,450	74.6	15,473	28,768	53.8	27,117	34,184	79.3
1967	21,177	32,489	65.2	24,021	31,330	76.7	14,832	27,611	53.7	24,430	33,048	73.9

Sources: David Swinton, "The Economic Status of African Americans: 'Permanent' Poverty and Inequality," in Janet Dewart, ed., *The State of Black America 1991* (New York: National Urban League, 1991), Table 5, page 32, and U.S. Department of Commerce, Bureau of the Census, *Money Income of Households, Families, and Persons in the United States, 1991*, Series P-60, No. 180, August 1992, Table 13, pp. 41-42.

163

$20,124, respectively. The South resumed its historical position as the region with the lowest incomes for the first time since 1986.

White incomes were substantially higher than black incomes in all regions. Equality was greatest in the West, where the index of equality was 75.2 percent. Inequality was highest in the Midwest—as it was throughout the Reagan-Bush era—with a B/W index of only 54.6 percent. Black median income was 61.1 percent of white median income in the Northeast and 57.1 percent of white income in the South.

For the Reagan-Bush years as a whole, black family income increased relative to 1980 income in the Northeast and the South, remained about constant in the West, and declined in the Midwest. The average median family income was significantly higher in the Northeast ($24,044 versus $22,927) and the West ($27,478 versus $24,732) during the 11 Reagan-Bush years than in the pre-Reagan-Bush period. The average income in the South was slightly higher ($19,842 versus $19,530), and the average income in the Midwest was significantly lower ($20,076 versus $26,047).

During this period, family income inequality as measured by the B/W index was on average higher in the Midwest, South, and Northeast than it was in the pre-Reagan-Bush period. In the South, the average inequality index between 1969 and 1981 was 59.2 percent; this average fell to 57.1 percent in the Reagan-Bush years. In the Northeast, the average fell from 61.1 percent to 59.0 percent. Inequality rose sharpest in the Midwest, where the B/W index dropped from 70.1 percent to 53.7 percent. In fact, the Midwest was the most equal region in the pre-Reagan-Bush period, while it became the most unequal region during the Reagan-Bush era. Finally, inequality declined by the B/W measure in the West as the index increased from an average of 67.9 percent in the pre-Reagan-Bush years to 72.3 percent during the Reagan-Bush years. In any case, overall inequality remained high in all regions throughout the Reagan-Bush era.

Income of Households by Selected Characteristics

Table 12 contains data which summarize the income recipiency of African-American and white households by selected characteristics for 1991. The reader can peruse this table to note the distribution of black and white households across the various characteristics listed and how their median incomes vary with these characteristics. Clearly there are still some major differences in the characteristics of white and black households: they have differing residential patterns, household types, age distributions, household sizes, numbers of earners, and work experience. Moreover, black households have lower income than white households for every characteristic. These differences in circumstances—many of which increased during the Reagan-Bush years—imply that the interests and needs of the two populations may often be divergent.

164

Table 12
Percent of Households and Median Income of Households by Selected Characteristics and Race

Characteristics	Households Black	Households White	Median Income Black	Median Income White	B/W
Number of Households					
(millions)	11,083	81,675			
All Households	100.0	100.0	$18,807	$31,569	9.6
Type of Residence					
Nonfarm Residence	99.8	98.1	18,838	31,594	59.6
Inside Metro Areas	84.8	76.7	20,211	33,988	59.5
Inside Metro Areas—Large	59.5	48.0	21,534	36,732	58.6
Inside Central Cities	40.7	16.4	18,243	30,027	60.8
Outside Central Cities	18.8	31.6	29,776	40,652	73.2
Inside Metro Areas—Small	25.3	28.7	17,260	29,995	57.5
Inside Central Cities	16.5	11.4	15,963	26,885	59.4
Outside Central Cities	8.8	17.3	20,066	31,871	63.0
Outside Metro Areas	5.2	23.3	13,120	25,804	50.8
Type of Household					
Family Households	69.6	70.1	22,203	38,229	58.1
Married-Couple Family	32.8	57.7	33,369	41,584	80.2
Single-Male Headed	4.5	2.9	26,428	31,634	83.5
Single-Female Headed	32.3	9.5	12,196	21,213	57.5
Nonfamily Households	30.4	29.9	12,202	18,461	66.1
Male Householder Nonfam.	14.4	12.8	15,223	24,531	62.1
Female Householder Nonfam.	16.0	17.1	9,520	14,790	64.4
Age of Householder					
Under 65	82.4	77.2	21,606	36,766	58.8
15-24	6.3	4.9	8,603	19,803	43.4
25-34	24.0	20.4	19,284	32,315	59.7
35-44	23.8	22.4	26,233	41,202	63.7
45-54	15.5	16.3	27,526	46,215	59.6
55-64	12.8	13.2	20,103	35,550	56.5
65 and over	17.6	22.8	10,466	17,794	58.8
65-74	11.2	13.0	11,555	21,087	54.8
75+	6.3	9.9	9,151	14,343	63.8
Number of Persons in household					
One	26.3	25.1	10,650	15,985	66.6
Two	26.0	33.2	19,230	32,527	59.1
Three	18.7	16.9	23,285	40,330	57.7
Four	15.0	15.2	26,187	45,240	57.9
Five	7.9	6.4	24,371	42,519	57.3
Six	3.3	2.0	25,251	40,274	62.7
Seven or More	2.7	1.1	23,806	38,033	62.6
Number of Earners					
No Earners	25.4	21.4	6,332	12,771	49.6
One Earner	38.8	32.5	17,230	26,147	65.9
Two Earners or more	35.7	46.1	37,268	47,100	79.1
Two Earners	27.8	35.7	33,991	44,056	77.2
Three Earners	6.4	7.7	45,882	56,228	81.6
Four Earners or More	1.6	2.8	59,256	69,305	85.5
Work Experience of Householder					
Total	100.0	100.0	18,807	31,569	59.6
Worked	66.1	72.6	26,424	38,814	68.1
Worked Year-round, Full-time	44.5	52.6	31,866	43,572	73.1
Did Not Work	33.9	27.4	7,494	15,488	48.4

Source: U.S. Department of Commerce, Bureau of the Census, *Money Income of Households, Families, and Persons in the United States: 1991*, August 1992, Table 1.

165

Blacks, for example, were much more likely to live in the central city; 57.2 percent of blacks compared to 27.8 percent of whites lived in the central city of large and small metropolitan areas. Whites were more likely to live in nonmetropolitan areas (23.3 percent of whites versus 15.2 percent of blacks), and the suburbs of metropolitan areas (48.9 percent of whites versus 27.6 percent of blacks). Because of their heavier concentration in large metropolitan areas and central cities, blacks clearly have a stronger interest in policies that assist such areas.

Median household income for African Americans ranged from a low of $13,120 in nonmetropolitan areas to a high of $29,776 in the suburbs of large metropolitan areas. Black incomes in all other residences ranged between $15,963 and $20,066. Whites also had their highest incomes in the suburbs of large metropolitan areas ($40,652) and their smallest incomes in nonmetropolitan areas ($25,804).

However, although both blacks and whites had higher incomes in metropolitan areas than in nonmetropolitan areas, in large rather than in small metropolitan areas, and in suburbs rather than in central cities, blacks had smaller incomes than whites in all locations. Equality for blacks was generally greater in large rather than in small metropolitan areas. The B/W index of the large areas was 60.8 percent versus 57.5 percent in smaller metropolitan areas. The reader may note by comparing the other B/W indexes that equality was least in nonmetropolitan areas with a B/W index of 50.8 percent and was greatest in the suburbs with a B/W index of 73.2 percent. In all other types of residence, the B/W index ranged between 57.5 percent and 63.0 percent.

We will not go through all of the other characteristics in detail; the reader may observe the differences for him/herself. Blacks generally had fewer married-couple family households; they had somewhat younger householders; their households were slightly larger; they had fewer earners; and they had less work experience. Moreover, for every type of characteristic, blacks had lower earnings. Income equality was greatest when blacks had more earners, such as for married-couple households. Income inequality varied very little for characteristics that were not highly correlated with the number of earners.

We performed some calculations to derive the maximum extent to which reducing the differences in the black and white characteristics could reduce racial inequality. These calculations, however, are not intended to imply any causal connection between any given characteristic and the economic status of blacks. We particularly warn against the relatively common error of considering the smaller proportion of African-American married-couple families as a cause of their economic disadvantage. It is more likely, in our view, that the economic disadvantages of African Americans are a cause of the smaller proportion of married-couple families. The estimates are derived by calculating average black medians, using black median incomes and black distributions as weights and comparing them to average black medians using black median incomes and white population distributions as weights. These two medians are then compared to average white median income.

The results of this exercise suggest that most of the inequality would remain even if blacks had white characteristics, so long as the median income differences at each characteristic remained. The gap in median incomes from eliminating the differences in black and white distributions across places of residence would be reduced by only 10 percent. The B/W index would rise from 60.0 percent to 64.11 percent. The gap could be reduced by a maximum of about 39 percent if blacks had the same family type distributions. The black age distribution is slightly favorable. The estimated gaps are actually increased by giving blacks the white age distribution. Similarly, the calculations show that the size of household distribution is also favorable for black income. The estimates suggest that the B/W index would decline slightly and the inequality gap would be reduced by 1.4 percent if the size distributions were equalized. Finally, as one might expect, equalizing the number of earners or work experience would reduce inequality. These changes could increase the B/W index and reduce the inequality gap by 23 percent and 34 percent, respectively. In summary, although the black characteristics are unfavorable, they cannot explain most of the racial inequality. Moreover, the unfavorable characteristics are not independent causes of inequality rather than effects or symptoms of the black disadvantage.

Poverty Trends

Poverty is another way to view the economic status of blacks. Poverty by definition is the lack of sufficient income to attain standard consumption levels. The income trends previously discussed result in blacks having high rates of poverty during the Reagan-Bush years. These data are reviewed in the next two tables.

Table 13 contains the latest data as well as historical data on numbers of persons in poverty and poverty rates for all persons, children, and persons in female-headed families. The numbers and rates increased for African Americans and whites in all three categories. For African Americans, the numbers in poverty were at all-time highs in each category. In total, 10,242,000 African Americans were in poverty. This was up by 405,000 persons from 1990. The number of children in poverty in 1991 reached 4,637,000—up 87,000 from the previous year. But the number of persons in poverty among female-headed families rose by 552,000, indicating that this category accounted for all of the rise and more during 1991. Poverty rates also rose in each category during 1991. The total persons poverty rate rose from 31.9 percent in 1990 to 32.7 percent in 1991; the poverty rate for children rose

Table 13
Selected Poverty Rates by Race for Selected Years

Persons in Poverty

	Number (Millions)		Percent			Poverty Gap (Millions)
	Black	White	Black	White	B/W	
1991	10,242	23,747	32.7	11.3	2.9	6.70
1990	9,837	22,326	31.9	10.7	3.0	6.53
1989	9,302	20,785	30.7	10.0	3.1	6.28
1988	9,356	20,715	31.3	10.1	3.1	6.33
1987	9,520	21,195	32.4	10.4	3.1	6.46
1986	8,983	22,183	31.1	11.0	2.8	5.80
1985	8,926	22,860	31.3	11.4	2.7	5.67
1984	9,490	22,955	33.8	11.5	2.9	6.26
1983	9,882	23,984	35.7	12.1	3.0	6.53
1982	9,697	23,517	35.6	12.0	3.0	6.42
1981	9,173	21,553	34.2	11.2	3.1	6.17
1980	8,579	19,699	32.5	10.2	3.2	5.89
1979	8,050	17,214	31.0	8.9	3.5	5.73
1978	7,625	16,259	30.6	8.7	3.5	5.47
1977	7,726	16,416	31.3	8.9	3.5	5.54
1976	7,595	16,713	31.1	9.1	3.4	5.37
1975	7,545	17,770	31.3	9.7	3.2	5.20
1974	7,182	15,736	30.3	8.3	3.7	5.21
1973	7,388	15,142	31.4	8.3	3.8	5.43
1972	7,710	16,203	33.3	9.0	3.7	5.62
1971	7,396	17,780	32.5	9.9	3.3	5.15
1970	7,548	17,484	33.5	9.9	3.4	5.31
1969	7,095	16,659	32.5	9.5	3.4	5.06
1968	7,616	17,395	32.2	10.0	3.2	4.87
1967	8,486	18,983	39.3	11.0	3.6	6.11

Children in Poverty

	Number (Millions)		Percent			Poverty Gap (Millions)
	Black	White	Black	White	B/W	
1991	4,637	8,316	45.6	16.1	2.8	3.00
1990	4,550	8,232	44.8	15.9	2.8	2.88
1989	4,375	7,599	43.7	14.8	3.0	2.85
1988	4,296	7,435	43.5	14.5	3.0	2.81
1987	4,385	7,788	45.1	15.3	2.9	2.84
1986	4,148	8,209	43.1	16.1	2.7	2.56
1985	4,157	8,253	43.6	16.2	2.7	2.58
1984	4,413	8,472	46.6	16.7	2.8	2.80
1983	4,398	8,862	46.7	17.5	2.7	2.70
1982	4,472	8,678	47.6	17.0	2.8	2.84
1981	4,237	7,181	45.2	15.2	3.0	2.79
1980	3,961	6,193	42.3	13.9	3.0	2.64
1979	3,833	6,193	41.2	11.8	3.5	2.70
1978	3,830	5,831	41.5	11.3	3.7	2.77
1977	3,888	6,097	41.8	11.6	3.6	2.79
1976	3,787	6,189	40.6	11.6	3.5	2.69
1975	3,925	6,927	41.7	12.7	3.3	2.72
1974	3,755	6,223	39.8	11.2	3.6	2.68
1970	3,922	6,138	41.5	10.5	4.0	2.90

168

Table 13 (Cont.)
Selected Poverty Rates by Race for Selected Years

Persons Female-Headed Families

	Number (Millions)		Percent			Poverty Gap (Millions)
	Black	White	Black	White	B/W	
1991	6,557	6,806	54.8	31.5	1.7	2.79
1990	6,005	6,210	50.6	29.8	1.7	2.47
1989	5,530	5,723	49.4	28.1	1.8	2.38
1988	5,601	5,950	51.9	29.2	1.8	2.45
1987	5,789	5,989	54.1	29.6	1.8	2.62
1986	5,473	6,171	53.8	30.6	1.8	2.36
1985	5,342	5,990	53.2	29.8	1.8	2.35
1984	5,666	5,866	54.6	29.7	1.8	2.59
1983	5,736	6,017	57.0	31.2	1.8	2.60
1982	5,698	5,686	58.8	30.9	1.9	2.71
1981	5,222	5,600	56.7	29.8	1.9	2.48
1980	4,984	4,940	53.4	28.0	1.9	2.37
1979	4,816	4,375	53.1	25.2	2.1	2.53
1978	4,595	4,371	54.2	25.9	2.1	2.46
1977	4,712	4,474	55.3	26.8	2.1	2.37
1976	4,415	4,463	55.7	28.0	2.0	2.20
1975	4,168	4,577	54.3	29.4	1.8	1.91
1974	4,116	4,278	55.0	27.7	2.0	2.04
1973	4,064	4,003	56.5	28.0	2.0	2.05
1972	4,139	3,770	58.1	27.4	2.1	2.19
1971	3,587	4,099	56.1	30.4	1.8	1.64
1970	3,656	3,761	58.7	28.4	2.1	1.89
1969	3,225	3,577	58.2	29.1	2.0	1.61
1968	3,312	3,551	58.9	29.1	2.0	NA
1967	3,362	3,453	61.6	28.5	2.2	NA

Source: U.S. Department of Commerce, Bureau of the Census, *Poverty in the United States: 1991*, August 1992, Tables 2 and 3.

from 44.8 percent to 45.6 percent, while that rate for persons in female-headed families rose from 50.6 percent to 54.8 percent.

As the B/W index indicates, racial inequality remained high during 1991. However, the indicator declined slightly for the total poverty rate because of increases in poverty among whites. For all persons, the B/W index stood at 2.9 in 1991, indicating that black persons were 2.9 times as likely to be in poverty. For children, the inequality index stood at 2.8, and for female-headed families, 1.7. As the last column shows, record poverty gaps existed in 1991. About 6,700,000 additional African-American persons and 3,000,000 additional children were in poverty than would be expected if black poverty rates were equal to white poverty rates. Among female-headed families, an excess of 2,790,000 persons were in poverty during 1991.

Taken as a whole, the Reagan-Bush era has resulted in increased numbers of persons in poverty and poverty rates for blacks and whites. The annual average number of African Americans in poverty during this period was 9,492,000, which was up from an average of 7,668,000 persons in the 11-year pre-Reagan-Bush period. The African-American poverty rate for all persons rose from a pre-Reagan-Bush average of 31.7 percent to a Reagan-Bush average of 32.8 percent. The number of whites in poverty rose also, from 16,947,000 to 22,347,000; the poverty rate for whites increased from 9.2 percent to 11.1 percent.

Poverty numbers and rates also averaged higher for children and persons in female-headed families during the Reagan-Bush years for both blacks and whites. For African-American children, the average was up—from 3,863,000 to 4,370,000, and the rate increased from an average of 41.3 percent to an 45.0 percent. For persons in African-American female-headed families, the average number in poverty increased from 4,296,000 to 5,693,000, while their poverty rate actually went down slightly—from 55.5 percent to 54.1 percent. The number of white children in poverty increased from 6,224,000 to 8,093,000, and their rate of poverty averaged 15.9 percent in the Reagan-Bush era, up from 11.8 percent in the previous period. The number of poor persons in white female-headed families increased from 4,283,000 to 6,001,000, while their rate of poverty increased from 27.7 percent to 30.0 percent.

Clearly, during the Reagan-Bush years, poverty rose. Relative inequality as measured by the B/W index declined for all categories. For all persons, the B/W index dropped from 3.5 in the pre-Reagan-Bush era to an average value of 3.0 during the Reagan-Bush years. The children inequality index decreased from 3.5 to 2.5, and the index for persons in female-headed families dropped from 2.0 to 1.8. However, it is important to note that these declines in relative inequality were brought about solely by a slightly faster rate of increase in poverty among whites from a lower base. As noted, black poverty rates and numbers also increased. Indeed, the absolute poverty gaps averaged much higher during the Reagan-Bush period. The average excess number of African Americans in poverty was 6,290,000 under Reagan-Bush and 5,450,000 in the earlier period. The excess poverty among African Americans in female-headed families increased to 2,530,000 from 2,150,000.

Table 14 contains data on poverty rates by region. As these data show, the black poverty rate varied substantially by region. During 1991, poverty for blacks was lowest in the West at 24.0 percent and highest in the Midwest at 37.7 percent. African-American poverty rates in the Northeast and the South were 28.1 percent and 33.6 percent, respectively. This pattern of regional differences persisted throughout the Reagan-Bush era.

Table 14
Poverty Rates by Regions:
Selected Years, 1970-1991

	Northeast			Midwest		
	Black	White	B/W	Black	White	B/W
1991	28.1	10.0	2.8	37.7	9.9	3.8
1990	28.9	9.2	3.1	36.0	9.5	3.8
1989	24.7	8.0	3.1	36.4	9.0	4.0
1988	22.9	8.4	2.7	34.8	8.7	4.0
1987	28.8	8.9	3.2	36.6	9.9	3.7
1986	24.0	8.9	2.7	34.5	10.6	3.3
1985	28.0	9.8	2.9	35.3	11.4	3.1
1984	NA	NA	NA	NA	NA	NA
1983	32.5	11.0	3.0	39.2	12.1	3.2
1982	32.2	10.7	3.0	37.9	11.5	3.3
1981	33.2	9.5	3.5	32.4	10.0	3.2
1980	30.7	8.9	3.4	33.3	8.9	3.7
1979	27.6	8.4	3.3	29.6	7.6	3.9
1978	29.1	8.2	3.5	24.8	7.4	3.4
1977	27.1	8.5	3.2	32.1	7.6	4.2
1976	29.5	8.3	3.6	29.7	7.9	3.8
1975	24.5	8.8	2.8	25.5	8.1	3.1
1974	25.4	7.1	3..6	26.3	7.2	3.7
1973	NA	NA	NA	NA	NA	NA
1972	NA	NA	NA	NA	NA	NA
1971	NA	NA	NA	NA	NA	NA
1970	20.0	7.7	2.6	25.7	8.9	2.9

	South			West		
	Black	White	B/W	Black	White	B/W
1991	33.6	11.7	2.9	24.0	13.5	1.8
1990	32.6	11.6	2.8	23.7	12.2	1.9
1989	31.6	11.4	2.8	23.5	11.3	2.1
1988	34.3	11.6	3.0	23.6	11.3	2.1
1987	34.5	11.5	3.0	24.3	11.5	2.1
1986	33.6	11.8	2.8	21.7	12.3	1.8
1985	32.7	11.9	2.7	20.1	12.1	1.7
1984	NA	NA	NA	NA	NA	NA
1983	37.5	12.3	3.0	25.6	13.1	2.0
1982	33.6	12.0	2.8	26.6	11.8	2.3
1981	37.1	12.9	2.9	23.7	11.5	2.1
1980	35.1	12.2	2.9	19.0	10.4	1.8
1979	33.9	10.6	3.2	23.6	8.7	2.7
1978	34.1	10.2	3.3	26.1	8.9	2.9
1977	33.3	10.3	3.2	25.6	8.8	2..9
1976	33.1	10.8	3.1	25.8	9.0	2.9
1975	36.6	11.4	3.2	26.2	10.6	2.5
1974	34.9	10.8	3.2	22.1	9.3	2..4
1973	NA	NA	NA	NA	NA	NA
1972	NA	NA	NA	NA	NA	NA
1971	NA	NA	NA	NA	NA	NA
1970	42.6	12.4	3.4	20.4	10.6	1.9

Source: United States Department of Commerce, Bureau of the Census, *Poverty in the United States: 1991*, August 1992, Table 9.

White poverty also varied by region; however, the range of variation is narrower and the pattern less consistent. During 1991, the white poverty rate was lowest in the Midwest at 9.9 percent and highest in the West at 13.5 percent. This is just the opposite of the situation for blacks. White poverty in the Northeast was 10.0 percent and 11.7 percent in the South during 1991. Throughout the Reagan-Bush years, the Midwest and the Northeast swapped positions as the regions with the lowest and next to lowest white poverty rates, while the West and the South swapped positions as the regions with the highest and next highest poverty rates.

In comparison with the pre-Reagan-Bush period, black poverty rates were higher on average in the Midwest and the Northeast and perhaps on average slightly lower or about the same in the South and the West. White poverty rates were generally higher in all regions.

Finally, racial inequality as measured by the B/W gap remained high in all regions. The B/W index was highest in the Midwest at 3.8, which indicates that black poverty in that region was almost four times white poverty. The index had its lowest value in the West, at 1.8, indicating that black poverty rates in the West were less than two times white poverty rates. According to the B/W index of 2.8 and 2.9 in the Northeast and the South, respectively, poverty rates for blacks in those two regions were about three times white poverty rates. However, we note that relative poverty rates declined in all regions except the Midwest during the Reagan-Bush era because of the increase in white poverty rates in all regions. Reagan-Bush provided equal opportunities to increase poverty rates.

SOURCES OF INCOME AND INCOME INEQUALITY

The extensive inequality in income and poverty rates is the consequence of the limited ownership discussed earlier. This limited ownership of wealth, businesses, and human capital has direct and indirect impacts on the income generated by African Americans. Limited ownership of financial assets and businesses limits the amount of income earned from self-employment and property income. Moreover, to the extent that claims to pensions and social security benefits can be considered assets, limited ownership of these assets limits earnings of these types of income. Limited educational capital directly limits wage and salary income. In addition, limited ownership indirectly limits opportunities to employ labor and other resources. Public assistance is the only type of income not significantly determined by ownership of wealth or capital.

Tables 15 and 16 display data on the income received by blacks from various sources. These data represent the situation at the close of the Reagan-Bush era. We can see from the tables that the income sources received by the largest proportion of the black and white populations were wage and salary income. According to Table 15, 69.68 percent of African

Table 15
Percentage of Persons with Income and Aggregate Per Capita Income by Race, 1991

	Black					White					B/W	B%/W%
	Number with Income	Percent with Income	Mean Income	Aggregate Income (Billions)	Percent of Income	Number with Income	Percent with Income	Mean Income	Aggregate Income (Billions)	Percent of Income	Mean Income	with Income
Wage & Salary	13,706	69.68	$16,478	$225.8	78.34	106,563	68.62	$22,223	$2,368.1	72.62	74.15	101.55
Nonfarm Self-Employed	598	3.04	12,328	7.4	2.56	11,320	7.29	17,044	192.9	5.92	72.33	41.71
Farm Self-Employed	30	0.15	-	-	0.00	1,630	1.05	9,947	16.2	0.50	-	14.53
Property Income	5,878	29.88	1,077	6.3	2.20	100,585	64.77	2,355	236.9	7.26	45.73	46.14
Govt. Transfer Payments	7,541	38.34	5,133	38.7	13.43	48,963	31.53	6,771	331.5	10.17	75.81	121.60
Pensions	944	4.80	7,847	7.4	2.57	13,547	8.72	9,199	124.6	3.82	85.30	55.02
Soc. Security or RR Ret.	3,439	17.48	5,195	17.9	6.20	31,713	20.42	6,454	204.7	6.28	80.49	85.62
Public Assistance or SSI	3,047	15.49	3,333	10.2	3.52	5,992	3.86	3,366	20.2	0.62	99.02	401.48
All Income Sources[1]	19,670	100.00	14,656	288.3	100.00	155,299	100.00	20,997	3,260.8	100.00	69.80	100.00

[1]The components do not add to the total because of overlapping categories.

Aggregate Income is number with income * mean income.

Source: Calculated by author from data in U.S. Department of Commerce, Bureau of the Census, *Money Income of Households, Families, and Persons in the United States: 1991*, August 1992, Table 34.

Americans and 68.62 percent of whites received wage and salary income. Thus, as indicated by the B/W value of 101.55, slightly higher proportions of blacks "worked for a living."

The earnings of workers also contributed more than any other source to black and white aggregate income. In 1991, black workers earned $225.8 billion, which accounted for 78.34 percent of black aggregate income. The contributions of white workers accounted for only 72.62 percent of their income. Thus, a higher percentage of black income was derived from "working for a living."

However, mean earnings of black wage and salary workers were only $16,478, substantially less than the $22,223 mean income earned by whites. The B/W index for wage and salary means, in fact, was only 74.15 percent. Wage and salary income as determined by comparing the B/W index for the other sources was the most equal of the "earned" income sources and less equal than the "transfer" income sources.

Only 3.19 percent of black persons had income from self-employment in 1991. This contrasted with 8.34 percent of whites. Thus, blacks were only 38.25 percent as likely to have income from self-employment. Moreover, less than 5 percent of the black self-employed but almost 13 percent of the white self-employed were engaged in the farm sector.

On average, the black self-employed in the nonfarm sector had mean earnings of $12,328. This contrasted with $17,044 mean earnings for the white self-employed. The B/W index of 72.33 indicates that equality in self-employment earnings was only slightly less equal than wage and salary earnings. Self-employment contributed $7.4 billion, or 2.56 percent, of black aggregate income. On the other hand, the earnings of the white self-employed contributed 5.92 percent of their aggregate earnings.

Almost 30 percent of blacks received some form of property income: their mean receipts were $1,077, contributing $6.3 billion—2.2 percent—to their aggregate income. The inequality indexes indicate that African Americans were only 45.14 percent as likely as whites to have property income and have average receipts that were only 45.73 percent of the average receipts of whites. This makes property income the most unequal of the income sources, which is to be expected given the large ownership gaps previously discussed.

Government transfer income was the most equal of the three sources. Over 38 percent of blacks and 31 percent of whites received this source; thus, blacks were more likely than whites to receive government transfers. However, this was due entirely to the high rate of receipt of welfare income among blacks. As can be seen, over 15 percent of blacks but only about 4 percent of whites received welfare income. A higher proportion of whites than blacks received social security income (20.42 percent versus 17.48 percent). A larger proportion of whites also received pension income (8.72 percent versus 4.80 percent).

174

Blacks had lower mean incomes for each of the transfer types—including welfare income. Black mean income was $5,133 for all government transfers, $7,847 for pensions, $5,195 for social security, and $3,333 for welfare income. The corresponding numbers for whites were $6,771, $9,199, $6,454, and $3,366, respectively. The mean transfer inequality index ranged from 75.81 for all transfer income to 99.02 for public assistance and supplemental security income.

Government transfer income contributed 13.43 percent to black aggregate income and 10.17 percent to white aggregate income. Again, the advantage for blacks was because of the high contribution of welfare—3.52 percent compared to a contribution of only 0.62 percent to white income. Blacks received $10.2 billion from public assistance and supplemental security income and $17.9 billion from social security in 1991. Private pensions contributed 3.82 percent to white income but only 2.57 percent, or $7.4 billion, to African-American income.

In general, black income disadvantages arose from (1) lower proportions receiving each type of income except welfare, and (2) wage and salary incomes and lower mean income for all types of income. The net impacts of these two factors on per capita and aggregate income are shown in Table 16.

The first thing that stands out from this table is that the per capita contribution of each income source other than welfare was much lower for blacks than whites. Black per capita income from wages and salary was only $7,183.90 versus white per capita wage and salary income of $11,263.71.

Table 16
Per Capita Income and Per Capita Income Gaps by Source of Income

	Black Per Capita	White Per Capita	B/W	Per Capita Gap	Aggregate Gap (Billions)	% of Gap
Wage & Salary	$7,183.90	$11,263.71	63.8	$4,079.81	$128.3	64.4
Self-Employment	234.50	917.68	25.6	683.18	$21.5	10.8
Property Income	201.37	1,126.67	17.9	925.30	$29.1	14.6
Govt. Transfer Payments	1,231.25	1,576.86	78.1	345.61	$10.9	5.5
Other Income	318.90	625.00	51.0	306.10	$9.6	4.8
Soc. Security or RR Ret.	569.37	973.62	58.5	404.25	$12.7	6.4
Public Assistance or SSI	324.45	96.08	337.7	(228.37)	($7.2)	-3.6
Pensions	235.48	592.64	39.7	357.16	$11.2	5.6
Total[1]	9,169.91	15,509.51	59.1	6,339.60	$199.3	100.0

[1]Components do not sum to total because of overlaps in categories and rounding. First five categories sum to total.

Black Per Capita = Number with income * mean income divided by population.

Aggregate Gap = per capita gap * 1991 population (black = 31,438,000; white = 210,246,000).

Source: Calculated by author from data in U.S. Department of Commerce, Bureau of the Census, *Money Income of Households, Families, and Persons in the United States: 1991*, August 1992, Table 34.

The B/W index shows that black per capita wage and salary income was only 63.8 percent of the income received by whites. This inequality implies that African-American workers earned $4,079.81 less per person. In the aggregate, their contribution to per capita income was $128.3 billion less than would be required for wage and salary parity. Inequality in wage and salary income accounted for 64.4 percent of the overall income gap.

As can be seen from the table, black per capita self-employment income of $234.50 was only 25.6 percent as much as white per capita self-employment income. Earnings from property ownership were $201.37 per capita for blacks, only 17.9 percent of the per capita property income of whites. The per capita gaps from these two sources were $683.18 and $925.30, while the aggregate gaps were $21.5 billion and $29.1 billion, respectively. The gap in self-employment income accounted for 10.8 percent, while the disparity in property income accounted for 14.6 percent of the overall aggregate income gap.

Transfers also contributed to inequality, although the relative equality in transfers was greater. The black per capita income from government transfers of $1,576.86 was 78.1 percent of white per capita income from transfers. Altogether, inequality in government transfers caused a per capita gap of $345.61 and an aggregate gap of $10.9 billion. Inequality in government transfers accounted for 5.5 percent of the aggregate gap.

However, this relatively high degree of equality was due to the excess per capita income received from welfare. Black per capita public assistance or supplemental security income of $324.45 was 337.7 percent of white per capita income from this source. This excess welfare income reduced the per capita income gap by $228.37 and the aggregate income gap by $7.2 billion. Because of welfare income, the overall gap was reduced by 3.6 percent.

Other transfers were not equalizing. Black per capita income from social security was $569.37—only 58.5 percent of white per capita. Black per capita income from pensions was $235.48 versus $592.64 for whites, resulting in a B/W index of 39.7 for pensions. Social security inequality added $404.25 to the per capita gap and $12.7 billion to the aggregate income gap. Pensions added $357.16 to the per capita gap and $11.2 billion to the aggregate gap. Inequality in social security income accounted for 6.4 percent of the aggregate gap; inequality in pensions accounted for 5.6 percent of the aggregate gap.

The catchall category, "Other Income," includes all sources other than those in the first four categories. As can be seen, these residual sources were also unequal. Black per capita income of $318.90 was only 51 percent of white per capita income of $625. Inequality in this category added $306.10 to the per capita gap and $9.6 billion to the aggregate gap. This source accounted for 4.8 percent of the overall inequality.

We can now develop a rough estimate of the direct loss due to lower ownership of wealth, capital, and businesses. First, we note that 35.6

percent of the aggregate gap was due to nonwage and salary earnings. Since the ability to earn most of this other income was attributable to property ownership or rights, it seems reasonable to attribute at least 75 percent of this gap to lower ownership. This implies that at least $53.2 billion of current income was directly due to lower nonhuman wealth ownership. We have already estimated that the loss of wage and salary income due to human capital shortfall was, at a minimum, $46.4 billion. Combining these two estimates produces a rough estimate of $99.6 billion for the direct loss of current income due to capital shortages. This was about 50 percent of the overall gap. The remainder of the gap was due to quality differences in black and white capital, discrimination, and demographic factors. Equalizing ownership would also eliminate that part of the gap due to discrimination and quality differences. Moreover, this would also eliminate any demographic differentials generated by the historic economic disadvantages over the long run.

CURRENT AND RECENT LABOR MARKET TRENDS

As earlier recounted, labor market earnings accounted for the largest share of income for both blacks and whites. Moreover, continuing inequality in wage and salary income explained the largest share of current income inequality.

Labor market earnings depended on the rate of employment and the rate of earnings. In this section, we will examine data on employment, unemployment, occupational distribution, and wage or earnings rates. The data for this review will be presented in the remaining tables.

National Employment and Unemployment Rates

Table 17 contains the latest data on the employment rates of African Americans. This table covers the period from June to October 1992. As can be seen, 54.5 percent of African Americans were employed during October. The employment rate for the population as a whole and for each of the subgroups shown had fallen slightly since August. However, employment rates generally fluctuated in a fairly narrow range since June. African-American men, women, and teenagers had employment ratios in October of 63.0 percent, 53.9 percent, and 21.2 percent, respectively.

We can also see from this table that whites overall and in each subgroup were more likely to be employed than blacks. In October, for example, the white employment rate was 62.2 percent for the total population. As the B/W indicator suggests, blacks were only 87.6 percent as likely as whites to be employed during October. Black men were only 86.7 percent as likely as white men to be employed, and black teenagers were less than half as likely to be employed. The employment population ratio for black women was only slightly less than it was for white women.

Table 17
Civilian Employment—Population Ratio
by Race, Sex, and Age:
1992

Total Population

	Black	White	B/W
October	54.5	62.2	87.6
September	54.9	62.2	88.3
August	55.2	62.3	88.6
July	54.5	62.4	87.3
June	54.7	62.3	87.8

Men (20 years and over)

	Black	White	B/W
October	63.0	72.7	86.7
September	63.4	72.8	87.1
August	63.6	72.9	87.2
July	63.1	73.0	86.4
June	63.6	72.9	87.2

Women (20 years and over)

	Black	White	B/W
October	53.9	54.6	98.7
September	54.1	54.6	99.1
August	54.1	54.8	98.7
July	53.6	55.1	97.3
June	53.5	55.1	97.1

Both Sexes (16 to 19 years old)

	Black	White	B/W
October	21.2	45.9	46.2
September	22.5	46.3	48.6
August	25.0	45.2	55.3
July	23.0	44.1	52.2
June	22.8	43.2	52.8

Data are seasonally adjusted.

Source: U.S. Department of Labor, Bureau of Labor Statistics, *Employment Situation, November 1992*, Table A-2.

Table 18 contains annual employment population data for the Reagan-Bush and pre-Reagan-Bush periods. The data show that employment rates for the total African-American population and for both adult cohorts declined again during 1992. The employment rates for the total black population and for black women have declined each year since 1989, while the employment

Civilian Employment—Population Ratio by Race, Sex, and Age: Selected Years

	Total Population			Men (20 years +)			Women (20 years +)			Both Sexes (16 to 19 years)		
	Black	White	B/W	Black	White	B/W	Black	White	B/W	Black	White	B/W
*1992	54.5	62.4	0.873	63.2	72.9	0.867	53.2	55.0	0.967	23.0	45.2	0.509
1991	55.1	62.6	0.880	64.9	73.4	0.884	53.5	54.8	0.976	22.9	46.6	0.491
1990	56.2	63.6	0.884	66.1	75.0	0.881	54.2	55.3	0.980	26.6	49.8	0.534
1989	56.8	63.8	0.890	66.9	75.4	0.887	54.6	54.9	0.995	28.8	51.5	0.559
1988	56.3	63.1	0.892	67.0	75.1	0.892	53.9	54.0	0.998	27.5	51.0	0.539
1987	55.6	62.3	0.892	66.4	74.7	0.890	53.0	53.8	0.985	27.1	49.4	0.549
1986	54.1	61.5	0.879	65.1	74.3	0.877	51.6	52.0	0.992	25.1	48.8	0.514
1985	53.4	61.0	0.876	64.6	74.3	0.869	50.9	51.0	0.999	24.6	48.5	0.508
1984	52.3	60.5	0.865	64.1	74.3	0.863	49.8	50.2	0.992	21.9	48.0	0.457
1983	49.5	58.9	0.840	61.6	72.6	0.848	47.4	48.9	0.970	18.7	45.9	0.407
1982	49.4	58.8	0.840	61.4	73.0	0.841	47.5	48.4	0.981	19.0	45.8	0.415
1981	51.3	60.1	0.854	64.3	75.2	0.855	48.5	48.6	0.998	21.9	48.8	0.448
1980	52.2	60.1	0.868	65.6	75.7	0.867	49.1	47.9	1.024	23.8	50.8	0.468
1979	53.8	60.7	0.886	69.0	77.4	0.892	49.4	47.4	1.041	25.3	52.7	0.481
1978	53.6	60.0	0.893	69.1	77.2	0.895	49.3	46.1	1.069	25.2	52.4	0.481
1977	51.4	58.7	0.876	67.4	74.8	0.901	46.9	44.4	1.056	22.2	50.2	0.442
1976	50.8	57.6	0.882	66.7	76.0	0.877	46.3	43.1	1.075	22.3	47.9	0.466
1975	50.1	56.6	0.885	66.4	75.8	0.877	44.8	41.9	1.069	23.1	46.6	0.495
1974	53.5	58.3	0.918	71.8	78.6	0.914	46.9	42.2	1.112	25.9	49.3	0.524
1973	54.5	58.2	0.936	73.6	79.2	0.930	47.2	41.6	1.134	27.3	49.0	0.557
1972	53.7	57.4	0.936	73.0	79.0	NA	46.5	40.6	1.145	25.2	46.4	0.543

*: Average of the first three quarters of 1992.

Sources: David Swinton, "The Economic Status of African Americans: Limited Ownership and Persistent Poverty," in Billy Tidwell, ed., *The State of Black America 1992* (New York: National Urban League, 1992), Table 18, page 83, and U.S. Department of Labor, Bureau of Labor Statistics, *Handbook of Labor Statistics, June 1985*, pp. 46–47; and *Employment and Earnings, January 1992 and October 1992.*

rate for black men has declined slightly each year since 1988. There was a very slight increase in the employment rate of African-American teenagers; however, the rate was still only 23.0 percent.

Inequality also worsened slightly during 1992 for the total black population and for both black men and women. For all three groups, inequality as measured by the B/W index has been worsening for five consecutive years. Inequality for black youth improved slightly; black youth were still only about half as likely as white youth to be employed. For the first nine months of 1992, black males 20 years and over were only 86.7 percent as likely to be employed as white men. The gap in the black male adult employment rate in 1992 cost black males roughly 864,000 jobs. Black women were 96.7 percent as likely as white women to be employed during the same period. This difference in employment rates translated into about 199,000 jobs. Black teenagers had an employment ratio of only 23.0 percent versus 45.2 percent for white teenagers. This disparity translates into a job shortfall of about 461,000 jobs. Overall, the aggregate job shortfall for blacks is currently nearly 1,564,000 jobs.

A perusal of the data in Table 18 for the entire period reveals that, for all African-American groups, the Reagan-Bush years have been somewhat of a roller-coaster ride for employment rates. The rates generally declined from 1980 through 1982-83 for each group. This was true for whites as well. The employment rate then increased through 1988-89 for most groups and, as mentioned, the employment rate has generally declined since 1988-89.

However, in comparison to the decade preceding the Reagan-Bush era, women of both races had higher average employment population rates. For black women, the Reagan-Bush average was 51.5 percent, and the pre-Reagan-Bush average was 47.4; for white women, the corresponding averages were 52.2 percent and 43.9 percent, respectively. Thus, women continued the long-term trend of increasing their employment rates. However, the data also show that black women continued to lose ground relative to white women during the Reagan-Bush watch. In the pre-Reagan-Bush period, black women had a higher average employment population ratio than white women (47.4 percent versus 43.9 percent). The B/W index was 1.08 in the pre-Reagan-Bush years; this fell to 0.99 during the Republicans' watch.

Further, the employment rate for black and white men continued their historic decline during Reagan-Bush. For black men, the average employment population ratio of 64.6 percent was 4.6 percentage points below the pre-Reagan-Bush average of 69.2 percent. The white male average fell from 77.1 percent to 74.2 percent. Thus, relative inequality increased for males as the B/W index declined, from an average value of 90 percent in the pre-Reagan-Bush era to 87 percent during Reagan-Bush.

The employment population rate average for teenagers was also slightly lower during the Reagan-Bush era. For blacks, an average of 24.5 percent of teenagers was employed pre-Reagan-Bush; during Reagan-Bush, it fell to 23.9 percent. Racial inequality as measured by the B/W ratio remained constant, averaging 49 percent during each period.

Overall, because of the increase for black women, the average employment rate for the total population was up slightly during the Reagan-Bush years. It averaged 53.7 percent compared to an average of 52.6 percent in the prior years. However, because the average increased more for whites, inequality

Table 19
Unemployment Rates by Sex, Race, and Age:
Selected Months
1992

| | Total Population | | |
	Black	White	B/W
October	13.9	6.5	2.14
September	13.7	6.7	2.04
August	14.3	6.6	2.17
July	14.6	6.7	2.18
June	14.9	6.8	2.19
	Men (20 years and over)		
October	13.7	6.4	2.14
September	13.2	6.4	2.06
August	13.9	6.4	2.17
July	13.7	6.4	2.14
June	13.8	6.6	2.09
	Women (20 years and over)		
October	10.8	5.5	1.96
September	10.6	5.7	1.86
August	11.9	5.7	2.09
July	12.3	5.7	2.16
June	12.7	5.4	2.35
	Both Sexes (16 to 19 years old)		
October	42.5	15.1	2.81
September	43.3	17.3	2.50
August	36.9	16.9	2.18
July	40.7	18.1	2.25
June	41.6	20.6	2.02

Note: Data are seasonally adjusted.

Source: U.S. Department of Labor, Bureau of Labor Statistics, *Employment Situation: November 1992*, Table A-2.

as measured by the B/W ratio was also up during Reagan-Bush: the index of equality declined from 90 percent to 87 percent.

The latest unemployment data are shown in Tables 19 and 20. As can be seen from Table 19, black unemployment has been very high for the last five months. Overall, the October unemployment rate was 13.9 percent for the total African-American population. African-American men experienced 13.7 percent joblessness, while women experienced a 10.8 percent rate. The unemployment rate for black teenagers was at 42.5 percent. Inequality was rampant. All groups continued to experience a 2-to-1 disadvantage in unemployment. The B/W ratio for black teenagers was at 2.81 in October; for men, 2.14; for women, 1.96.

As can be seen by the annual data in Table 20, unemployment rates rose sharply during 1992 for all black subgroups. The 1992 unemployment rate rose from 12.4 percent in 1991 to 14.6 percent in 1992 for the total African-American population. Unemployment was up almost 2 percentage points for black men, rising from 11.7 percent in 1991 to 13.6 percent in 1992. For women, the increase was to 11.6 percent, up from 10.2 percent; the teenage unemployment rate rose, from 36.2 percent to 39.8 percent.

Although white unemployment also rose, black unemployment rose faster. The overall B/W index increased to 2.2 from 2.1. The B/W index remained constant for black women and dropped slightly for black teenagers. The aggregate impact of the differential in unemployment rates during 1992 was to create excess unemployment of 1,059,000 persons. This was made up of 471,000 men, 415,000 women, and 173,000 teenagers.

The pattern of unemployment during the Reagan-Bush era mirrored the pattern discussed for the employment population ratio. Unemployment rates rose sharply for all groups from 1980 through 1982-83. Unemployment then declined for all groups through 1989-90; it has been rising since then. Throughout the Reagan-Bush period, blacks had high unemployment rates in comparison to the previous period. Over the Reagan-Bush years, the unemployment rate for the total population averaged 14.5 percent. The lowest rate for blacks during that entire period was 11.3 percent in 1990. Black unemployment averaged 12.4 percent in the pre-Reagan-Bush years shown in the table.

Each group experienced higher average unemployment rates during the Reagan-Bush era. For black men, the rate averaged 13.0 percent versus 9.4 percent in the immediately preceding period. The corresponding numbers for black women and teenagers were 12.3 percent versus 10.6 percent and 37.7 percent versus 36.0 percent, respectively.

Not only was the unemployment rate absolutely higher during Reagan-Bush, but also inequality in unemployment rates increased. For the total population, the average B/W index was 2.36 during Reagan-Bush versus 2.16 in the earlier period. The differential for men averaged 2.2 to 1 in the pre-

Selected Years

	Total Population			Men (20 Years +)			Women (20 Years +)			Both Sexes (16 to 19 Years)		
	Black	White	B/W	Black	White	B/W	Black	White	B/W	Black	White	B/W
*1992	14.6	6.5	2.2	13.6	6.4	2.1	11.6	5.4	2.1	39.8	17.2	2.3
1991	12.4	6.0	2.1	11.7	5.8	2.0	10.2	4.9	2.1	36.2	14.9	2.4
1990	11.3	4.7	2.4	10.4	4.3	2.4	9.8	4.1	2.4	31.1	13.4	2.3
1989	11.4	4.5	2.5	10.0	3.9	2.6	9.8	4.0	2.5	32.4	12.7	2.6
1988	11.7	4.7	2.5	10.1	4.1	2.5	10.4	4.1	2.5	32.5	13.1	2.5
1987	13.0	5.3	2.5	11.1	4.8	2.3	11.6	4.6	2.5	33.4	13.3	2.5
1986	14.5	6.0	2.4	12.9	5.3	2.4	12.4	5.4	2.3	39.3	15.6	2.5
1985	15.1	6.2	2.4	13.2	5.4	2.4	13.1	5.7	2.3	40.2	15.7	2.6
1984	15.9	6.5	2.4	14.3	5.7	2.5	13.5	5.8	2.3	42.7	16.0	2.7
1983	19.5	8.4	2.3	18.1	7.9	2.3	16.5	6.9	2.4	48.5	19.3	2.5
1982	18.9	8.6	2.2	17.8	7.8	2.3	15.4	7.3	2.1	34.6	14.4	2.4
1981	15.5	6.7	2.3	13.3	5.6	2.4	13.4	5.9	2.3	41.5	17.3	2.4
1980	14.1	6.3	2.2	12.2	5.2	2.3	11.7	5.6	2.1	38.6	15.5	2.5
1979	12.2	5.1	2.4	9.1	3.6	2.5	10.8	5.0	2.2	15.5	17.4	0.9
1978	12.8	5.2	2.5	9.3	3.7	2.5	11.2	5.2	2.2	48.0	20.4	2.4
1977	13.9	6.2	2.2	10.5	4.6	2.3	12.2	6.2	2.0	41.1	15.4	2.7
1976	13.8	7.0	2.0	11.2	5.4	2.1	11.6	6.8	1.7	39.3	16.9	2.3
1975	14.7	7.8	1.9	12.4	6.2	2.0	12.1	7.5	1.6	39.4	17.9	2.2
1974	10.4	5.0	2.1	7.3	3.5	2.1	8.7	5.0	1.7	34.9	14.0	2.5
1973	9.3	4.3	2.2	5.9	2.9	2.0	8.5	4.3	2.0	31.4	12.6	2.5
1972	10.4	5.1	2.0	7.0	3.6	1.9	9.0	4.9	1.8	35.4	14.2	2.5

*: 1992 data represent average of first three quarters.

Source: U.S. Department of Labor, Bureau of Labor Statistics, *Handbook of Labor Statistics*, June 1985, pp. 69, 71 - 73; *Employment and Earnings, August 1992*, Table 5; *Employment Situation: November 1992*.

Reagan-Bush era and 2.36 to 1 afterwards. The inequality index for black women grew from 1.92 to 2.32 during Reagan-Bush. The ratio of black-to-white teenager unemployment averaged 2.27 in the period before Reagan-Bush but 2.47 during the Reagan-Bush years. Thus, the racial disparity in unemployment increased sharply for all black population groups.

Employment and Unemployment Rates in Regions and Places

Tables 21 through 24 contain the most currently available employment and unemployment data for regions and places in 1991. Because the employment situation continued to worsen in 1992, the current situation has changed in many of the regions and places. Nonetheless, these are the best available data to assess how African Americans are faring below the national level.

Table 21 has employment population ratios for the four census regions. The ratios generally declined in each region for the total African-American population and in each of the subgroups in comparison to 1990 levels. The only exception was a very slight increase from 65.1 percent to the 65.3 percent shown in the table for black men in the West. During 1991, the black employment rate for the total population once again was lowest in the Midwest, where only 49.7 percent of the African-American population was employed. The ratio was highest in the West, where 57.6 percent of the population was employed. The black employment population rate in the South was 56.7 percent, and 53.5 percent in the Northeast.

The pattern discussed for the total population holds for African-American men as well. They had their lowest employment rates in the Midwest (55.1 percent) and their highest rate in the West (65.3 percent). Their rate in the South was 62.4 percent and 58.1 percent in the Northeast. The reader can observe the numbers for women and teenagers from this table. We note that for African-American women, the South and West changed positions; otherwise, the pattern held. The South was also the region with the highest employment-to-population ratio for black teenagers, with the West taking second place. However the Northeast replaced the Midwest as the region with the lowest employment rate for teenagers. In general, the relative position of the regions remained unchanged from the previous year.

The table shows that white employment population rates were higher than black rates for the total population and for each of the subgroups in every region. As the pattern of B/W values shows, inequality for the total population was highest in the Midwest, where blacks were only 76.8 percent as likely as whites to be employed, followed by the Northeast, where they were 87.8 percent as likely. The West and the South tied for the region with the least inequality in employment rates, each having a B/W index of 91.7. The order of inequality from highest to lowest inequality for men was the Midwest, Northeast, South, and West. The order for both women and teenagers from most inequality to least inequality was Midwest, Northeast, West, and

Table 21
Employment Population Ratios by Sex and Race by Regions, 1991

	Total Population			Men (20 Years+)			Women (20 Years+)			Both Sexes (16 to 19 Years)		
	Black	White	B/W	Black	White	B/W	Black	White	B/W	Black	White	B/W
Northeast	53.5	60.9	87.8	58.1	70.0	83.0	49.8	52.7	94.5	18.1	44.0	41.1
Midwest	49.7	64.7	76.8	55.1	73.1	75.4	45.5	56.9	80.0	21.7	53.1	40.9
South	56.7	61.8	91.7	62.4	71.2	87.6	52.1	53.3	97.7	24.2	44.3	54.6
West	57.6	62.8	91.7	65.3	71.7	91.1	50.5	54.1	93.3	22.8	44.7	51.0

Source: U.S. Department of Labor, Bureau of Labor Statistics, *Geographic Profile of Employment and Unemployment: 1991*, August 1992, Table 1.

Table 22
Unemployment Rates by Regions, 1991

	Total Population			Men (20 Years+)			Women (20 Years+)			Both Sexes (16 to 19 Years)		
	Black	White	B/W	Black	White	B/W	Black	White	B/W	Black	White	B/W
Northeast	12.2	6.7	1.821	14.4	7.3	1.973	10.0	6.0	1.667	35.6	16.6	2.145
Midwest	16.3	5.5	2.964	17.8	6.0	2.967	14.8	4.9	3.020	42.7	14.4	2.965
South	11.4	5.6	2.036	11.2	5.7	1.965	11.7	5.4	2.167	34.8	17.0	2.047
West	11.1	6.5	1.708	11.4	6.9	1.652	10.6	6.0	1.767	29.8	18.0	1.656

Source: 'U.S. Department of Labor, Bureau of Labor Statistics, *Geographic Profile of Employment and Unemployment: 1991*, August 1992, Table 1.

South. In general, inequality as measured by the B/W index increased in all regions for the total population and for each subgroup since 1990. The exception again was the West, where the B/W measure improved for the total population, men, and women.

Table 22 displays data on the unemployment rates in the regions for 1991. First, it should be noted that the unemployment rate was uniformly higher for the total black population and for all subgroups in each of the regions in comparison to the situation in 1990. It was also higher for all white groups in every region. For the total African-American population, the unemployment rate was highest in the Midwest at 16.3 percent; it was followed, in order, by the Northeast (12.2 percent), the South (11.4 percent), and the West (11.1 percent). The unemployment rate was also highest for each black subgroup in the Midwest. It was 17.8 percent for men, 14.8 percent for women, and 42.7 percent for teenagers. It is interesting to note that the Midwest had the lowest unemployment rates for whites in 1991. Black men had their lowest unemployment rate in the South; even so, it was still 11.2 percent. Their unemployment rate in the West was 11.4 percent and 14.4 percent in the Northeast. For African-American women, the unemployment rate was lowest in the Northeast at 10.0 percent, followed by the West at 10.6, percent and the South at 11.7 percent. Black teenagers did best in the West, where their unemployment rate was 29.8 percent, followed by the South (34.8 percent), and the Northeast (35.6 percent).

Although unemployment remained highest in the Midwest during 1991 for all black groups, between 1990 and 1991, unemployment increased most in percentage and absolute terms in the Northeast and the West. For the total African-American population, the unemployment rate in the Northeast increased by 2.4 percentage points, or 24 percent, over the 1990 rate; in the West, the unemployment rate increased by 1.5 percentage points, or 16 percent. The increase in the Midwest was 1.2 percentage points, or 8 percent, while the increase was six-tenths of 1 percentage point, or 6 percent, in the South. Unemployment increased by 21 percent, 30 percent, and 25 percent, respectively, for black men, women, and teenagers in the Northeast, and by 12 percent, 19 percent, and 21 percent, respectively, for the corresponding groups in the West. In the Midwest, the rates increased by only 8 percent, 9 percent, and 14 percent, respectively, for black men, women, and teenagers. Their rates increased least in the South—7 percent, 5 percent, and 15 percent, respectively.

As can be seen from Table 22, the greatest inequality existed in the Midwest, where all black categories had almost three times the unemployment rates of the corresponding white groups. The B/W indexes in the Midwest ranged from 2.964 to 3.020. Inequality in the Midwest was also greatest for adults, with adult females experiencing slightly more inequality than adult males. The South generally had the next highest level of inequality as measured by B/W, with the index ranging from 1.965 for adult males to 2.167 for adult females. The Northeast was generally the next most unequal region except for females. The B/W index ranged from 1.667 for females to 2.145 for teenagers. In general, the West had the least inequality: the B/W index ranged from 1.652 for men to 1.767 for women. It is noteworthy that women experienced the highest levels of inequality in every region except the Northeast.

We conclude by noting that the relative degree of inequality as measured by the B/W index declined during 1991 for all categories in every region. This decline was caused by the unemployment rate for blacks rising relatively slower than that for whites. However, in most categories, the absolute increase in the unemployment rate for blacks was higher in each region. In general, this pattern suggests that black unemployment will worsen in each region in absolute and relative terms for the next couple of years.

Tables 23 and 24 contain data on the employment situation in selected large places with significant numbers of African Americans. We note that Minneapolis-St. Paul, MN, and Rochester, NY, are new additions to the list, while San Francisco and Sacramento, CA, have left the list. As Table 23 illustrates, black employment rates ranged from a high of 75.8 percent in Hartford to a low of 38.4 percent in Buffalo-Niagara Falls, which was the only place in which the black employment-population ratio was under 40 percent. Blacks had nine places in which the employment-population ratio was less than 50 percent and 20 places in which it was less than 55 percent. On the other hand, there are only six places with ratios above 65 percent. As has been the case in recent years, blacks have their lowest employment rates in the large metropolitan areas of the Northeast and the industrial heartland in the Midwest. Blacks fared best generally in the moderate-size areas of the West and the South.

In most places, blacks had lower employment-population ratios than whites. The average on the list is 56.3 percent for blacks and 64.2 percent for whites. Whites had no places with an employment-population ratio less than 50 percent and only two with less than 55 percent (New York and Ft. Lauderdale). At the other end, the white employment-to-population ratio was higher than 65 percent in 18 places.

As indicated by the B/W value of less than 1, African Americans generally had lower employment-to-population ratios than did whites in most places. The index ranged from a low of 0.653 in Buffalo-Niagara Falls to a high of 1.175 in Hartford. There were six places for which the index was under 0.75, 11 places between 0.75 and 0.85, another 14 places between 0.85 and 0.95, and seven between 0.95 and 1.0. Blacks had higher employment rates than whites in only five of the 43 places listed.

The employment picture in places worsened somewhat during the course of the year. However, the pattern was not uniform. In the 41 places for which

Table 23
Employment-to-Population Ratios for Selected SMSAs
by Race, 1991

Metro Area	Black Emp/Pop Ratio	White Emp/Pop Ratio	B/W
Hartford, CT	75.8	64.5	1.175
Phoenix, AZ	70.7	64.1	1.103
Seattle, WA	68.7	68.7	1.000
Charlotte, NC	68.0	69.1	0.984
Dallas-Ft. Worth, TX	65.3	72.9	0.896
Kansas City, KS	65.2	68.9	0.946
Washington, DC	64.7	72.3	0.895
Fort Lauderdale, FL	64.4	54.1	1.190
Atlanta, GA	63.8	71.3	0.895
Norfolk, VA	63.6	66.7	0.954
Denver-Boulder, CO	63.2	71.6	0.883
Louisville, KY	60.9	64.4	0.946
Houston, TX	60.6	68.4	0.886
Bergen-Passaic, NJ	60.1	61.7	0.974
Newark, NJ	59.4	62.5	0.950
Nassau-Suffolk, NY	59.3	60.9	0.974
Tampa-St. Petersburg, FL	58.9	57.9	1.017
San Antonio, TX	58.2	57.1	1.019
Baltimore, MD	57.7	66.3	0.870
Riverside, CA	57.2	57.6	0.993
Rochester, NY	57.1	66.7	0.856
Minneapolis-St. Paul, MN	56.5	73.8	0.766
Columbus, OH	55.6	67.1	0.829
Memphis, TN	53.7	63.3	0.848
Los Angeles, CA	53.3	61.8	0.862
Cleveland, OH	53.1	59.9	0.886
Miami, FL	52.5	60.7	0.865
Pittsburgh, PA	52.4	55.8	0.939
Dayton, OH	51.9	62.1	0.836
Oakland, CA	51.6	65.3	0.790
Cincinnati, OH	51.5	67.2	0.766
Philadelphia, PA	50.9	62.2	0.818
St. Louis, MO	50.3	63.1	0.797
New York, NY	50.2	53.5	0.938
Indianapolis, IN	49.6	67.3	0.737
Boston, MA	49.3	64.1	0.769
New Orleans, LA	49.0	62.8	0.780
Milwaukee, WI	48.9	69.1	0.708
Providence, RI	46.7	61.5	0.759
Chicago, IL	46.3	66.9	0.692
Oklahoma City, OK	43.8	64.7	0.677
Detroit, MI	42.6	62.1	0.686
Buffalo-Niagara Falls, NY	38.4	58.8	0.653

Source: U.S. Department of Labor, Bureau of Labor Statistics, *Geographic Profile of Employment and Unemployment: 1991*, Table 23.

Table 24
Unemployment Rates for Selected SMSAs
by Race, 1991

Metro Area	Black	White	B/W
Phoenix, AZ	4.6	5.7	0.807
Bergen-Passaic, NJ	5.0	6.1	0.820
Hartford, CT	7.0	7.8	0.897
Washington, DC	8.0	3.7	2.162
Denver-Boulder, CO	8.3	3.9	2.128
Atlanta, GA	8.4	3.5	2.400
Seattle, WA	8.7	4.6	1.891
Columbus, OH	8.8	4.0	2.200
Charlotte, NC	9.8	4.7	2.085
Dallas-Ft. Worth, TX	9.8	4.8	2.042
San Antonio, TX	9.9	8.0	1.238
Indianapolis, IN	10.1	4.6	2.196
Norfolk, VA	10.1	5.3	1.906
Minneapolis-St. Paul, MN	10.5	4.8	2.188
New York, NY	10.5	7.6	1.382
Houston, TX	11.0	4.5	2.444
Louisville, KY	11.1	4.3	2.581
Los Angeles, CA	11.1	8.2	1.354
Riverside, CA	11.1	9.4	1.181
Miami, FL	11.2	7.4	1.514
Dayton, OH	11.9	5.7	2.088
New Orleans, LA	12.0	3.9	3.077
Kansas City, KS	12.2	5.4	2.259
Baltimore, MD	12.2	4.6	2.652
Nassau-Suffolk, NY	12.3	6.0	2.050
Cleveland, OH	12.5	4.9	2.551
Pittsburgh, PA	12.5	6.2	2.016
Newark, NJ	12.5	6.0	2.083
Oakland, CA	13.8	7.1	1.944
Tampa-St. Petersburg, FL	14.0	6.6	2.121
Buffalo-Niagara Falls, NY	14.2	6.6	2.152
Philadelphia, PA	14.3	5.0	2.860
Fort Lauderdale, FL	14.6	7.5	1.947
Memphis, TN	15.4	5.0	3.080
Cincinnati, OH	16.6	4.8	3.458
Oklahoma City, OK	16.6	5.1	3.255
Boston, MA	17.0	7.8	2.179
St. Louis, MO	17.6	5.6	3.143
Chicago, IL	18.3	5.3	3.453
Milwaukee, WI	20.1	3.6	5.583
Rochester, NY	20.7	5.4	3.833
Providence, RI	22.0	8.6	2.558
Detroit, MI	22.3	7.2	3.097

Source: U.S. Department of Labor, Bureau of Labor Statistics, *Geographic Profile of Employment and Unemployment: 1991*, Table 23.

1990 data were available, the employment-population ratio for blacks increased in 17 places, decreased in 23 places, and remained the same in the other place. Inequality was also up between 1990 and 1991 in more places than it was down as measured by the B/W indicator: it fell in 26 places and rose in 16 places.

Table 24 contains the data on the unemployment rate for places. As can be seen, black unemployment rates ranged from a low of 4.6 percent in Phoenix to a high of 22.3 percent in Detroit—one of four places in which the black unemployment rate was over 20 percent. There were 13 places in which the unemployment rate was greater than 14 percent, and 19 additional places in which it was between 10 and 14 percent. On the other hand, there were only four places with rates of 8 percent or lower. As has been the case recently, blacks had their highest unemployment rates in the large older metropolitan areas in the industrial heartland in the Northeast and Midwest. Blacks fared best generally in the newer, more moderate-size economically diverse areas of the West and the South.

In most places, blacks had higher unemployment rates than whites. The average of the rates was 12.6 percent for blacks and 5.7 percent for whites. Whites have no places with an unemployment rate greater than 10 percent and only four with rates of at least 8 percent. At the other end, the white unemployment rate was less than 6 percent in 28 places.

As indicated by a value of B/W greater than 1, African Americans generally had higher unemployment rates than whites in most places. The B/W index ranged from a low of 0.807 in Phoenix to a high of 5.583 in Milwaukee. The Milwaukee B/W indicates that African Americans in that city were at least five times more likely than whites to be unemployed. Besides Phoenix, there were two other places on the list for which the B/W index was under 1.0, nine places for which it was between 1.0 and 2.0, another 22 places between 2.0 and 3.0, and nine places over 3.0. Blacks had lower unemployment rates than whites in only three of the 43 places listed.

The unemployment picture in places worsened somewhat during the course of the year. However, the pattern was not uniform. In the 41 places for which 1990 data were available, the unemployment rate for blacks increased in 25 places and decreased in the other 16. Inequality in unemployment as measured by the B/W indicator went down between 1990 and 1991 in more places than it rose: fell in 29, increased in 12. This phenomenon was caused by higher relative increases or lower relative declines in white unemployment rates. Obviously, however, the data in Table 24 and the above discussion make it clear that inequality in unemployment was still rampant in most places.

Occupational Distributions

Table 25 contains the latest data on the distribution of employed blacks and whites across major occupational groups. In addition to the persisting unemployment and employment disadvantages, the table illustrates the persistence of occupational disadvantages as well at the end of the Reagan-Bush era. It should also be noted that the black disadvantage is understated by the fact that the broad occupational categories included some very disparate groupings. For example, the sales category includes cashiers at

Table 25
Occupational Percent Distribution of Employed Workers, 1991

	Male			Female		
	Black	White	B/W	Black	White	B/W
Exec., Admin., & Managerial	7.2	14.7	0.49	7.2	12	0.60
Professional Specialty	6.7	12.6	0.53	11.5	16.1	0.71
Technicians & Related						
Support	2.3	3	0.77	3.4	3.5	0.97
Sales Occupations	6.2	11.8	0.53	9.4	13.3	0.71
Administrative Support	8.9	5.4	1.65	26.3	27.9	0.94
Private Household	0.1	-	NA	2.7	1.3	2.08
Protective Service	4.6	2.6	1.77	1.3	0.5	2.60
Other Service	14.2	6.4	2.22	23.6	14.8	1.59
Precision Pro., Craft, & Repair	15.2	19.5	0.78	2.2	2.1	1.05
Mach. Operators, Assem., &						
Inspectors	10	7	1.43	9.2	5.2	1.77
Trans. and Material Movers	11.9	6.6	1.80	1.1	0.8	1.38
Handlers, Cleaners, Helpers,						
Laborers	9.4	5.7	1.65	1.9	1.5	1.27
Farming, Forestry, & Fishing	3.5	4.7	0.74	0.3	1.2	0.25

Note: Data are not shown where base is less than 35,000. NA means not applicable.

Source: U. S. Department of Labor, Bureau of Labor Statistics, *Employment and Earnings, January 1992*, Table 21.

discount stores in the same broad grouping as high-powered industry representatives. The pay and conditions of work vary widely among these occupations, and blacks tended to be concentrated in the least desirable subgroups in each broad category.

In any case, as can be seen from the data, blacks were underrepresented in the most desirable occupations and overrepresented in the less desirable occupations. Black males were only about half as likely as white men to be employed in three top groups—Executive, Administrative, and Managerial; Professional and Related Specialties; and Sales Occupations. Black women were between 60 percent and 71 percent as likely as white women to be employed in these occupations. Black men were also only about three-fourths as likely to be employed in Technicians and Related Support, or Precision Production, Craft, and Repair occupations. Black men were more likely to be employed in all of the other occupations except farming. These other occupations tended to be lower paying, dirtier, riskier, more subservient, or otherwise less desirable. Black women were also overrepresented in the least desirable categories, as can be derived from examining the table.

The underrepresentation of black males in good jobs resulted in an aggregate gap of 1.412 million good jobs:

- 441,000   managerial job gap;
- 347,000   professional job gap;
- 42,000   technician job gap;
- 329,000   sales job gap; and
- 253,000   craftsman job gap.

The gap for black women was about 897,000 good jobs:

- 287,000   managerial jobs;
- 275,000   professional jobs;
- 6,000   technician jobs;
- 233,000   sales jobs; and
- 96,000   administrative support jobs.

Combining the estimates for men and women yielded a total gap for African Americans of 2,309,000 good jobs.

Trends in Earnings and Wage Rates

The impact of the poor occupational distributions and the widespread employment and unemployment rates are reflected in lower earnings and wage rates. The last three tables provide information on trends in earnings and wage rates during the Reagan-Bush era. Table 26 contains data on the median weekly earnings of full-time wage and salary workers. These data were close to weekly wages; they were not available for blacks prior to 1979. Thus, the information in this form is available only for the last two years of the Reagan-Bush period.

However, the table does show trends during the entire Reagan-Bush period. It indicates that wages generally declined for black and white males and rose for black and white females. Black males had weekly wages of $374

Table 26
Median Weekly Earnings of Full-time Wage and Salary Workers
by Race and Sex, 1979-1991
(1991 Dollars)

Year	Both Sexes			Males			Females		
	Black	White	B/W	Black	White	B/W	Black	White	B/W
1991	$348	446	0.78	374	09	0.73	323	374	0.86
1990	343	445	0.77	375	518	0.72	321	370	0.87
1989	350	449	0.78	382	529	0.72	331	367	0.90
1988	362	454	0.80	400	535	0.75	332	366	0.91
1987	361	459	0.79	391	540	0.72	330	368	0.90
1986	362	460	0.79	396	538	0.73	326	366	0.89
1985	350	450	0.78	385	528	0.73	319	356	0.90
1984	348	445	0.78	399	529	0.76	318	346	0.92
1983	349	435	0.80	405	537	0.75	313	344	0.91
1982	345	429	0.80	390	522	0.75	299	339	0.88
1981	349	433	0.81	391	522	0.75	302	325	0.93
1980	339	433	0.78	402	523	0.77	300	332	0.90
1979	373	462	0.81	442	560	0.75	309	337	0.92

Source: U.S. Department of Labor, Bureau of Labor Statistics, *Handbook of Labor Statistics, June 1985*, p. 94; *Employment and Earnings, January 1986-1991*, Table 54.

during 1991. This wage has been declining since 1988 and was substantially lower than the median wage for black males when the Reagan-Bush era started. The wages for black females increased slowly during the Reagan-Bush years. That wage during 1991 was $323, up from the wages prevailing at the start of the Reagan-Bush period. The wage gains for females offset the losses for males so that the median wage for the total African-American population was about the same at the end of Reagan-Bush as it was at the beginning in 1981.

It is apparent from the table that white workers received higher wages than black workers. While blacks had median earnings of $348 in 1991, the median wage for the white population was $446. As the B/W index shows, black male median weekly earnings were only about 73 percent of the white male weekly earnings. Black female median wages were about 86 percent of white female median weekly wages. Assuming that the differences between the mean earnings of blacks and whites were at least as large as the differences in median earnings, we estimate that black males working full-time for wages or salaries lost about $34 billion, and black females lost about $11 billion. The combined losses due to lower weekly wages for full-time workers were at least $45 billion annually.

B/W ratios for males, females, and the total population declined during the Reagan-Bush era. The B/W ratio for males fell about 2 to 3 percentage points. The female B/W index declined more, by about 5 to 7 percentage points. For the total population, the B/W was in the range of 0.77 to 0.78 at the end of the period, and was in the 0.80 to 0.81 range at the beginning of the period. Thus, racial inequality in wage rates appears to have increased during the Reagan-Bush era.

Table 27 provides information on the proportion of the population that worked year-round full-time. This information helps to place the full-time wage data in context. It is apparent from the table that black males were much less likely to work full-time year-round than were white males. In 1991, only 40.57 percent of black males worked year-round full-time compared to 52.55 percent of white males. According to the B/W index, black males were about 77.2 percent as likely as white males to work full-time year-round. On the other hand, black females were slightly more than white females to work year-round full-time during 1991. As can be seen, 32.62 percent of black women versus 31.89 percent of white women worked year-round full-time.

As can be seen from the last two rows of this table, the proportion of both black and white males working full-time averaged slightly higher during the Reagan-Bush period. However, the average inequality for males also improved, albeit the changes for males were very small.

Both female groups increased their proportions working full-time year-round during the Reagan-Bush era. The averages for both black and white

194

Table 27
Percent of Civilian Non-Institutional Population
Working Year-round Full-time

	Males			Females		
	Blacks	Whites	B/W	Blacks	Whites	B/W
1991	40.57	52.55	77.20	32.62	31.89	102.28
1990	43.31	54.21	79.89	32.32	31.29	103.29
1989	43.76	55.43	78.95	33.25	31.05	107.10
1988	41.88	54.60	76.70	33.81	31.18	108.42
1987	40.84	53.68	76.07	31.21	30.31	102.97
1986	40.56	52.84	76.76	30.29	28.87	104.93
1985	40.49	52.26	77.48	30.45	28.02	108.67
1984	37.75	51.94	72.69	29.90	27.37	109.22
1983	36.55	49.83	73.34	27.68	26.53	104.34
1982	34.11	48.87	69.79	26.68	25.21	105.83
1981	38.57	51.82	74.42	26.02	25.09	103.73
1980	37.74	52.15	72.36	26.13	24.85	105.15
1979	40.03	53.24	75.18	25.33	24.44	103.61
1978	38.02	52.18	72.86	25.22	23.31	108.20
1977	38.25	50.45	75.82	23.71	21.75	109.02
1976	37.31	49.85	74.86	22.52	20.78	108.41
1975	35.88	49.51	72.48	21.97	20.31	108.16
1974	37.99	51.05	74.42	21.15	20.08	105.30
1973	42.76	53.93	79.30	23.00	20.64	111.46
1972	42.13	53.09	79.34	23.89	20.17	118.44
1971	40.93	51.96	78.77	21.63	19.91	108.66
1970	42.35	52.21	81.11	22.17	19.64	112.88
1969	45.11	54.64	82.57	21.87	19.96	109.57
1968	46.47	55.76	83.33	23.00	19.74	116.51
1967	46.30	56.07	82.57	22.99	19.65	117.01
Reagan-Bush	39.85	52.55	75.75	30.38	28.80	105.52
Pre-Reagan-Bush	39.40	51.78	76.05	23.34	21.44	109.03

Source: U.S. Department of Commerce, Bureau of the Census, *Money Income of Households, Families, and Persons in the United States: 1991,* Current Population Reports, Series P-60, No. 180, U.S. Government Printing Office, Washington, DC, 1992, Tables B-14 and B-17.

women increased substantially. For black females, the gain was from 23.34 percent to 30.38 percent; for white females, it was from 21.44 percent to 28.80 percent. Black women lost much of the advantage they had in full-time year-round work at the beginning of the Reagan-Bush period. The B/W index averaged 105.52 for women during the Reagan-Bush years, and 109.03 in the years preceding that period. We should note that the averages understate both the gains for women and the decline in the black woman advantage. The employment rates for black and white women exceeded the Reagan-Bush average at the end of the period, while the B/W index was lower than the period average.

Finally, Table 28 shows the median annual earnings for full-time year-round workers for the last 24 years. The median earnings of black males who worked year-round full-time inched up slightly in 1991; this small improvement ended three straight years of falling earnings for them. White male earnings had also been falling off since 1986; they increased slightly during 1991. Earnings continued to decline during 1991 for both black and white females.

At the end of the period, these data show that black males and females had lower median annual earnings than did whites. Black males received only $22,075 compared to $30,266 for white males. Black females also continued to earn less than white females, with median annual earnings of $18,270 compared to $20,794 for white females.

Average median annual earnings for both male groups were slightly lower than during the period before Reagan-Bush. However, it should be noted that both groups had income gains during this period, and neither group made any gains during the Reagan-Bush era. Moreover, wages during the Reagan-Bush period for both male groups were generally lower than in the latter half of the preceding era. Thus, it is accurate to say that males lost ground during the last 12 years. Racial inequality for males, although averaging slightly lower than in the pre-Reagan-Bush period, was also up relative to the latter half of the earlier period.

Average median earnings were significantly higher for both female groups during the Reagan-Bush years. The gains for black women were much smaller than they were in the immediately preceding period. Median income of black women working full-time year-round increased by 27 percent in the period before Reagan-Bush and increased by only 6 percent during the Reagan-Bush years. The corresponding increases for white women were 6 percent during the period before Reagan-Bush and 11.4 percent during the Reagan-Bush era. Thus, black women made substantial gains in reducing earnings inequality during the period before Reagan-Bush and lost ground during the Reagan-Bush years. The B/W index for females declined significantly during the Reagan-Bush era.

CONCLUSIONS

The review of the trends in African-American economic status shows that after 12 years of Reagan-Bush policies, extensive racial inequality persists

Table 28
Median Annual Income of Year-round Full-time Workers

	Males			Females		
	Black	White	B/W	Black	White	B/W
1991	$22,075	$30,266	72.94%	$18,720	$20,794	90.03%
1990	22,002	30,096	73.11	18,799	20,892	89.98
1989	22,436	31,349	71.57	19,100	20,784	91.90
1988	23,453	31,348	74.81	19,040	20,515	92.81
1987	22,927	31,807	72.08	18,885	20,472	92.25
1986	22,790	32,219	70.73	18,310	20,408	89.72
1985	22,125	31,723	69.74	18,111	19,995	90.58
1984	21,808	31,411	69.43	17,985	19,537	92.06
1983	22,089	30,655	72.06	17,353	19,235	90.22
1982	22,087	30,776	71.77	17,284	18,749	92.19
1981	22,262	31,300	71.12	16,929	18,303	92.49
1980	22,419	31,703	70.72	17,661	18,663	94.63
1979	23,261	32,033	72.62	17,345	18,829	92.12
1978	24,907	32,274	77.17	17,799	19,018	93.59
1977	22,510	32,455	69.36	17,450	18,689	93.37
1976	23,186	31,672	73.21	17,541	18,697	93.82
1975	23,525	31,636	74.36	17,539	18,208	96.33
1974	22,878	31,801	71.94	17,223	18,422	93.49
1973	22,738	33,230	68.43	15,833	18,566	85.28
1972	22,396	32,495	68.92	15,789	18,399	85.81
1971	21,075	30,523	69.05	15,845	17,858	88.73
1970	21,001	30,416	69.05	14,665	17,848	82.17
1969	20,326	30,199	67.31	13,859	17,554	78.95
1968	19,198	28,432	67.52	12,598	16,546	76.14
1967	17,924	27,750	64.59	11,984	16,055	74.64
Reagan-Bush	22,369	31,177	71.76	18,229	19,971	91.29
Pre-Reagan-Bush	22,718	31,840	71.35	16,790	18,472	90.85

Source: U.S. Department of Commerce, Bureau of the Census, *Money Income of Households, Families, and Persons in the United States: 1991*, Current Population Reports, Series P-60, No. 180, U.S. Government Printing Office, Washington, DC, 1992, Tables B-14 and B-17.

throughout the American economy. Whether we reviewed data on income, jobs, or wealth, we found the gaps remained very large at the end of the Reagan-Bush period. We also found very few areas in which African Americans made any substantial progress.

This poor record of progress against racial inequalities certainly suggests that the strategy followed during the past 12 years was lacking. The Reagan-Bush approach appeared to rely on a color-blind approach to policy with an emphasis on market processes and individual action. Indeed, there was no significant attempt to address explicitly the problem of racial inequality. In fact, many of the strategies aimed explicitly at reducing racial inequality from the period before Presidents Reagan and Bush were abandoned or emasculated. For example, the equal opportunity enforcement effort abandoned the class-action approach, while civil rights agencies became guardians against so-called reverse discrimination.

Although it is apparent that the black population lacked the internal wealth and controls to achieve equality through internal efforts alone, so-called self-help efforts were widely advocated by Reagan-Bush supporters. However, no policies were advocated or developed to create the internal resources to make the self-help strategy a realistic option.

Now at the beginning of a new administration, the African-American population can only hope that the Clinton-Gore administration will accord a higher priority to resolving its problems. Racial inequality derives from the history of racism in this country. As we have indicated, the historical pattern of slavery, Jim Crowism, and discrimination not only impacted the generation against which these practices were directed but also continues to impact their descendants because it reduced their inheritances of human and nonhuman wealth. The tremendous wealth gaps discussed earlier were a direct consequence of the earlier pattern of racism. Moreover, once they were established, they were automatically self-perpetuated by the workings of the market.

The wealth disparities are the primary reason for the inability of blacks to overcome racial inequality on their own. The wealth gaps have the direct impact of lowering black earnings and an indirect impact of creating dependency and vulnerability to discrimination. This is why we have stressed the importance of eliminating the very large wealth gaps in the previous editions of this paper. A permanent solution to the problem of racial inequality cannot be achieved as long as the current wealth ownership disparities persist. The high rate of unemployment and poverty, the low levels of income, the restricted occupations, and many other problems are symptoms or consequences of the underlying problem of limited ownership.

We hope that the Clinton-Gore team will pay some attention to the problem of racial inequality. If it does, we hope it will not devote all of its time to treating the symptoms rather than the underlying cause of the persistence of racial inequality. General policies to promote national economic recovery are fine. However, history teaches us that recovery by itself will not resolve the underlying problem of racial inequality. During a recovery, all boats may rise, but the black boat will remain a small canoe next to the white yacht. The swings in the black economic status attributable to the stages of the business cycle are only a few percentage points. General policies will not result in secular improvements for the black population.

We hope Bill Clinton will take a close look at policies to build parity in wealth ownership. Only when blacks own enough to be equal participants in the nation's economy will they be able to ensure their own prosperity and equality. If Clinton-Gore do not choose to call such policies reparations, that is fine. We warn, however, that the magnitude of capital infusions necessary is very large. A 20-year program to build systematically ownership among blacks investing $50 billion per year would be a minimal program. We note that since blacks are a part of this society, this would not be a social cost but merely a social transfer. In any case, in the absence of a meaningful effort to address the ownership disparities, blacks will be no better off at the end of the Clinton-Gore administration than they are now at the end of the Reagan-Bush era.

* * *

The author thanks Ms. Patricia Chaffin for her expert and helpful research assistance. My secretary, Ms. Bridgett Jones, deserves a special thanks for her diligent efforts in producing the final manuscript and tables. The author assumes sole responsibility for the contents and opinions expressed in this paper.

REFERENCES

Swinton, David H. 1992. "The Economic Status of African Americans: Limited Ownership and Persistent Inequality," *The State of Black America 1992*, ed. Billy J. Tidwell. New York: National Urban League, Inc.

_____. 1991. "The Economic Status of African Americans: 'Permanent' Poverty and Inequality," *The State of Black America 1991*, ed. Janet Dewart. New York: National Urban League, Inc.

_____. 1989. "Economic Status of Black Americans," *The State of Black America 1989*, ed. Janet Dewart. New York: National Urban League, Inc.

_____. 1989. "Racial Parity under Laissez Faire: An Impossible Dream," *Race: Twentieth Century Dilemmas—Twenty-First Century Prognoses*, ed. Winston A. Van Horne. Madison: The University of Wisconsin System.

U.S. Department of Commerce, Bureau of the Census. 1992. *Money Income of Households, Families, and Persons in the United States: 1991*. Washington, DC: U.S. Government Printing Office.

_____. 1992. *Money Income and Poverty Status in the United States: 1991*. Washington, DC: U.S. Government Printing Office.

_____. 1992, *Poverty in the United States: 1991*. Washington, DC: U.S. Government Printing Office.

_____. 1990. *Household Wealth and Asset Ownership: 1988*. Washington, DC: U.S. Government Printing Office.

_____. 1990. *The Statistical Abstract of the United States, 1990*. Washington, DC: U.S. Government Printing Office.

_____. 1987. *Survey of Minority-Owned Businesses: Black, 1987*. Washington, DC: U.S. Government Printing Office.

U.S. Department of Labor, Census Bureau. 1992. *Employment and Earnings, January, August, and October 1992*. Washington, DC: U.S. Government Printing Office.

_____. 1992. *Employment Situation: November 1992*. Washington, DC: U.S. Government Printing Office.

_____. 1992. *Geographic Profile of Employment and Unemployment: 1991*. Washington, DC: U.S. Government Printing Office.

_____. 1985. *Handbook of Labor Statistics, June 1985*. Washington, DC: U.S. Government Printing Office.

CASE STUDIES

The preceding articles elucidate some of the serious problems facing Black America in the 1990s and recommend progressive public policy initiatives to alleviate them. At the same time, we have stressed the need for African Americans to be more reflective, resolute, and resourceful concerning their own development and preparation to meet the challenges ahead.

The point is made with keen awareness of the many laudable self-development efforts being pursued by African-American organizations, groups, and communities around the country. The case studies that follow represent just two examples of the kinds of community-based, self-development activities and programs that might be multiplied and reinforced to realize more far-reaching benefits.

Programs for Progress and Empowerment: The Urban League's National Education Initiative

Michael B. Webb, Ed.D.

INTRODUCTION

Throughout its more than 80-year history, the National Urban League has recognized the important role of education in the economic and social development of all citizens. In 1985, the Urban League Movement confronted the realization that the nation's progress toward assuring educational excellence for all African-American children had stalled.

It was not that this progress had yielded results of which the nation could be proud. Indeed, the growing tide of mediocre student outcomes chronicled within the pages of a plethora of national reports did not even begin to address the lack of development of those most underserved by public education, particularly African Americans, Latinos, and the poor.

Rather, it was becoming increasingly clear among African Americans that for the first time in generations, children were unlikely to surpass their parents' educational attainments. The evidence was compelling and urgently demanded a response.

Not only were college-going rates among African Americans in decline, but also ever-increasing numbers of students were abandoning the classroom altogether. Moreover, children and youth were becoming more engaged in other behaviors that threatened to consign them to poverty, such as early childbearing and illicit drug use.

HOW HAS THE NATIONAL URBAN LEAGUE RESPONDED?

Faced with these alarming trends, the Urban League Movement recognized that individual, local efforts alone would be inadequate. What was needed was an all-out effort to develop African-American children. The Urban League's **National Education Initiative** (NEI) was born as a result of this realization.

During the 1985 National Urban League Conference, the Delegate Assembly—comprising representatives of 114 local affiliates—adopted a resolution "to develop and support a Movement-wide program that would involve every Urban League affiliate." While the resolution went on to recognize that a single national model approach would not work in a movement comprising 114 local affiliates of varying resources and capacities, each affiliate was challenged to organize its programs and services in accordance with its situation.

The resolution further called upon affiliates to make a measurable difference in the educational achievement of African-American students who predominantly attend the nation's public schools.[1]

ORGANIZATION OF NEI

The Delegate Assembly directed the Urban League Movement to implement NEI programs in every League city by September 1986. It was determined that although each affiliate's education intervention strategies would differ according to local needs and resources, certain essential elements should be included in all NEI programs:

- a written plan
- provisions for parent/adult involvement
- identified target groups
- measurable objectives and a system for collecting and reporting data
- a five-year time frame

Seven program areas were targeted for action: (1) tutoring, enrichment, and test preparation; (2) guidance and counseling; (3) parent involvement; (4) coalition-building among parents, schools, and community; (5) cultural enrichment; (6) early childhood development; and (7) mathematics, science, and technological literacy. What bound these program areas together was that, collectively, they would constitute the services, interventions, and framework required to ensure that all students would progress toward academic excellence, regardless of their economic or social circumstances.

LEVEL OF AFFILIATE INVOLVEMENT IN NEI

A midpoint assessment of NEI conducted in 1988 revealed that of the 107 affiliates responding, 87 had fully operational programs.[2] The remaining 20 affiliates, while not conducting fully operational programs, were engaged at some level of implementation. Three years later, all affiliates reported conducting NEI programs. NEI represented the first time that the Urban League Movement had committed itself to one education initiative.

According to the 1990 census, approximately 10 million African Americans were 18 years of age or younger. Affiliates report that, together, their education programs serve slightly more than 300,000 students and parents. While this number does not take into account the indirect impact of Urban

League programs and services (for example, impact on families and peers of participating students), clearly, NEI has reached only a small number of the target population. In order to broaden the impact of NEI, affiliates have increasingly turned to strategies to change local education policies.

WHO IS INVOLVED IN NEI PROGRAMS AND ACTIVITIES?

NEI was conceived as an initiative to focus on public school students in grades pre-K through 12 and their parents or guardians. Table 1 presents an overview of the populations served by affiliate NEI programs, based upon surveys conducted in 1988 and 1991.

Table 1
Percent of Populations Served by Affiliate Programs,
1991 and 1988 Surveys

TARGET POPULATION	1991: 150 ANSWERS FROM 28 AFFILIATES	1988: 704 ANSWERS FROM 76 AFFILIATES
Elementary/Middle School Students	31%	35%
High School/Higher Education Students	36	29
Adults/Parents	22	14
School Professionals	7	16
Community-Based Organizations	4	6

As one can see from Table 1, it is likely that significant shifts have occurred in the target population of Urban League NEI programs.[3] Programs increasingly target high school and college students and parents. The data suggest that the percentage of programs targeting elementary/middle school students and school professionals has declined. This shift would mirror trends in society at large.

For example, the African-American adolescent population today faces an unparalleled crisis. Among African-American adolescents and teens, dramatic increases in the incarceration rate (especially among males), escalating violence, lack of employment opportunities, and vulnerability to disease and chronic health problems are factors that have necessitated emergency action, particularly on the part of frontline community-based organizations.

Another trend has to do with new and concerted efforts to involve parents and guardians, and particularly those from low-income backgrounds, in education. Research and practice in the last several years have emphasized the importance of the parental or guardian role in student success. Indeed, recent legislation has reflected this emphasis (for example, Chapter 1).

Despite the shifts, significant NEI programming and activities continue to focus on elementary and middle school students.

As Table 2 reflects, more than half of the 315 students who responded to a 1991 survey of 47 Urban League NEI programs (51 percent) had been involved in NEI activities for one year or less.

Table 2
Number of Years Student Participated in NEI,
1991 Survey

NUMBER OF YEARS PARTICIPATING	PERCENT (TOTAL = 315)
One Year or Less	51%
Two Years	23
Three Years	11
Four Years	7
Five or More Years	8

Note: Based upon a sample of 47 Urban League affiliates.

The length of time that students spend participating in Urban League programs is often a product of the nature of funding cycles, which tend to be 12 months. The obvious fact is that commitment to long-term and sustained interventions is often compromised by the whims and changing priorities of funding agencies.

ESTEEM, CONFIDENCE, AND EMPOWERMENT

In calling for a national initiative, the Delegate Assembly enjoined students, parents, and other members of African-American communities to take responsibility for the educational destinies of our people. Underlying the spirit of the resolution was a belief that empowerment represents a necessary condition for the educational development of African Americans.

The fragile self-concept of African-American students is a topic that has been much discussed by educators and researchers. Lack of effort in school and involvement in counterproductive or even destructive behaviors have been correlated with African-American students' perceptions of their individual worth and chances for academic success.

As a response, the majority of affiliates have focused on the building of students' and their families' confidence and self-esteem as the philosophical engines to drive programs and activities. These efforts have been predicated on an assumption, validated in educational and psychological research, that self-esteem and confidence are prerequisites for empowerment.

Researchers and educators have long known that a relationship exists among the variables of expectations, self-esteem, and academic achievement. Recent research conducted by the Urban League and the Educational Testing Service on ability grouping is highly suggestive of a link between expectations and performance/behavior. Mathematics classes in six urban school districts were included in the study, *On the Right Track: The Consequences of Mathematics Course Placement Policies and Practices in the Middle Grades.* Students were grouped in these classes based on varying criteria: teacher decision, test scores in math and test scores in two or more subjects. Classroom observations and interviews with parents, students, teachers, and administrators yielded data on how students were grouped for mathematics instruction and the effects of grouping policies on students' attitudes about mathematics.

Students in high-ability classes were found to be the most confident, most positive about math, and were the most likely to report that they were good at math. The converse was true for students in low-ability math classes.

The same study revealed that students in low-ability classes were more likely to be involved in fights, not to care about class, and to feel left out of classroom activities. Nonwhite students were also much more likely to be overrepresented in the low-level math classes. These findings are consistent with other research (see, for example, Braddock, 1989; Oakes, 1985; Slavin, 1987).

The study also found that while students in "low-ability classes spent considerable time on basic arithmetic, high-ability classes were likely to be working on word problems and learning algebra." Level of grouping (i.e., high, medium, and low ability) correlated with the type of interaction between teachers and students, i.e., teacher praise. White students in the low- and high-ability groups experienced more favorable interactions with their teachers.

Expectations of low performance create a "self-fulfilling prophecy." Despite little or no evidence that ability grouping results in higher achievement levels, students are routinely sorted and the message that is communicated by assigning a student to a low-level track is clear: "You are dumb." Traditional expectations about human intelligence—who has it and who doesn't—are in fact, unsubstantiated. The gross products of such beliefs are lack of confidence and self-esteem and a lack of establishment in students of adequate connections between their actions and consequences (Howard and Hammond, 1985).

Low self-esteem and low expectations are actually antecedents for a number of harmful behaviors, including delinquency and acting out, substance abuse, and low achievement (Dryfoos, 1990). Expectations are an insidious predictor of the level of commitment a student will assume toward his or her education.

When students are involved in programs and classes for "academic excellence," they perform much better than when they are involved in programs characterized as "basic," or "remedial" (Black Issues in Higher Education, 1992). It is clear that when students are stigmatized as low achievers, they do not look to their school experiences for esteem; rather, they must look elsewhere (Ogbu, 1974; Steele, 1992).

Today, nearly seven years later, how successful has the education initiative been in empowering students to take responsibility for higher levels of achievement? Several studies have been undertaken by the League's Education and Career Development Cluster over the 1988 to 1992 period to assess the effectiveness of NEI programs and activities. While the studies have targeted only a sample of students and parents participating in NEI programs, they nonetheless present an important indication of the efficacy of Urban League efforts to build student success.

Table 3 presents student participation data from the 1991 survey of a sample of 47 NEI programs. In several areas (math activities, self-esteem, test-taking, after-school homework help), student and parent perceptions of participation differed markedly. This may possibly be explained as a result of parent perception of the type of services that are provided by League affiliates. Parents may assume that the League's affiliates provide more assistance in interpersonal areas (e.g., mentoring, building self-esteem, role models) and less in some of the academic areas because of their perception of the role of the National Urban League.

Table 3
Student Participation in NEI Activities
Student and Parent Perceptions

ACTIVITY	STUDENT SELF-REPORT (N = 315)	PARENT PERCEPTION (N = 141)
Math Activities	44%	34%
Self-esteem	41	49
Test-taking	41	25
Reading	34	36
Career Guidance	32	32
Computers	24	20
Black History	24	28
College Admission/- Financial Aid	21	28
Science	19	19
Mentoring	18	21
Course Selection	16	23

Note: Based on a sample of 47 Urban League affiliates.

More than half (52 percent) of the affiliate education specialists identified student self-esteem building as the kind of help students need. One hundred and twenty-nine of the 315 students responding to the same survey (41 percent) reported participating in self-esteem building activities (e.g., through knowledge of self, efficacy), despite the fact that only 25 percent of the students indicated that they actually needed to build self-esteem.

Table 4 provides parent and student self-reported data on the perceived helpfulness of NEI program activities. Nearly all the students considered their participation helped them to feel good about themselves.

Table 4
Helpfulness of Program Activities,
Student and Parent Perceptions

AREA	STUDENT SELF-REPORT N = 315	PARENT PERCEPTION N = 141
Feeling Good About Themselves	90%	93%
Getting Better Grades	85	87
Getting Better Test Scores	79	79
Getting Along Better With Teacher	71	75
Better School Attendance	75	73
Choosing School Courses	60	62

Note: Based on a sample of 47 Urban League affiliates.

Affiliate assessments of student impact are congruous with the self-reported data included in Table 4: 92 percent of the affiliate education specialists responded that students know themselves better as a result of their participation in NEI programs and activities. Ninety-six percent of the specialists also responded that students participating in their programs have grown academically.

Self-reported responses, summarized in Table 5, indicated ambivalence regarding students' locus of control; that is, how students attributed their success or lack of success. For example, nearly one-third agreed that chance and luck are very important for what happens in their life. However, more than 80 percent responded that their efforts would determine the level of success they experienced in school. Nearly three-fourths of the students reported a high degree of confidence that they could do things as well as other people. This is in contrast with slightly more than half (56 percent) who reported that "every time I try to get ahead, something or somebody stops me."

While the reasons for this ambivalence are unclear, one possible reason may be a lack of congruity between messages students received as a result of the participation in Urban League programs and the level of reinforcement they received in their school, community, or home. Students may not experience elsewhere the same level of support and encouragement for success that they experience from interacting with Urban League staff and their peers participating in the program.

Table 5
Student Sense of Power and Self-Confidence

	AGREE (of 315)	DISAGREE (of 315)
Chance and luck are very important for what happens in my life	32%	39%
Every time I try to get ahead something or somebody stops me	24	56
I am able to do things as well as most other people	74	12
If I go to school every day, pay attention in class and apply myself, I can succeed in school	83	13

Note: Based on a sample selected from 47 Urban League affiliates. Does not include percent of students responding "Don't Know."

ANALYSIS OF STUDENT SURVEY DATA

Written goals of NEI programs typically include a reference to building student self-esteem. Many programs also link self-esteem to knowledge of African-American culture. However, according to a review of descriptions included in the Urban League's *1990-1991 Summary of Affiliate Programs*, only five programs identified student self-esteem as the **major** program goal. An unstated assumption appears to be that the development of student self-esteem will be a product of increased student success or performance in an academic area (e.g., reading, math, or science), on tests, or through better decisionmaking.

In addition to supplementing what students learn in school, Urban League programs provide opportunities for students to experience success. Program staff exhibit high expectations for student success. Most programs are nongraded and almost all programs conduct one or more student recognition events on an annual basis. The goal of student self-esteem was often implicit rather than explicit. This factor may account for the fact that fewer than half (41 percent) the students responding to the 1991 survey reported that they were participating in self-esteem building activities.

Slightly more than half (51 percent) of the affiliate education specialists surveyed identified student self-esteem building as the greatest kind of help needed by students. Only 15 percent of the specialists identified tutoring as the greatest kind of help needed; 10 percent identified guidance in course selection.

The results of the 1988 and 1991 surveys do not reflect the recent, rapid growth of mathematics and science programs since 1990 as part of the second phase of NEI. For example, there are 84 education programs with mathematics and science components across 108 Urban League affiliates.

In conclusion, NEI programs focus explicitly or implicitly on the goal of improved student self-esteem. Students participating in programs and activities overwhelmingly report feeling good about themselves as a result of their participation. They also report better school attendance and getting better grades and test scores.

PARENT EMPOWERMENT INITIATIVES

A recent National PTA report (1992) cites more than 50 major research studies that draw a clear relationship between parent/guardian (PG) involvement and increased student achievement. *The evidence is beyond dispute: parent involvement improves student achievement. When parents are involved, children do better in school, and they go to better schools* (Henderson, 1987).

As community-based organizations, many Urban League affiliates have recognized that successful efforts to involve parents or guardians in education are often the result of programs or services that focus on PG needs—not on the specific needs of their children. Experience shows that parent involvement programs, and especially programs for economically poor PGs, are likely to fail if they are too narrow in focus. For example, a narrow focus on school reform communicates to low-income parents a lack of appreciation for the difficulties in their lives. Parents sometimes view education as a secondary priority as they struggle to maintain basic needs.

An illustration of factors that must be addressed when reaching out to low income parents is provided by a recent Manpower Demonstration Research Corporation (1991) study of a training program involving 930 young mothers who were on welfare and had left school prior to completion:

> On a widely used measure administered at baseline, half of the young women registered scores indicating that they were at risk of a diagnosis of depression, and half of these had scores indicating that they were at high risk of such a diagnosis. Program staff noted that many young women lacked self-confidence.[4]

During two recent Urban League national parent focus group sessions, participants corroborated the importance of personal variables as determinants of a PG's ability to be involved effectively in education. Nine of 42 responses to three questions indicated that PGs' confidence and self-esteem were major determinants in their ability to be involved in their children's education.

Prior to the implementation of NEI, only ten affiliates reported conducting formal parent education programs. Today, approximately 70 affiliates sponsor formal parent education activities. Increased parental involvement in education has been reported as one of the most significant NEI outcomes.

In one respect, however, numbers are an inadequate indicator of the level of affiliates' efforts to involve PGs. In addition to formal parent programs, affiliates often develop relationships with PGs of participating students by sharing information, involving parents as volunteers, and involving them in special and ongoing education activities.

Numerous examples and anecdotes indicate that as grade level increases, PGs become less and less welcome at the schoolhouse door. Far too many educators believe that a parent's job is simply to get the child to school on time.

Fewer than half the 38 school superintendents who responded to a 1991 Urban League survey considered parent participation in school board meetings to be very important (47 percent) or somewhat important (45 percent). Slightly more than half (55 percent) felt that parents should work to promote new state education policies. Superintendents almost unanimously indicated that sending children to school well-rested and well-fed and attending open house and parent-teacher conferences were the most important parent roles.

Based upon the need to focus on the parent/guardian as a whole person before attempting to involve him or her in support of education, many Urban League affiliates have reconceptualized the nature of parent involvement programs. The League and several of its affiliates have designed a series of materials plus training and program development strategies for parent empowerment.

THE BEGINNING: LISTENING TO PARENT/GUARDIAN CONCERNS

New, reconceptualized Urban League PG programs begin with questions, not information. Through the use of nominal or focus groups, small group discussion, personal inventories, and other strategies, affiliate staff attempt to gain a better perspective of the person behind the PG role. Often, PG needs are identified that can be met through linkage to other Urban League programs and services—for example, health, housing, employment, or training—or through referral.

The focus group process was recently introduced as a national strategy to develop local affiliate PG programs. The National Urban League's staff conducted six regional focus groups involving a total of approximately 60 parents.

A series of open-ended questions provided a framework for examining PG perspectives and needs:

- What are the most important things parents need to do to be involved in their children's education?
- Which of these things are parents most likely to do? Why? Which of these things are parents least likely to do? Why?
- What have you found to be the easiest in dealing with teachers and administrators?
- What kinds of problems have you had with teachers and administrators?
- What do you think parents should do to make sure their child has a good school experience?
- What discourages parents from doing these things?

One outcome of the focus groups was trust-building among the participants. Participants did not identify themselves in terms of education or professional affiliation—a factor that diminished status differentiation. In each focus group, participants emerged with a sense of common purpose. Many remarked that "it felt good to be heard," or "I felt that people were really listening to me." Evaluations of the focus group sessions indicated that participants had developed a sense of belonging to something important.

Information from the focus groups was used to make referrals to Urban League and non-Urban League services, and program planning decisions: goals of the program, meeting days and times, and training priorities (e.g., child/PG, teacher/PG communication).

INFORMATION ON WHICH TO ACT

In 1988, the Urban League published *What Students Need to Know*. This manual makes specific recommendations, gives instructions, and provides the necessary how-to's on developing closer collaboration between PGs and schools in order to improve student performance. The manual avoids educational jargon and states explicitly what students need to know and to be able to do for success in school and in the world of work. More than 8,000 copies of the manual have been distributed.

What Students Need to Know also includes information on planning and conducting PG workshops (goals and objectives, format, publicity, agenda, evaluation, etc.), information on tests, and resource materials. The manual has been used as a training tool in more than half the Urban League affiliate PG programs.

Another example of an action manual for training PGs is *Parent Empowerment Training: Meaningful Strategies in Changing Times*, developed by the Urban League of Greater Cincinnati.

ANALYSIS OF PARENT SURVEY DATA

A 1991 survey of 208 parents participating in affiliate programs revealed that:

- Sixty-seven percent believed the Urban League had helped them become partners with the schools.
- Ninety-one percent viewed the Urban League as a partner in education.
- Fifty-four percent responded the Urban League had helped them deal with school-related problems.
- Sixty-one percent reported that the Urban League had helped them understand school plans.

In conclusion, the Urban League has emerged as a leading organization working to enable parents and guardians to contribute effectively to the education of their children. The number of formal PG programs conducted by Urban League affiliates has grown rapidly; these programs have utilized new strategies for reaching parents and families in greatest need.

PGs participating in Urban League programs consistently cite the Urban League as a partner in their efforts to support their children's education.

Eleven parent councils have been established to recruit PGs for Urban League programs and to plan, coordinate, and conduct training activities. In November 1992, the first annual National Parents Council was held in Washington, DC. Approximately 200 parents attended representing affiliates nationwide.

The Urban League will continue to expand its efforts to assess the impact of NEI programs and activities on self-esteem, confidence, and empowerment. The data presented in this paper suggest that NEI has resulted in some early successes.

* * * *

The author wishes to acknowledge the valuable contributions of the staff of the League's Education and Career Development Department—Adrian Lewis, Sydney Lancaster, and Dr. Gwendolyn Rippey—and Dr. John Cardwell of EVAXX in the preparation of this paper.

REFERENCES

Academy for Educational Development. 1991. *Strengthening Education Reform: The Family and the Community.* Washington, DC.

Black Issues in Higher Education. 1992. "Minority Math Scores Higher When Excellence Stressed," June 18.

Braddock, J. 1989. *Tracking of Black, Hispanic, Asian, Native American, and White Students: National Patterns and Trends.* Baltimore: Johns Hopkins University, Center for Research on Effective Schooling for Disadvantaged Students.

Dryfoos, J. 1990. *Adolescents at Risk: Prevalence and Prevention.* New York: Oxford University Press.

Education and Career Development. 1992. *Report to the Delegate Assembly.* New York: National Urban League, Inc.

Education and Career Development. 1991. *Report to the Delegate Assembly.* New York: National Urban League, Inc.

Education and Career Development. 1991. *Summary of Affiliate Programs.* New York: National Urban League, Inc.

Education and Career Development. 1988. *Report to the Delegate Assembly.* New York: National Urban League, Inc.

Education and Career Development. 1988. *What Students Need to Know.* New York: National Urban League, Inc.

Education and Career Development. 1986. *Report to the Delegate Assembly.* New York: National Urban League, Inc.

Ekstrom, R. et al. 1991. *On the Right Track: The Consequences of Mathematics Course Placement Policies and Practices in the Middle Grades.* New York: Educational Testing Service and the National Urban League, Inc.

Henderson, A. 1987. *The Evidence Continues to Grow.* Columbia, MD: National Committee for Citizens in Education.

Howard, J. and Hammond, R. 1985. "Rumors of Inferiority." *The New Republic,* September 9.

LeMelle, W. 1992. *Parents Are Best Hope for Reform of Inner City Schools.* New York: Phelps-Stokes Fund.

National PTA. 1992. *Proceedings: National Parent Involvement Summit.* Chicago.

Oakes, J. 1985. *Keeping Track: How Schools Structure Inequality.* New Haven: Yale University Press.

Ogbu J. 1974. *The Next Generation: The Ethnography of Education in an Urban Neighborhood.* New York: Academic Press.

Quality Education for Minorities Project. 1990. *Education That Works: An Action Plan for the Education of Minorities.* Cambridge, MA: Massachusetts Institute of Technology.

Quint, J., Fink, B., and Rowser, S. 1991. *New Chance: Implementing a Comprehensive Program for Disadvantaged Young Mothers and Their Children.* San Francisco: Manpower Demonstration Research Corporation.

Slavin, R. 1987. *Effects of Ability Grouping on Black, Hispanic, and White Students.* Baltimore: Johns Hopkins University, Center for Research on Elementary and Middle Schools and Center for Research on Effective Schooling of Disadvantaged Students.

Steele, C. 1992. "Race and the Schooling of Black Americans." *The Atlantic Monthly*, April.

Urban League of Greater Cincinnati. 1992. *Parent Empowerment Training: Meaningful Strategies in Changing Times*. Cincinnati: Urban League of Greater Cincinnati.

ENDNOTES

[1] Education and Career Development, *Report to the Delegate Assembly* (New York: National Urban League, Inc., 1986).

[2] Education and Career Development, *Report to the Delegate Assembly* (New York: National Urban League, Inc., 1988).

[3] Because of the relatively small number of affiliates participating in the 1991 survey, results—though suggestive—should be considered inconclusive.

[4] J. Quint, B. Fink, and S. Rowser, *New Chance: Implementing a Comprehensive Program for Disadvantaged Young Mothers and Their Children* (San Francisco: Manpower Demonstration Research Corporation, 1991).

Coordinated Community Empowerment: Experiences of the Urban League of Greater Miami

T. Willard Fair

INTRODUCTION

The first Africans arrived in North America 373 years ago. Since landing in Jamestown, Virginia, in 1619, black Americans have come up the rough side of the mountain, sustained by faith and an indomitable spirit of self-preservation

The first black immigrants came as indentured servants. However, later arrivals were condemned to slavery and the peculiarly American enslavement process. Unlike the European indentured service system and the slave system in South America, American slavery was totally dehumanizing—converting men into brutes; robbing them of every liberty; working them without wages; restricting their relations with their fellow man; beating them with sticks and flogging them with the lash; burning their flesh; loading their limbs with irons; hunting them with dogs; selling them at auctions; and, as if this were not enough, sundering their families.[1]

American slaves were subjected to such dehumanizing experiences in order to effectuate their complete submission and obedience to their white masters. For nearly two and a half centuries, the agricultural economy of the South was nourished by the misery of black slaves who trusted no future and simply acted in the living present.

From 1865 to 1954, despite being declared emancipated, black Americans continued to have their dignity, self-respect, self-worth, and self-confidence undermined by *de jure* and *de facto* segregation. Undergirded by the dogma of white supremacy and the pseudo-religious principle of manifest destiny, Jim Crowism effectively maintained the long-standing master-slave relationship between the races.[2]

The 1954 school desegregation decision, along with subsequent judicial and legislative actions, brought the end of legal, institutionalized, racial subjugation and cruelty. While racism has not been eradicated, its overt manifestation is illegal. Furthermore, today's black population and the majority of white Americans no longer tolerate the type of blatant discrimination we once knew.

In my judgment, however, black Americans continue to believe in the absurd dogma of white racism. And I submit that this circumstance, perhaps more than anything else, limits their ability to take full advantage of opportunities created by the civil rights revolution. Thus, black Americans still harbor self-doubts and -deprecation. Their protracted experience with racism has induced an insidious estrangement—physical, mental, and spiritual—causing Black America today to be, in some ways, in the worst state of its history.

The signs of malaise are widespread. Too many black Americans are hypnotized by television, mesmerized by music, and anesthetized by drugs and alcohol. Racism has victimized us to the point where high rates of divorce, teenage pregnancy, black-on-black crime, and other detriments to progress pervade our existence. Add the fact that the primary messages and values in our community are coming less and less from the heart and the God above, and one can understand my conclusion that, at a time when we should be at our *strongest*, we are at our *weakest*.

This is not to disregard the sterling traditions of kinship, communal values, collective effort, self-reliance, and self-determination that have infused the black experience. Even under the harsh oppression of slavery, black Americans exhibited human development attributes that are admirable by any standard; there have been impressive examples since of efforts toward self-empowerment, based on individual responsibility and collective commitment.[3]

The point is that this proud heritage—the traditions that enabled those who preceded us to survive and surmount the meanest forms of oppression—has lost influence. It is time to reaffirm it; time to return to the basics; time to conquer the adversities of the present and define the parameters of the future. In this connection, I suggest that the salvation and well-being of the black community at this moment in history are linked to the following propositions:

1. Unless there is a revival of spiritual values and an acceptance of divine principles, we will never maximize the use of what we have but will only continue to complain about what we do not have.
2. Economic well-being and advancement are and will continue to be moot issues to a generation that can curse with eloquence but cannot do calculus.
3. Excessive reliance on others and lack of reliance on ourselves is stifling and counterproductive, as it should not be the primary responsibility of anybody to take care of us, however poor we might be or however severe the economic difficulties we face.

4. The future welfare and security of our children are contingent upon the determination to develop them and ourselves to the fullest.

These propositions have guided the Urban League of Greater Miami in developing programs for and delivering services to its constituents. We call the approach "coordinated community empowerment." It did not originate overnight, but evolved through an extended process of assessment and reassessment—of our institutional mission, community needs, and program initiatives. The process and outcomes reflect my view of what is required to reverse the conditions of degeneration and decline that characterize so many black communities. I believe there are important lessons to be shared. Here is our story.

THE MISSION

From 1943 to 1972, the stated mission of the Urban League of Greater Miami was: "To work to eliminate from all forms of community life segregation and discrimination based on race or color and to secure equal opportunity for every Negro citizen in Miami." In 1972, as we began to think about a strategic planning process that would give legitimacy and relevancy to our institutional presence in the twenty-first century and beyond, we decided that the first step would be the development of a new mission statement.

Based on a careful review of the past, we concluded that the eradication of all legal and most social prohibitions that had denied blacks equal opportunity had been accomplished. Therefore, the next area of Black Miami's concentration had to be development. The small group of staff and volunteers who initiated our "New Directions" discussions believed that to continue to do business as usual would be self-serving and of no real value to the constituency we professed to serve.

The review of program initiatives that had been pursued from 1943 to 1972 disclosed that service delivery by the organization was constantly changing. In what direction, how rapidly, how profoundly, how permanently, and the degree to which a given change was evolutionary or revolutionary could not be clearly determined. As Soren Kierkegaard noted, "Life is lived forward, but understood backward."[4] However, as we pondered the historical changes in service patterns and the mission statement, directions for future change became more apparent. Thus, analysis of the paradigm shifts and the seeming paradoxes between what we were doing and what we should be doing on behalf of black Dade Countians suggested that not only was a new mission statement warranted but also a new operating philosophy, strategy, and methodology as well.

In 1979, after seven years of intensive review, analysis, refocusing, and restructuring, the Urban League of Greater Miami announced a new mission and modus operandi in response to what we considered to be the 21st century needs of black Dade Countians. The new mission was: "To enable blacks to cultivate their potential and exercise their full human rights as American citizens." The key to the modified mission was the elimination of other people's negative attitudes and behaviors toward us; the imperative was to focus on personal and intellectual development.

As we debated the ways and means to carry out the new mission, the concept of "coordinated community empowerment" was adopted as the central plank of our development-oriented service delivery strategy. Coordinated community empowerment was defined as "an enabling process to maximize personal and intellectual development and to realize environmental and institutional changes necessary thereto."

Since the definition of coordinated community empowerment included the critical role of institutions in personal and intellectual development, we formulated a set of implementation strategies geared to influencing public policy and institutional change. Our specific objectives:

- To intervene into the social and economic structure of Dade County where the interests of blacks are at stake.
- To assist members of the black community in developing strategies and techniques to bring about positive change in policies and institutions that adversely affect their lives.
- To make existing institutions more responsive to the needs of blacks.
- To mobilize and organize community groups toward the development of alternatives to established systems that are determined to be inadequate.
- To conduct specialized programs and/or provide discrete services toward strengthening the growth and development of individuals and families, the areas of activity to include: education, housing, employment, economic development, urban affairs, community development, legal and consumer affairs, social welfare, and citizenship education.
- To research and publicize the social and economic needs of our clientele for policy development purposes.

Since its initial conceptualization in 1972, implementation of the coordinated community empowerment process has been influenced by a number of significant events, the most impactful of which were the riots that occurred in 1980. The riots were a kind of man-made disaster that spawned the belief that if communities were empowered, they would be better able to control their destiny. The Urban League of Greater Miami was a strong advocate of this belief and undertook another very intense community-wide planning process to develop a five-year plan that would put the empowerment principle into practice. The plan addressed eight major areas of activity and service as they related to black families in Dade County: employment, housing, health, education, children and youth, older adults, crime, and civic and political participation.[5]

The plan prescribed a limited set of goals and objectives believed to be achievable over a five-year period. Specific recommended actions to accomplish the stated objectives encompassed a variety of activities deemed appropriate for the Urban League. While the final mix of goals and objectives was expected to remain the League's pivotal focus for the next five years, the strategies and initiatives to achieve them were reevaluated periodically in response to changes in resources, institutional policies, and environmental conditions.

The goals and objectives of the five-year plan were not claimed to be unique to the Urban League. We fully recognized that many of them also represented the concerns of other community groups. However, our plan sought to establish a clearly identifiable and measurable role for the League toward the achievement of common goals through the coordinated community empowerment strategy.

The League would continue to press for broad public policy changes to improve the quality of life of all black families in Dade County and that of other similarly situated families. At the same time, services would be designed to mobilize and use the skills, resources, and strengths of black families to foster appropriate self-help activity. Other direct services would be provided to compensate for a need-meeting deficiency in the larger human services system or to demonstrate a model for some specialized service that might be incorporated into the larger system. Finally, economic development would be pursued to expand employment opportunity, without which other efforts to enhance functioning might have very little lasting benefit.

While the Urban League recognized that the black poor have the greatest problems and needs, the League's services would not be targeted exclusively to poor families. For the most part, the needs of poor families stem from the structure and operation of our social and economic systems and, therefore, cannot be totally resolved through service provision and the limited resources available to community-based organizations. Thus, the effectuation of changes in public policy was deemed paramount to meeting the needs of the poor and moving them toward economic self-sufficiency.

Given the size of metropolitan Dade County and the diversity of its black communities, it was felt that the effectiveness of the coordinated community empowerment strategy could be assessed more easily if the initiative were carried out in selected target areas rather than county-wide. Consequently, West Little River, Liberty City, and Overtown were designated initial target areas for the program.

However, the target area designations still presented serious complications, as the three black communities chosen were very different. Measuring the outcomes of the coordinated community empowerment thrust under such conditions with any degree of accuracy was thought to be too problematic. Therefore, in 1985, we shifted from a multi-neighborhood approach to a single-neighborhood approach, confining the target area to Liberty City.

THE NEED

Demographic analysis disclosed that the condition of black female household heads and their children in Miami's Liberty City community was very disconcerting. As Table 1 shows, in 1986, black single female-headed families with children less than 18 years of age represented 69 percent of all such families in the Miami area.

Table 1
Proportion of Female-Headed Families
with Children under 18 Years in Poverty,
by Race and Hispanic Origin: 1986

Race/Ethnicity	Percent of all families
Total	46.2
Black	69.0
Hispanic*	43.5
Other	47.5

*: Persons of Hispanic origin may be of any race.
Source: Dade County Research Department.

Focusing specifically on Liberty City, we found the incidence of poverty among female-headed families with children to be alarmingly high. In 1986, seven out of ten such families were poor. The poverty rate was higher still among those having related children under age six, falling just short of 90 percent. In addition, the data revealed that the poverty problem among female-headed families had worsened substantially since 1980. For example, the proportion of poor families with children under six soared by nearly 30 percentage points during the six-year period (Table 2).

222

Table 2
Percent of Female-Headed Families in Poverty
in Liberty City by Selected Characteristics:
1980 and 1986

	Percent in poverty	
Characteristic	1980	1986
All female-headed households	45.6	53.2
Householder worked	33.7	41.6
With children under 18	51.0	70.5
With children under 6	58.6	87.7

Sources: Bureau of the Census and Dade County Research Department.

A closer look at the conditions of the typical black child in Liberty City deepened the concern. The child lived in substandard housing—usually a small-size apartment unit dubbed a "concrete monster"—with few single family homes or duplexes in his/her neighborhood. The environment was replete with abandoned cars that were often crime scenes and vacant apartment buildings used by crack addicts for shelter and for drug trafficking. Solid waste and garbage littered the neighborhood, blighting the community, and posing serious public health risks.

The typical black child was involved with the criminal justice system early and often. He/she had perpetrated a serious crime by the age of 14; had served time in a correctional facility; had more than one prior adjudication; had participated in a wide range of serious and nonserious offenses; and was an academic underachiever and school dropout. As a dropout, the child had left school during the first two years of high school; had been retained at least one year between grades 1 and 6; had a negative self-image; had been labeled "at risk"; and had not benefited from positive parental involvement in his/her educational experience.

Service to this target population of female household heads and their children was coined the "Liberty City Renaissance," a term that reflected the desire for a more personalized treatment of the myriad problems impairing the quality of life in this particular black community. It also prompted a nostalgia for the way community life was when it was "colored," and linked it with the realization that improvement is possible, given a highly motivated, well-coordinated community effort. The renaissance theme suggested to the community and its residents the opportunity to make a difference through their own resourcefulness.

The essence of the "Liberty City Renaissance," then, was to be personal: "There is nothing wrong with us that we cannot fix!" became the battle cry.

THE PROGRAMS

The challenge to the Urban League was to ensure that empowerment be self-controlled, that personal energy be focused on fixing the problem and not the blame, that spiritual growth be the foundation for personal growth, and that racism no longer be recognized as our most formidable foe. To undergird the effort, the League promulgated a set of values that included self-sacrifice, self-discipline, self-respect, and respect for others. Collectively, these values would guide the development and implementation of programs in the Liberty City Renaissance area. They also would reflect the League's expectations, foremost among which were the desire and willingness of the residents and public and private sector entities to work together to improve the quality of life in Liberty City.

The philosophy and vision associated with the Liberty City Renaissance were consistent with the urgent need to improve the conditions of the community's single female heads of household and their children. Forging viable partnerships between internal and external institutions would be essential to advancing the well-being of a given family and to the overall success of the coordinated community empowerment strategy. At the broadest level, the efficacy of the organizational initiatives would be measured in terms of three outcomes: (1) the amount of direct financial support provided to the League and/or the client families, (2) the amount of financial and in-kind resources flowing into the Liberty City area from public and private sources, and (3) the degree of legitimacy and favor accorded to the League's initiatives by the intended beneficiaries.

All Liberty City Renaissance projects were developed to mirror the common vision. For example, there is a common recognition of the critical need for affordable housing, decent schools, safe recreational facilities, and quality child care. Tasks associated with a given project are discussed with both the public and private partners in the enterprise, and each partner is expected to draw upon the strengths of the other. Financial partners are to provide needed funding, while the League designs and implements the programs that enable residents to develop their personal and intellectual capabilities.

Thus, the overriding goal of each program initiative is to assist in creating an environment conducive to the self-empowerment process and, most important, to promote the view that our attitudes and self-perceptions must change as well as the institutions with which we interface. The comprehensive, systematic application of empowerment principles, involving diverse groups and interests, drives the League's concerted efforts on behalf of Liberty City mothers and their children. Parents, children, businesspersons, religious leaders, government officials, human service administrators, law enforcement personnel, media, and staff of other community organizations have participated actively in planning and implementation. The collaborations ensure the availability of vital resources while confirming community ownership of the programs.

The following demonstration projects are important parts of the broader community empowerment and renewal strategy. Each seeks to strengthen relationships among Liberty City residents, service providers, and public policymakers—within a value system that accentuates the positive.

M&M Maison I

This 30-unit townhouse project provides affordable housing and career advancement opportunities for female household heads with children. The project was made possible by the city of Miami's willingness to write down the cost of the development site to zero and the Urban League's success in securing $710,000 in financing through the Metropolitan Dade County Documentary Surtax Program. Other funding sources included Greater Miami Neighborhoods, Inc., and Homes for South Florida, Inc.—which represented a consortium of five local banks (North Carolina National Bank, Sun Bank, Barnett Bank, Southeast Bank, and Citicorp Savings of Florida).

The development consists of 24 two-bedroom, two-bath units and 6 one-bedroom units, measuring 950 and 780 square feet, respectively. The monthly rent is $250 for the one-bedroom unit and $350 for the two-bedroom unit. Tenants are selected from mothers who the League feels fit the unique profile of the "marginal poor": female household heads who are one step away from welfare, work hard every day, are independent-minded, and are pursuing child support through the family court system. If these women were to become sick or otherwise physically impaired, they would have to resort to public assistance to survive.

The mothers selected had to meet the following eligibility criteria:

- Have an annual income of $13,000 or less and be currently employed.
- Have no more than two children, with the older not being over the age of 12.
- Exhibit a strong desire to better their lives and the lives of their children.
- Commit to working with the Urban League through development of a Family Service Plan, which serves as the guide to achieving stated goals and solving identified problems.
- Commit to increasing their competitiveness in the labor market by continuing their education.

Upon selection, each mother is assigned a Family Service Provider who assists her in developing the Family Service Plan and an individualized prescription for increased economic independence and marketability. The latter provides for the participant's continued education. The Family Service Provider also explains or clarifies the program's rules and regulations as set forth in the covenants of the lease agreement.

There are high expectations of the women who participate in the M&M Maison program. Among these are: (1) that they will work toward making sure that the fathers of their children pay child support; (2) that they will not get pregnant; and (3) that they will not allow men to reside with them. Expectations (2) and (3) are the most controversial. The League's rationale for the pregnancy prohibition is that another child, whether planned or unplanned, would adversely affect the participant's ability to follow her individualized empowerment prescription. The ban on cohabitation was instituted as a further safeguard against problems that might restrict the mother's progress. In any case, the penalty for violating any of these rules is eviction. (If a participant marries, she loses her eligibility to stay in the program, and the couple is expected to make alternative housing arrangements—which enables the League to assist another family in the target group.)

This demonstration project has proved to be ideal for model-testing. For one thing, the residents of M&M Maison constitute a relatively homogeneous group. Also, the environment is self-contained and manageable, with the League providing necessary services and amenities. Such conditions enable us to observe in practice the idea that collective people power can be harnessed to check the breakdown of values and related problems experienced by single female household heads.

After two years of operation, the League has begun to see the fruits of development. Positive peer pressure within the complex has increased, and participants are more rigorously abiding by a set of accepted norms and standards of behavior. Also, some participants have improved their marketability to such an extent that they have been afforded the opportunity to move to a newly built Urban League apartment complex in the suburbs.

The Rainbow Club

This project seeks to extend and build upon the natural social group to which participants belong as residents of the Liberty Square Housing Project and the surrounding area. The program is designed on a "club" format, and all participants are considered to be club members who might affiliate with one of several "chapters." The member concept communicates an expectation of personal responsibility, involvement, and commitment to the goals of the program.

The Rainbow Club was established to promote the physical, intellectual, emotional, and social development of children through family-centered activities. Presently serving 75 families with young children, the program includes home visiting, parent-child interaction groups, information and support groups, and referral services.

Centers for Child Development and Learning

These centers provide a variety of services to support mothers in their parenting role and to assist in the development of infants, toddlers, and children in grades two through five. The Clara B. Knight Early Childhood Learning and Development Center offers affordable, high-quality child care for children through age five. It operates on a 24-hour basis seven days a week, a schedule that fully accommodates clients who need child care during irregular hours or on weekends and holidays. The center was established to help mothers break away from the cycle of welfare dependency. It is virtually impossible to be gainfully employed if one cannot make adequate arrangements for the care of young children.

In the Miami area, as elsewhere across the nation, the need for affordable child care is critical; presently, 5,000 children are on waiting lists for government-subsidized child care. Because of the level of need in the Liberty City Renaissance area, a second Clara B. Knight Center is scheduled to open in 1993.

The Parent Assistance and Mobilization Center is a community-based program designed to increase parental involvement in the education of children. The program concentrates on parents of second through fifth grade students who have been identified as being "at risk." There are nine participating elementary schools which are part of the Miami Northwestern Senior High School Feeder Pattern. The parents are involved in a variety of classes, workshops, and family activities. The program builds upon the strengths of families, with service interventions occurring at the earliest signs of distress.

Black-on-Black Crime

Public awareness and education activities are carried out to promote community support for and participation in crime prevention and control. The need is compelling; for example, a review of 1986 statistics for Liberty City revealed that black males accounted for more than eight out of ten juvenile arrests for Part One Index Crimes—homicide, rape, robbery, aggravated assault, burglary, larceny, and motor vehicle theft. Further, the data showed that black males were prone to commit violent crimes while whites were more likely to commit property crimes.[6]

The anti-crime program includes public forums, workshops, and training sessions to educate residents on the incidence and effects of criminal activity in their community. In addition, community-wide initiatives are developed and implemented to provide positive alternative opportunities for youth.

Through club-type activities, youth are exposed to positive role models, involved in projects that enhance their self-esteem, and afforded other experiences that help them to make sound decisions and deal with community problems. Finally, a special task force meets regularly to discuss the overall direction of the program and to consider any new strategies or initiatives that might be worthwhile.

Operation POP (Push Out the Pusher)

Created in 1985, Operation POP was undertaken for the immediate purpose of reducing the frequency of street drug sales in Liberty City. The program consists of a well-organized network of municipal agencies, community groups, and landlords. It has drawn widespread public attention through such activities as "Hands Around Germ City," in which residents joined hands to signify that the area belongs to the people, not the dealers.

To combat the drug trade, a cooperative plan was developed with the city manager, mayor, chief of police, fire department chief, sanitation administrator, and the state's attorney. Specific actions included increasing the number of arrests, introducing "park and walk" patrols, obtaining written permission from landlords for police to search premises without a search warrant, evicting drug dealers from private and public rental units, clearing empty lots, removing abandoned cars, and cutting back trees. In short, there has been an all-out effort to make the neighborhood less attractive to drug dealers.

A task force meets once a month to set goals and to report on progress. The task force's monitoring function covers the activities of major municipal departments—i.e., police, fire, planning, building and zoning, sanitation, parks and recreation—as well as the city manager's office and the Urban League. The President of the League conducts additional on-site review by surveying the area in the company of a POP police officer. This practice also helps to make the program visible in the community and serves as a concrete link among the police, the Urban League, and local residents. It has succeeded in improving relations and communication on all sides. More generally, the use of task forces, committees, and the team approach has been crucial to the success of Operation POP.

It bears emphasizing that Operation POP does not expect open support from residents, as the violence of the drug trade in Liberty City is so intense that they could easily endanger themselves. However, citizens are encouraged to make anonymous reports to the police or to the Urban League. This type of support has been indispensable.

Over the past two years, the scope of Operation POP has been expanded to include advocacy for better housing, medical care, pregnancy and parenting counseling, and other services. The expansion recognizes the multifaceted nature of the drug problem.

Black Men Connecting

This project is designed to demonstrate how to cultivate community concern about the relative absence of black males, especially in terms of the effects on the socialization of male children. The Urban League studied in-depth the problems of young black males in the nation's inner cities. In Liberty City, we found that the conditions of these youth had deteriorated seriously during the past two decades—unemployment had soared, access to quality education had diminished, and the feeling of being "trapped" with no way out had taken hold.

Young black males in Liberty City did not relish what we call the "American dream," and they were not fooling themselves when they decided to take routes to maturity that were self-destructive. Their material deprivations and unwholesome day-to-day experiences suggested to them that they had little choice but to succumb to the perverse influence of the streets. The League was convinced that the antisocial, self-defeating attitudes and behaviors of many young black males were becoming as dysfunctional as the structural and economic conditions that gave rise to them. Their expectations of failure, low self-esteem, and exaggerated sense of victimization had to be addressed if any self-improvement program was to succeed. However, we also realized that such debilitating attitudes and insecurities were very difficult to overcome in an environment that feeds and sustains them.

Against this backdrop, the Black Men Connecting initiative seeks to create an environment in which young black males are afforded opportunities to learn to make responsible decisions and appropriate choices as they move toward adulthood. The program serves youth up to 18 years of age. Participants attend monthly meetings, are mentored by adult role models sponsored by a local bank, and engage in coordinated recreational activities. The program interfaces with the Urban League's education initiative.

African Square Park

This facility is the most exciting amenity involved in the Liberty City Renaissance. It supports the efforts of families and the community in socializing and inculcating positive attitudes toward conformity and achievement. The park is the locus of many of the Urban League's youth empowerment initiatives.

The League identified wholesome recreation as being one of the most important missing elements in the social life of Liberty City. Specifically, we observed that the local park had never realized its full potential as a center of recreational and leisure activities for black children in the area. African Square Park was established in the mid-1970s as an outdoor flea market, with concrete booths for vendors and a sunken amphitheater for concerts and other programs. The flea market concept never took off and the park deteriorated through lack of use and maintenance. Worse yet, the vendor booths became outdoor bathrooms; drug dealers conducted business behind a wall on the premises; drug users shot up under the slide and in the amphitheater; older boys gambled boisterously; cursing and fighting were commonplace. The children of the neighborhood saw and heard it all.

It took the League seven years to rescue and rehabilitate African Square Park. In 1985, we formed a task force that was charged with developing a plan to make the park a viable, community-controlled recreation and leisure center that would cater to children 12 and under. In 1987 and 1988, the special Miami police task force involved in the POP program cleared the park of most of the illegal activity. In 1990, the park underwent $600,000 in renovations—$400,000 of which was financed by the city, $200,000 by the state. Trees and grass were planted, sand was put down, and a six-foot iron fence was installed. In addition, short basketball goals were erected and the amphitheater and administration building were rehabilitated.

The park reopened in 1991. Shortly thereafter, in February 1992, the city executed a contract that allowed the Urban League to manage the facility. Following the development plan, we imposed age and activity restrictions and proceeded to implement programs designed to stimulate academic achievement, to cultivate leadership skills, and to foster respect for authority.

It is important to point out that program-related partnerships have been formed with other agencies and organizations. For example, United Teachers of Dade assisted by encouraging its members to volunteer instruction time for needy students. Currently, 25 teachers tutor kids in reading, math, science, and music. The Miami Police Community Benevolent Association joined with the League in implementing the PeeWee Kiddie Patrol, a program in which children patrol the park. Finally, discussions have been held with management of the Miami Heat basketball team regarding the possibility of running a youth basketball league in the park. We have also talked with wives of the Heat players about conducting charm classes.

Partners in Education Initiative

This project was inspired by the Urban League's keen appreciation of the primacy of education in personal and intellectual development. Created in 1985, the Partners in Education Initiative is a cooperative effort with the Dade County public school system, Miami Dade Community College, United Teachers of Dade, and the Wolfson Foundation. A principal objective has been to reform the Northwestern Feeder Pattern.

Comprised of one senior high school, two junior high schools, and nine elementary schools, the Northwestern Feeder Pattern is predominantly black and operates in the Liberty City area. Specific actions to improve the academic performance of children in this system include holding classes on

Saturday; instituting the Black Student Opportunity Program, a scholarship program to enable graduating seniors to attend the local junior college; and establishing the Parent Assistance and Mobilization Center, designed to increase parental involvement in the educational process.

In 1992, the Urban League articulated the need for a new approach to teaching black children and petitioned the Dade County school board for its endorsement and funding support. The new approach is called "Efficacy." Developed by The Efficacy Institute in Lexington, Massachusetts, the process involves mobilizing available resources to solve problems and to promote development in an educational setting. (It is worth noting that the Efficacy concept also applies to the National Urban League's changed mission and the coordinated community empowerment strategy.)

The Efficacy initiative recognizes that the capacity and inclination to mobilize our own resources and know-how to enhance the education of black children are constrained by a dysfunctional and unfounded set of beliefs. Chief among these is the idea that only a small percentage of black children is intelligent enough to excel. In this connection, intelligence is viewed as an attribute one is born with and can do very little to change. Black children are disproportionately underachievers, the thinking goes, because they are disproportionately unintelligent. The Efficacy model obliterates such beliefs, replacing them with the concept that "Smart is not something that you just are, smart is something that you can *get*."

The Efficacy approach is being implemented—in grades 4 through 6—in a Liberty City elementary school. Children are being taught to believe in themselves, to work hard, and to pursue high goals. The process is buttressed by several practices and regulations that accord with the community empowerment thrust. In particular, students wear a standard uniform; the wearing of earrings by male students is prohibited, as is the wearing of excessive jewelry by either sex; boys are not to have lines cut into their hair; and attendance at personal appearance and hygiene classes is mandatory.

A local financial institution, First Union National Bank, has provided 22 black role models to interact with the 240 black male students at least one-half day per week. Also, the children may participate in the ACE Club. Co-sponsored by the local Department of Housing and Urban Development, ACE is an incentive program to motivate students and to recognize those who excel in the areas of attendance, conduct, and effort.

Housing Development and Conservation

One of the most significant conclusions from the League's "New Directions" discussions was that "a powerless institution cannot empower a powerless people." Accordingly, the realization of self-sufficiency, through political and economic empowerment, has been our overriding organizational goal. As we developed a coordinated empowerment strategy to serve our constituents, we also formulated an institutional self-sufficiency action plan. The cornerstone of the plan is housing development, conservation, and management.

To date, the League has created nine affiliate corporations that have independent income-producing capacity for the organization. Seven of the corporations are not-for-profit, while two are profit-making. Their business concentrates on expanding the inventory of low- and moderate-income housing in and around the Liberty City Renaissance area for female household heads and their children.

CONCLUSION

In a relatively short time, the projects outlined above have replaced the Urban League's traditional program initiatives and have effectuated a significant amount of real community empowerment. As we go forward, the League continues to examine critically the evolution and impact of our new strategy and methodologies. We also remain steadfast in stressing service based on our current state and not on past victimization.

In large part, the Liberty City Renaissance can be viewed as a concerted attempt to restore traditional value systems within a modern, urban context. Responsive and responsible advocacy on behalf of single female heads of household and their children, together with concrete programs to enhance their quality of life in different areas, is central to the process. Additional strategical adjustments and service delivery innovations are anticipated as we strive to keep abreast of changing needs in a changing environment.

By any measure, the past 20 years have been a very challenging and eventful period for the Urban League of Greater Miami. We have wrestled intently with the formidable issues and problems that have rendered the American dream elusive to black Americans. Our coordinated community empowerment initiative, we believe, is succeeding in making the dream more attainable for blacks in Liberty City. Key to the outcome is establishing the premise that we all are human—even those who have been treated inhumanely—and when our humanity is respected and nurtured, we are moved to reach our full potential.

Above all else, our experiences during the last two decades—the setbacks as well as the progress—have affirmed categorically the importance of *development*. Thus, I am more convinced than ever that access to opportunity in the modern era is less a function of race than of the extent to which black Americans develop themselves—intellectually, spiritually, and morally. And as we pursue development, we must fix the holes in the road to prosperity. We must rid ourselves of the bad habits, hopelessness, low valuation of education, poor judgments, lack of belief in self, and dependency on others that have limited our individual and collective progress. Ideally, we should not repair the holes, but build a new road, using the machinery of coordinated community empowerment.

Finally, I close with the proclamation that no strategy to improve the human condition in Liberty City will succeed if it is devoid of a commitment to regenerate a consciousness of God. Again, the primary messages and values of too many Liberty City mothers no longer emanate from the heart and the God above. Consequently, many of their children have no sense of struggle and have a warped perspective on survival and success. A kind of moral degeneracy has combined with such long-standing problems as unemployment, poverty, poor housing, and crime to assure virtually a bleak future for these youth.

The God who brought us through the dark passage, the dehumanization of slavery, the humiliation of segregation, and the disillusionment of integration is being reduced to a convenience figure for casual use. We all must realize that any person or institution that professes to care about the future of Black America must challenge it to return to God.

ENDNOTES

[1] See Stanley M. Elkins, *Slavery: A Problem in American Institutional and Intellectual Life* (Chicago: University of Chicago Press, 1959). See also Kenneth M. Stampp, *The Peculiar Institution: Slavery in the Ante-Bellum South* (New York: Vintage Books, 1956).

[2] C. Vann Woodward, *The Strange Career of Jim Crow* (New York: Oxford University Press, 1966).

[3] Notable examples include the works of Booker T. Washington, Marcus Garvey, and Elijah Muhammad. For relevant discussion, see Edward Peeks, *The Long Struggle for Black Power* (New York: Charles Scribner's Sons, 1971).

[4] Quoted in Sack Green and Steven Mastrofki, *Community Policing: Rhetoric or Reality* (New York: Praeger, 1988), p. 28.

[5] See T. Willard Fair and Maxine Thurston, *The Next Five Years: 1985-1990—Building Strong Black Families* (Miami: Urban League of Greater Miami, Inc., 1984).

[6] Data obtained from the Florida Department of Law Enforcement, Juvenile Arrests Office.

Recommendations

With the new national leadership, the recommendations in the 1993 edition of *The State of Black America* assume special significance. A new president, committed to positive change, and a largely new Congress, rejuvenated by more diverse representation, inspire hopes of completing the unfinished business of racial justice and preparing the nation to meet the formidable challenges of the 21st century.

There is also a renewed sense of potency and purpose within the African-American community. After 12 years of "malign neglect" and retarded progress, African Americans welcome the changed political environment with genuine, albeit guarded, optimism. In addition, African Americans are disposed to be more assertive toward the advancement of their own interests.

Thus, conditions are in place that promise more attention to the nation's pressing domestic needs and the unfulfilled aspirations of African Americans. The new political leadership appears to realize that the national security in post-Cold War America depends on our economic strength and ability to compete in the global marketplace. There also seems to be a clearer recognition that tapping the talents of all racial and ethnic groups in our increasingly diverse society is key to maximizing the nation's economic competitiveness. At last, perhaps, racism and racial disadvantage may be perceived for what they are—national liabilities that we can no longer afford.

As we bring in the new year and, hopefully, a new era, the National Urban League is poised to work even more vigorously on behalf of African Americans and the common good—with President Clinton and his administration, members of Congress, state and local elected officials, corporate leaders, nonprofit organizations, and any other like-minded groups. Progressive public policies and propitious private initiatives are the vehicles. At the same time, we are, more than ever, dedicated to reinvigorating the self-directed development of the African-American community.

AFRICAN-AMERICAN SELF-DEVELOPMENT

Responsive public policy initiatives clearly are necessary to improve the contemporary well-being of African Americans and their prospects for the future. However, the National Urban League continues to believe that governmental action is insufficient to overcome the barriers to progress confronting the African-American community. Thus, the African-American community itself, inspired and guided by its proud tradition of self-preservation, must be more forceful and strategic in furthering its own development. As disadvantaged as African Americans continue to be, their collective resources, talents, and influence are substantial. History has demonstrated that when these assets are effectively mobilized and focused, African Americans are able to make impressive advances, to surmount the most intransigent obstacles.

As we anticipate the more taxing, complex demands of the 21st century, there has never been a more critical time for African Americans to re-energize and come together around their compelling mutual interests. There has never been a more critical time for African Americans to emphasize legacy. Thus, as Jeff Howard stresses in the article, "The Third Movement: Developing Black Children for the 21st Century," there has never been a more critical time for African Americans to undertake a new movement to control their own destiny.

The National Urban League believes that this new movement must, above all else, center on developing all African-American children into "21st century citizens." This concept recognizes the manifold perils our children face as well as their unlimited potential to excel, given the proper nurturance. We call upon the broader African-American community to join us in bringing the concept to reality. The following operational principles are integral to the plan of action:

- That every African-American child graduate from high school with the ability to do calculus.
- That every African-American child be fluent in a foreign language.
- That every African-American child be able to research, organize, and write a 25-page essay on a challenging topic.
- That every African-American child live by strict, high ethical standards.

We have no illusions about the ease with which these conditions can be achieved. They require fundamental institutional changes. They require a revolutionary, nothing-less-will-do mind-set. Most important, they require that each African-American individual, family, organization, and community be actively involved in the campaign. The mission will not be easy, but the consequences of failure are totally unacceptable.

Again, public policies favoring African-American advancement are essential. The new government must operate with the type of enlightenment to which we alluded at the outset. Much is at stake, for both the African-American community and the nation as a whole. Accordingly, the policy proposals set forth below should be included in the enlightened national agenda to "rebuild America."

236

MARSHALL PLAN FOR AMERICA

The National Urban League calls upon the president and the Congress to enact legislation establishing the League's Marshall Plan for America as the cornerstone of a comprehensive strategy to increase the nation's economic productivity and competitiveness. The Marshall Plan for America is a coordinated, targeted, and accountable economic investment program predicated on the need to improve the nation's human and physical capital. It recognizes that lack of public investment in these areas largely accounts for America's deteriorated position in the global economy and the concomitant decline in our standard of living. It recognizes, further, that African Americans and the urban centers in which they remain concentrated must be principal targets of efforts to develop our human resources and upgrade the physical infrastructure that supports economic activity. In his article, "Promoting Priorities: African-American Political Influence in the 1990s," Charles Hamilton clarifies that this type of "dual agenda" initiative, i.e., one that serves both the needs of African Americans and the broader national interests, is not uncharacteristic of the National Urban League. Policy deliberations on implementing the Marshall Plan and the specific proposals detailed in the report, *Playing to Win: A Marshall Plan for America*, should be informed by the following principles:

- That the Marshall Plan initiative be designed to achieve both long-term economic productivity goals and short-term stimulation toward economic recovery.
- That the Marshall Plan initiative be designed to maximize returns by concentrating on groups and areas in greatest need.
- That the Marshall Plan initiative be designed to facilitate sustained, programmed collaborations on the part of the government, the private sector, and nonprofit organizations.
- That the Marshall Plan initiative be designed to operate under rigorous accountability systems for monitoring, assessing, and adjusting results over time.

WORK-FORCE PREPARATION

American workers are challenged to participate more productively in a labor market that is increasingly dominated by the dynamics of global economic competition. The new administration and Congress must seize the moment and institute policies and programs that ensure adequate preparation of all of our youth (whether in-school or out-of-school) and adults (whether unemployed, underemployed, or employed) to meet the changing demands. As Billy Tidwell explains in "African Americans and the 21st Century Labor Market: Improving the Fit," the imperative has special relevance with respect to the needs of African Americans. Accordingly, the National Urban League recommends:

- That the findings and recommendations of the SCANS Commission concerning work-force competencies be adopted as a framework for the formulation of individual and institutional performance standards for skills development.
- That the related work-force recommendations of the Commission on the Skills of the American Workforce, as codified in S. 1790, be enacted into law.

EDUCATION

The public education system desperately needs reform, as it too frequently fails to afford children a quality education. The shortcomings are particularly distressing in urban school districts in which African-American and other disadvantaged students tend to be concentrated. In "Programs for Progress and Empowerment: The Urban League's National Education Initiative," Michael Webb discusses the League's concerted efforts, as a community-based organization, to improve the public education of African-American children. More affirmative steps to alleviate observed deficiencies and inequities also must be taken by the federal government. In particular, the National Urban League recommends:

- That the U.S. Department of Education take a more active role to ensure the equitable distribution of federal fiscal support of public education.
- That the 103rd Congress reauthorize Chapter One of the 1965 Elementary and Secondary Education Act at a level of funding more commensurate with the need and institute more potent safeguards for allocating funds to the neediest schools.

HEALTH

During the 102nd Congress, numerous health care proposals were introduced, but no agreement on health care reform legislation could be reached. As the number of uninsured persons and families continues to rise, the need for health care reform has become critical. In addition, health care costs have escalated so rapidly as to hinder economic growth. Failure to act soon, therefore, endangers the physical well-being of a large segment of the population and the fiscal well-being of the nation as a whole. The National Urban League firmly supports the call for comprehensive health care reform that provides coverage for all Americans, especially the least advantaged among us. Specifically, we recommend that such a plan include the following:

238

- high quality, easily accessible general health services for all persons and families, regardless of ability to pay;
- catastrophic health insurance for the elderly and disadvantaged;
- increased funding for programs such as Healthy Start, which seek to help in the battle against infant mortality, as well as mandated immunization programs for all children;
- financial assistance for valued inner-city hospitals and community health centers that are at risk of closing for lack of resources.

In addition, we call upon the 103rd Congress to reintroduce the Family and Medical Leave Act and move swiftly to pass it on for the president's signature.

CIVIL RIGHTS

Despite the eventual passage of the 1991 Civil Rights Act, the past 12 years have been a period of retrenchment and regression in the area of civil rights. It is now time to complete the business of realizing racial and social justice for all groups, especially in terms of the race-based economic inequalities so extensively documented in David Swinton's "The Economic Status of African Americans During the Reagan-Bush Era: Withered Opportunities, Limited Outcomes, and Uncertain Outlook." The civil rights issue, in all of its complexity, must be restored to the national agenda. In particular, the National Urban League recommends:

- That the 1989 decision in *City of Richmond v. Croson*, which attacked the validity of minority set-aside programs, be reversed.
- That the Equal Remedies Act, which would eliminate caps on employment discrimination damages awards under Title VII, be passed.

VOTER REGISTRATION

The National Urban League strongly advocates national voter registration legislation that would break down barriers to exercising the franchise. The evidence shows that many people do not vote because of overly restrictive voter registration procedures. Furthermore, the great majority of those registered to vote actually do vote on election day. Voting is a right, not a privilege, and voter registration reform should be regarded as mandatory to guarantee that all citizens are able to participate fully in this basic democratic process. Hamilton, in "Promoting Priorities . . .," leaves no doubt about the strategic importance of the franchise to African Americans. Therefore, the National Urban League endorses legislation that provides for:

- registration by mail, without notarization, on a form that is available in convenient places;
- conjunctive registration with application for a driver's license or photo identification card;
- registration at state agencies, including libraries, schools, welfare bureaus, unemployment offices, and the like;
- prohibiting states from removing persons from registration lists for failure to vote.

CRIME AND CRIMINAL JUSTICE

Violent crime and drug abuse continue to be enormous and costly social problems that have become closely related. Violent crime rates are exceptionally high in African-American communities, and the data show that African Americans are disproportionately victimized. Likewise, the high incidence of drug abuse is tragically ruining the lives of far too many African-American individuals and families, while casualties of the drug business—including innocent bystanders—continue to mount. Moreover, the prevalence of crime in general is one of the most serious problems facing commercial enterprises in these communities. In light of the numerous other constraints on African-American business development, as discussed in Lenneal Henderson's article, "Empowerment through Enterprise: African-American Business Development," the crime problem severely worsens the situation. Whether drug-related or not, many of the violent crimes in African-American communities involve the use of handguns. Law enforcement agencies, as well as the African-American community itself, must be more aggressive in combating these conditions. At the same time, racial inequities in the criminal justice system must be addressed, including the great disparity in the imposition of the death penalty. Specifically, the National Urban League recommends:

- That federal assistance for fighting crime in local communities be increased, concentrating on those that are high crime areas.
- That the Crime Insurance Program, established under the 1968 Housing and Community Development Act to underwrite insurance coverage for minority business owners in high crime areas who are unable to acquire insurance from private carriers, be reauthorized and operationalized throughout the country.
- That the "Brady Bill," which would better regulate the acquisition of handguns, be enacted into law.
- That the so-called War on Drugs be reinforced vis-a-vis both the supply and demand sides of the problem.
- That the Racial Justice Act, allowing defendants to challenge death sentences that may be influenced by racial bias, be passed.

ENVIRONMENT

Numerous environmental hazards impair the well-being of African Americans. One of the most prevalent and deleterious conditions is lead poisoning. Indeed, exposure to toxic quantities of lead is the predominant environmental problem experienced by African-American children. Consumed even in small doses, lead can cause irreversible learning and behavioral disabilities. African-American children are disproportionately at risk of contamination. More effective prevention of this health problem is vital.

A second pressing environmental issue is the inordinate frequency with which toxic waste dumps, landfills, and incinerators are situated in or near African-American communities. (In *The State of Black America 1992*, Robert Bullard terms this practice "environmental racism.") The National Urban League recommends federal action that provides for:

- an increase in federal funding to test for lead poisoning in children and mandated public education programs on lead hazards and safety;
- a requirement for full lead disclosure before a dwelling is sold or rented;
- the establishment of stricter regulations for lead levels in drinking water;
- increased federal authority to enforce testing of schools and day care centers for lead paint and soil hazards.

HOUSING

African Americans and other disadvantaged groups are severely affected by the shortage of affordable, decent housing. Even many working families find themselves unable to meet their housing needs. The problem has reached crisis proportions, and it is having an especially adverse impact on the development and well-being of children. In the case of African Americans, the general problem is aggravated by the persistence of mortgage lending discrimination—a subject William Bradford discusses authoritatively in his article, "Money Matters: Lending Discrimination in African-American Communities." As a matter of national priority, both the general housing crisis and the discrimination problem must be more effectively addressed. Accordingly, the National Urban League recommends:

- That the HOME program be strengthened by increasing the authority of state and local administrators.
- That the low-income housing tax credit be permanently extended.

- That funding for the Community Development Block Grant (CDBG) program be increased.
- That a nationwide network of community-based banks be established to provide financing for affordable housing and community development loans to help revitalize economically depressed urban areas.
- That there be stricter enforcement of provisions in the Community Reinvestment Act (CRA), the Home Mortgage Disclosure Act (HMDA), and related legislation, and that the coverage capability of designated enforcement agencies be increased.
- That nonprofit antidiscrimination agencies be established in metropolitan areas across the country.
- That state agencies responsible for enforcement be required to abolish caps on damages plaintiffs can receive in lending discrimination cases.

INCOME SECURITY

Safety net programs are integral to the general welfare of any modern society. In the past 12 years, however, the safety net in this country has shrunk, even as the need for such programs has escalated. Countless families and individuals have been snared by poverty and deprivation, without the institutional supports needed to move toward economic self-sufficiency. In her article, "Toward Economic Self-Sufficiency: Independence Without Poverty," Lynn Burbridge examines the particularly stifling experiences of African-American women in this regard. T. Willard Fair describes some promising initiatives undertaken to assist African-American AFDC and other mothers in his article, "Coordinated Community Empowerment: Experiences of the Urban League of Greater Miami." The National Urban League remains in the forefront in advocating a more functional and humane income support system for the poor. In particular, we call for a system that:

- provides the services and supports necessary to enable public assistance recipients to secure unsubsidized employment;
- is explicitly dedicated to strengthening family units and, therefore, provides income support at the level and for the duration necessary to ensure their subsistence;
- repudiates provisions that tie eligibility for public assistance to recipient behaviors—such as child truancy, giving birth to another child, or relocating.
- stresses the crucial role of community-based organizations in program planning and service delivery, operating in conjunction with public and private social welfare agencies.

APPENDIX

Fast Facts:
African Americans in the 1990s

Billy J. Tidwell, Ph.D.
Monica B. Kuumba, M.S.
Dionne J. Jones, Ph.D.
Betty C. Watson, Ph.D.

"Knowledge is power." As hackneyed as this adage may seem, it has become increasingly relevant to the well-being and aspirations of African Americans. The African-American condition in the 1990s is characterized by persisting disadvantages and new challenges. There are also potential opportunities for advancement. In a sense, the collective status of African Americans has never been more complex, and never has their future seemed more uncertain. What is certain is that reliable empirical knowledge about present conditions is essential to support further progress— to overcome the residual disadvantages, to meet the new challenges, and to seize the emerging opportunities.

Since its inception nearly two decades ago, *The State of Black America* has been dedicated to empowerment through knowledge, showcasing the expertise and wisdom of some of the most erudite scholars in the country. The 1993 volume reaffirms the publication's commitment to promote informed public policy as well as sound initiatives by African Americans themselves on behalf of their own development. Likewise, this appendix was produced to serve as a ready reference source of statistical information for all of those who are concerned about the problems confronting today's African-American community.

The data presented below address some of the most noteworthy aspects of the contemporary African-American experience. The presentation was not intended to be comprehensive or to offer in-depth discussion of the selected information. Its chief purpose is to provide "fast facts" that are likely to command broad public interest.

For added convenience, the data are organized in three sections—General Profile, The State of Young Black America, and The State of Urban Black America. In addition to the statistical information, each section includes a prefacing statement and concise narrative representations of the data.

The project was carried out within the framework of the National Urban League's Census Data Analysis and Dissemination (CDAD) program, a co-operative venture with the Bureau of the Census that specializes in data user services. Deborah Searcy provided much-needed production support, and Marcus Gordon developed the graphs.

GENERAL PROFILE

Racial disparities in well-being remain a distinguishing feature of American social and economic life. While the forms that racial inequalities take and the levels on which they are manifest have changed over time, they are far from eliminated, as they continue to define and delimit the relative status of African Americans. As the following data show, disparities in such vital areas as education, health, income, and employment still take their toll. Moreover, the adverse effects of the inequality in any one area are compounded by their interaction with similar effects in the others. Magnified through these interactive and cumulative effects that cut across the various levels, persisting racial disparities have consequences that extend beyond their individual impacts.

Of course, African Americans have made status gains, in both absolute and relative terms, over the long-run. Achieved against great odds, this progress can be neither disregarded nor belittled. Nevertheless, the fact that they have yet to realize racial parity in key dimensions of well-being is the dominant reality facing African Americans in the 1990s. This point takes on added significance in light of the profound demographic changes underway in this society and what they imply for the future welfare of the entire nation. As they comprise a growing share of the U.S. population, African Americans become an increasingly important national resource. They must be enabled to produce and progress to their full potential, for the benefit of themselves and of the common good.

In any case, the general profile data presented here suggest that the contemporary African-American condition is incompatible with the long-standing ideal of racial justice as well as the changing national interests.

244

Table 1
Population Percentages, by Race and Hispanic Origin:
1990 and Projections to 2010

Group	1990	2000	2010
White	83.9%	81.7%	79.6%
African American	12.3	12.9	13.6
Hispanic*	9.0	11.1	13.2
Asian	3.0	4.5	5.9
American Indian	0.8	0.9	0.9

*: Persons of Hispanic origin may be of any race.

Source: Bureau of the Census, *Population Projections of the United States, by Age, Sex, Race, and Hispanic Origin: 1992-2050*, Current Population Reports, Series P25-1092 (draft), Table 1, p. 12.

- African Americans are accounting for an increasing share of the U.S. population. At 12.3 percent in 1990, their proportion is projected to rise to nearly 14 percent in 2010.

- The proportion of whites is expected to continue declining, from 84 percent in 1990 to 80 percent in 2010. This trend and the higher growth rates of African Americans and other minorities presage an even more diverse population in the years ahead.

Table 2
Life Expectancy, by Race and Sex: 1991

	Total U.S.	African American	White American
Both Sexes	75.7	70.0	76.4
Male	72.2	65.6	73.0
Female	79.1	74.3	79.7

Source: U.S. Department of Health and Human Services, National Center for Health Statistics, "Annual Summary of Births, Marriages, Divorces, and Deaths: United States, 1991," *Monthly Vital Statistics Report*, Vol. 40, No. 13 (September 30, 1992), Table 7, p. 16.

- The average life expectancy of African Americans is six-plus years less than that of whites.

- As a result of the multitude of hazards and social ills experienced by African-American males, their life expectancy continues to be among the lowest of all groups in the nation. African-American males live only 65.6 years, a life span that is almost a decade shorter than the 73-year average for white males.

Table 3
Death Rates, by Race and Sex: 1991
(per 100,000 population)

	Total U.S.	African American	White American
Both Sexes	854.0	835.4	880.1
Male	909.1	961.5	924.3
Female	801.6	721.3	837.6

Source: U.S. Department of Health and Human Services, National Center for Health Statistics, "Annual Summary of Births, Marriages, Divorces, and Deaths: United States, 1991," *Monthly Vital Statistics Report*, Vol. 40, No. 13 (September 30, 1992), Table 4, p. 13.

- In 1991, African Americans as a group experienced a death rate of about 835 persons per 100,000. Their overall death rate was 5 percent lower than the rate for whites.

- The African-American death rate differed greatly by sex. African-American males had a 33 percent higher death rate than African-American females. They also experienced a 4 percent higher rate than white males. Among whites, the male death rate was only 10 percent higher than that of females.

Table 4
Death Rates for HIV Infection, by Race and Sex: 1991
(per 100,000 population)

	Total U.S.	African American	White American
Both Sexes	11.8	30.4	9.4
Male	21.1	50.4	17.6
Female	2.9	12.2	1.5

Source: U.S. Department of Health and Human Services, National Center for Health Statistics, "Annual Summary of Births, Marriages, Divorces, and Deaths: United States, 1991," *Monthly Vital Statistics Report*, Vol. 40, No. 13 (September 30, 1992), Table 10, p. 21.

• The incidence of death from AIDS differs sharply by race. Overall, African Americans were 3.2 times more likely than whites to die from the HIV infection in 1991. The racial differential was especially pronounced among females, with African-American females being 8.1 times more likely to fall victim to the ravages of the AIDS virus.

• African-American males are hardest hit by the AIDS epidemic. Their 1991 death rate from HIV infection was over four times the national average, while African-American females virtually matched the national rate.

Table 5
Death Rates for Homicide and Legal Intervention,
by Race and Sex: 1989
(per 100,000 population)

	Total U.S.	African American	White American
Both Sexes	9.2	35.8	5.4
Male	14.6	61.1	8.2
Female	4.1	12.9	2.8

Source: U.S. Department of Health and Human Services, National Center for Health Statistics, "Advance Report of Final Mortality Statistics, 1989," *Monthly Vital Statistics Report*, Vol. 40, No. 8, Supplement 2, Table 11, pp. 28-29.

• Violence in the United States is also disproportionately felt by African Americans. The problem is clearly indicated by the frequency of deaths by homicide and legal intervention. In 1989, close to 11,000 African Americans died from these causes.

- African-American males are most susceptible to violent death. They are more than seven times as likely as white males to die by homicide or legal intervention. Among females, the racial disparity is smaller but still significant, as African-American females are nearly five times as likely as their white counterparts to die from these causes.

Table 6
Prisoners under Sentence of Death, by Race and Hispanic Origin: Spring 1991

Race	Number	Percent
Total	2,588	100.0%
White American	1,316	50.9
African American	1,008	40.0
Hispanic*	185	7.2
Native American	47	1.8
Other	32	1.2

*: Persons of Hispanic origin may be of any race.

Source: U.S. Department of Justice, Bureau of Justice Statistics, *Sourcebook of Criminal Justice Statistics - 1991*, Table 6.140, p. 703.

- Historically, the criminal justice system has impacted African Americans in disproportionate numbers. The ultimate indicator is the frequency with which African Americans are sentenced to death. Forty percent of all prisoners on death row are African American.

- The total number of African Americans on death row in spring 1991 was more than five times the number of Hispanics, the second largest minority group.

Table 7
Marital Status of African Americans 15 Years and Older, by Sex: 1991

Marital Status	African American		White American	
	Male	Female	Male	Female
Never married	44.8%	38.7%	28.0%	20.8%
Married	43.1	38.4	62.4	59.0
Widowed	3.3	11.9	2.5	11.2
Divorced	8.8	11.0	7.1	8.9

Source: Bureau of the Census, *The Black Population in the United States: March 1991*, Current Population Reports, Series P-20-464, Table C, p. 5.

- Corresponding to the high incidence of single female-headed families in the African-American community, African-American females are much less likely than white females to be married.

- Among both African-American males and females, about the same proportion is married as is in the never-married category, while whites of both sexes are distinctly more likely to be married than never married.

Table 8
Years of School Completed by Persons 15 Years and Older, by Race: 1991

Years Completed:	Total U.S.	African American	White American
4 years high school	74.4%	66.7%	87.5%
1 or more years college	37.2	29.0	46.3
4 or more years college	18.5	11.5	25.2

Source: Bureau of the Census, *Educational Attainment in the United States: March 1991 and 1990*, Current Population Reports, Series P-20, No. 462, pp. 15-28.

- The educational level of African Americans continues to lag behind that of whites. As of 1991, two-thirds of African Americans ages 15 and older had completed high school, compared to almost nine out of ten whites.

- In terms of higher education, African Americans had completed 4 or more years of college at less than half the rate of whites.

Table 9
Percent Distribution of Degrees Conferred
on African Americans, by Sex and Degree Type: 1989-1990*

Degree	Total	Male	Female
Associate	7.9%	7.0%	8.5%
Bachelor's	5.8	4.7	6.8
Master's	4.8	3.6	5.8
Doctor's	3.0	2.2	4.4
First-Professional	4.8	3.8	6.5

*: Table entries are percentages of all degrees conferred in each category.

Source: National Center for Education Statistics, *Digest of Education Statistics, 1992*, Tables 246, 249, 252, 255, and 258, pp. 270-282.

- African Americans are severely underrepresented among recipients of degrees beyond high school. In 1989-90, they accounted for 8 percent of all associate degrees and a much lower 3 percent of all doctorates awarded.

- African-American males are less likely than females to receive higher degrees of any type. At the highest level, the proportion of doctorates conferred upon African-American females in the 1989-90 school year doubled the proportion received by African-American males.

Table 10
Distribution of Family Income, by Race: 1991

Income	African American	White American
Under $5,000	11.4%	2.5%
$5,000 to $9,999	15.0	4.8
$10,000 to $14,999	11.1	6.7
$15,000 to $24,999	18.4	15.7
$25,000 to $34,999	14.5	15.9
$35,000 to $49,999	14.8	20.3
$50,000 and over	14.9	34.1
Median Income	$21,548	$37,783

Source: Bureau of the Census, *Money Income of Households, Families, and Persons in the United States: 1991*, Current Population Reports, Series P-60, No. 180, Table 20, pp. 84-85.

- While African-American families have experienced some gains, their income level continues to lag well behind that of white families. Overall, African-American family income in 1991 averaged just 57 percent of white income.

- At the extremes, about 11 percent of African-American families received less than $5,000 in income, compared to only 2 percent of white families. Conversely, African-American families were less than half as likely as whites to receive $50,000 or more.

Table 11
Official and Hidden Unemployment Rates,
by Age, Race, and Sex: 1991

All Races	African American	White American
Official Unemployment Rates		
Both Sexes	6.7%	12.4%	6.0%
Male	7.0	12.9	6.4
Female	6.3	11.9	5.5
Hidden Unemployment Rates*		
Both Sexes	12.9	23.1	11.5
Male	11.8	21.4	10.6
Female	14.2	24.6	12.6

*: Estimates from the National Urban League's Hidden Unemployment Index, which factors in discouraged and involuntary part-time workers.

Source: Prepared by the National Urban League from unpublished Bureau of Labor Statistics data.

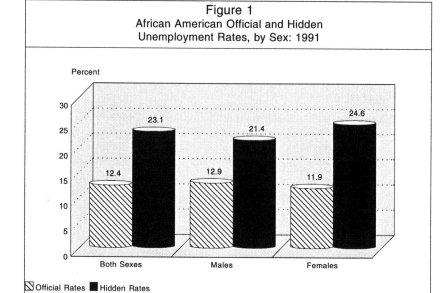

**Figure 1
African American Official and Hidden
Unemployment Rates, by Sex: 1991**

Percent

Official Rates ☒   Hidden Rates ■

Source: Prepared by National Urban League from
unpublished Bureau of Labor Statistics data.

- Joblessness remains an overriding concern in the African-American community. By official estimates, the overall African-American unemployment rate in 1991 was more than double the rate for whites.

- The Urban League's Hidden Unemployment Index put the actual level of African-American joblessness in 1991 at a catastrophic 23 percent.

THE STATE OF YOUNG BLACK AMERICA

Today's African-American youth face tremendous odds, and an alarming number is at risk of failure and of being trapped in a web of debilitation and dependency. Their problems have both internal and external sources. Internally, many African-American youth have little self-esteem and -confidence, having internalized low appraisals and expectations ascribed to them by others. Additionally, too many lack vision and seem unable to picture a future for themselves beyond the age of 30, if that far. They tend to exhibit a low value for human life—whether their own or the lives of others—and eschew setting self-development goals.

In terms of their external situation, many African-American children live in poverty-stricken families that are unable to provide the material and emotional support necessary for wholesome development. Furthermore, far

252

too many of these children are in communities where poverty, unemployment, crime, drug abuse, and other adverse conditions are commonplace.

Of particular concern is the manner in which African-American children are treated by the public institutions charged with promoting their development. Thus, far too many receive highly negative messages in school, the most vital development institution outside the family. African-American students, for example, are disproportionately placed in lower academic tracks where they have limited experience with tasks involving critical and analytic thinking skills. Many remain in low track placements throughout their school career.

In short, there is a complex of internal and external factors that interact to limit the well-being of African-American children and jeopardize their future. Remedying these conditions requires more responsive policy initiatives as well as more concerted and strategic actions by the African-American community itself. The overriding objective should be to prepare *all* African-American children to be productive members of their community and the society at large. The following selected statistical data highlight some of the conditions that must be improved.

Table 12
Distribution of African-American Population
Ages 1-to-24 Years, by Sex: 1990
(numbers in thousands)

	Both Sexes		Male		Female	
	Number	Percent	Number	Percent	Number	Percent
Total Pop.	29,986	100.0	14,170	100.0	15,816	100.0
Under 5 yrs.	2,786	9.3	1,408	10.0	1,377	8.7
5-9 yrs.	2,671	8.9	1,350	9.5	1,321	8.4
10-14 yrs.	2,602	8.7	1,314	9.3	1,287	8.1
15-19 yrs.	2,658	8.9	1,342	9.5	1,316	8.3
20-24 yrs.	2,579	8.6	1,259	8.9	1,320	8.4

Source: Bureau of the Census, *Statistical Abstract of the United States: 1992*, Table No. 18, p. 18.

- The African-American population is relatively young. African-American children ages 19 years and younger represent more than one-third of the of the total African-American population.

- The proportion of African-American males is somewhat greater than the proportion of females in the younger age groups.

Table 13
Living Arrangements of Children Under 18 Years,
by Race: 1991

	Total U.S.	African American	White American
Living with:			
Two Parents	71.7%	35.9%	78.5%
One Parent	25.5	57.5	19.5
Mother Only	22.4	54.0	16.5
Father Only	3.1	3.5	3.0
Other			
Relatives	2.2	5.5	1.5
Nonrelative only	0.6	1.0	0.5

Source: Bureau of the Census, *Marital Status and Living Arrangements: March 1991*, Current Population Reports, Series P-20, No. 461, Table F, p. 8.

- African-American children are over three times as likely as white children to live in female-headed households. More than 50 percent of African-American children under 18 years live with their mother only, compared to just 16 percent of their white counterparts.

- Just one out of three African-American children lives with two parents, compared to three out of four white children.

Table 14
Poverty Rates of Persons under 18 Years,
by Household Type and Race: 1991

	All Races	African American	White American
Total	21.8%	45.9%	11.3%
In married-couple families	10.6	15.1	9.8
In female-headed households	55.5	68.2	47.2

Source: Bureau of the Census, *Poverty in the United States: 1991*, Current Population Reports, Series P-60, No. 181, Table 5, pp. 10-15.

- In 1991, more than two-thirds of all African-American children living in female-headed households were poor, a poverty rate that was about 20 percentage points higher than the rate for white children in similar households.

254

- African-American children in married-couple families tend to fare far better than those living in female-headed households. In 1991, the poverty rate for African-American children in married-couple families was only 15 percent.

Table 15
Juveniles in Public Facilities, by Race
and Hispanic Origin: 1989

Race	Number	Percent
Total	56,123	100.0
White	22,201	39.6
African-American	23,836	42.5
Hispanic*	8,671	15.5
Other	1,415	2.5

*:   Persons of Hispanic origin may be of any race.

Source: Bureau of Justice Statistics, *Sourcebook of Criminal Justice Statistics: 1991*, Table 6.22, p. 604.

- African-American juveniles are greatly over-represented as tenants of public facilities, accounting for 42 percent of the total population in 1989.

- Hispanics, the next largest minority, were only 36 percent as likely as African Americans to be in public facilities for juveniles in 1989.

Table 16
Number of Children Ever Born to Teenaged Women,
by Race and Marital Status: 1990

	All Races	African American	White American
Born to women ever married:			
None	19.0%	13.0%	20.0%
One	23.0	21.0	23.0
Two or more	58.0	66.0	57.0
Born to women never married:			
None	82.0	53.0	89.0
One	10.0	20.0	7.0
Two or more	8.0	26.0	4.0

Source: Bureau of the Census, *Statistical Abstract of the United States: 1992*, Table 94, p. 71.

- The proportion of African-American teenagers who have been married and gave birth to one or more children is somewhat higher than the proportion of white teenagers with the same marital status.

- Birth rates differ sharply among never married teenagers, as African Americans in this group are more than four times as likely as their white counterparts to bear one or more children.

Table 17
Infant Mortality Rates, by Race and Sex: 1989
(per 1,000 live births)

	All Races	African American	White American
Both Sexes	9.8	18.6	8.1
Male	10.8	20.0	9.0
Female	8.8	17.2	7.1

Source: National Center for Health Statistics, "Annual Summary of Births, Marriages, Divorces, and Deaths: United States, 1991," *Monthly Vital Statistics Report*, Vol. 40, No. 13, September 30, 1992, Table 11, p. 22.

- Racial disparities in life chances begin very early in the life cycle. Infant mortality among African Americans continues at more than twice the mortality rate among whites.

- The racial disparity in infant mortality rates is wider among females. African-American female infants are nearly 2.5 times as likely as white infants to die before their first birthday.

Table 18
Death Rates for Persons Ages 1-to-24 Years,
by Race: 1989
(per 100,000 population)

Age	African American Male	African American Female	White American Male	White American Female
Under 1 year	2,179.0	1,863.9	909.4	716.0
1-4 years	88.4	72.5	47.8	38.4
5-9 years	39.3	28.6	24.8	18.6
10-14 years	44.3	27.6	31.7	19.0
15-19 years	76.2	48.6	115.3	49.8
20-24 years	00.7	86.8	149.5	48.1

Source: National Center for Health Statistics, "Advance Report of Final Mortality Statistics, 1989," *Monthly Statistics Report*, Vol. 40, No. 8, Supplement 2, January 7, 1992, Table 2, p. 15.

- African-American children between 1 and 14 years of age have a death rate that is about 1.5 times that of whites in the same age group.
- The racial gap in death rates is largest for persons under 1 year and those 20-to-24. The death rate for African-American males in these age groups is twice the rate for their white counterparts.

Table 19
Percent of High School Dropouts among
16- to 24-Year Olds, by Race and Sex: 1991

	All Races	African American	White American
Both Sexes	12.5%	13.6%	8.9%
Male	13.0	13.5	8.9
Female	11.9	13.7	8.9

Source: National Center for Education Statistics, *Digest of Education Statistics, 1992*, Table 98, p. 109.

- The high school dropout rate for African-American youth is 53 percent higher than the rate for whites.
- There is little difference in dropout rates between African-American males and females in the 16-to-24 age group.

Table 20
Percent of High School Graduates Enrolled
in College, by Race and Sex: 1980 and 1991

| | 1980 | | 1991 | |
	African American	White American	African American	White American
Both Sexes	28.3%	32.5%	31.8%	42.0%
Male	27.0	34.3	32.2	41.9
Female	29.2	30.9	31.4	42.1

Source: Bureau of the Census, *Statistical Abstract of the United States: 1992*, Table 258, p. 163.

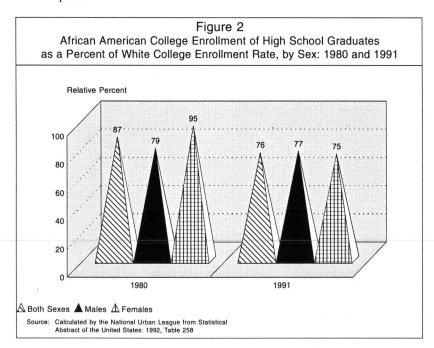

Figure 2
African American College Enrollment of High School Graduates as a Percent of White College Enrollment Rate, by Sex: 1980 and 1991

Relative Percent

△ Both Sexes ▲ Males ⚠ Females

Source: Calculated by the National Urban League from Statistical Abstract of the United States: 1992, Table 258

- The proportion of African-American high school graduates enrolled in college, relative to the proportion of white graduates, declined during the past decade. The African-American proportion was 76 percent that of whites in 1991, down from 87 percent in 1980.

- The rate percentage increase in college enrollment for African-American males from 1980 to 1991 was larger than the percentage increase for African-American females.

Table 21
African-American College Enrollment of Persons
Ages 14-to-34 Years, by Sex: 1991
(numbers in thousands)

	Number	Percent of Total Enrollment
Both Sexes	1,190	10.3%
Male	523	4.5
Female	667	5.8

Source: National Center for Education Statistics, *Digest of Education Statistics, 1992*, Table 198, p. 208.

- In the 14-to-34 year age group, African Americans accounted for 10 percent of all persons enrolled in college in 1991.

- The African-American college enrollment rate for females was 22 percent higher than the rate for males.

Table 22
Official and Hidden Teenaged Unemployment Rates,
by Race and Sex: 1991

	All Races	African American	White American
Official Unemployment Rates			
Both Sexes	18.6%	36.3%	16.4%
Male	19.8	36.5	17.5
Female	17.4	36.1	15.2
Hidden Unemployment Rates*			
Both Sexes	33.6	57.0	29.9
Male	34.5	56.9	30.8
Female	32.6	56.9	29.0

*: Estimates from the National Urban League's Hidden Unemployment Index, which factors in discouraged and involuntary part-time workers.

Source: Prepared by the National Urban League from unpublished Bureau of Labor Statistics data.

- Exceptionally high levels of joblessness continue to plague African-American youth. Official estimates for 1991 show unemployment among African-American teenagers to be more than double the rate among white teens.

- Joblessness among African-American youth is sharply higher when discouraged and underemployed workers are taken into account. The Hidden Unemployment Index put the level of African-American teen unemployment in 1991 at nearly 60 percent.

THE STATE OF URBAN BLACK AMERICA

While important social and economic inequalities continue to characterize Black America in general, such disparities are particularly pronounced among African Americans in urban areas. Indeed, the data indicate that urban African Americans not only fare worse than their white counterparts but also are significantly worse off than their fellow African Americans who reside in suburban communities. In other words, the widely recognized adversities and disadvantages African Americans experience take their most acute form in the nation's urban centers where the group remains heavily overrepresented.

These observations have serious implications for public policy. In particular, they underscore the need for targeted initiatives within any larger strategy to promote African-American advancement. Also, the interrelationships among urban problems are such as to require a well-coordinated, holistic approach to intervention.

In any case, as the April 1992 riots in South Central Los Angeles reminded us, conditions in urban Black America remain combustible, set to explode when the right spark occurs. More importantly, these conditions are counterproductive, inasmuch as they stifle human potential. Rather than being bastions of dependency, our urban areas can and should be revitalized into centers of economic opportunity and advancement. The following selected data help to emphasize that without more effective policy initiatives, the forces and processes at work in urban Black America are sure to produce further disadvantage and decline. By the same token, urban African Americans themselves must intensify their efforts to alleviate some of the serious social problems that exist in their communities.

Table 23
Distribution of Population,
by Area of Residence and Race: 1991

Area of Residence	Total	African American	White American
Metropolitan areas	77.6%	83.0%	76.4%
Inside central cities	30.1	56.3	25.7
Suburbs	47.5	26.7	50.7
Nonmetropolitan Areas	22.4	17.0	23.6

Source: Bureau of the Census, *The Black Population in the United States: March 1991*, Current Population Reports, Series P-20, No. 464, Table 3, p. 33.

- While the trend towards urbanization has decelerated among white Americans, African Americans continue to live disproportionately in urban areas. Approximately 56 percent of all African Americans, but only 26 percent of whites, live in cities.

- Conversely, only 27 percent of African Americans reside in suburban areas, compared to 51 percent of whites.

Table 24
Top 10 Metropolitan Areas with Largest Number
of African Americans: 1990
(numbers in thousands)

Metropolitan Area*	Number	Percent of Total
New York, NY	3,289	18.2%
Chicago, IL	1,548	19.2
Los Angeles, CA	1,230	8.5
Philadelphia, PA	1,100	18.7
District of Columbia	1,042	26.6
Detroit, MI	975	20.0
Atlanta, GA	736	26.0
Houston, TX	665	17.9
Baltimore, MD	616	25.9
Miami, FL	591	18.5

Source: Bureau of the Census, *Statistical Abstract of the United States: 1992*, Table 35, p. 33.

*: Consolidated Metropolitan Statistical Area (CMSA).

- African Americans tend to be concentrated in larger metropolitan areas. For example, about 3.3 million live in New York, 1.5 million in Chicago, and 1.2 million in Los Angeles.
- Of these top 10 metropolitan areas, at least one out of every four persons is African-American in three of these areas: the District of Columbia (26.6 percent), Atlanta (26.0 percent), and Baltimore (25.9 percent).

Table 25
Top 10 Cities with Largest Proportion
of African Americans: 1990
(numbers in thousands)

City	Number	Percent of Total
Inglewood, CA	57	51.9
Macon, GA	55	52.2
Memphis, TN	610	54.8
Jackson, MS	109	55.7
New Orleans, MS	497	61.9
Birmingham, AL	266	63.3
District of Columbia	607	65.8
Atlanta, GA	394	67.1
Detroit, MI	1,028	75.7
Gary, IN	94	80.6

Source: Bureau of the Census, *Statistical Abstract of the United States: 1992*, Table 38, pp. 35-37.

- African Americans constitute an overwhelming majority of the population in several U.S. cities. For example, they are 81 percent of the population in Gary, Indiana; 76 percent in Detroit, Michigan; and 67 percent in Atlanta, Georgia.

- Most of the cities in which African Americans are a majority are in the southern part of the country; Atlanta, Birmingham, and New Orleans are prominent.

Table 26
Unemployment Rates, by Area of Residence and Race: 1991

	Total Metro	Central City	Suburbs
All Races	6.7%	8.1%	5.8%
African American	12.7	13.9	10.6
White American	5.8	6.7	5.4

Source: Bureau of Labor Statistics, *Employment and Earnings*, Vol. 39, No. 1, January 1992, Table A-76, p. 83.

- For a number of decades, cities have been losing jobs. African Americans in the central cities are unemployed at 1.3 times the rate of African Americans in the suburbs.
- Interestingly, the black/white employment gap is only slightly wider in the central city than in the suburbs.

Table 27
Labor Force Participation Rates,
by Area of Residence and Race: 1991

	Total Metro	Central City	Suburbs
All Races	66.8%	64.4%	68.3%
African American	63.1	60.2	69.3
White American	67.4	65.8	68.2

Source: Bureau of Labor Statistics, *Employment and Earnings*, Vol. 39, No. 1, January 1992, Table A-76, p. 83.

- Persistent unemployment is highly correlated with psychological discouragement and withdrawal from the labor force. Thus, it is not surprising that the labor force participation rate of African Americans in central cities is well below that of their suburban counterparts.

- African Americans in the central city participate in the labor force at a significantly lower rate than their white counterparts.

Table 28
Median Family Income, by Area of Residence
and Race: 1991

Area of Residence	African American	White American	AA/Wh Ratio
Metro	$23,226	$40,671	.57
One million persons or more	24,741	43,700	.56
Central city	20,559	35,874	.57
Suburb	32,722	47,035	.69
Under 1 million	20,659	36,203	.57
Central city	19,591	33,930	.57
Suburb	23,695	37,149	.63

Source: Bureau of the Census, *Money Income of Households, Families, and Persons in the United States: 1991*, Current Population Reports, Series P-60, No. 180, Table 13, pp. 40-43.

Figure 3
African American Family Income as Percentage of White Family Income
in Metropolitan Areas with 1 Million or more Persons

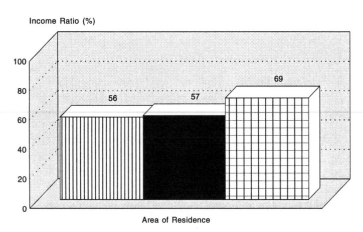

Income Ratio (%)

Area of Residence

☐ Metropolitan ■ Central City ☐ Suburban

Source: Calculated by the National Urban League from Current Population Reports
"Money Income Households, Families, and Persons in the United States: 1991"

- The loss of jobs and hope of African Americans in urban areas is reflected in the fact that central-city African Americans have a much lower family income than both suburban African Americans and central-city whites.

- In metro areas of 1 million or more persons, African-American family income in the central cities is only 57 percent that of their white counterparts. The racial income gap is substantially smaller in the suburbs.

Table 29
Living Arrangements of African-American Children
under 18 Years, by Area of Residence: 1991

	Total Metro	Central City	Suburbs
Living with:			
Both parents	38.3%	32.8%	47.0%
Mother only	60.1	63.0	49.0
Father only	4.2	4.1	4.0

Source: Bureau of the Census, *Marital Status and Living Arrangements: March 1991*, Current Population Reports, Series P-20, No. 461, Table 6, p. 51.

- Nearly half of all African-American children in the suburbs live with both parents compared to just one out of three children in central cities.

- Almost two-thirds of central-city African-American children live with their mother only, a much higher frequency than occurs among African Americans in the suburbs.

Chronology of Events
1992[1]

Nineteen ninety-two was a very eventful year—around the world and across the country. Indeed, there was seemingly an uncommon number of significant, if not dramatic, developments that history may record as having lasting effects. Not the least of these, of course, were the outcomes of the 1992 national elections, which could presage a markedly new day in American politics.

As usual, *The State of Black America* has tried to capture the events that are of particulalr interest to African Americans. The listing is by no means exhaustive. Moreover, it almost certainly includes items that might not be as worthy of mention as others that were omitted.

Nevertheless, we believe this "Chronology of Events" is a worthwhile and an informative representation of the year in review from the perspective of Black America. It should be a valuable resource for policymakers, educators, students, news media, community leaders, and others who desire to be well informed about the contemporary African-American experience.

* * *

Jan. 1:   The special investigator of news leaks about **Anita Hill's** allegations of sexual harassment against U.S. Supreme Court Justice **Clarence Thomas** asks National Public Radio reporter **Nina Totenberg** to make a formal deposition in the case, reports *The Washington Post*. Totenberg and **Timothy Phelps** of *Newsday* reported Oct. 6, 1991, that Hill, an Oklahoma University law professor, told the FBI that Thomas had sexually harassed her when she worked for him at the U.S. Department of Education and at the Equal Employment Opportunity Commission.

Jan. 1:   The Equal Employment Opportunity Commission (EEOC) asserts that the new Civil Rights Act does not apply to thousands of cases filed before the law was enacted, reports *The Washington Post*. The EEOC's policy reflects the **Bush** administration's continuing efforts to enforce a conservative interpretation of the Civil Rights Act.

---

[1] This chronology is based on news reports. In some instances, the event may have occurred a day or so befor the news item was reported.

Jan. 5: **Sean Combs,** a 22-year-old promoter of the celebrity basketball game at City College in New York, tells a city investigator that crowd violence had begun an hour before nine young people were fatally crushed and that the police had failed to stop it, despite his pleas to disperse and control the crowd, reports *The New York Times.*

Jan. 8: More than a month before votes are cast in New Hampshire in the 1992 presidential primaries, Virginia Gov. **L. Douglas Wilder** drops out of the Democratic field, leaving the other five candidates to scramble for black votes that Wilder failed to lock up, reports *The New York Times.*

Jan. 8: A significant number of minority infants are being classified in death as white, a mistake that dramatically underestimates minority infant mortality rates, according to an article published in the *Journal of the American Medical Association*, reports *The Washington Post.*

Jan. 8: The difference in life expectancy between black and white Americans widened in 1989, continuing a trend that has been evident for half a decade, according to the National Center of Health Statistics, reports *The Washington Post.*

Jan. 11: Portraying violence against the only state not to honor the nonviolent legacy of Dr. **Martin Luther King, Jr.,** or civil rights, a music video arouses anger and fascination in Phoenix, AZ, reports *The New York Times.* Depicting the assassination of local politicians, the video, "By the Time I Get to Arizona," by **Public Enemy**, gets repeated airplay on Phoenix news programs and elicits discussions on the front pages and in editorial columns of newspapers statewide.

Jan. 14: **Steven Johnson**, former press secretary to U.S. Sen. **Charles Robb** (D-VA), agrees to plead guilty to disclosing illegally contents of a tape recording secretly made in 1988 of a phone conversation between Virginia Gov. **L. Douglas Wilder** and a political supporter, reports *The Washington Post.*

Jan. 17: After passing up a $30 million NBA contract, Louisiana State University basketball star **Shaquille O'Neal** says he's just in school having fun: "I'm not in any hurry for college to be over," he tells *The Washington Post.* "I don't want to pay any bills."

Jan. 17: Lawyers for former Washington, DC, Mayor **Marion Barry** file suit in federal court in Richmond, VA, seeking $5.5 million in damages from six prison officials they accuse of violating Barry's rights, according to *The Washington Post*. The Bureau of Prisons investigated and disciplined Barry for alleged sexual misconduct while he was visiting with a guest in prison.

Jan. 17: Striving to see beyond a recent spate of racially motivated attacks, New York Mayor **David Dinkins** spends a day spotlighting the pain of hate and demanding tolerance by meeting with the governor, state legislators, and religious and community leaders, reports *The New York Times*.

Jan. 17: **Rodney King**, victim of a notorious beating by Los Angeles police officers in March 1991, tells investigators that he heard several racial epithets, including "How do you feel now, nigger?" and "Shut up, nigger" while he was struck repeatedly with police batons, reports *The Washington Post*.

Jan. 18: In an Atlanta ceremony honoring the achievements of Dr. **Martin Luther King, Jr.**, the slain civil rights leader's daughter, Rev. **Bernice King**, asks, "How dare we celebrate when the ugly face of racism still peers out at us?" President **Bush** impassively sat several yards from Miss King at the Martin Luther King, Jr. Center for Nonviolent Social Change, reports *The Washington Post*.

Jan. 18: Birmingham, AL, Mayor **Richard Arrington, Jr.**, the first black mayor of the city that was at the heart of the most violent civil rights demonstrations of the 1960s, is cited for contempt of court for failing to honor a federal grand jury subpoena for his appointment logs, reports *The New York Times*.

Jan. 19: Prosecutors ask a judge to reconsider her ruling barring testimony in former heavyweight boxing champion **Mike Tyson**'s rape trial from a South Carolina psychologist who also was enlisted for the William Kennedy Smith trial, reports *The Washington Post*. Marion County, IN, Superior Court Judge **Patricia Gifford** is expected to rule Jan. 21 on the appeal of her decision denying testimony by **Dean Kilpatrick**, director of the Crime Victims Research and Treatment Center at the Medical University of South Carolina in Charleston.

Jan. 20: After a decade of reports that the percentage of blacks entering college was regressing or barely inching forward, black college enrollment posted its first significant gains between 1988 and 1990, according to an American Council of Education study, reports *The Washington Post*.

Jan. 20: Democratic presidential candidates pay respect to the late Dr. **Martin Luther King, Jr.**: Arkansas Gov. **Bill Clinton** attends a ceremony at Thomas Jefferson High School in Brooklyn; Nebraska Sen. **Bob Kerrey** speaks to students at St. Paul's School in Concord, NH, and later attends a ceremony at Notre Dame College in Manchester, NH, with former Massachusetts Senator **Paul Tsongas**, reports *The Washington Post*.

Jan. 21: The **National Urban League** reports that black Americans are in an economic depression and that neither President **Bush** nor his Democratic challengers have come up with adequate proposals to help, reports *The New York Times*. "Every indicator of economic well-being shows that African Americans are doing far worse than whites," observes **John Jacob**, president and chief executive officer of the League, in its 17th annual report on *The State of Black America*. "We were in a recession before this recession hit, and now we are in a deep economic depression." Jacob restates the League's demand for a domestic Marshall Plan of economic support for education, job training, transportation, water supplies, waste treatment, and telecommunications technology.

Jan. 21: The Florida Supreme Court orders Judge **John Santora** to step down as chief judge after he says that black youths have a tendency to fight and form gangs, have difficulty coping in public schools, and commit rapes, reports *The Washington Post*. Santora also said he would not want any of his children married to a black, Asian, Chinese, or Puerto Rican; referred to female colleagues as girls; and said more Jews should be judges so they could work on Christmas day.

Jan. 22: Unlike the 1991 rape trial of William Kennedy Smith, the *State of Indiana v. Michael "Mike" Gerard Tyson* trial will not be televised, reports *The Washington Post*. Former boxing champion **Mike Tyson** will be tried for the July 1991 rape of an 18-year-old contestant in the Miss Black America beauty pageant.

Jan. 22: The U.S. Justice Department rejects as racially discriminatory a redistricting plan approved last year by the Georgia legislature, reports *The New York Times*. The move raises the possibility of a battle between black and white legislators over how to draft a new plan.

Jan. 23: Democratic presidential candidate **Bill Clinton** returns to Little Rock to oversee the execution by lethal injection of **Ricky Ray Rector**, a 40-year-old black man convicted of killing a white police officer, reports *The Washington Post*. Rector suffered brain damage when he shot himself in the head after killing the police officer, but was tried anyway. Clinton is expected to allow the execution over the strong objections of the National Coalition to Abolish the Death Penalty and the NAACP Legal Defense and Educational Fund.

Jan. 24: **Richard Arrington, Jr.**, the first black mayor of Birmingham, AL, is imprisoned for refusing to turn over personal records to federal prosecutors investigating City Hall corruption, reports *The Washington Post*. Arrington, four-term mayor of Birmingham, told defiant supporters that he was being hounded by federal attorneys demanding that he yield telephone logs and his daily appointment calendar for several years in a probe of bribery and kickbacks.

Jan. 24: Ten hours before he was scheduled to die in Virginia's electric chair, convicted killer **Herbert Bassette, Jr.,** is saved when Gov. **L. Douglas Wilder** issues a commutation order, saying he has doubts about Bassette's guilt, reports *The Washington Post*. Bassette, 47, a Richmond, VA, native, was the second person whose death sentence was commuted by Wilder, who, in his two years as governor, allowed five other executions to proceed.

Jan. 28: The Rev. **Al Sharpton** launches his campaign in New York for the U.S. Senate by marching across the Brooklyn Bridge and saying, "I intend to formally throw my hair into the ring," reports *The Washington Post*.

Feb. 5: **Michael Jordan** is suspended for the first time in his NBA career and fined $5,000 for one game for bumping a referee in Chicago's triple-overtime loss to the in Utah Jazz, reports *The Washington Post*. The suspension cost him one game's pay—about $40,000.

Feb. 5: **Willie Gary**, 44, a prosperous Florida lawyer, pledges $10 million to his alma mater, Shaw University in Raleigh, NC, reports *The New York Times.*

Feb. 6: Amid concern about fair-trial procedures, hundreds of prospective jurors gather as jury selection begins in the trials of four Los Angeles police officers accused of assaulting **Rodney King**, the black motorist whose roadside beating was captured on videotape in March 1991.

Feb. 6: A federal appeals court challenges the constitutionality of a scholarship program for black students at the University of Maryland, a ruling that calls into question scholarships based on race as a way to correct past discrimination, reports *The New York Times.*

Feb. 8: Former heavyweight champion **Mike Tyson** testifies in an Indianapolis court that he never forced an 18-year-old beauty pageant contestant to engage in sex, and that she willingly accepted his physical advances on a date in July, reports *The Washington Post.*

Feb. 10: **Alex Haley**, the award-winning author whose 12-year search for his African ancestry produced the best-selling novel, *Roots*, and subsequent television miniseries, "Roots: The Saga of an American Family," dies in Seattle after a heart attack.

Feb. 10: **Earvin "Magic" Johnson** is named the Most Valuable Player of the National Basketball Association All-Star Game, finishing with 25 points and 9 assists in 20 minutes at the Orlando Arena in Florida. With his performance, he fulfilled a personal quest and strengthened his determination to increase AIDS awareness and to fight HIV, the virus that causes AIDS, through his words and his deeds, reports *The New York Times.*

Feb. 12: **Benjamin Hooks**, Executive Director of the NAACP, urges blacks not to buy Japanese cars, saying that Japanese auto makers are reluctant to establish dealerships owned by blacks and unwilling to build plants in inner cities, reports *The New York Times.*

Feb. 16: **Benjamin Hooks** announces he will resign as Executive Director of the National Association for the Advancement of Colored People. The leadership of the nation's oldest civil rights organization split publicly in an angry debate over limiting the terms of its officers, reports *The New York Times.*

Feb. 19: The **Center for Constitutional Rights** goes into a New York federal court to seek a bigger voice for minority voters, reports *The New York Times*. The civil rights organization is charging that the way Supreme Court justices are nominated and elected in New York violates the Voting Rights Act.

Feb. 21: As many as 20 graves in a colonial-era cemetery for black New Yorkers are uprooted by construction workers, notwithstanding repeated assurance by federal officials that the critical archeological site in lower Manhattan would be spared such destruction, reports *The New York Times*.

Feb. 21: The U.S. Supreme Court rules that a beating or other use of excessive force by a prison guard may violate the Constitution, even if it does not result in serious injury to the prisoner, reports *The New York Times*. The vote was 7 to 2, with a dissenting opinion by Associate Justice **Clarence Thomas**, who said that the Eighth Amendment's prohibition against cruel and unusual punishment "is not and should not be turned into a national code of prison regulation."

Feb. 26: **Wayne Rudd**, the U.S. Attorney in Boston, is poised to be named to the third highest position in the Justice Department, overseeing the department's civil, antitrust, tax, civil rights, and land division, reports *The Washington Post*.

Feb. 27: The **Congressional Black Caucus** seeks a meeting with Secretary of Health and Human Services **Louis Sullivan** to discuss remarks by top department mental health official **Frederick Goodwin** that appeared to liken violence by inner-city youth to the behavior of "male monkeys" in the jungle. An HHS spokesman says Sullivan "personally and sternly reprimanded" Goodwin for his "offensive and insensitive remarks," reports *The Washington Post*.

Feb. 27: More than 250 professors and students at the City University of New York sue New York State, contending that the way it finances public higher education is racially discriminatory, reports *The New York Times*.

Feb. 28: Reelection campaign officials for Sen. **Jesse Helms** (R-NC) sign a consent decree to settle a U.S. Justice Department complaint that the 1990 campaign was involved in a mailing to intimidate black voters, reports *The New York Times*. The investigation began after postcards were sent to 125,000 North Carolinians, most of them eligible black voters, suggesting to them that they were not eligible and warning that if they went to the polls, they could be prosecuted for voter fraud.

Feb. 28:   In an unusual challenge to Harvard Law School, **Derrick Bell**, the law professor who took a leave of absence to protest the school's failure to hire and give tenure to a black woman on its faculty, asks Harvard to change its rule on leave time to allow him to continue his protest, reports *The New York Times*. Bell, Harvard's first black law professor, says he will challenge the two-year limit on grounds that the rule "doesn't apply to people who have walked away for reasons of conscience."

Feb. 28:   **Frederick Goodwin**, head of the government's Alcohol, Drug Abuse, and Mental Health Administration, resigns after a firestorm of criticism for his remarks that appeared to liken violence by inner-city youth to the behavior of "male monkeys" in the jungle, reports *The Washington Post* [see Feb. 27]. In his letter of resignation to President **Bush**, Goodwin said his remarks had been distorted and twisted to appear as if they were a racial insult.

Feb. 28:   The **U.S. Civil Rights Commission** plans to issue a report criticizing New York Mayor **David Dinkins'** handling of the boycott of a Korean grocery store by black shoppers in Brooklyn two years ago, reports *The New York Times*. Administration officials say the criticism will be a small part of a federal agency's study deploring what it describes as increasing acts of bigotry against Asian-Americans throughout the United States.

Feb. 28:   Discrimination against blacks trying to rent apartments in the Washington, DC, area has increased for the third consecutive year, according to the Fair Housing Council of Greater Washington, reports *The Washington Post*. The council says its black apartment seekers encountered bias 67 percent of the time when they tried to rent a unit.

Feb. 28:   Civil rights activist **Jesse Jackson** takes the high road in reaction to a minor flap involving Arkansas Gov. **Bill Clinton**, reports *The Washington Post*. After an erroneous report that Jackson was supporting Democratic presidential candidate **Tom Harkin**, the senior U.S. Senator from Iowa, Clinton called it "an outrage; a dirty double-crossing, back-stabbing thing to do." Jackson, however, said the campaign is about defeating the Bush-Quayle team and getting past side issues and back to real issues in the campaign.

Feb. 29: New York Mayor **David Dinkins** defends his handling of a black-led boycott of a Korean market in 1990 after the release of a federal report that repeated the criticism that he did not respond quickly enough to the crisis, reports *The New York Times*.

Feb. 29: Democratic politicians in New York lambast Vice President **Dan Quayle** and call his criticism of the state and its welfare system little more than a thinly disguised appeal to racism. Gov. **Mario Cuomo** says Quayle's stinging rebuke of New York's "liberal economics" and its welfare system was part of a calculated political effort to blame the recession on the unemployed.

Feb. 29: Lt. Col. **Joseph Perry, Jr.**, a black career officer who rose through the ranks of the still nearly all-white Connecticut State Police, is named the department's commander—the first minority officer to ever hold the top job. He takes over the 991-member force during a time of fiscal and morale troubles, reports *The New York Times*.

Mar. 1: In his first four months on the U.S. Supreme Court, Associate Justice **Clarence Thomas** voted as conservatively as any justice, delighting activists who battled to secure his confirmation and dashing the hopes of some liberals who thought his experiences with poverty and segregation might temper his judicial philosophy, reports *The Washington Post*.

Mar. 1: In the first presidential primary season since 1980 that **Jesse Jackson** has not been a candidate, Southern black voters show little excitement for the five major Democratic candidates, reports *The Washington Post*. However, the one candidate who has repeatedly campaigned for black votes, Arkansas Gov. **Bill Clinton**, seems to be a favorite in Georgia.

Mar. 3: Spurred by the shooting deaths of two students at Thomas Jefferson High School, New York Mayor **David Dinkins**, a coalition of black ministers, and **Bill Cosby** go to the school and invoke the imagery of the Civil Rights Movement in a call for East New York residents to be in an antiviolence crusade, reports *The New York Times*.

Mar. 3: In his new autobiography, *Darryl*, **Darryl Strawberry** accuses Mets management of racial bias and blames the Mets for making him a scapegoat for everything that was wrong with the baseball team and exploiting his personal problems in order to reduce his market value, reports *The New York Daily News*.

Mar. 7: The final episode of the "The Cosby Show" finishes taping; this last broadcast will air on April 30, reports *The New York Times*. Since its premier Sept 30, 1984, this show—created by comedian/entertainer/philanthropist **Bill Cosby**—has been watched by more people than any other situation comedy in the history of television.

Mar. 9: More than 300 college students from throughout the country march to the U.S. capitol to protest a **Bush** administration proposal to ban minority scholarships and to call on Congress to enact legislation requiring that every eligible student receive a federal grant for study, reports *The Washington Post*.

Mar. 10: Representatives of the American Federation of Government Employees and the American Federation of State, County, and Municipal Employees meet with organizers of a campaign to recall DC Mayor **Sharon Pratt Kelly**, reports *The Washington Post*. The two unions have more than 14,000 DC government employees.

Mar. 12: After the Federal Communications Commission doubles the number of radio stations that a single company may own, abstaining Commissioner **Andrew Barrett**, the only black member, accuses his colleagues of paying "lip service" to minority broadcasters and leaving him out of last-minute negotiations. Barrett also argues that the Commission was "grossly altering" the ownership structure of the industry, reports *The New York Times*.

Mar. 14: Arkansas Gov. **Bill Clinton** tells a predominantly black audience at Pleasant Grove Baptist Church in Detroit: "I come here to challenge you to reach out your hand to them [whites], for we have been divided too long," reports *The Washington Post*. Clinton's deputy campaign manager says that Clinton believes the country cannot succeed without racial healing.

Mar. 14: Actor **Sidney Poitier** is awarded the 20th American Film Institute's Life Achievement Award in honor of a career that has been distinguished in its own merit and groundbreaking for blacks in the entertainment industry, reports *The Washington Post*.

Mar. 16: Internationally renowned dancer **Katherine Dunham** is prepared to starve to death to protest the treatment of Haitian refugees who are being sent back to their homeland. Her fast has lasted more than 40 days, reports *The Washington Post*.

Mar. 17: About half of all white American youth believe it is whites, not minorities, who are more likely to be denied opportunities because of race, while most black and Hispanic youths say their groups are most likely to face discrimination, according to a new study by People for the American Way, reports *The Washington Post*.

Mar. 18: A longtime friend of award-winning author **Alex Haley**, three banks, an engineering firm, and a funeral home have filed claims totaling $238,143 against his estate, reports the *Associated Press*. "I would anticipate the debt is massive, but the assets are massive also," said Haley's son, **William**. "We're an honorable family. If my father has debts, we will do what we can to dispose of them."

Mar. 18: Blacks became slightly less segregated during the 1980s, but Hispanics were more likely to live in segregated neighborhoods at the end of the decade than at the beginning, a team of statisticians said in a study, reports *The Washington Post*.

Mar. 20: The Los Angeles police sergeant who supervised the beating of black motorist **Rodney King**, says the action of his officers was "violent and brutal" but fully justified by King's action, reports *The Washington Post*. "It was done to control a violent and combative suspect," says Sgt. **Stacey Koon** during the trial in Simi Valley, CA.

Mar. 22: A Stanford University surgeon, accused of harassing black female colleague **Frances Conley**, is demoted and agrees to undergo gender sensitivity training, reports *The Washington Post*. **Gerald Silverberg**, former acting chairman of the neurosurgery department, demonstrated a "troubling insensitivity" in his working relationships with women students and doctors, said David Korn, dean of the medical school.

Mar. 22: Basketball megastar **Michael Jordan** says he never bet on NBA games or any other sports events, reports *The Washington Post*. "I am no Pete Rose," Jordan says in response to questions about gambling debts he was said to have paid off. "I can safely say this is not a Pete Rose matter."

Mar. 26: Minorities are hit hardest by AIDS but are overlooked by prevention efforts, says a report by the National Minority AIDS Council, reports *USA Today*. The council called on Congress to reinstate $14 million for AIDS prevention that was cut from the federal budget by the **Bush** administration.

Mar. 26: Former heavyweight champion **Mike Tyson** is ordered to begin serving a six-year prison term. He was sentenced to 10 years on each of three rape convictions, with four years suspended.

Mar. 27: **Clarence Chance** and **Benny Powell** are released from prison after 17 years for what a California judge calls a concocted murder conviction, reports *The New York Times*. Seventeen years earlier, Los Angeles police officers coerced witnesses and manufactured the testimony of a prison informer to convict the two men in the killing of a California highway patrol officer.

Mar. 27: Dr. **Louis Sullivan**, Secretary of Health and Human Services, unveils a new AIDS education campaign that is comprised of a collection of ads warning that the disease can strike anyone. Groups representing people with AIDs, however, criticize the plan because it says nothing about safe sex, condoms, drug needles, or measures to prevent the spread of the disease, reports *The New York Times*.

Mar. 31: L. **Douglas Wilder, Jr.**, son of Virginia Governor **L. Douglas Wilder**, launches his own political career by announcing his candidacy for the House of Delegates. He will be a Democratic candidate for the seat left vacant by the death of **Roland "Duke" Ealey** (D-Richmond), reports *The Washington Post*.

Apr. 1: Ruling in a major school desegregation case, the U.S. Supreme Court gives hundreds of formerly segregated school districts a potentially new legal tool for returning to local control after decades of operating under federal court supervision, reports *The New York Times*. The 8-0 ruling, in a case from an Atlanta suburb, allows school districts to win release from court control bit by bit as they achieve racial equality in various facets of their operations.

Apr. 1: After meeting with **Michael Jordan** and his attorneys in New York, Commissioner **David Stern** says the National Basketball Association finds no cause for disciplining him following an investigation into reports that linked him to high-stakes gambling, reports *The New York Times*.

Apr. 4: Former Los Angeles Laker **Earvin "Magic" Johnson** becomes so fed up with the **Bush** administration's handling of the AIDS crisis that he vows to step down from the President's National Commission on AIDS "if things don't change," reports *The Washington Post*.

Apr. 7: The government is not doing enough to discover why diabetes strikes minorities far more often than white Americans, according to congressional investigators. The National Institutes of Health targets only a small number of research projects to Hispanic and black communities, and almost all the research on American Indians is devoted to a single Arizona tribe, reports *The Washington Post*.

Apr. 8: **Arthur Ashe**, the first black man to win one of tennis' Grand Slam tournaments, announces he has AIDS, the result of receiving contaminated blood more than a decade ago when he underwent quadruple bypass surgery at St. Luke's Hospital in New York after suffering a heart attack.

Apr. 9: A national network of 60 colleges, universities, public school systems, and professional organizations called Quality Education for Minorities unveils an $18 billion plan aimed at solving the lack of minority engineers, scientists, and mathematicians, reports *The Washington Post*. The eight-year plan includes identifying minorities who are interested in math, science, and engineering and providing them with after-school and Sunday academic programs; ensuring that predominantly black schools have up-to-date science laboratories; and financially rewarding prospective minority teachers.

Apr. 11: For 30 years, blacks with serious ailments have been much more likely than whites to be rejected for benefits under social security disability programs, according to a congressional investigative agency, reports *The New York Times*.

Apr. 16: **Willie Williams**, 48, commissioner of police in Philadelphia, is appointed to head the Los Angeles police force, becoming the city's first black chief of police.

Apr. 16: Pianist **Sammy Price**, 83, the "King of Boogie Woogie," dies at his home in Harlem, reports *The New York Times*.

Apr. 20: Actor **Denzel Washington** says the film "Malcolm X" will be the most controversial film of the decade, underlining the anticipation in Hollywood for **Spike Lee**'s forthcoming film about the slain black nationalist, reports *The New York Times*.

Apr. 20: Tightened standards issued by the U.S. military are expected to have a profound effect on the poor and many minorities who saw the military as a way to move up the economic ladder, reports *The Washington Post*.

Apr. 20: **Johnny Shines**, 76, one of the last of the original "Delta Blues" guitarists and singers who was nominated for a Grammy Award in 1980 for "Hanging On," a recording with Robert Junior Lockwood, dies in Tuscaloosa, AL.

Apr. 22: The FBI and lawyers for more than 300 black agents reach an agreement to settle the agents' claims of bias, reports the *Associated Press*. Six black agents will be promoted to supervisory positions and will receive back pay, and another 67 black agents will be given new positions or special training.

Apr. 24: Leaders of the Senate Rules Committee end attempts by a special Senate counsel to compel testimony from journalists who disclosed sexual harassment charges against U.S. Supreme Court Justice **Clarence Thomas** during his confirmation hearings, reports *The Washington Post*.

Apr. 27: "The Cosby Show" desensitizes whites to the nation's racial inequalities because it features an affluent black family, according to a study financed by **Bill Cosby**, reports *The Associated Press*. The findings renew debate over whether the 8-year-old program has set back race relations.

Apr. 29: Los Angeles police officer **Laurence Powell**, who struck most of the baton blows in the videotaped beating of **Rodney King**, said he does not regret his conduct and labeled King a "political puppet" who was "no victim at all," reports *The Washington Post*.

Apr. 30: A jury of 11 whites and one Asian American acquits three white Los Angeles police officers in the beating of black motorist **Rodney**

King and fails to reach a verdict on a single count involving a fourth officer, reports *The Washington Post*. Despite evidence of a videotape showing more than 50 baton blows and kicks directed at King as he lay on the ground after being stopped for traffic violations March 3, 1991, the jury acquitted Sgt. **Stacey Koon** and officers **Timothy Wind**, 32, and **Theodore Briseno**, 39, of assault charges.

The acquittal results in the nation's largest city becoming a war zone. Thousands of National Guard troops and police are deployed in riot gear to try to stop the spread of looting and destruction. The casualty toll rose to at least 17 people dead and 200 injured. Mayor **Tom Bradley** declares a dusk-to-dawn curfew for the entire city and announces that lawbreakers will be arrested and punished, reports *The Washington Post*.

Apr. 30: **"The Cosby Show"** airs its last show after eight salutary seasons on NBC. "It's arguably the saddest because the show was arguably the happiest," writes Tom Shales, television critic for *The Washington Post*.

May 1: Los Angeles Congresswoman **Maxine Waters** (D-CA) blames the police department and the White House for the ensuing riots after the acquittal of those police officers in the **Rodney King** beating trial. Although she condemns the violence, she says: "People are acting out of frustration and hopelessness. People who are thinking that way don't think rationally. They act. Until you can send a message that there is some kind of justice, I think things could get even worse before they get better," reports *The Washington Post*.

May 1: **Howard University** lobbies to roll back a federally imposed 50 percent tuition surcharge on international students that it says drives away prospective students and jeopardizes Howard's reputation as a mecca for students from developing countries, reports *The Washington Post*.

May 2: **Rodney King**, the unemployed construction worker whose beating by police set off the events leading to the Los Angeles riots, addresses the public for the first time in 14 months. Choking back tears, he pleads for an end to the violence. "People," he says haltingly, "I just want to say, can we all get along? Can we stop making it horrible for the older people and for the kids?" reports *The Los Angeles Times*.

May 4:   The **University of Maryland** graduates more black baccalaureates than any other predominantly white university, reports *The Washington Post.*

May 4:   The **U.S. Conference of Mayors** calls on President **Bush** and **Congress** to name a commission to study the Los Angeles rioting, saying deteriorating conditions of cities demand an investigation not only of "the visible riots, but also to stem the 'quiet riots' of poverty and injustice in America's cities," reports *The Washington Post.*

May 4:   Four slayings in Los Angeles increase the death toll to 49 since violence began in that city on April 30, reports *The Washington Post.*

May 4:   After three days of terror, Los Angeles hopes to return to normal, with schools set to reopen, a curfew lifted, and utilities and transportation services ready to be restored, reports *The Washington Post.*

May 5:   Twelve historically black colleges head the list of higher learning institutions which graduate the most blacks. **Howard University** tops the list, reports *The Associated Press.*

May 5:   The number of black Ph.D.'s may be rising after a decade of decline, according to the National Research Council study that showed a 13 percent increase in the number of blacks earning Ph.D.'s from 1989 to 1991, reports *The New York Times.*

May 6:   **Spelman College** in Atlanta will receive a $37 million gift, the largest ever to a historically black college. The gift, the principal of a fund set up by **DeWitt Wallace**, was established in 1980 with $1 million in *Reader's Digest* stock, reports *The New York Times.*

May 6:   A U.S. Court of Appeals orders the suspension of part of the District of Columbia program that reserves contracts for minority-owned businesses, ruling in favor of a white-owned firm that claimed it had been prohibited from bidding on city road construction contracts, reports *The Washington Post.* The ruling could lead to an end to the city's 15-year-old minority contracting law, experts agree. DC Mayor **Sharon Pratt Kelly** later tries to find a way to retain the program, but some members of the DC City Council criticize her for not acting sooner to forestall the legal challenge.

May 7: As President **Bush** sees the face of violence, rage, and poverty in Los Angeles, he sets aside his speech to say, "We should take nothing but sorrow out of all that," reports *The Washington Post.* Entering a world he rarely sees, Bush hears the rage of a black construction worker unable to find work and of Korean business owners who lost everything in the looting and fires of recent rioting.

May 7: Citing the riots that followed the verdict in the **Rodney King** beating case, a Miami state judge orders a change of venue in the second trial of a Miami police officer who was convicted of killing two black motorists in 1989, reports *The New York Times.*

May 10: A week after the acquittal of four white police officers in the beating of a black motorist, a sense of betrayal sweeps even the most prosperous blacks in Los Angeles and across the nation, reports *The New York Times.* The frustration prompts a renewed solidarity among some blacks who plan to close their accounts at white banks and start new ones at black-owned institutions. Others are returning to the old neighborhood, lecturing at inner-city schools to inspire impoverished children or to take their own children on tours of charred city blocks for a tragic life lesson.

May 11: A week after the rioting in Los Angeles, certain facts remain unknown. The coroner guesses that 58 people died, but police estimate 53. About 40 people died of gunshots; others were stabbed or strangled. Among the dead; 15 young men and an 89-year-old woman. About 26 were black; 18 Hispanics, 10 whites, and two Asians. The dead were wealthy and poor, educated and ignorant, hopeful and bitter, reports *The Washington Post.*

May 11: Most Americans view the riots in Los Angeles as a "warning" about the state of race relations, and say it is time for a new emphasis on the problems of minorities and cities, according to a *New York Times*/CBS News poll.

May 14: **Ramona Africa** is released from prison seven years after she ran screaming from a bombed Philadelphia row house. Miss Africa, 36, is the only adult to survive the 1985 confrontation between police and the radical MOVE organization that resulted in a fire that killed 11 organization members, including five children, reports the *Philadelphia Inquirer.*

May 16: Los Angeles police officer **Laurence Powell**, principal assailant in the beating of black motorist **Rodney King**, will be tried again on a felony assault charge, rules Superior Court Judge **Stanley Weisberg**, reports *The Washington Post.*

May 17: A federal jury directs the owner of a suburban Virginia housing development to pay $850,000 to a group of plaintiffs for having used only white people as models in the development's advertising, reports *The New York Times.* Legal experts say the verdict might be the largest award ever made by a jury in a housing discrimination case.

May 18: About 1,600 businesses were severely damaged in the Los Angeles riots, most of them in South-Central Los Angeles, reports *The New York Times.* City officials estimate the losses at nearly $800 million. A large proportion of the businesses was owned by Koreans, a group blacks charge was exploiting their poverty.

May 19: **Michael Jordan**, overcoming what he called "individual adversity," is named the National Basketball Association's Most Valuable Player for the 1991-92 season. Jordan led the defending champion Chicago Bulls to an NBA-best 67-15 record that also was the best in franchise history.

May 21: Four black men in Los Angeles plead not guilty in the televised beating of **Reginald Denny**, a white truck driver. A judge sets bail for them, saying he found no reason to believe they would be a threat to others, reports *The Washington Post.* Denny was dragged from his truck and nearly killed April 30 as rioting began hours after 10 not-guilty verdicts were announced in the trial of four white Los Angeles police officers accused of assaulting black motorist **Rodney King**.

May 28: A Washington, DC, real estate management firm agrees to pay $350,000 to a black woman who complains that she is unable to rent an apartment at the Charlestowne North complex in Greenbelt, MD, because of racial bias, reports *The Washington Post.* The promised payment to **Carolyn Jackson** is a record sum for a housing discrimination claim in the District of Columbia, Maryland, and Virginia.

June 8: In the days after the acquittal of four white Los Angeles police officers charged in the beating of black motorist **Rodney King**, black and white opinions were uncharacteristically in sync on a racial question. Large majorities of whites and overwhelming majorities of blacks told pollsters that the verdict was wrong and justice had not been served, reports *The Washington Post*. But when asked if the verdict "shows that blacks cannot get justice in this country," 78 percent of blacks said yes, compared to only 25 percent of the whites.

June 8: The New York borough of Queens is believed to be the largest political subdivision where blacks and whites share a common median income, according to *The New York Times*.

June 10: Former Washington, DC, Mayor **Marion Barry** announces he will run for the DC City Council seat in Ward 8, the district's most impoverished area, reports *The Washington Post*.

June 10: **Larry Riley**, 39, a featured actor in the nighttime soap opera "Knots Landing," dies of AIDS in Burbank, CA. Riley won the 1991 *Soap Opera Digest* Award for best supporting actor in a prime-time drama.

June 13: The Minnesota Supreme Court rules that a black girl should be adopted by her grandparents, not the white couple who have cared for her nearly since her birth and fought for two years to adopt her, reports *The Washington Post*.

June 14: The Rev. **Joseph Lowery**, one of the founding ministers in the 1960s Civil Rights Movement, retires as Executive Director of the Southern Christian Leadership Conference with an angry sermon targeting government indifference as the cause of America's social woes, reports *The Washington Post*. "It is not our economy we need to be worried about. What's imperiled today in America is her soul," Lowery tells about 1,500 people who packed Atlanta's Cascade United Methodist Church.

June 14: Democratic presidential hopeful **Bill Clinton** stuns members of the **Rainbow Coalition** by criticizing it for giving a public forum to rap singer **Sister Souljah**, whose words in the aftermath of the Los Angeles riots Clinton said were "filled with hatred," reports *The Washington Post*.

June 15: **Dominique Dawes** is set to become the first black woman gymnast to compete in the Olympics for the United States, while **Jair Lynch** is poised to become the third black male gymnast to represent the United States, reports *The Washington Post*.

June 17: Responding to criticism by Arkansas Gov. **Bill Clinton** that remarks she made in a newspaper interview were hate-filled and divisive, rap artist **Sister Souljah** characterizes the Arkansas governor as a hypocrite and calls his remarks "a poor excuse for an agenda-less candidate," reports *The New York Times*.

June 17: In a decision described as a significant step toward desegregating New Jersey's schools, a state appeals court rules that the State Board of Education has the power and obligation to eliminate school segregation, even across district lines, reports *The New York Times*.

June 18: The Governor of Georgia and the primary plaintiffs in lawsuits challenging the way state judges are selected reach an agreement that will change the system from elective to appointive and pave the way for an immediate and dramatic increase in the number of black judges, reports *The New York Times*.

June 18: Nearly two months after the Los Angeles riots, efforts by the **Bush** administration and **Congress** to adopt a sweeping urban aid package and to get money into the pipeline by midsummer are bogged down because of partisan bickering, reports *The Washington Post*.

June 19: Federal job recruiters tend to bypass the nations 117 historically black colleges and universities, and many students on those campuses say they cannot find information about government job opportunities in their schools, reports *The Washington Post*.

June 19: A group of black business people, including Washington Redskins halfback **Joe Washington**, accuses an American-owned distributor of Toyota franchises of discriminating against minorities who seek to open dealerships, reports *The Washington Post*.

June 19: Six years after ruling that the prosecution cannot exclude people from serving on juries on the basis of race, the U.S. Supreme Court extends the same rule to criminal defendants, reports *The New York Times*. The decision, based on the constitutional guarantee of equal protection of the laws, requires the defense to provide a "racially neutral explanation" for any pattern of challenges to potential jurors that suggests a racial motivation.

June 20: **Carl Lewis**, considered by many to be the greatest track and field athlete ever, fails to make the 1992 U.S. Olympic team in the 100 meters and will not run the event (in which he holds the world record) at the Summer Olympics in Barcelona, reports *The Washington Post*.

June 21: **Bill Cosby, Janet Jackson, Michael Jordan, Magic Johnson, Prince, Oprah Winfrey**, and Washington, DC, philanthropist **Peggy Cooper Cafritz** come to the aid of filmmaker **Spike Lee**, who runs over budget in his epic filming of "Malcolm X," reports *The Washington Post*.

June 21: The Pentagon's largest new weapons program—the F-22 stealth fighter—is becoming nearly as invisible to small and minority-owned defense firms, reports *The Washington Post*. In a plan approved by the Air Force, **Lockheed Corp**. allocates only $16 million of its $3.2 billion share of the F-22 work to small businesses, about one half of 1 percent. For minority-owned businesses, the share was $694,000.

June 22: Declaring that the First Amendment prohibits the government from "silencing speech on the basis of its content," a five-member majority of the U.S. Supreme Court rules that legislatures may not single out racial, religious, or sexual insults or threats for prosecution as "hate speech" or "bias crimes," reports *The New York Times*.

June 25: **Reginald Davis**, facing his own troubles with an impending criminal drug trial in a Washington, DC, Superior Court, ends his campaign to have Mayor **Sharon Pratt Kelly** recalled, reports *The Washington Post*. Davis, a student at the University of the District of Columbia, started the drive to unseat Kelly less than two years into her first term, accusing the mayor of being unresponsive to residents.

June 29: Virginia Gov. **L. Douglas Wilder** arrives in South Africa for a nine-day visit in the midst of a major political crisis for the country, reports *The Washington Post*.

June 30: Mayor **Tom Bradley** of Los Angeles says that the city should settle a pending multimillion-dollar lawsuit filed by **Rodney King**, victim of a beating by Los Angeles police, reports *The Washington Post*.

July 1: People gather on Springfield Avenue in Newark, NJ, for the groundbreaking ceremonies for the new $5 million Loews Newark Sixplex Theater, scheduled to open in December 1992, reports *The New York Times*. The theater stands where the riots began in 1967 and is, except for a two-year-old supermarket, the first major business to open in Central Ward in 25 years.

July 1: A new era begins in riot-scarred Los Angeles as police chief **Willie Williams** takes over the helm of a demoralized force with promises to help heal the city's wounds and eliminate "racism" and "sexism" from the Los Angeles Police Department, reports *The Washington Post* [see April 16].

July 1: Democratic presidential hopeful **Bill Clinton** meets with members of the **Congressional Black Caucus** and appears to win over members of the group who were miffed because the Arkansas governor canceled previously scheduled meetings, reports *The Washington Post*. After a closed-door session in the Rayburn House Office Building, Rep. **Edolphus Towns** (D-NY) says, "I felt very good about the meeting." Towns had criticized Clinton for controversial comments about rap singer **Sister Souljah** and for playing golf at an all-white country club in Little Rock.

July 2: To settle a major housing discrimination suit, New York City's Housing Authority agrees to set aside 1,900 apartments for Hispanics and blacks who allegedly were denied housing in order to keep selected housing projects mostly white, reports *The New York Times*.

July 5: *The New York Times* reports that Mayor **David Dinkins** has mastered the art of mayor by trimming $2 billion from New York City's vast bureaucracy in a single year, achieving a $500 million surplus despite a recession, moving aggressively against possible police corruption, standing up to the city's labor unions, and demonstrating toughness and guile in outwitting state legislators.

July 5: **John O'Bryant**, who became the first black member of the Boston School Committee and served amid turbulent white protests over court-ordered school busing, dies at Carney Hospital in Boston after suffering a heart attack, reports *The New York Times*.

July 6: Black public colleges face an uncertain future after a U.S. Supreme Court ruling that some schools in Mississippi were unlawfully kept separate and inferior, reports *The Associated Press*. Some predict the ruling will bring increased funds and upgraded degree programs at historically black schools. Others say it will sound a death knell for black colleges in states that would rather close them than improve them.

July 7: A Mark Twain scholar, **Shelley Fisher Fishkin**, links the voice of Huckleberry Finn to a 10 year-old black servant Twain met just before starting to work on the book. Tracing Huck's voice to a black source could change the way the book is taught and revises the current debate over multiculturalism, reports *The New York Times*. "This shows a real black root in a white consciousness," said **Dave E.E. Sloane**, a professor of English at the University of New Haven.

July 7: A $3.1 million multipurpose center that will stand as a tribute to blues singer **Bessie Smith** is set to open next September in Chattanooga, TN, where the singer sang for nickels and dimes as a youngster, reports *The Washington Post*.

July 7: Minorities continue to be underrepresented in the teaching profession and only 28 percent of teachers are male, the smallest percentage in at least three decades, according to a survey by the National Education Association, reports *The Washington Post*.

July 9: Virginia Gov. **L. Douglas Wilder** says he will endorse Arkansas Gov. **Bill Clinton** for president before the upcoming Democratic national Convention begins, reports *The Richmond Times-Dispatch*. Wilder, who at one time opposed Clinton for the nomination, says his late endorsement should not be interpreted as a slap at Clinton.

July 12: **Benjamin Hooks** plans to deliver his final executive speech at the NAACP's national convention in Nashville. Facing retirement, Hooks, 67, says he has been the victim of unfair criticism of his leadership, reports *The Atlanta Journal/Constitution*.

July 15: The Democratic presidential ticket of **Bill Clinton** and **Al Gore** wins support from former President **Carter**, the last Democrat to occupy the White House, but only modest support from **Jesse**

Jackson, who ran unsuccessfully in 1984 and 1988, reports *The Associated Press.*

July 15: Philip Morris, Inc., donated more than $17 million to schools, hospitals, and cultural and charity groups last year, targeting minority organizations that might help defeat tax and anti-smoking bills, reports *The Washington Post.*

July 15: Since Al Campanis' infamous "necessities" remark, major-league baseball teams have made 52 managerial changes, naming four minorities as managers, reports *The Richmond Times-Dispatch.* One, **Frank Robinson**, was fired in Baltimore. Others are **Cito Gaston** in Toronto, **Hal McRae** in Kansas City, and **Felipe Alou** in Montreal. There are no black general managers in the major leagues.

July 15: **Marilyn DeShields**, 22, of Petersburg, VA, is crowned Miss Black America in Indianapolis, IN.

July 16: **Buck Buchanan**, an NFL Hall of Fame defensive lineman for the Kansas City Chiefs (1963-1975), dies of lung cancer at the age of 51, reports *The New York Times.*

July 19: An FBI agent screening a prominent black lawyer for a federal judgeship forces the lawyer to submit a footprint, then posts the print and jokes it was a stunt, reports *The Boston Herald.* The agent and his supervisor were suspended for the prank.

July 19: Efforts by La Crosse, WI, officials to assign and bus children to elementary schools based on family income was designed to break up the concentration of poor children in a few schools and to ensure efforts to improve test scores and upgrade skills. Voters reacted by recalling four of the nine school board members who supported the plan, reports *The Washington Post.*

July 20: **Ronald Brown**, the chairman of the Democratic National Committee, is hailed as one of the party's greatest conciliators for choreographing what turns out to be the most conflict-free convention in years, reports *The New York Times.*

July 23: Virginia Gov. **L. Douglas Wilder** outlaws an Air National Guard squadron's use of the Confederate battle flag, a symbol that many African-American airmen reportedly find offensive, reports *The Richmond Times-Dispatch.*

July 24: In Fort Leavenworth, KS, Joint Cheifs of Staff Chairman **Colin Powell** dedicates a 13-foot statue of a black soldier, rifle in hand, riding a horse along an avenue leading to the base, reports *The Associated Press*. The memorial honors black military men dubbed "Buffalo Soldiers" for their animal-skin coats and fierce fighting skills. About 100 original members attend the dedication, including the oldest survivor, 109-year-old **Jones Morgan** of Richmond, VA.

July 24: The long-standing income gap between black and white households in the United States remained wide in the 1980s, narrowing only slightly according to the 1990 Census, reports *The New York Times*. Black households fare better in the Northeast and on the West Coast, while being hard hit in the Midwest. Nationally, the 1989 median household income for whites was $31,435, and for blacks, $19,758.

July 24: High school graduation rates among blacks have doubled over the past two decades, significantly narrowing the racial gap in educational attainment, according to 1990 Census figures, reports *The Washington Post*. Among blacks 25 and older, 63 percent are high school graduates, up from 31 percent in 1970. The 1990 figure for the total population is 75.2 percent.

July 26: **Mary Wells**, the singer who helped break pop music barriers with 1960s Motown hits such as "My Guy," dies of throat cancer at the age of 49, reports *USA Today*.

July 26: Maryland Democrats elect Baltimore City Councilmember **Vera Hall**, 55, as the first African-American woman to lead the state party and one of only a few women to hold such a post nationally, reports *The Washington Post*.

July 26: The case of **William Andrews**, convicted of a grisly murder as a teenager and condemned to die by lethal injection as he approaches middle age, becomes a rallying point for Utah's tiny black population who are angry over his treatment and what they say are innumerable past slights and injustices, reports *The Washington Post*.

July 26: The **National Urban League** kicks off its annual convention in San Diego, CA, with the convention theme, "Making A Difference in the '90s: Bringing the Future into Focus." It is expected to attract more than 18,000 people, including presidential candidates Bill Clinton and Ross Perot.

President and chief executive officer **John Jacob**, says in his keynote address that the League's Marshall Plan, unveiled two years ago, "can be the engine that pulls this nation out of recession and onto a long-term growth path. . . ."America cannot survive in a global economy when it has far more poverty than its competitors, when it has much greater inequality than its competitors, when it writes off the minorities it depends on to outproduce it."

July 27: "It's time to rebuild America and to provide the American dream for all persons living in America," says Democratic presidential nominee **Bill Clinton**, who suggests that those twin goals can be met by merging the common strategies in the National Urban League's Marshall Plan for America and his "Rebuild America" plan. Clinton addresses a standing-room-only crowd at the opening plenary session of the League's annual conference in San Diego, CA.

July 27: The Rev. **Al Sharpton** surprises a lot of people in his U.S. Senate campaign race in New York as he restyles himself and runs a serious, if quixotic, campaign, reports *The New York Times*. Sharpton insists that mainstream America, not himself, has changed. "After Rodney King and LA, after such blatant acts, people say, 'Well, maybe Sharpton is not crazy, maybe there is something wrong in the justice system.'"

Aug. 2: **Gail Devers** wins the women's 100-meter race in the Summer Olympics in Barcelona, Spain.

Aug. 2: **Lem Barney** and **John Mackey** are enshrined in Canton, Ohio's National Football League Hall of Fame.

Aug. 3: **Jackie Joyner-Kersee** becomes the first woman ever to repeat as Olympic heptathlon champion when she wins the two-day, seven-event marathon by nearly 200 points over **Irina Belova** of the Unified Team during the Summer Olympics in Barcelona, Spain.

Aug. 4: **Ralph Cooper, Sr.**, the founder of Harlem's Apollo Theater Amateur Night and the host of the legendary "Wednesday Amateur Night," dies after a bout with cancer in New York City. Cooper, once considered a matinee idol for his movie roles as a black cowboy, was also the first African American to host a television variety show in New York.

Aug. 6: In an Olympic long-jump competition, **Carl Lewis** wins the gold medal with a 1-1/4" jump longer than that of **Mike Powell**, who—for the second Games in a row—has to settle for the silver during the Summer Olympics in Barcelona, Spain.

Aug. 6: Federal civil rights charges are leveled against the four policemen whose acquittals on most state charges in the beating of motorist **Rodney King** led to deadly riots, reports *The Associated Press.* Indictments charge officers **Laurence Powell**, **Timothy Wind**, and **Theodore Briseno** with aiding and abetting each other in beating, stomping, and kicking King under cover of law. The fourth defendant, Sgt. **Stacey Koon**, is charged with failing to prevent an unlawful assault.

Aug. 8: Outstanding Louisiana State University star **Shaquille O'Neal**, chosen first in the 1992 National Basketball Association draft, signs a contract with the Orlando Magic reportedly worth $40 million over seven years, reports *The New York Times.* The deal is believed to be the most lucrative in team sports history.

Aug. 8: **Lee Brown**'s departure after 2-1/2 years as New York City's top police official is somewhat typical of an emerging pattern across the nation. With increasing frequency, police chiefs are lasting only a short time on the job, reports *The New York Times.* Brown, who said the job had grown far more demanding, is retiring to spend more time with his seriously ill wife.

Aug. 8: **Kevin Jackson** narrowly defeats **Elmadi Jabraijloy** in the 180.5 pound wrestling class, winning a gold medal in the Summer Olympics in Barcelona, Spain.

Aug. 9: **Carl Lewis** anchors a world-record 400-meter relay, winning his eighth gold medal in three Olympics, while the U.S.A.'s Dream Team beats Croatia 117-85 during the 1992 Summer Olympics in Barcelona, Spain.

Aug. 10: Asserting that all women owe a debt of gratitude to **Anita Hill**, **Hillary Clinton**, wife of Democratic presidential candidate **Bill Clinton**, praises the Oklahoma University law professor for her "courageous" testimony before the Senate Judiciary Committee last October about sexual harassment by then-Supreme Court nominee **Clarence Thomas**. Mrs. Clinton gave the keynote address at the American Bar Association luncheon during which Professor

Hill was honored by the ABA's Commission on Women in the Profession, reports *The Associated Press.*

Aug. 13: *The Afro-American* newspaper group, which includes black newspapers in Richmond, Washington, and Baltimore, reaches a century of telling stories others often would not, reports *The Associated Press. The Afro-American*, which once printed 13 editions with a circulation of 225,000 from New Jersey to South Carolina, was one of three major newspaper chains for blacks in the first half of the century. The paper, founded by **John H. Murphy, Sr.**, a former slave, now has a circulation of about 50,000, up from a low of 25,000 in the mid-1980s.

Aug. 14: Black motorist **Rodney King** will not be prosecuted on charges of drunken driving, the district attorney's office in Orange County, CA, announces, saying evidence from his arrest is not strong enough to convince a jury of his guilt, reports *The Associated Press.*

Aug. 16: Although they traditionally are labeled as liberals, a third of the blacks in a recent Joint Center for Political Studies survey call themselves conservatives, reports *The Washington Post.* A quarter said they are political independents, not Democrats. Nearly half support capital punishment and limits on abortion rights. A majority thought people who possess drugs should be evicted from public housing and that women who have more children while on welfare should not necessarily get more money.

Aug. 20: Companies that make clothes, cosmetics, sports equipment, and other products persist in using white models almost exclusively in magazine ads, contends **Mark Green**, New York City's consumer affairs commissioner. The finding is reported in *The Detroit News,* which publishes excerpts from Green's latest report, "Still Invisible," a sequel to his "Invisible People," which found in July 1991 that only 3.4 percent of the models in 11,391 ads in 27 magazines were African American.

Aug. 21: If 1991 was a breakthrough year for black-oriented movies, 1992 has been a comedown, reports *The Los Angeles Times.* Last year, about 20 major films dealing with African-American themes were released out of the roughly 140 films distributed by major film companies. The number is reported to be half that for 1992.

Aug. 22: **Derrick Bell**, the first black faculty member at Harvard Law School, says there is no evidence that his two-year leave of absence to protest racial discrimination in hiring practices did any good, reports *The New York Times*. "If the measure is getting women of color on the law school faculty, it was not very successful," he said. A constitutional scholar at the school for 22 years, Bell said it did not appear that he would return to the school after his request to continue his protest a third year was denied.

Aug. 23: Racism is costing America money, reports *The Associated Press*. Bigotry subtracts from economic growth in the toll of welfare and unemployment, in the high cost of crime that demands more police and prisons, in the tariff exacted by what often seems to be self-destructive violence. Racism deprives the nation of energy, know-how, drive, and dollars. "Unless we get a handle on racism, foreign competitors are going to eat our lunch," says **Edward Irons**, dean of business at Clark Atlanta University and a consultant to federal and international agencies on banking and economic development.

Aug. 23: President **Bush** and Democratic nominee **Bill Clinton** are able to skirt issues such as health care and poverty because they are not being forced to address them, agree several journalists during a panel discussion at the **National Association of Black Journalists** convention in Detroit. "This election year, poor people are really not on the agenda, and we will not see a lot of campaigning among blacks by either side this fall," says **Michael McQueen**, a political reporter for the *Wall Street Journal*.

Aug. 23: **Frederick O'Neal**, an award-winning actor who was the first black president of the Actors' Equity Association, dies at his home in Manhattan at age 86, reports *The New York Times*. A character actor who avoided typecasting, O'Neal performed on stage and in television and film. He made his Broadway debut in 1944 in the role of the comic bully Frank in "Anna Lucasta." For his performance, he won the Clarence Derwent Award as most promising newcomer of the theater season, the New York Drama Critics Award for best supporting performance of 1944, and the Donaldson Award for the 1944-45 season.

Aug. 25: **JoAnn Price**, head of the National Association of Investment Companies—a trade group representing 150 minority venture-capital firms—seeks to raise $250 million for minority-owned firms to create a huge superfund of investment capital, reports

USA Today. The money would be funneled to venture capitalists and other groups that would invest in promising minority businesses.

Aug. 25: New York Gov. **Mario Cuomo** says he will nominate **George Bundy Smith**, a judge on the Appellate Division of the State Supreme Court in Manhattan, to be an associate judge on New York State's highest court, reports *The New York Times.* If confirmed, Bundy would replace Judge **Fritz Alexander, II**, who resigned to work as New York City's Deputy Mayor for Public Safety.

Aug. 29: Dr. **Mae Jemison** will become the first African-American woman astronaut and the first woman of color in space when she flies aboard the Space Shuttle *Endeavour* in early September, reports the Richmond *Afro-American.* Dr. Jemison, of Decatur, AL, is the National Aeronautics and Space Administration's (NASA's) first science mission specialist. She will conduct 40 experiments, including one she designed that will look at the effects of the space environment on bone cells.

Sept. 4: **Harold Fleming**, 70, president emeritus of the Potomac Institute—an organization devoted to eliminating racial discrimination—and an influential figure in the Civil Rights Movement for more than 40 years, dies of an apparent heart attack at his Washington, DC, home, reports *The Washington Post.*

Sept. 8: Democratic party officials say they have reached an agreement to enlist **Jesse Jackson** to help the Clinton-Gore presidential ticket by heading a grass-roots effort aimed at aggressively recruiting black voters for the fall elections, reports *The Los Angeles Times.*

Sept. 8: Milestone Media's **Michael Davis, Derek Dingle, Denys Cowan**, and **Dwayne McDuffie** launch a deal with DC Comics, Inc., publisher of "Batman" and "Superman," to distribute nationally comic books featuring a world of minority superheros and villains. The deal is unprecedented in comic book history, reports *The Washington Post.*

Sept. 9: The **W.E.B. Du Bois Preparatory School,** Detroit's first Afrocentric high school, opens as an expansion of the Aisha Shuttle: The Affirmative School for Gifted Students, reports *The (Detroit) Monitor.* The school will emphasize that education is for self-reliance, and that their knowledge and skills should be taken back into the community to help rebuild them.

Sept. 10: Experts on race say that barriers of discrimination are smaller in rural regions, at least outside the South, than they are in urban centers, and that the income gap between whites and blacks in places like Billings, MT, is much smaller than those in urban areas, reports *The New York Times.*

Sept. 12: The president of the **State University of New York's College at Oneonata** says official letters of apology will be sent to all 125 black men who are students there, whose names were given to the police investigating an assault case, reports *The New York Times.* The commander of the local state police troop apologizes for insensitivity by law enforcement officials who asked for the list when investigating an attempted rape, burglary, and assault Sept. 4 in Oneonata. The only description of the suspect was that he was a black man with cuts on his hands and arms.

Sept. 13: More than 20,000 Washington-area African Americans and others explore black culture on the grounds of the Washington Monument during the seventh annual **Black Family Reunion**, which draws families from throughout the East Coast, reports *The Washington Post.*

Sept. 14: Sixty-eight years after Pvt. **Alonzo Johnson** dies at the age of 78, a military officer delivers an American flag to Johnson's family in Northeast Washington, DC. Johnson was 17 when he ran away from slavery to fight for emancipation. After the war, there was no token of appreciation from the government and no flag to cover Johnson's coffin, reports *The Washington Post.*

Sept. 15: Two federal appeals court judges in Washington, DC, draw on some unlikely sources in pop culture to buttress their conflicting conclusions on a drug and gun conviction, reports *The Washington Post.* Circuit Judge **David Sentelle**, known as a staunchly conservative appointee of former President Reagan, cites rap star **Ice-T**, his song "Cop Killer," and his album "Body Count" to support the conviction of a district man. Just as improbably, Circuit Court Judge **Stephen Williams**, another Reagan appointee, says a portion of the conviction should be reversed, and he looks to the movie "Boyz 'N the Hood" for authority.

Sept. 16: A study of kidney patients suggests that blacks in the United States may be less likely than whites to get some expensive new drugs, even when both carry similar insurance, reports *The Washington Post.*

Sept. 16: Although Los Angeles' predominantly black rival gangs, the Bloods and the Crips, have been killing each other less frequently since their highly publicized truce in May, law enforcement authorities say the pact does nothing to curb street violence victimizing neighborhoods there daily, reports *The Washington Post*.

Sept. 17: Former Washington, DC, Mayor **Marion Barry** wins a landslide victory over **Wilhelmina Rolark** in the Democratic primary in Ward 8, reports *The Washington Post*. Barry finishes with nearly 70 percent of the vote, three times as much as Rolark, who has represented the ward for 16 years.

Sept. 20: A federal judge reverses the Senate's 1989 conviction of former U.S. District Judge **Alcee Hastings** on corruption charges, ruling that Hastings was tried improperly by a committee instead of the full Senate, reports *The Washington Post*. Hastings is running for Congress from a new predominantly black district.

Sept. 22: African Americans are moving into the ranks of the nation's top financial executives, reports *USA Today*. *Black Enterprise* magazine profiles 25 of them in its October issue. All earn at least $300,000 to as much as $1 million a year.

Sept. 23: With New York City's mayoral race 14 months away, Mayor **David Dinkins** and his likely Republican rival, **Rudolph Giuliani**, are squaring off in an unusually bitter and racially charged political battle that began when Giuliani spoke before thousands of angry police officers at a demonstration near City Hall, reports *The New York Times*. Giuliani and the mayor or his aides have accused one another of appealing to racial bias for political advantage. Each side has also suggested that the other is pandering to its natural political base, sacrificing racial harmony in the process.

Sept. 24: Filmmaker **Spike Lee** files a countersuit asking that he be allowed to use the **Rodney King** beating videotape, shot by plumbing store manager **George Holliday** in his upcoming film "Malcolm X," reports *The Washington Post*. Holliday had previously sued Lee, charging that Lee's arrangement with Holliday's former attorney was invalid.

Sept. 25: Mayor **Tom Bradley**, politically scarred by the Los Angeles riots and a pervasive anti-incumbent mood, announces he will not seek a sixth term, reports *The Washington Post*.

Sept. 25: At the annual meeting of the **Congressional Black Caucus Foundation**, black conservative **Robert Woodson**, president of the National Center for Neighborhood Enterprise, criticizes what he terms the racial "bait and switch game," in which he says some black leaders use racism and the plight of the less fortunate to argue for programs that wind up benefiting upper income blacks.

Sept. 26: Basketball superstar **Earvin "Magic" Johnson** resigns from the National Commission on AIDS after criticizing President **Bush** for fighting the disease with "lip service and photo opportunities," reports *The Washington Post*.

Sept. 27: While black-white income disparities have persisted throughout the post-Civil Rights Movement era, two-parent black families in which both spouses work have made the greatest gains toward matching the income of their white counterparts, according to the Census Bureau, reports *The Washington Post*. Black families with husbands and wives working made $85 for every $100 earned by whites in 1990, up from $72 in 1967, the report said. Median income in constant 1990 dollars for these families with two working spouses was $28,700 in 1967, but $40,040 in 1990, compared with $40,040 for whites in 1967 and $47,250 in 1990.

Sept. 27: Hundreds of officials and activists gathered for the annual **Congressional Black Caucus** legislative weekend plot strategy to turn out the black vote in November, but complaints continue that Democratic presidential nominee **Bill Clinton** has taken black votes for granted, reports *The Washington Post*.

Sept. 28: Former U.S. Rep. **Shirley Chisholm** (D-NY) and Dr. **Gloria Toote** are honored by the National Political Congress of Black Women for their contributions "to the political progress of African-American women," reports *The Washington Post*.

Sept. 28: California Gov. **Pete Wilson** vetoes a landmark civil rights bill that would have banned housing and job discrimination against homosexuals, minorities, the disabled, and non-English speakers, reports *The Washington Post*.

Sept. 29: An admissions policy that gives special treatment to minority candidates at the law school of the University of California at Berkeley violates federal law, according to the Department of Education, reports *The Washington Post*.

Oct. 1: **Earvin "Magic" Johnson** announces his return to the NBA after a year's absence following his resignation due to his HIV infection status. He signs a $14.6 million one-year contract extension with the Los Angeles Lakers, the largest single-season salary in team sports reports the *Los Angeles Times*.

Oct. 2: A Nashville, TN, car dealer and his landlord sue **Ford Motor Co.** for $100 million, putting a national focus on industrywide problems for minority-owned dealerships. **Anthony Kennedy**, a black dealer, and his white landlord, **Robert Frensley**, allege that Ford lured them into opening a dealership and then failed to provide reasonable assistance, reports *The Washington Post*.

Oct. 2: **Alex Haley**'s literary works are auctioned with the manuscript of his first major work, the 1964 *Autobiography of Malcolm X*, selling for $100,000. The manuscript, with editing notes by Haley and the Black Muslim leader, was sold to **Gregory Reed**, a Detroit entertainment lawyer representing singer **Anita Baker**, reports *The New York Times*.

Oct. 5: As Los Angeles becomes increasingly a city of minorities, a struggle for political power intensifies among ethnic groups, the most recent being a battle between a black and a Hispanic candidate for the post of interim Superintendent of Schools, reports *The New York Times*. The candidates are **Sidney Thompson**, who is black—like 14 percent of the students; and **Ruben Zacarias**, a Hispanic who reflects the background of 64 percent of the students.

Oct. 5: **Eddie Kendricks**, 52, a founding member of The Temptations and the falsetto lead for such hits as "The Way You Do The Things You Do," dies of lung cancer at a hospital in his native Birmingham, AL.

Oct. 10: **Tony Williams**, the original lead singer of The Platters whose renditions of "Only You" and "The Great Pretender" propelled the R&B group to stardom in the 1950s, dies at age 64 in New York.

Oct. 14: **Cleveland Dennard**, 63, founding president in 1968 of Washington Technical Institute, now part of the University of the District of Columbia, dies at a hospital in Atlanta, reports *The Washington Post*. Dr. Dennard had been a management consultant and acting chief operating officer at the Martin Luther King Center for Nonviolent Social Change since 1984.

Oct. 16: In Jackson, MS, justices consider whether to allow prosecutors to try, for the third time, 71-year-old white supremacist **Byron De La Beckwith** for the 1963 murder of civil rights leader **Medgar Evers**, reports *USA Today*. Twice in 1964, all-white Mississippi juries failed to reach a verdict against Beckwith, despite evidence showing Beckwith's fingerprint on the .30-caliber rifle that killed Evers.

Oct. 18: **Jesse Jackson** tours the country in a joint Rainbow Coalition and Democratic National Committee effort to boost voter turnout and leads about 150 people to the Denver Election Commission to vote in a process known as "early voting," reports *The Washington Post*.

Oct. 18: New York City's new Police Commissioner, **Raymond Kelly**, whose appointment was greeted warily by some black community leaders, says that the first and "most vital" item on his agenda is the recruitment of more black officers to the force, reports *The New York Times*.

Oct. 18: Los Angeles Mayor **Tom Bradley** and former police chief **Daryl Gates** are singled out for criticism in an inquiry into the city's failure to contain the violence of the spring riots, reports *The New York Times*. The five-month study was led by **William Webster**, former director of the FBI, and **Hubert Williams**, president of the Police Foundation.

Oct. 18: Several incidents at the University of Massachusetts' Amherst campus have heightened racial tensions to the point where a U.S. Justice Department mediation team has been brought in to help heal the campus of 23,000 students, reports *The New York Times*.

Oct. 20: The only son of former Alabama Governor **George Wallace**, **George Wallace, Jr.**, appears poised to win a hard-fought race for Congress, thanks in large part to his overwhelming support among blacks, reports *The Washington Post*. "Time moves on," said the younger Wallace as he campaigns as the Democratic nominee in the 2nd Congressional District in Southeast Alabama.

Oct. 21: **David Eaton**, 59, a former president of the DC Board of Education, senior pastor emeritus of All Souls Unitarian Universalist Church, and a major player on Washington's political stage for nearly three decades, dies at Howard University Hospital of complications related to hepatitis B, a viral condition affecting the liver, reports *The Washington Post.*

Oct. 22: **Cleavon Little**, the popular actor who starred regularly on television and who played the sheriff in "Blazing Saddles," dies of colon cancer at the age of 53, reports *The Washington Post.*

Oct. 26: Racism still exists in Hollywood, actress **Cicely Tyson** tells *The Washington Post.* "All you have to do is go to the movies. They are predominately white, with blacks only in nonfeatured roles. But if one turns the television on, one would gather that blacks in the industry are doing extremely well because every network has its black show."

Oct. 27: A group seeking to build the first national monument honoring black Revolutionary War soldiers will have to abandon the effort if it doesn't raise $5.2 million, says **Maurice Barboza**, president of the Black Revolutionary War Patriots Foundation, reports *The Associated Press.*

Oct. 28: Mortgage applications from blacks and Hispanics are still rejected roughly twice as often as applications from whites and Asians, according to a second annual Federal Reserve report, reports *The Associated Press.*

Nov. 3: **Carol Moseley Braun**, the Cook County, IL, Recorder of Deeds, becomes the first black woman ever elected to the U.S. Senate, beating **Richard Williamson** handily in a race where symbolism was as important as strategy, reports *The New York Times.*

Nov. 4: **Pearl Stewart**, a former writer for the *San Francisco Chronicle*, is named editor of the *Oakland Tribune*, thus becoming the first black woman to edit a metro daily newspaper in a major city. *The Tribune* was sold to the Alameda Newspaper Group last month by **Robert Maynard**, who was the first black owner and publisher of a major daily.

Nov. 3: Democrat **William Jefferson "Bill" Clinton**, 46, is elected president of the United States in an election that brushed aside Republican warnings and embraced, in addition to Democrats, women, minorities, and others out of power, reports *USA Today.* "It's a new world, it's a different country," says Democratic National Committee Chairman **Ron Brown**. "You have to change with the times."

Nov. 4: A record number of minorities ran for Congress and a record number won, making the House and Senate more reflective of the nation's population than ever before in history, reports *USA Today*. Early returns indicate that 67 of the 97 minority candidates who ran claimed victory. **Jesse Jackson** says the numbers reflects a "coalition for change." The 26-member Congressional Black Caucus will increase to 40; and the 11-member Congressional Hispanic Caucus will add eight members.

Nov. 9: The University of Massachusetts announces it will recruit more minority students and faculty and take other steps in an effort to ease racial tensions at the school, reports *The Washington Post.*

Nov. 9: An outline for a speech given by **Martin Luther King, Jr.**, is auctioned in Beverly Hills, CA, for $35,000, despite a lawsuit by the King estate contesting ownership, reports *The Washington Post.* The suit asks for the return of the document and $5 million in punitive damages. According to King biographer **David Garrow**, the speech, given during a Southern Christian Leadership Conference staff retreat on Nov. 14, 1966, "is probably the most significant handwritten King document not in an archive." King delivered most of his sermons extemporaneously.

Nov. 9: Officials with the University of Virginia's graduate school of business say they will investigate black students' allegations of "systematic and institutional racism" at the school, reports *The Washington Post.* The students' report followed allegations in May by a Darden student committee that there was a hostile environment toward female faculty members and problems with leadership, hiring practices, and relationships within the faculty.

Nov. 9: NBA star **Michael Jordan**, 29, will earn $36 million in 1992, catapulting him to the top of *Forbes* magazine's list of the 40 best-paid athletes. A $20 million contract with Nike, Inc., helped boost Jordan's income, reports *The New York Times.*

Nov. 9: Detroit prosecutors plan to issue warrants to police officers suspected of beating black Detroit motorist **Malice Green** to death on November 5. Police officials say two plainsclothes officers beat Green with a flashlight as five others watched or took part. Detroit's new police chief, **Stanley Knox**, acted swiftly to assure a complete investigation and suspended without pay all seven black and white officers involved in the beating, reports *The Associated Press.*

Nov. 9: Democratic Party Chairman **Ron Brown** expresses pride and pleasure for his role in unifying the party and putting together an organization that helped **Bill Clinton** engineer a stunning victory over President **Bush**, reports *USA Today*. "It gives me an enormous feeling of completion," Brown says. Brown is being considered for a high-level post in the new Clinton administration, a prospect he welcomes.

Nov. 13: **Riddick Bowe** earns the world heavyweight title after he defeats heavyweight champion **Evander Holyfield** in a unanimous, 12-round decision.

Nov. 15: Once known as the largest segregated city in the nation, Birmingham, AL, has never been able to escape its past completely. But, the dedication of the $12 million **Birmingham Civil Rights Institute** may be a sign that the city, once called "an incurable sore" by the writer James Agee, is ready to heal itself, reports *The New York Times*.

Nov. 16: A federal judge rules that the seniority system in place during the early 1970s at a Du Pont plant in Louisville, KY, was intentionally discriminatory. Blacks were stuck in poor-paying, dead-end jobs, Judge **Carl B. Rubin** said, and the company owes money to an estimated 154 workers or their survivors with the amount of damages yet to be determined, reports *The New York Times*.

Nov. 18: Filmmaker **Spike Lee**'s long-awaited movie, "Malcolm X," opens in theaters throughout the country. Actor **Denzel Washington**, who portrays the slain Nation of Islam leader, is expected to earn an Oscar for his role, reports the *Los Angeles Times*.

Nov. 19: Mary Washington College student **Faith Christmas** tells more than 400 students at the Fredericksburg, VA, institution that she never felt so "degraded" or "humiliated" until she answered a pay phone outside her dormitory Nov. 1 and heard a voice say, "Tell the three niggers on the fifth floor that they're dead," reports *The Richmond Times-Dispatch*. Ms. Christmas said the threat was directed at her and two other black women in her dormitory. President **William Anderson, Jr.,** calls the incident "deplorable" and pledges to pursue new ways to attack bigotry.

Nov. 20: Prominent Washington lawyer **Vernon Jordan, Jr.**, 57, is named co-chairman of President-elect **Bill Clinton**'s transition team and may be in line for a permanent job in the new administration, reports *USA Today*. Jordan is a former Executive Director of the National Urban League.

Nov. 22: **Betty Shabazz**, the widow of **Malcolm X**, is suing the brother of the late **Alex Haley** for at least half the money the author's estate made on the sale of the original manuscript of *The Autobiography of Malcolm X*, reports *The Associated Press*.

Nov. 24: New York Mayor **David Dinkins** plans to deliver a televised address on race relations in order to place the tumult over the Crown Heights verdict behind him, reports *The New York Times*. The case involved a teenager accused of fatally stabbing a Jewish scholar during disturbances in Crown Heights in August 1991. The teen was acquitted.

Nov. 25: **Ron Dickerson**, 44, becomes the only black to head a Division I-A football team when he is named to head Temple University's football team. Dickerson, a former Clemson University defensive coordinator, replaces **Jerry Berndt**. Entertainer **Bill Cosby**, a Temple alumnus, played a key role in Dickerson's hiring, reports *USA Today*.

Nov. 30: Blacks 55 years and older should be immunized against a blood infection caused by a certain type of pneumonia, according to a study in the *American Journal of Public Health*, reports *USA Today*.

Nov. 30: Alabama's black legislators say they will boycott the Dec. 12 rededication of the Alabama state capitol to protest the decision of Gov. **Guy Hunt** to fly the Confederate battle flag over the newly renovated building, reports *The Washington Post*. At least a half-dozen chambers of commerce, the Alabama State Employees Association, the Montgomery Hotel-Motel Association, and prominent state historians joined the legislators' opposition.

Dec. 2: President-elect **Bill Clinton** selects **Metropolitan AME Church**, a downtown Washington landmark with a distinguished history in national black political and religious life, as the site of his inaugural morning prayer service, reports *The Washington Post*.

Dec. 3: Celebrated poet **Maya Angelou** is asked to compose a poem to read at **Bill Clinton**'s swearing-in ceremony. She accepts, saying, "It is fitting, at the risk of taking away from the fact that he really likes my poetry, that he asks a woman and a black woman to write a poem about the tenor of the times," Ms. Angelou tells *The Washington Post*.

Dec. 5: In the nation's capital, a federal judge certifies a class-action suit against the giant utility **PEPCO** that could cost the company millions in damages if a jury finds that it discriminated against black employees and job applicants, reports *The Washington Post*. The ruling transforms the case from one affecting a few dozen plaintiffs to more than 8,400 potential plaintiffs.

Dec. 9: Baseball outfielder and two-time National League Most Valuable Player **Barry Bonds** signs a $43.75 million contract for six years with the **San Francisco Giants**, making him the game's highest paid player.

Dec. 10: Poverty and the ills it produces are keeping many black women from marriage, according to researchers in a study, "Marriage, Divorce, and Remarriage in the 1990s," reports *The Associated Press*. One black woman in four reaches 40 without ever having married, and fewer black men are available primarily because of poverty and many of the difficulties that follow from that, notes the report.

Dec. 13: President-elect **Bill Clinton** selects Democratic National Committee Chairman **Ronald Brown** to head the Commerce Department, reports *The Washington Post*.

Dec. 13: Recent racial slurs by Cincinnati Reds owner **Marge Schott** alerted the country to lingering racism in sports, **Jesse Jackson** tells Jewish leaders as he renews a threat to organize a boycott of professional baseball unless owners take steps to hire more minorities, reports *The Washington Post*. Schott apologized for making racially insensitive remarks but faces possible disciplinary action from fellow owners.

Dec. 14: "Clustering" white students in the same classes at a Richmond, VA, elementary school sparks a debate over how far a majority-black school system should go to attract and keep white students, reports *The Washington Post*.

Dec. 14: The U.S. Supreme Court agrees to decide whether states may give longer prison sentences and higher fines to assailants who chose a victim based on race, religion, or sexual orientation, reports *The Washington Post*. The case of *Wisconsin v. Mitchell* presents a major First Amendment problem and gives the court a chance to clarify the law on "hate crimes" which state officials say are increasing.

Dec. 15: A man fatally beaten by police in Detroit was hit so hard that part of his scalp was torn off, a pathologist testifies at a preliminary hearing to determine if four officers should stand trial, reports *The Associated Press*. At least 14 blows to **Malice Green**'s face and head ripped loose part of his scalp, damaged his brain, and finally caused his heart and lungs to fail. Undercover officers **Larry Nevers** and **Walter Budzyn** are charged with second-degree murder.

Dec. 17: A bitterly divided Mississippi Supreme Court refuses to block the trial of **Byron De La Beckwith**, paving the way for him to be tried for the third time for the 1963 murder of civil rights leader **Medgar Evers**, reports *The New York Times*.

Dec. 17: **Dusty Baker** becomes one of four black managers in major league baseball when he is named manager of the San Francisco Giants, reports *The New York Times* [see July 15].

Dec. 18: The United States has a higher infant mortality rate for black children than for children of all races in 31 other nations, including Cuba and Kuwait, reports *The Washington Post*.

Dec. 18: **"Mother" Clara Hale**, the woman who—at the age of 65—started Hale House for babies of drug addicts in New York, dies after a lengthy illness at the age of 88, reports *The New York Times*. Mothe Hale had garnered national praise, including White House honors, for caring for more than 800 so-called "boarder babies" since founding Hale House.

Dec. 18: In Mineola, Long Island, NY, **Alfred Jermaine Ewell**, the black high school football star who was beaten in a racial attack, urges that one of his attackers "be shown the same consideration and compassion that he showed me that night—absolutely none," reports *The New York Times*. Moments later, Judge **Donald Belfi** sentences the white attacker, **Shannon Siegel**, to 7 to 21 years in prison, the maximum penalty for first-degree assault.

Dec. 19: In Nashville, TN, two white police officers are fired for using excessive force to subdue a black motorist who turns out to be **Reggie Miller**, an undercover officer working on a prostitution sting, reports *The Associated Press*.

Dec. 19: **John Lucas** is tapped as head coach for the San Antonio Spurs, reports *The Associated Press*. Lucas, the first overall pick in the 1976 draft by Houston, was in and out of rehabilitation for cocaine use during his playing career but has since devoted his life to fighting drug abuse.

Dec. 19: **Georgia McMurray**, a leader in developing services for children in New York City, dies at her home in Manhattan at age 58, reports *The New York Times*. A quadriplegic, she had suffered from a progressive nervous disease. Ms. McMurray was a former Commissioner of the New York City Agency for Child Development and deputy general director for programming of the Community Service Society of New York. A contributor to *The State of Black America 1990*, she was teaching at Fordham University at the time of her death. Last April, she was presented the Essence Award by *Essence* magazine and cited for distinguished service by the Children's Aid Society.

Dec. 20: Tennis legend **Arthur Ashe** is named *Sports Illustrated*'s "Sportsman of the Year." Ashe, who revealed in April that he has AIDS, becomes the first athlete to win the award after his playing days are over [see April 8].

Dec. 20: UCLA's **Natalie Williams** is the nation's best collegiate volleyball player and has the school's highest career rebounding average (12.2) in basketball, reports *The Washington Post*.

Dec. 22: **Shoney's, Inc.**, officials deny reports that **Leonard Roberts** was forced to resign as chairman because of his push for affirmative action, but an industry analyst says Roberts' effort to change the Shoney's "culture" probably alienated his fellow officers so that they wanted to get rid of him. His resignation came six weeks after the Nashville-based restaurant chain settled a racial discrimination lawsuit for $105 million, reports *The Washington Post*.

Dec. 22: Former Social Security Commissioner **Gwendolyn King** becomes the first woman to be elected to the board of directors of Bethesda-based Martin Marietta Corp., making her one of very few women to sit on defense boards, reports *The Washington Post*.

Dec. 23: **Albert King**, blues guitarist and singer who became a major figure in postwar American music, dies after suffering a heart attack in Memphis at age 69, reports *The New York Times*. An intense performer, his sound was filled with bent and crying notes. As a singer, he used his smooth voice, made passionate by a steady vibrato, to project doom and authority. His songs often were about anger, loss, and failed relationships.

Dec. 23: Rep. **Ronald Dellums** (D-CA), an impassioned opponent of many military programs even as he rose in the ranks of the House Armed Services Committee, is in line to succeed Rep. **Les Aspin** (D-WI) as chairman of the traditionally hawkish panel, reports *The Associated Press*. Aspin, head of the committee for eight years, has been selected by President-elect **Bill Clinton** as Secretary of Defense.

Dec. 23: The Detroit-based **Kresge Foundation** pledges $15 million, its largest grant ever, to the **United Negro College Fund** for the renovation and construction of buildings, reports *The Associated Press*. The Kresge grant is earmarked for a $100 million construction and renovation program for the fund's 41 historically black colleges. The black college fund had already raised $36 million, and the Kresge grant is contingent upon raising the $49 million from other sources.

Dec. 24: Three Detroit police officers are ordered to stand trial in the fatal beating of black motorist, **Malice Green**, 35, outside a suspected crack house on Nov. 5. But a judge dismisses a felony charge against a sergeant accused of failing to stop the attack, reports *The Associated Press*.

Dec. 26: *The New York Times* reports blacks selected to fill top-level posts in the Clinton administration include **Ronald Brown**, Secretary of Commerce; **Jesse Brown**, Secretary of Veterans' Affairs; **Hazel O'Leary**, Energy Secretary; **Mike Espy** (D-MS), Secretary of Agriculture; **Clifton Wharton, Jr.**, Deputy Secretary of State; and Dr. **Jocelyn Elders**, Surgeon General.

Dec. 28: Wake Forest University football coach **Jim Caldwell** says he doesn't feel any extra pressure as the first black head coach in the 40-year history of the Atlantic Coast Conference, reports *The Associated Press*. "I think the emphasis on the plight of black coaches in the '90s really did give me an opportunity to interview for the job, but that wasn't a primary reason (for being selected)," he said.

Dec. 29: A federal judge in Washington, DC, strikes down the District's minority contracting law as unconstitutional, declaring that the District cannot rely on general allegations of discrimination to defend setting aside about one-third of all contracts for minority-owned firms, *The Washington Post* reports. U.S. District Court Judge **John Garrett Penn** ruled—following a pattern set in other recent court decisions on such programs—that the District must provide statistical evidence of past discrimination to justify the contracting law.

INDEX OF AUTHORS AND ARTICLES

In 1987, the National Urban League began publishing *The State of Black America* in a new, smaller, typeset format. By so doing, it became easier to catalog and archive the various essays by author and article name. The 1993 edition of *The State of Black America* is the first to contain an index of the authors and articles published since the 1987 conversion. The authors are alphabetically listed first in this section; their contributions are listed chronologically, beginning with the most recent. The articles are listed in the second half, alphabetically by title, irrespective of year of publication.

Reprints of the articles catalogued herein will be available beginning in March 1993.

Index of Authors

THE STATE OF BLACK AMERICA: 1987-1993

313

Darity, Jr., Dr. William A. (with Dr. Samuel L. Myers, Jr.), *The State of Black America 1992*, "Racial Earnings Inequality into the 21st Century," pp. 119-139.

Edelin, Dr. Ramona, *The State of Black America 1990*, "Toward an African-American Agenda: An Inward Look," pp. 173-183.

Edelman, Marian Wright, *The State of Black America 1989*, "Black Children in America," pp. 63-76.

Fair, T. Willard, *The State of Black America 1993*, "Coordinated Community Empowerment: Experiences of the Urban League of Greater Miami," pp 217-233.

Glasgow, Dr. Douglas D., *The State of Black America 1987*, "The Black Underclass in Perspective," pp. 129-144.

Gray, Sandra T., *The State of Black America 1992*, "Public-Private Partnerships: Prospects for America . . . Promise for African Americans," pp. 231-247.

Hamilton, Dr. Charles V., *The State of Black America 1993*, "Promoting Priorities: African-American Political Influence in the 1990s," pp. 59-69; *The State of Black America 1989*, "On Parity and Political Empowerment," pp. 111-120.

Hamilton-Lee, Dr. Muriel (with Drs. James P. Comer and Norris M. Haynes), *The State of Black America 1990*, "School Power: A Model for Improving Black Student Achievement," pp. 225-238.

Hare, Dr. Bruce R., *The State of Black America 1988*, "Black Youth at Risk," pp. 81-93.

Haynes, Dr. Norris M. (with Drs. James P. Comer and Muriel Hamilton-Lee), *The State of Black America 1990*, "School Power: A Model for Improving Black Student Achievement," pp. 225-238.

Henderson, Dr. Lenneal J., *The State of Black America 1993*, "Empowerment through Enterprise: African-American Business Development," pp. 91-108; *The State of Black America 1992*, "Public Investment for Public Good: Needs, Benefits, and Financing Options," pp. 213-229; *The State of Black America 1991*, "Budgets, Taxes, and Politics: Options for the African-American Community," pp. 77-93; *The State of Black America 1990*, "Budget and Tax Strategy: Implications for Blacks," pp. 53-71; *The State of Black America 1987*, "Blacks, Budgets, and Taxes: Assessing the Impact of Budget Deficit Reduction and Tax Reform on Blacks," pp. 75-95.

Hill, Dr. Robert B., *The State of Black America 1992*, "Urban Redevelopment: Developing Effective Targeting Strategies," pp. 197-211; *The State of Black America 1989*, "Critical Issues for Black Families by the Year 2000," pp. 41-61.

Holden, Jr., Dr. Matthew, *The State of Black America 1990*, "The Rewards of Daring and the Ambiguity of Power: Perspectives on the Wilder Election of 1989," pp. 109-120.

Howard, Dr. Jeff P., *The State of Black America 1993*, "The Third Movement: Developing Black Children for the 21st Century," pp. 11-34.

Kornblum, Dr. William (with Dr. Terry Williams), *The State of Black America 1991*, "A Portrait of Youth: Coming of Age in Harlem Public Housing," pp. 187-207.

Leffall, Jr., Dr. LaSalle D., *The State of Black America 1990*, "Health Status of Black Americans," pp. 121-142.

Lincoln, Dr. C. Eric, *The State of Black America 1989*, "Knowing the Black Church: What It Is and Why," pp. 137-149.

McHenry, The Honorable Donald F., *The State of Black America 1991*, "A Changing World Order: Implications for Black America," pp. 155-163.

McAlpine, Robert, *The State of Black America 1991*, "Toward a Development of a National Drug Control Strategy," pp. 233-241.

McBay, Dr. Shirley M., *The State of Black America 1992*, "The Condition of African-American Education: Changes and Challenges," pp. 141-156.

McKenzie, Dr. Floretta Dukes, *The State of Black America 1991*, "Education Strategies for the '90s," pp. 95-111.

McMurray, Georgia L., *The State of Black America 1990*, "Those of Broader Vision: An African-American Perspective on Teenage Pregnancy and Parenting," pp. 195-211.

Malveaux, Dr. Julianne M., *The State of Black America 1992*, "The Parity Imperative: Civil Rights, Economic Justice, and the New American Dilemma," pp. 281-303.

Massey, Dr. Walter E., *The State of Black America 1992*, "Science, Technology, and Human Resources: Preparing for the 21st Century," pp. 157-169.

Mendez, Jr., Dr. Garry A., *The State of Black America 1988*, "Crime Is Not a Part of Our Black Heritage: A Theoretical Essay," pp. 211-215.

Miller, Jr., Dr. Warren F., *The State of Black America 1991*, "Developing Untapped Talent: A National Call for African-American Technologists," pp. 111-127.

Murray, Sylvester, *The State of Black America 1992*, "Clear and Present Danger: The Decay of America's Physical Infrastructure," pp. 171-182.

Myers, Jr., Dr. Samuel L. (with Dr. William A. Darity, Jr.), *The State of Black America 1992*, "Racial Earnings Inequality into the 21st Century," pp. 119-139.

National Urban League Research Staff, *The State of Black America 1992*, "African Americans in Profile: Selected Demographic, Social, and Economic Data," pp. 309-325.

Nobles, Dr. Wade W., *The State of Black America 1989*, "Drugs in the African-American Community: A Clear and Present Danger," pp. 161-181.

Pemberton, Dr. Gayle, *The State of Black America 1991*, "It's the Thing That Counts, Or Reflections on the Legacy of W.E.B. Du Bois," pp. 129-143.

Persons, Dr. Georgia A., *The State of Black America 1987*, "Blacks in State and Local Government: Progress and Constraints," pp. 167-192.

Pinderhughes, Dr. Dianne M., *The State of Black America 1992*, "Power and Progress: African-American Politics in the New Era of Diversity," pp. 265-280; *The State of Black America 1991*, "The Case of African Americans in the Persian Gulf: The Intersection of American Foreign and Military Policy with Domestic Employment Policy in the United States," pp. 165-186; *The State of Black America 1988*, "Civil Rights and the Future of the American Presidency," pp. 39-60.

Primm, Dr. Beny J., *The State of Black America 1987*, "Drug Use: Special Implications for Black America," pp. 145-158; and "AIDS: A Special Report," pp. 159-166.

Robinson, Dr. Eugene S., *The State of Black America 1990*, "Television Advertising and Its Impact on Black America," pp. 157-171.

Robinson, Dr. Sharon P., *The State of Black America 1987*, "Taking Charge: An Approach to Making the Educational Problems of Blacks Comprehensible and Manageable," pp. 37-47.

Schexnider, Dr. Alvin J., *The State of Black America 1988*, "Blacks in the Military: The Victory and the Challenge," pp. 115-128.

Solomon, Dr. Barbara Bryant, *The State of Black America 1987*, "Social Welfare Reform," pp. 113-127.

Sudarkasa, Dr. Niara, *The State of Black America 1988*, "Black Enrollment in Higher Education: The Unfulfilled Promise of Equality," pp. 7-22.

Swinton, Dr. David H., *The State of Black America 1993*, "The Economic Status of African Americans During the Reagan-Bush Era: Withered Opportunities, Limited Outcomes, and Uncertain Outlook," pp. 135-200; *The State of Black America 1992*, "The Economic Status of African Americans: Limited Ownership and Persistent Inequality," pp. 61-117; *The State of Black America 1991*, "The Economic Status of African Americans: 'Permanent' Poverty and Inequality," pp. 25-75; *The State of Black America 1990*, "Economic Status of Black Americans During the 1980s: A Decade of Limited Progress," pp. 25-52; *The State of Black America 1989*, "Economic

Status of Black Americans," pp. 9-39; *The State of Black America 1988*, "Economic Status of Blacks 1987," pp. 129-152; and *The State of Black America 1987*, "Economic Status of Blacks 1986," pp. 49-73.

Thomas, Jr., Dr. R. Roosevelt, *The State of Black America 1991*, "Managing Employee Diversity: An Assessment," pp. 145-154.

Tidwell, Dr. Billy J., *The State of Black America 1993*, "African Americans and the 21st Century Labor Market: Improving the Fit," pp. 35-57, and with Monica B. Kuumba, Dr. Dionne J. Jones, and Dr. Betty C. Watson, "Fast Facts: African Americans in the 1990s," pp. 243-265; *The State of Black America 1992*, "Serving the National Interest: A Marshall Plan for America," pp. 11-30; *The State of Black America 1991*, "Economic Costs of American Racism," pp. 219-232; *The State of Black America 1990*, "The Unemployment Experience of African Americans: Some Important Correlates and Consequences," pp. 213-223; *The State of Black America 1988*, "Black Wealth: Facts *and* Fiction," pp. 193-210; *The State of Black America 1987*, "A Profile of the Black Unemployed," pp. 223-237.

Watson, Dr. Bernard C., *The State of Black America 1992*, "The Demographic Revolution: Diversity in 21st Century America," pp. 31-59; *The State of Black America 1988*, "Tomorrow's Teachers: Who Will They Be, What Will They Know?," pp. 23-37.

Webb, Dr. Michael B., *The State of Black America 1993*, "Programs for Progress and Empowerment: The Urban League's National Education Initiative," pp. 203-216.

Williams, Dr. Terry M. (with Dr. William Kornblum), *The State of Black America 1991*, "A Portrait of Youth: Coming of Age in Harlem Public Housing," pp. 187-207.

Willie, Dr. Charles V., *The State of Black America 1988*, "The Black Family: Striving Toward Freedom," pp. 71-80; *The State of Black America 1987*, "The Future of School Desegregation," pp. 37-47.

Wilson, Dr. Reginald, *The State of Black America 1989*, "Black Higher Education: Crisis and Promise," pp. 121-135.

Wirschem, David, *The State of Black America 1991*, "Community Mobilization for Education in Rochester, New York: A Case Study," pp. 243-248.

317

Index of Articles

THE STATE OF BLACK AMERICA: 1987-1993

"A Changing World Order: Implications for Black America," Donald F. McHenry, **1991**, pp. 155-163.

"Civil Rights and the Future of the American Presidency," Dianne M. Pinderhughes, **1988**, pp. 39-60.

"Clear and Present Danger: The Decay of America's Physical Infrastructure," Sylvester Murray, **1992**, pp. 171-182.

"Community Mobilization for Education in Rochester, New York: A Case Study," David Wirschem, **1991**, pp. 243-248.

"The Condition of African-American Education: Changes and Challenges," Shirley M. McBay, **1992**, pp. 141-156.

"Coordinated Community Empowerment: Experiences of the Urban League of Greater Miami," T.Willard Fair, **1993**, pp. 217-233.

"Crime in the Black Community," Lee P. Brown, **1988**, pp. 95-113.

"Crime Is Not a Part of Our Black Heritage: A Theoretical Essay," Garry A. Mendez, **1988**, pp. 211-215.

"Critical Issues for Black Families by the Year 2000," Robert B. Hill, **1989**, pp. 41-61.

"Critical Perspectives on the Psychology of Race," Price M. Cobbs, **1988**, pp. 61-70.

"The Demographic Revolution: Diversity in 21st Century America," Bernard C. Watson, **1992**, pp. 31-59.

"Developing Untapped Talent: A National Call for African-American Technologists," Warren F. Miller, Jr., **1991**, pp. 111-127.

"Drugs in the African-American Community: A Clear and Present Danger," Wade W. Nobles, **1989**, pp. 161-181.

"Drug Use: Special Implications for Black America," Beny J. Primm, **1987**, pp. 145-158.

"Economic Costs of American Racism," Billy J. Tidwell, **1991**, pp. 219-232.

"The Economic Status of African Americans: Limited Ownership and Persistent Inequality," David H. Swinton, **1992**, pp. 61-117.

"The Economic Status of African Americans: 'Permanent' Poverty and Inequality," David H. Swinton, **1991**, pp. 25-75.

"The Economic Status of African Americans During the Reagan-Bush Era: Withered Opportunities, Limited Outcomes, and Uncertain Outlook," David H. Swinton, **1993**, pp. 135-200.

"Economic Status of Black Americans," David H. Swinton, **1989**, pp. 9-39.

"Economic Status of Black Americans During the 1980s: A Decade of Limited Progress," David H. Swinton, **1990**, pp. 25-52.

"Economic Status of Blacks 1987," David H. Swinton, **1988**, pp. 129-152.

"Economic Status of Blacks 1986," David H. Swinton, **1987**, pp. 49-73.

"Education Strategies for the '90s," Floretta Dukes McKenzie, **1991**, pp. 95-111.

"The Elusive Quest for Racial Justice: The Chronicle of the Constitutional Contradiction," Derrick Bell, **1991**, pp. 9-23.

"Empowerment through Enterprise: African-American Business Development," Lenneal J. Henderson, **1993**, pp. 91-108.

"Fast Facts: African Americans in the 1990s," Billy J. Tidwell (with Monica B. Kuumba, Dionne J. Jones and Betty C. Watson), **1993**, pp. 243-265.

"The Future of School Desegregation," Charles V. Willie, **1987**, pp. 37-47.

"Health Status of Black Americans," LaSalle D. Leffall, Jr., **1990**, pp. 121-142.

"Housing Opportunity: A Dream Deferred," Phillip Clay, **1990**, pp. 73-84.

"Interagency and Intergovernmental Coordination: New Demands for Domestic Policy Initiatives," Henry A. Coleman, **1992**, pp. 249-263.

"It's the Thing That Counts, Or Reflections on the Legacy of W.E.B. Du Bois," Gayle Pemberton, **1991**, pp. 129-143.

"Knowing the Black Church: What It Is and Why," C. Eric Lincoln, **1989**, pp. 137-149.

"The Law and Black Americans: Retreat from Civil Rights," Julius L. Chambers, **1987**, pp. 15-30.

"Managing Employee Diversity: An Assessment," R. Roosevelt Thomas, Jr., **1991**, pp. 145-154.

"Money Matters: Lending Discrimination in African-American Communities," William D. Bradford, **1993**, pp. 109-134.

"On Parity and Political Empowerment," Charles V. Hamilton, **1989**, pp. 111-120.

"The Parity Imperative: Civil Rights, Economic Justice, and the New American Dilemma," Julianne M. Malveaux, **1992**, pp. 281-303.

"A Portrait of Youth: Coming of Age in Harlem Public Housing," William Kornblum and Terry Williams, **1991**, pp. 187-207.

"Power and Progress: African-American Politics in the New Era of Diversity," Dianne M. Pinderhughes, **1992**, pp. 265-280.

"Preventing Black Homicide," Carl C. Bell, **1990**, pp. 143-155.

"A Profile of the Black Unemployed," Billy J. Tidwell, **1987**, pp. 223-237.

"Understanding African-American Family Diversity," Andrew Billingsley, **1990**, pp. 85-108.

"The Unemployment Experience of African Americans: Some Important Correlates and Consequences," Billy J. Tidwell, **1990**, pp. 213-223.

"Urban Infrastructure: Social, Environmental, and Health Risks to African Americans," Robert D. Bullard, **1992**, pp. 183-196.

"Urban Redevelopment: Developing Effective Targeting Strategies," Robert B. Hill, **1992**, pp. 197-211.

"Valuing Diversity: The Myth and the Challenge," Price M. Cobbs, **1989**, pp. 151-159.

Acknowledgments

As usual, *The State of Black America 1993* is the product of a herculean collective effort, led by the fine work of the authors who contributed to the publication. The editor extends his deepest appreciation to each of them. The unqualified commitment to excellence of Paulette Robinson, associate editor, permeates the volume. Assistant editors Johnnie Griffin and Michele Long Pittman provided their customary superb support. Bonnie Stanley, who compiled the "Chronology of Events 1992," was industrious in this taxing task. Under the wise oversight of President/Chief Executive Officer John E. Jacob and Executive Vice President Frank Lomax III, the National Urban League staff maintained the tradition of unselfish, superlative performance. Acknowledgment goes to the significant contributions of Richard W. Keough and members of the Public Relations and Communications Department—Ernie Johnston, Jr.; B. Maxwell Stamper; Farida Syed; Faith J. Williams; and Denise Wright. Also, Daniel S. Davis and Betty Ford in the Office of the President were very helpful. In addition, we acknowledge the assistance of the Programs staff, with special thanks to Anne Hill and Janet Zobel.

The staff of the Washington Operations office met the challenge with enthusiasm and confidence. Robert McAlpine, Director of the Policy and Government Relations Department, was helpful throughout, and his staff—Suzanne Bergeron, Lisa Bland-Malone, and Robin Doroshow—took major responsibility for developing the National Urban League's policy recommendations. The administrative assistance of Gwendolyn Duke, Arnold Hall, and Thea Sanders is also recognized. In addition to co-authoring the appendix, researchers Dionne Jones, Monica Kuumba, and Betty Watson provided valuable technical support. Kathleen Daley of the Research Department was diligent in carrying out her administrative duties, while Deborah Searcy deserves special mention for having served so meticulously as the project's chief production assistant.

A special acknowledgment for the production and printing of this volume is owed to Zale S. Koff and his wonderfully cooperative staff at Astoria Graphics, Inc.

To all of those who, directly or indirectly, shared the burden, many thanks for a job well done.

Order Blank

National Urban League Publications
500 East 62nd Street
New York, NY 10021

	Per Copy	# of Copies	Total
The State of Black America 1993 $24.95		_____	_____

Recent Volumes in series:

	Per Copy	# of Copies	Total
The State of Black America 1992	$24.95	_____	_____
The State of Black America 1991	$19.95	_____	_____
The State of Black America 1990	$19.00	_____	_____
The State of Black America 1989	$19.00	_____	_____
The State of Black America 1988	$18.00	_____	_____
The State of Black America 1987	$18.00	_____	_____

Postage and handling:
Individual volumes-- $ 2.00/book rate   _____   _____
                            $ 3.00/first class   _____   _____

Total amount enclosed $ _____

"New Generations"

The limited-edition, numbered lithograph of "New Generations" is signed by the artist, Elizabeth Catlett. "New Generations" is the seventh in the "Great Artists" series on African Americans commissioned for the National Urban League by the House of Seagram; proceeds benefit League programs. The unframed lithograph measures 38-1/2"x25". The four-color poster costs $1,000, which includes postage and handling.

For more information or to order, contact:

National Urban League, Inc.
Office of Development
500 East 62nd Street
New York, NY 10021

Please make check or money order payable to:
National Urban League, Inc.

Founded in 1910, the National Urban League is the premier social service and civil rights organization in America. The League is a nonprofit, nonpartisan community-based organization headquartered in New York City, with 112 affiliates in 34 states and the District of Columbia. The mission of the National Urban League is to assist African Americans in the achievement of social and economic equality. The League implements its mission through advocacy, bridge building between the races, program services, and research. The League also has an office in Washington, D.C. that oversees the activities of Congress and the federal government as they pertain to African Americans and minorities and maintains a renowned Research Department.

The National Urban League is governed by an interracial Board of Trustees composed of outstanding men and women from the professions, business, labor, civic and religious communities. Another hallmark of the League is its highly trained professional staff at the national and local levels.

John E. Jacob is the President and Chief Executive Officer and Reginald K. Brack, Jr. is Chairman of the Board of Trustees.

Today, while the National Urban League continues to provide assistance in traditional areas of concern, such as employment, housing, education and social welfare, it has been a leader in a number of new areas—African American male development, AIDS education, political empowerment and crime in the black community.

The National Urban League has sought to emphasize greater reliance on the unique resources and strengths of the African-American community to find solutions to its own problems. To accomplish this, the League's approach has been to utilize fully the tools of advocacy, research, program service and bridge building. The result has been an organization with strong roots in the community, which serves more than a million individuals each year.

327

Notes